PRIVATE ACTORS AS PARTICIPANTS IN INTERNATIONAL LAW

This book examines the status of private actors as subjects of law under the rules of the international law of the sea. Providing a methodology for the notion of a single legal personality, it provides a clear understanding of membership in international law in order to establish to what extent private actors can be rights-holders or duty-bearers. It does this by taking a theoretical perspective which allows the reader to interpret their relevance in international law. This unique and innovative work makes a significant contribution to the current scholarly debates on private actors in international law.

Volume 85 in the series Studies in International Law

Studies in International Law

Recent titles in this series

Asylum Control and Access to Protection: Admission, Readmission and Human Rights
Mariagiulia Giuffré

Intertemporal Linguistics in International Law: Beyond Contemporaneous and Evolutionary Treaty Interpretation
Julian Wyatt

The Responsibility to Protect and the Failures of the United Nations Security Council
P M Butchard

The Role of Multilateral Environmental Agreements: A Reconciliatory Approach to Environmental Protection in Armed Conflict
Britta Sjostedt

Prosecutorial Discretion at the International Criminal Court
Anni Pues

Judicial Deference in International Adjudication: A Comparative Analysis
Johannes Hendrik Fahner

Human Rights Commitments of Islamic States: Sharia, Treaties and Consensus
Paul McDonough

Intervention in Civil Wars: Effectiveness, Legitimacy, and Human Rights
Chiara Redaelli

General Principles as a Source of International Law: Art 38(1)(c) of the Statute of the International Court of Justice
Imogen Saunders

The Law of Humanity Project: A Story of International Law Reform and State-making
Ukri Soirila

Extraterritoriality and Climate Change Jurisdiction: Exploring EU Climate Protection under International Law
Natalie L Dobson

International Law and the War with Islamic State: Challenges for Jus ad Bellum and Jus in Bello
Saeed Bagheri

Private Actors as Participants in International Law: A Critical Analysis of Membership under the Law of the Sea
Armando Rocha

For a complete list of titles in this series, see www.bloomsburyprofessional.com/uk/series/studies-in-international-law

Private Actors as Participants in International Law

A Critical Analysis of Membership under the Law of the Sea

Armando Rocha

•HART•
OXFORD • LONDON • NEW YORK • NEW DELHI • SYDNEY

HART PUBLISHING

Bloomsbury Publishing Plc

Kemp House, Chawley Park, Cumnor Hill, Oxford, OX2 9PH, UK

1385 Broadway, New York, NY 10018, USA

29 Earlsfort Terrace, Dublin 2, Ireland

HART PUBLISHING, the Hart/Stag logo, BLOOMSBURY and the Diana logo are trademarks of Bloomsbury Publishing Plc

First published in Great Britain 2021

A catalogue record for this book is available from the British Library.

Library of Congress Cataloging-in-Publication data

Names: Rocha, Armando Luis Silva, author.

Title: Private actors as participants in international law : a critical analysis of membership under the Law of the Sea / Armando Rocha.

Description: Oxford, UK ; New York, NY : Hart Publishing, an imprint of Bloomsbury Publishing, 2021. | Series: Studies in international law; volume 85 | Based on author's thesis (doctoral – Universidade Católica Portuguesa, 2018) issued under title: Private actors as rights-holders under the international law of the sea. | Includes bibliographical references and index.

Identifiers: LCCN 2021016644 (print) | LCCN 2021016645 (ebook) | ISBN 9781509948048 (hardback) | ISBN 9781509948130 (paperback) | ISBN 9781509948062 (pdf) | ISBN 9781509948055 (Epub)

Subjects: LCSH: Non-state actors (International relations) | Law of the sea.

Classification: LCC KZ3925 . R63 2021 (print) | LCC KZ3925 (ebook) | DDC 341.4/5—dc23

LC record available at https://lccn.loc.gov/2021016644

LC ebook record available at https://lccn.loc.gov/2021016645

ISBN: HB: 978-1-50994-804-8
ePDF: 978-1-50994-806-2
ePub: 978-1-50994-805-5

Typeset by Compuscript Ltd, Shannon

To find out more about our authors and books visit www.hartpublishing.co.uk. Here you will find extracts, author information, details of forthcoming events and the option to sign up for our newsletters.

Acknowledgements

To the memory of my father,

HAVING BEEN BORN in the middle of the Atlantic Ocean (in the Azores), it was just natural to do a doctoral research in the law of the sea. This book is the result of that journey and is based on the PhD dissertation that I submitted and defended at the Lisbon School of Law of Universidade Católica Portuguesa.

This was challenging research that could not have been concluded if it were not for the support from my mother, sister and family, and from my friends and colleagues, who assisted me in the harshest moments on this path.

I am particularly thankful to Prof Maria da Glória Garcia and Prof Irini Papanicolopulu, who supervised my work as a PhD student and were always an example of resilience, courage, and creative thinking. Their words of wisdom and constant support were fundamental to the conclusion of this research.

I also owe acknowledgement to Professor Catherine Redgwell and Professor Fernando Loureiro Bastos, who examined my PhD dissertation and whose insightful comments were important in bringing this book to life.

I am also thankful to my colleagues at Católica. Special thanks are owed to Ana Taveira da Fonseca, André Salgado de Matos, António Cortês, Elsa Vaz Sequeira, Henrique Sousa Antunes, Jan Dalhuisen, Joana Arnaut, João Gama, Jorge Pereira da Silva, Luís Barreto Xavier, Marta Sá Rebelo, Miguel Correia, Pedro Garcia Marques, Rita Lynce de Faria and Tito Rendas. Their support was more important than they probably know.

Contents

Acknowledgements ... *v*
Table of Cases ... *xi*
Table of Treaties ... *xix*

1. Introduction ... 1
1. Setting the Scene ... 3
1.1. The Position of Private Actors in the LOSC ... 5
1.2. An Historical Account of Private Actors' Apartheid from International Law and the Law of the Sea ... 7
1.2.1. The Gradual Building of the Vattelian Premise ... 7
1.2.2. The Ongoing Erosion of the Vattelian Premise ... 11
1.3. Private Actors' Participation through Interpretation ... 13
2. Scheme of the Book ... 15

2. Participation of Private Actors as Subjects of Law ... 18
1. The Epistemological Function of Legal Personality ... 19
2. The Concept of Legal Personality in the Theory of Law ... 21
3. States' International Legal Personality: A Historical Redundancy ... 24
3.1. States as the Centrepiece of International Law ... 24
3.2. Reaffirming the Redundancy: States-only Conception of International Legal Personality ... 27
3.3. The Advent of Private Actors: Individuals-only Conception of International Legal Personality ... 30
4. Criteria for Assessing the International Legal Personality of Private Actors ... 32
4.1. The Criteria Adopted by the ICJ ... 32
4.2. A Composite Concept of International Legal Personality of Private Actors ... 33
4.3. A Procedural Concept of International Legal Personality ... 36
4.4. A Formal Concept of International Legal Personality ... 38
5. The Source of a Misconception: Legal Personality and Legal Capacity ... 41
5.1. The Ordeals of Private Actors' International Legal Personality ... 42
5.2. Single (Not Multiple) Legal Personality ... 45
5.3. Legal Personality as a Status Prior to a Given Legal Order ... 46
5.4. An Open and Empty Concept(ion) ... 48
5.5. An Inclusive Concept(ion) ... 48
6. Conclusion ... 49

3. Unveiling Private Actors' Entitlements **51**
1. Entitlements Deriving from Freedom of Navigation 51
1.1. The Right of Innocent Passage 53
1.2. The Role of Nationality of a Vessel as a Condition for the Enjoyment of Navigational Entitlements 58
2. The Puzzling Reference to Ships 61
2.1. Ships as Apparent Rights-holders 61
2.2. The Pragmatic Reason for Assigning Rights to Ships 64
3. States *and* Private Actors Navigational Rights-holders 64
3.1. States as Navigational Rights-holders 64
3.2. Private Actors as Navigational Rights-holders 66
3.2.1. The Structure and Obligational Scope of the LOSC's Provisions 67
3.2.2. Conferral of Rights Irrespective of Direct Effect 71
4. Intertwining the Position of Ship-owners and Flag States 75
4.1. The Genuine Link Requirement 77
4.2. The Indirect Responsibility of the Flag State 81
4.3. The Obligation of Due Diligence 84
5. Right to Compensation 87
5.1. The Grounds for Lawful Interference with Navigation 88
5.2. The Holder of the Right to Compensation 90
6. Conclusion 93

4. The Narrow Reading of Explicit Private Actors' Entitlements **95**
1. Rights Emerging from the Activities in the Area 96
1.1. The Ontological Function of the (State-like) Authority 97
1.2. The Participation of Private Miners in Activities in the Area 98
1.3. Entitlements of Private Miners 101
1.3.1. Pre-contractual Rights of the Applicants 101
1.3.1.1. Selection of the Contractor. Right to the Approval of the Plan of Work 102
1.3.1.2. Procedural Entitlements of the Applicants 102
1.3.2. Contractual Entitlements of Private Miners 104
1.3.3. The *Locus Standi* of Private Miners in Disputes Arising Out of Deep Seabed Mining 108
1.4. The Responsibility of Private Miners, the Authority and Sponsoring States 111
1.4.1. The Accountability of Private Miners and the Authority 112
1.4.2. The Accountability of Sponsoring States 113

2. The *Locus Standi* of Private Actors in Prompt Release Applications 118
2.1. The Function of Prompt Release Proceedings in the Framework of the LOSC 118
2.2. The Submission of Applications on Behalf of the Flag State 123
2.3. The Importance of Having Remedies 131
3. Conclusion 134

5. Taking Systemic Interpretation Seriously 136
1. The Common Genetic Code of the Law of the Sea and Human Rights Law 137
2. The Application of Human Rights Treaties at Sea 143
2.1. Jurisdiction as a Precondition of Human Rights Application 143
2.2. Human Rights Jurisdiction at Sea 145
3. Human Rights in the LOSC: Particularly, Repression of Slavery and the Protection of Human Life 166
3.1. Repression of Slavery 169
3.1.1. What Amounts to Slavery? 169
3.1.2. The Obligational Scope of Articles 99 and 110(1)(b) of the LOSC 172
3.2. The Protection of Life at Sea 176
3.2.1. Protection of Life under Article 98 of the LOSC 177
3.2.2. Protection of Life under Article 146 of the LOSC 183
4. Conclusion 185

6. Conclusion 187

Bibliography *191*
Index *207*

Table of Cases

ECOWAS Court of Justice

Hadijatou Mani Koraou v The Republic of Niger (ECW/CCJ/JUD/06/08) Economic Community of West African States Community Court of Justice, Judgment 27 October 2008 171

European Court of Human Rights

Marckx v Belgium (App no. 6833/74) ECtHR 13 June 1979 160
Airey v Ireland (App no. 6289/73) ECtHR 9 October 1979 160
López Ostra v Spain (App no. 16798/90) ECtHR 9 December 1994 160
Loizidou v Turkey (Preliminary Objections) (App no. 15318/89) ECtHR 23 March 1995 149
Loizidou v Turkey (App no. 15318/89) ECtHR 18 December 1996 .... 149, 155
L.C.B. v United Kingdom (App no. 23413/94) ECtHR 9 June 1998 177
Osman v United Kingdom (App no. 23452/94) ECtHR 28 October 1998 180
Rigopoulos v Spain (App no. 37388/97) ECtHR (Decision) 12 January 1999 163–64
Drieman and Others v Norway (App no. 33678/96) ECtHR (Decision) 4 May 2000 161–62
Xhavara and Others v Italy and Albania (App no. 39473/98) ECtHR (Decision) 11 January 2001 166
Streletz, Kessler and Krenz v Germany (App nos. 34044/96, 35532/97 and 44801/98) ECtHR 22 March 2001 176
Cyprus v Turkey (App no. 25781/94) ECtHR 10 May 2001 .... 149, 154–56
Banković and Others v Belgium and Others (App no. 52207/99) [GC] Decision 12 December 2001 .... 148–50, 153–57
Pretty v the United Kingdom (App no. 2346/02) ECtHR 29 April 2002 177
Gentilhomme, Schaff-Benhadji and Zerouki v France (App nos. 48205/99, 48207/99 and 48209/99) ECtHR 14 May 2002 .... 150, 153
Federation of Offshore Workers' Trade Unions and Others v Norway (App no. 38190/97) ECtHR (Decision) 27 June 2002 158
Assanidze v Georgia (App no. 71503/01) ECtHR 8 April 2004 .... 149–50, 152–53, 156
Ilaşcu and Others v Moldava and Russia (App no. 48787/99) ECtHR 8 July 2004 .... 144, 149–50, 152–55, 160

Issa and Others v Turkey (App no. 31821/96) ECtHR 16 November 2004 ....144, 150, 153, 155, 157
Öneryildiz v Turkey (App no. 48939/99) ECtHR [GC] 30 November 2004 177
Öcalan v Turkey (App no. 46221/99) ECtHR [GC] 12 May 2005 157
Siliadin v France (App. no. 73316/01) ECtHR 26 July 2005 170–71
Saddam Hussein v Albania et al (App no. 23276/04) ECtHR (Decision) 14 March 2006 ....150, 157
Maria Isaak and Others v Turkey (App no. 44587/98) ECtHR (Decision) 28 September 2006 ....153, 157
Markovic and Others v Italy (App no. 1398/03) ECtHR [GC] 14 December 2006....157
Kontrová v Slovakia (App no. 7510/04) ECtHR 31 May 2007....180
Mansur Pad and Others v Turkey (App no. 60167/00) ECtHR (Decision) 28 June 2007....150, 157
Solomou and Others v Turkey (App no. 36832/97) ECtHR 24 June 2008,.... 144, 150, 153, 157
Branko Tomašić and Others v Croatia (App no. 46598/06) ECtHR 15 January 2009 180–81
Women on Waves and Others v Portugal (App no. 31276/05) ECtHR 3 February 2009....162, 164
Al-Saadoon and Mufdhi v United Kingdom (App no. 61498/08) ECtHR (Decision) 30 March 2009.... 152–53, 157, 159
Opuz v Turkey (App no. 33401/02) ECtHR 9 June 2009 181
Andreou v Turkey (App no. 45653/99) ECtHR 27 October 2009....157
Mikayil Mammadov v Azerbaijan (App no. 4762/05) ECtHR 17 December 2009....181
Rantsev v Cyprus and Russia (App no. 25965/04) ECtHR 7 January 2010.... 153, 170–71
Medvedyev and Others v France (App no. 3394/03) ECtHR 29 March 2010....145, 151, 163
Al-Skeini and Others v United Kingdom (App no. 55721/07) ECtHR [GC] 7 July 2011.... 148–53, 155, 157, 159
Al-Jedda v United Kingdom (App no. 27021/08) ECtHR [GC] 7 July 2011....144, 148, 157
Ivanţoc and Others v Moldova and Russia (App no. 23687/05) ECtHR 15 November 2011....155
Hirsi Jamaa and Others v Italy (App no. 27765/09) ECtHR [GC] 23 February 2012 ....144–45, 152–53, 157, 159, 161, 164–65, 182
Nada v Switzerland (App no. 10593/08) ECtHR 12 September 2012....144, 150, 153

Lambi Longa v Netherlands (App no. 33917/12) ECtHR 9 October 2012 ....144, 150, 153
Catan and Others v Moldova and Russia (Apps nos. 43370/04, 8252/05 and 18454/06) ECtHR [GC] 19 October 2012 .... 144, 153–55
C.N. v United Kingdom (App no. 4239/08) ECtHR 13 November 2012 171
Vassis and Others v France (App no. 62736/09) ECtHR 27 June 2013 164
Ali Samatar and Others v France (Apps nos. 17110/10 and 17301/10) ECtHR 4 December 2014 162–63
Hassan and Others v France (Apps nos. 46695/10 and 54588/10) ECtHR 4 December 2014 162–63
L.E. v Greece (App no. 71545/12) ECtHR 21 January 2016 171
Mozer v Moldova and Russia (App no. 11138/10) ECtHR [GC] 23 February 2016 154
Bakanova v Lithuania (App 11167/12) ECtHR 31 May 2016 154
Chowdury and Others v Greece (App no. 21884/15) ECtHR 30 March 2017 170–71
Apcov v Moldova and Russia (App no. 12463/07) ECtHR 30 May 2017 154
Soyma v Moldova, Russia and Ukraine (App no. 1203/05) ECtHR [GC] 30 May 2017 154
Vardanean v Moldova and Russia (App no. 22200/10) ECtHR 30 May 2017 154
N.D. and N.T. v Spain (Apps nos. 8675/15 and 8697/15) ECtHR 3 October 2017 144
Braga v Republic of Moldova and Russia (App no. 76957/01) ECtHR 17 October 2017 155
Draci v Republic of Moldova and Russia (App no. 5349/02) ECtHR 17 October 2017 155

Court of Justice of the European Union

Case C-308/06 *The Queen, on the Application of International Association of Independent Tanker Owners (Intertanko) and Others v Secretary of State for Transport* [2008] ECR I-04057 67

Inter-American Commission on Human Rights

The Haitian Centre for Human Rights and Others v United States [Decision, 13 March 1997] Inter-American Commission on Human Rights, Report no. 51/96 144
Victor Saldaño v Argentina [Decision, 11 March 1999] Inter-American Commission on Human Rights, Report No. 38/99 151

Inter-American Court of Human Rights

The Right to Information on Consular Assistance in the Framework of the Guarantees of the Due Process of Law [Advisory Opinion, 1 October 1999] ACtHR Series A, No. 16 167

International Court of Justice

Corfu Channel (United Kingdom v Albania) (Merits) [Judgment, 9 April 1949] ICJ Rep 4 .... 54–56, 168

Reparation for Injuries Suffered in the Service of the United Nations [Advisory Opinion, 11 April 1949] ICJ Rep 174 2

Barcelona Traction, Light and Power Company Limited (Belgium v Spain) (2nd Phase) [Judgment, 5 February 1970] ICJ Rep 3 .... 46, 169

Western Sahara [Advisory Opinion, 16 October 1975] ICJ Rep 12 .... 19, 33

Military and Paramilitary Activities in and against Nicaragua (Nicaragua v United States of America) (Merits) [Judgment, 27 June 1986] ICJ Rep 14 54

Arbitral Award of 31 July 1989 (Guinea-Bissau v Senegal) [Judgment, 12 November 1991] ICJ Rep 53 63

Legality of the Use by a State of Nuclear Weapons in Armed Conflict [Advisory Opinion, 8 July 1996] ICJ Rep 66 19

Legality of the Threat or Use of Nuclear Weapons [Advisory Opinion, 8 July 1996] ICJ Rep 226 132

Maritime Delimitation and Territorial Questions between Qatar and Bahrain (Qatar v Bahrain) (Merits) [Judgment, 16 March 2001] ICJ Rep 40 57

LaGrand (Germany v United States of America) [Judgment, 27 June 2001] ICJ Rep 466 38

Avena and Other Mexican Nationals (Mexico v United States of America) [Judgment, 31 March 2004] ICJ Rep 12 38

Legal Consequences of the Construction of a Wall in the Occupied Palestinian Territory [Advisory Opinion, 9 July 2004] ICJ Rep 136 .... 14, 150

Application of the Convention on the Prevention and Punishment of the Crime of Genocide (Bosnia and Herzegovina v Serbia and Montenegro) [Judgment 26 February 2007] ICJ Rep 43 69

Ahmadou Sadio Diallo (Republic of Guinea v Democratic Republic of Congo) (Preliminary Objections) [Judgment, 24 May 2007] ICJ Rep 582 44

Dispute regarding Navigational and Related Rights (Costa Rica v Nicaragua) [Judgment, 13 July 2009] ICJ Rep 214 14

Pulp Mills on the River Uruguay (Argentina v Uruguay) [Judgment, 20 April 2010] ICJ Rep 14 84

International Criminal Tribunal for the Former Yugoslavia

Prosecutor v Duško Tadić [Decision, 2 October 1995] ICTY Case No. IT-94-1-A........11, 140
Prosecutor v Duško Tadić [Judgment, 15 July 1999] ICTY Case No. IT-94-1-A........86
Prosecutor v Kunarac et al [Judgment, 22 February 2001] ICTY Case No. IT-96-23-T........171

International Tribunal for the Law of the Sea

M/V 'Saiga' Case (No. 1) (Saint Vincent and the Grenadines v Guinea) [Judgment, 4 December 1997] ITLOS Rep 16........120
M/V 'Saiga' (No. 2) (Saint Vincent and the Grenadines v Guinea) [Judgment, 1 July 1999] ITLOS Rep 10........3, 52, 168
'Camouco' (Panama v France) [Judgment, 7 February 2000] ITLOS Rep 10........118–20, 122–23, 125
'Monte Confurco' (Seychelles v France) [Judgment, 18 December 2000] ITLOS Rep 86........119–20, 123, 125
'Grand Prince' (Belize v France) [Judgment, 20 April 2001] ITLOS Rep 17........120, 125, 128–29
'Chaisiri Reefer 2' (Panama v Yemen) [Order, 13 July 2001] ITLOS Rep 82........125
'Volga' (Russian Federation v Australia) [Judgment, 23 December 2002] ITLOS Rep 10........119–21, 123, 125
'Juno Trader' (Saint Vincent and the Grenadines v Guinea-Bissau) [Judgment, 18 December 2004] ITLOS Rep 17........119, 123, 125, 168
'Hoshinmaru' (Japan v Russian Federation) [Judgment, 6 August 2007] ITLOS Rep 18........119, 123, 125
'Tomimaru' (Japan v Russian Federation) [Judgment, 6 August 2007] ITLOS Rep 74........119, 125, 168
Responsibilities and Obligations of States Sponsoring Persons and Entities with respect to Activities in the Area [Advisory Opinion, 1 February 2011] ITLOS Rep 10........83–85, 99
M/V 'Louisa' (Saint Vincent and the Grenadines v Kingdom of Spain) [Judgment, 28 May 2013] ITLOS Rep 4........168
M/V 'Virginia G' (Panama v Guinea-Bissau) [Judgment, 14 April 2014] ITLOS Rep 4........71, 77, 79, 81, 84, 124
Request for an Advisory Opinion Submitted by the Sub-Regional Fisheries Commission (SRFC) [Advisory Opinion of 2 April 2015] ITLOS Rep 4........69, 81–83
Enrica Lexie (Italy v India) [Order, 24 July 2015] ITLOS Rep 176........168

Permanent Court of International Justice

The Case of the SS 'Lotus' [Judgment, 7 September 1927] PCIJ Series A, No. 10 .... 3, 60, 146
Case concerning the Factory at Chorzów (Claim for Indemnity) (Merits) [Judgment, 13 September 1928] PCIJ Series A, No. 17 44
Case concerning the Payment of Various Serbian Loans Issued in France / Case concerning the Payment in Gold of the Brazilian Federal Loans Issued in France [Judgment, 12 July 1929] PCIJ Series A, Nos. 20/21 44
Jurisdiction of the Courts of Danzig (Pecuniary Claims of Danzig Railway Officials Who have Passed into the Polish Service, against the Polish Railways Administration) [Advisory Opinion, 3 March 1928] PCIJ Series B, No. 75 12
Legal Status of Eastern Greenland [Judgment, 5 April 1933] PCIJ Series A/B, No. 53 146

International Arbitral Tribunals' Awards and Decisions

In the Matter of an Arbitration pursuant to an Agreement to Arbitrate Dated 3 October 1996, between Eritrea and Yemen (Maritime Delimitation) (Award of the Arbitral Tribunal in the Second Stage of the Proceedings) [Award, 17 December 1999] PCA Case no. 1996-04 44
Guyana v Suriname [Award, 17 September 2007] PCA Case No. 2004-04 121
Arctic Sunrise Arbitration (The Netherlands v Russian Federation) (Merits) [Award, 14 August 2015] PCA Case No. 2014-02 168

United Nations Committee Against Torture

J.H.A. v Spain (CAT/C/41/D/323/2007) 21 November 2008 164

United Nations Human Rights Committee

Sergio Euben Lopez Burgos v Uruguay (Communication No. R.12/52) Human Rights Committee 29 July 1981, UN Doc. Supp. No. 40 (A/36/40) 151
Lilian Celiberti de Casariego v Uruguay (Communication No. 59/1979) Human Rights Committee 29 July 1981, UN Doc. CCPR/C/OP/1 151
Baboeram and others v Suriname (Communications nos. 146/1983 and 148 to 154/1983) Human Rights Committee 4 April 1985 UN Doc. Supp. No. 40 (A/40/40) 177

World Trade Organization Appellate Body

WTO, *United States: Standards for Reformulated and Conventional Gasoline* (20 May 1996) WT/DS2/AB/R..141
WTO, *United States: Import Prohibition of Certain Shrimp and Shrimp Products* (12 October 1998) WT/DS58/AB/R........................104

Table of Treaties

1910 Brussels International Convention for the Unification of Certain Rules of Law relating to Assistance and Salvage at Sea and Protocol of Signature (adopted 23 September 1910, entered into force 1 March 1913) *UKTS* 4 (1913), Cd. 6677 181

1926 Slavery Convention (adopted 25 September 1926, entered into force 9 March 1927) 60 *LNTS* 254 [Registration No. 1414] 169–70

Convention for the Protection of Human Rights and Fundamental Freedoms (adopted 4 November 1950, entered into force 3 September 1953) 213 *UNTS* 222 [Registration No. 2889] (ECHR) 17, 32, 35, 37, 43, 110, 130, 142–46, 149–51, 153–66, 170, 174–76, 181–83, 185, 189

1958 Convention on the Territorial Sea and the Contiguous Zone (adopted 29 April 1958, entered into force 10 September 1964) 516 *UNTS* 206 [Registration No. 7477] (TSC) 54–55

1958 Geneva Convention on the High Seas (adopted 29 April 1958, entered into force 30 September 1962, pursuant to Article 34) 450 *UNTS* 82 [Registration No. 6465] (HSC) 5, 62, 66, 77–78, 169, 172–73, 177

1963 Vienna Convention on Consular Relations (adopted 24 April 1963, entered into force 19 March 1967) 596 *UNTS* 261 [Registration No. 8638] 166

1969 Vienna Convention on the Law of Treaties (adopted 23 May 1969, entered into force 27 January 1980) 1155 *UNTS* 331 [Registration No. 18232] (VCLT) 1, 7, 13–15, 28–29, 51, 63, 78, 94, 127, 134–37, 141, 175, 186, 188–89

1969 International Convention on Civil Liability for Oil Pollution Damage (adopted 29 November 1969, entered into force 19 June 1975) 973 *UNTS* 3 [Registration No. 14097] 67, 70

1972 Convention on the International Regulations for Preventing Collisions at Sea (adopted 20 October 1972, entered into force 15 July 1977) 1050 *UNTS* 18 [Registration No. 15824] 55, 184

1973/1978 International Convention for the Prevention of Pollution from Ships (adopted 2 November 1973 and 17 February 1978, entered into force 2 October 1983) 1340 *UNTS* 62 [Registration No. 22484] (MARPOL) 62, 68, 148

1974 International Convention for the Safety of Life at Sea (adopted 1 November 1974, entered into force 25 May 1980) 1184 *UNTS* 278 [Registration No. 18961] (SOLAS)...............11, 61–62, 161, 177, 179–80, 184

1979 International Convention on Maritime Search and Rescue (adopted 27 April 1979, entered into force 22 June 1985) 1405 *UNTS* 119 [Registration No. 23489] (SAR).............. 161, 165, 177–78, 180, 182

1982 United Nations Convention on the Law of the Sea (adopted 10 December 1982, entered into force 16 November 1994) 1834 *UNTS* 397 [Registration No. 31363] (LOSC).................. 3, 5–7, 11–12, 16–17, 29, 33–34, 39–40, 51–73, 75–83, 86–93, 95–102, 104–37, 141–43, 146–50, 157–62, 164–89

1988 Convention for the Suppression of Unlawful Acts against the Safety of Maritime Navigation (adopted 10 March 1988, entered into force 1 March 1992) 1678 *UNTS* 221 [Registration No. 29004] (SUA) 62, 89, 91, 167

1988 United Nations Convention against Illicit Traffic in Narcotic Drugs and Psychotropic Substances (adopted 20 December 1988, entered into force 11 November 1990) 1582 *UNTS* 95 [Registration No. 27627] 61, 66, 163, 167

1989 International Convention on Salvage (adopted 28 April 1989, entered into force 14 July 1996) 1953 *UNTS* 165 [Registration No. 33479] 177–79, 182

1994 Agreement relating to the Implementation of Part XI of the United Nations Convention on the Law of the Sea of 10 December 1982 [adopted 28 July 1994, entered into force provisionally on 16 November 1994, in accordance with Article 7 (1), and definitively on 28 July 1996, in accordance with Article 6 (1)] 1836 *UNTS* 42 [Registration no. 31364] 97

1995 Agreement for the Implementation of the Provisions of the United Nations Convention on the Law of the Sea of 10 December 1982 relating to the Conservation and Management of Straddling Fish Stocks and Highly Migratory Fish Stocks (adopted 4 December 1994, entered into force 11 December 2001) 2167 *UNTS* 88 [Registration No. 37924].......................... 62, 82, 89, 91, 167

1996/2010 International Convention on Liability and Compensation for Damage in Connection with the Carriage of Hazardous and Noxious Substances by Sea (adopted 3 May 1996, not entered into force yet) 67

Agreement on Illicit Traffic by Sea, Implementing Article 17 of the United Nations Convention against Illicit Traffic in Narcotic Drugs and Psychotropic Substances (adopted 31 January 1995, entered into force 1 May 2000) *CETS* 156, 2136 *UNTS* 79 [Registration No. 37251] 66, 89–91
2000 Protocol against the Smuggling of Migrants by Land, Sea and Air, Supplementing the United Nations Convention against Transnational Organized Crime (adopted 15 November 2000, entered into force 28 January 2004) UN Doc. A/RES/55/25 (2000) of 15 November 2000, Annex III, 2241 *UNTS* 507 [Registration No. 39574] 167, 173
2001 International Convention on Civil Liability for Bunker Oil Pollution Damage (adopted 23 March 2001, entered into force 21 November 2008) 40 *ILM* 1493 67
2005 Protocol to the Convention for the Suppression of Unlawful Acts Against the Safety of Maritime Navigation (adopted 14 October 2005, entered into force 28 July 2010) 1678 *UNTS* 222 (Registration No. 29004) 62, 89, 91, 167

1

Introduction

ARE PRIVATE ACTORS rights-holders under international law? This topic is not alien to those interested in international law, but it remains a divisive question and international law is still bereft of an established notion or criteria of private membership. To some extent, the lack of a shared understanding of the role of private actors within the international legal system derives from two phenomena (if over-simplification is allowed): whereas some follow a State-to-State conception of international law (and therefore are inclined to exclude or limit private actors' participation in international law), others are eager to upgrade private actors to an enhanced category of international legal persons (and therefore are very inclusive with respect to private actors). However, if at first glance both approaches seem contradictory, in the end they suffer from the same handicap: they are mainly influenced by a prior bias of what *should be* international law (and, as a result, who should be the recipients of international law *rules*), not by the rules of legal science.

The goal of this book is to evidence that interpretation is a powerful tool to foster private participation in international law – which means, to begin with, that to boost the status of private actors in international law is not just a matter of drafting new treaty rules, but also of being neutral but open to private actors. This effort of openness exists in parallel with the interpretative process governed by Articles 31–33 of the Vienna Convention on the Law of Treaties (VCLT) but does not refer directly to 'treaty interpretation' under those provisions: being neutral but open to private actors is a commandment to awareness and avoidance of implicit interpretative biases that may impact the outcome of an interpretative process. But whereas Articles 31–33 of the VCLT establish the canons on how to read a treaty rule and its environment, they do not address the role of one's assumptions, beliefs, worldviews, biases and conceptions in the interpretative process.[1] However, sharing a States-only conception, for instance, interferes with that process inasmuch as it ends up driving the interpreter to consider States as rights-holders (and excluding private actors from that category) not because of the wording, context, object or purpose of the treaty provision, but rather as a result of following that conception of

[1] Ronald Dworkin, *Law's Empire* (Hart 2012) 70–72.

international law. Therefore, to assess private participation in international law, one needs to unveil the rights assigned to private actors under its rules hand in hand with assessing how an interpretative bias against private participation in international law may affect the reading of a treaty rule. Both efforts need to be performed in a coordinated manner. To that end, this book singles out three cases in which private actors can hold rights and duties under international law, which refer to three *modus operandi* of that interpretative bias: first, the exclusion of private actors in the face of an ambiguous wording of a provision; second, the exclusion or limitation of the private actors' role in spite of the clear wording of a rule; and finally, the lack of a proper understanding of systemic interpretation and cross-regime interaction.

To that end, the law of the sea is a curious case, not only because oratorical studies in favour of private membership do not exist, but especially because practice and the legal scholarship produced are deeply embedded in a State-centred conception of international law. The immediate result of such narrative is that the prevailing reading of the law of the sea rules excludes or limits the status of private actors as subjects of law – not because the wording of such rules excludes rights or duties of private actors, but rather because the interpreter is clouded by an implicit bias against private actors. Therefore, one can easily find in the law of the sea examples of those three *modus operandi*. For that reason, the law of the sea provides an opportunity to assess and evidence how an interpretative bias has affected the international legal status of private actors, on the one hand, and, based on that awareness, to unveil the entitlements held by private actors under the current law of the sea rules, on the other hand.

This, in brief, is the task of the next chapters. But before entering into the *corpus* of the book, some remarks are necessary. First, the terms 'subject of international law', 'international legal person' or 'international legal subject' are used interchangeably.[2] In legal theory, sometimes a difference is established between 'subjects' and 'persons', whose interest or relevance is not always clear. In any case, such difference appears to be connected with a methodologically inaccurate view of different degrees of legal personality. Second, the term 'private actors' is meant to be comprehensive and include individual human beings and juristic persons created under the aegis of domestic law, such as corporations, foundations, associations or non-governmental organisations (NGOs) (ie for-profit and non-profit entities). These entities share two qualities: they do not appear in the province of law under international law rules, as international organisations do; and they do not hold the typical public powers of authority to be qualified as State under international law.

[2] See also Robert McCorquodale, 'The Individual and the International Legal System', in Malcolm Evans (ed), *International Law* (5th edn, OUP 2018) 259, 284–85; Kate Parlett, *The Individual in the International Legal System – Continuity and Change in International Law* (CUP 2011) 29–30; Anne Peters, *Beyond Human Rights – The Legal Status of the Individual in International Law* (CUP 2016) 36. Already in 1949, see *Reparation for Injuries Suffered in the Service of the United Nations* [Advisory Opinion, 11 April 1949] ICJ Rep 174, 178.

1. SETTING THE SCENE

'All happy families are alike; each unhappy family is unhappy in its own way', wrote Tolstoy in the first line of *Anna Karenina*.[3] A similar idea could be expressed with regard to private actors and the international legal order: most domains have expressed some kind of enthusiasm with respect to their participation (even if limited), but each domain feels its own kind of illness when equipping private actors with rights and duties. The law of the sea, being the utmost example of a traditional realm of international law, 'govern[ing] the relations between independent States',[4] is a domain where private actors' participation is a cause of severe dyspepsia: here, private actors 'seem to occupy a space so small that it can be compared to that of a rock or a small island;'[5] and a perfunctory analysis of the Law of the Sea Convention (LOSC) suggests that its rules assign powers, rights or duties to sovereign States only, as if States were the *arche* of international law.

In this context, if 'the name is the archetype of the thing',[6] as the poet once said, an enquiry on the status of private actors in the inter*national* law of the sea could be doomed to fail. At most, private actors would be *objects* of protection or *beneficiaries* – but not subjects of law. Not surprisingly, it has been claimed that the only link between them and the law of the sea is the nationality of the *ship*: this is visible in the 'ship-as-a-unit' concept, as articulated by the International Tribunal for the Law of the Sea (ITLOS), according to which 'the ship, every thing on it, and every person involved or interested in its operations are treated as an entity linked to the flag State. The nationalities of these persons are not relevant'.[7]

Curiously, however, the terminology used to identify international law never refers directly to the *State*, but rather to concepts related to groups of *persons* such as *peoples* (eg *ius gentium*, *law of nations*, *Völkerrecht*, *volkenrecht*, or *folkeret*) or *nations* (eg *international law*, *droit international*, *derecho internacional*, *diritto internazionalle* or *direito internacional*). The expressions *inter-State* or *States' law* have hardly been used, and only within a very specific context of private international law.[8] International law thereby does not seem to be an eponymous legal system.

[3] Leo Tolstoy, *Anna Karenina* [1873–77] (Wordsworth 1995) 2.

[4] *The Case of the SS 'Lotus'* [Judgment, 7 September 1927] PCIJ Series A, No. 10, 18.

[5] Irini Papanicolopulu, 'The Law of the Sea Convention: No Place for Persons?' (2012) 27 *International Journal of Marine and Coastal Law* 867, 868.

[6] Jorge Luis Borges, 'The Golem', in a literary reference to Plato, *Cratylus*, 383a. [*Nova Antologia Pessoal* (Quetzal 2017) 30]

[7] *M/V Saiga (No. 2) (Saint Vincent and the Grenadines v Guinea)* [Judgment, 1 July 1999] ITLOS Rep 10, § 106.

[8] See generally Rolando Quadri, 'Cours général de droit international public' (1964-III) 113 *Collected Courses of the Hague Academy of International Law* 237, 247–48.

Neither does history support the view of international law as a law between States: only in the eighteenth century, after the gradual personification of the State, were private actors excluded from international law; and only in the nineteenth century, after the work of positivist legal scholars, was it established that the subjects of international law were 'solely and exclusively' the sovereign *States*.[9] Before that, scholars outlined a set of rights and duties held by private actors under *ius gentium* and acknowledged what in present-day taxonomy would be their international legal personality – but not of the State-like community. This implied the allocation of rights and freedoms to private actors (including freedom of navigation), and the imposition of duties upon individuals, notably after the 'colourful'[10] appearance of pirates under *ius gentium*; even law-making was at some point in history the task of what one would nowadays call the industry: maritime *lex mercatoria*, the forerunner of the law of the sea and maritime law, was based on local customs formed by traders.[11]

Thus, far from being an absolute dogma, the apparent apartheid of private actors from international law is a late formula of historical contingency. And the current state of the art is not exactly one of a 'States-only' international law. One cannot say in a sound, Camusian style 'aujourd'hui, l'État est mort', since States remain the major international rights-holders. However, the formula of international law is not one of an algorithm that always leads to inter-State positions: private actors have been accepted as proper subjects of law under international law, and, if one sets aside an interpretative bias against their international status, it is possible to discover and recover rights and duties held by private actors dormant in several fields of international law. Therefore, 'the old understanding of international law as something created solely by and for sovereigns is defunct',[12] not because States have disappeared, or lost the primary role in international law, but rather because they share this domain with other subjects, including private actors.[13] Even the very notion of international legal personality has proved to be plastic and evolutive in order to accommodate the sociological importance of the constituent members of international law. Nonetheless, even if private actors' membership should no longer be questioned, their status is governed by the rule of 'uncertainty'; even when accepted as proper legal persons, 'there is little consensus about what that means'.[14] The role of interpretative biases helps to explain such uncertainty.

[9] eg Lassa Oppenheim, *International Law – A Treatise* (2nd edn, Longmans, Green and Co. 1912) 19.
[10] René-Jean Dupuy, *Le droit international* [1963] (12th edn, Presses Universitaires de France 2001) 47.
[11] Jean Combacau and Serge Sur, *Droit international public* (12th edn, LGDJ 2012) 9–10; Vaughan Lowe, *International Law* (OUP 2007) 45; Aleksandra Thurman, *The Justification of the Law of the Sea in Early Modern Europe* (PhD dissertation, University of Michigan 2010) 7.
[12] Paul B Stephan, 'Privatizing International Law' (2011) 97 *Virginia Law Review* 1573, 1574.
[13] Dominique Carreau and Fabrizio Marrella, *Droit international* (11th edn, Pedone 2012) 367.
[14] Parlett, *Individual* (n 2) 3.

1.1. The Position of Private Actors in the LOSC

Taking into account the LOSC, one can claim that the law of the sea is deeply embedded in an orthodox narrative of international law, as it is mostly concerned with assigning powers, rights and the corresponding duties to flag, coastal, port and sponsoring States, even if States bear rights for their nationals;[15] and with reconciling conflicting States' interests and preserving States' sovereignty (defined not as a *power to*, but rather as a *freedom from*, purported to allow States to develop their existence without any interference apart from the rules of international law),[16] which is evidenced, inter alia, in the rule of primary or exclusive jurisdiction of the flag State on the high seas.[17]

Nonetheless, one can find in the LOSC concerns with interests that transcend States, as is particularly notorious in Part XI of the LOSC, where a principle of the common heritage of mankind is articulated. Moreover, the layout of the LOSC is not one of absolute apartheid of private actors. A careful reading of some of its provisions reveals that private actors are often conceived as objects of protection (eg human life is protected under Articles 98 and 146 of the LOSC, whereas Article 99 of the LOSC sets forth a prohibition of slavery), and one can unveil a more sophisticated participation of private actors as proper subjects of law (ie as rights-holders) as, in my view, is the case for navigational entitlements,[18] the rights of exploration and exploitation of resources in the Area (ie the sea-bed and ocean floor and subsoil thereof beyond national spatial jurisdiction), or the property rights over these resources.[19] And ultimately, private actors are the beneficiaries of all maritime activities.[20] However, it is visible how the LOSC is uncomfortable with framing rights or duties enjoyed

[15] See Article 116 of the LOSC. There is no reference in the preparatory works of the LOSC or the HSC regarding the exact meaning of the wording of this provision. However, in the works of the International Law Commission that prepared the ground for the United Nations Convention for the Law of the Sea (UNCLOS) I, it is explained that 'the term "nationals" denotes fishing boats having the nationality of the State concerned' [ILC, *1956 Articles concerning the Law of the Sea with Commentaries*, in *YILC* (1956-II) 265, 286].

[16] Jean Combacau, 'Pas une puissance, une liberté: La souveraineté internationale et l'État' (1993) 67 *Pouvoirs* 47; Emmanuelle Jouannet, *The Liberal-Welfarist Law of Nations – A History of International Law* (CUP 2012) 29 and 33.

[17] Article 92(1) of the LOSC.

[18] Articles 17ff, 37ff, or 52–54 of the LOSC.

[19] Article 137(3) of the LOSC.

[20] See generally Irini Papanicolopulu, 'Human Rights and the Law of the Sea', in David Joseph Attard, Malgosia Fitzmaurice and Norman A Martínez Gutiérrez (eds), *The IMLI Manual of International Maritime Law*, vol. I, *The Law of the Sea* (OUP 2014) 509, 517, and *International Law and the Protection of People at Sea* (1st edn, OUP 2018) 43; Bernard Oxman, 'Human Rights and the United Nations Convention on the Law of the Sea' (1998) 36 *Columbia Journal of Transnational Law* 399, 401; Budislav Vukas, 'Droit de la mer et droits de l'homme', in *The Law of the Sea – Selected Writings* (Martinus Nijhoff 2004) 71, 71–72. See also, *mutatis mutandis*, Laurent Lucchini and Michel Vœlckel, *Droit de la mer*, tome I, *La mer et son droit. Les espaces maritimes* (Pedone 1990) 124.

by private actors: the prohibition of slavery is apparently framed in terms of a duty incumbent on flag States,[21] not as a right of individuals; provisions regarding navigational entitlements are apparently framed in terms of rights held by ships, not States or private actors; and Article 137(3) of the LOSC (the best example of an international right held by a private actor), is written in a negative wording.

An immediate effect of the segregation of private actors from the law of the sea is their meagre procedural relevance. With regard to the upstream production of law (ie the adoption of international treaties, or the creation of international customs), private actors cannot make the law of the sea, since they cannot be parties to treaties and their conduct cannot per se create or be regarded as evidence of an international custom. One cannot ignore that international law comprises some creative mechanisms of private actors' participation in the negotiation of treaties, but confined to non-binding contributions, mainly from NGOs. With regard to the downstream production of the law of the sea (ie the creation of international legal rules at the moment of its enforcement and/or application),[22] the procedural relevance of private actors is also meagre. The drafters of the LOSC created an institutional apparatus responsible for keeping its integrity but tailored after the State-to-State matrix of international dispute settlement. Nevertheless, some exceptions can be found. On the one hand, Article 20(2) of the ITLOS Statute[23] determines that the ITLOS is open to entities other than States – unlike the International Court of Justice (ICJ), which is only open to States.[24] Accordingly, Article 292(2) of the LOSC and Article 110(1) of the ITLOS Rules establish that, in prompt release proceedings, an application may be submitted 'on behalf' of the flag State of the vessel, provided that they are duly authorised by the flag State. On the other hand, the SDC has jurisdiction over claims submitted by private actors against the staff of the International Seabed Authority ('the Authority'),[25] and over disputes between the Authority and a prospective contractor,[26] between the Authority and private actors arising from deep seabed mining contracts,[27] and between the Authority and private actors when it is alleged that the Authority has incurred liability.[28]

As with other domains of international law, private actors' participation in the law of the sea has increased during recent decades, rather because new rights and duties have been assigned to private actors, or because we are more aware that private actors can also derive entitlements from existing

[21] Article 99 of the LOSC.
[22] Stephan, 'Privatizing' (n 12) 1586.
[23] Annex VI of the LOSC.
[24] Article 34(1) of the Statute of the ICJ.
[25] Articles 153(2)(b) and 168(3) of the LOSC.
[26] Article 187(d) of the LOSC.
[27] Article 187(c) of the LOSC.
[28] Article 187 (e) of the LOSC.

provisions of the LOSC: the message to keep in mind is that 'there is more to the LOSC provisions than catches the eye'.[29]

Nonetheless, the prevailing narrative of international law in general (inclusive of the law of the sea) is still embedded in an orthodox conception of international law, whereby its norms (and therefore its rights and duties) are addressed to States and, more limitedly, to international organisations. In this context, one of the purposes of this book is to unveil an alternative narrative underpinning the law of the sea realm: one in which private actors have their own legal personality, and as a result can be (and in fact *are*) equipped with rights and duties under international law. If one follows a new narrative (ie one that is open to accepting private actors as subjects of law hand in hand with States), one will discover and recover rights and duties assigned to private actors in already existing rules of international law, as can be documented in the law of the sea. To follow that narrative, one needs only to be aware and set aside an interpretative bias against private actors' membership in international law, which impacts the reading of the existing treaty-based rules without any support in the rules of legal science or treaty interpretation set out in Articles 31–33 of the VCLT.

1.2. An Historical Account of Private Actors' Apartheid from International Law and the Law of the Sea

1.2.1. The Gradual Building of the Vattelian Premise

'In the beginning it was the State' – this could be a Biblical introduction to the Vattelian premise and the exclusion of private actors from international law, since there was a time when international law was defined as 'the science which teaches the rights subsisting between nations or states, and the obligations correspondent to those rights'.[30] This would suggest that the rights-holders under international law and the law of the sea have always been, and could only be, States. However, this was not the case in early international legal thought, and it is certainly not the current state of the art. The only idea safe to articulate is that the apartheid of private actors was a contingent evolution of international law in the eighteenth century, when Vattel introduced a concept of law of nations confined to the relations among States, therefore excluding private actors. As a result, private actors, far from being perceived as subjects of international law, were considered 'subjects of the State' or 'under its exclusive control'.[31]

[29] Papanicolopulu, 'The Law of the Sea Convention' (n 5) 871.

[30] Emer de Vattel, *The Law of Nations* [*Le droit des gens, Ou principes de la loi naturelle, appliqués à la conduit et aux affaires des nations et des souverains*: 1758] (Liberty Fund 2008) 67.

[31] Antonio Cassese, *International Law* (2nd edn, OUP 2005) 143.

In the law of the sea, the exclusion of private actors seems even more evident, for its major functions are the allocation of spatial authority to States and the promotion of States' cooperation in ocean governance. Borrowing Dupuy's words,

> The sea has always been lashed by two major contrary winds: the wind from the high seas towards the land is the wind of freedom; the wind from land towards the high seas is the bearer of sovereignties. The law of the sea has always been in the middle between those conflicting forces.[32]

This entails a difficulty for emancipating private actors under the law of the sea, since the fight for freedom, like the fight for authority, is a collective enterprise. In this sense, it should not come as a surprise that the history of the law of the sea – more than the history of international law – soon became a tale between States or State-like communities.

Nevertheless, States' appropriation of the seas was not visible in the early days of *ius gentium*. In the sixteenth and seventeenth centuries, scholars shared the assumption that private actors were the genuine subjects of their *ius gentium* (although one cannot refer to legal subjectivity in that period), and therefore were comfortable with assigning rights and duties to private actors – and not to the State, which as a legal fiction had not been formed yet. Even when referring to the entitlements of the community, the *ius gentium* of early international legal scholars was aimed at regulating the conduct of the ruling king or prince.[33] Full membership and legal personality of private actors could be implicit (if such notions existed) when those scholars invoked Roman law rules governing jural relations among individuals and outlined a set of rights held by private actors under *ius gentium*, including the right to property,[34] to wage war,[35] and navigational freedoms.[36]

This was possible because, at the time those scholars wrote, the State (as a legal fiction and social artefact) did not exist. Between the sixteenth and the eighteenth century, and especially after the Peace of Westphalia, the idea of a territorial, sovereign State was gradually built until full fruition after the French Revolution.

[32] René-Jean Dupuy, 'The Sea under National Competence', in René-Jean Dupuy and Daniel Vignes (eds), *A Handbook on the New Law of the Sea* (Martinus Nijhoff 1991) 247, 247.

[33] eg Emmanuelle Tourme-Jouannet, 'Des origines coloniales du droit international: à propos du droit des gens modern au 18ème siècle', in Pierre-Marie Dupuy and Vincent Chetail (eds), *The Roots of International Law / Les fondements du droit international – Liber Amicorum Peter Haggenmacher* (Martinus Nijhoff 2014) 649, 657.

[34] eg Vitoria, *De Indis*, in Anthony Pagden and Jeremy Lawrance (ed), *Vitoria – Political Writings* (CUP 2010) 246; Hugo Grotius, '*De Jure Belli ac Pacis*', in Richard Tuck (ed), *The Rights of War and Peace* (Liberty Fund 2005) chapters 2–4, and 6–10.

[35] eg Vitoria, *De Indis Relectio Posterior, sive de iure belli*, in Pagden and Lawrance (ed), *Vitoria* (n 34) 302; Grotius, *De Jure Belli*, III (n 34) 1374–80 and 1626–32, and *Commentary on the Law of Prize and Booty* [*De Iure Praedae Commentarius*: 1604–05] (Clarendon 1950) 271–72 and 274.

[36] eg Vitoria, *De Indis* (n 34) 278–80; Alberico Gentili, *De Iure Belli Libri Tres*, John C. Rolfe (ed) (Clarendon 1933) 91–92; Hugo Grotius, *Mare Liberum* [1604], in David Armitage (ed), *The Free Sea* (Liberty Fund 2004) 10.

In the eighteenth century, the magnetic force of the State was already so intense that soon the law of nations became a law governing the relations among sovereign States; the State moved from being a *creation* of philosophers, statesmen and legal scholars to being the *creator* and *sole subject* of the law of nations. The result, thus, was that an international society of patrimonial States and feudal relations gave way to an international society of territorial and sovereign States – and this meant that the law of nations was transformed from a broad *ius gentium* into a confined *ius inter gentes*.[37]

A pivotal step in this period was the depiction of the new territorial, political structures as legal subjects of their own, ie as holders of their own rights and duties.[38] Leibniz introduced for the first time a reference to States as *personae morales*,[39] in which he was followed by Pufendorf and Wolff, who looked at the State as an artificial or fictional legal person whose specificity was the possession of sovereignty.[40] As a consequence of providing sovereignty to States, private actors were excluded from international law. In the new framework of spatial governance of the world, the State became a tantalising legal concept, the centrepiece of a new legal order defined by reference to it.[41] Gradually legal scholars adopted a refined notion of the law of nations, confined to jural relations among nations, and thereby crafted a *new legal order*. This new legal order could only emerge because States, as juristic persons, already existed to be members: they were both the premises *and* the founding fathers of this new legal order. In the nineteenth century, the prominence of the sovereign State was so visible that international law could only be defined in an elliptical reference to the State: 'When we assert that there is such a thing as international law, we assert that there is a society of States; when we recognize that there is a society of States, we recognize that there is international law'.[42]

Under the new international law, only the sovereign State could hold rights and duties (which necessarily implied the wide acceptance of a States-only conception of international legal personality), whilst private actors could no longer be recipients of rights and duties. As a result of its influence, Vattel's treatise established what scholars qualify as the Vattelian premise:[43] States are the only subjects of international law, and thereby private actors are excluded from the international legal sphere; private actors have no interests autonomous

[37] Carl Schmitt, *Der Nomos der Erde im Völkerrecht des Jus Publicum Europaeum* (5th edn, Duncker and Humblot 2011) 99.

[38] eg Jouannet, *Liberal-Welfarist* (n 16) 34–35.

[39] *Codex Iuris Gentium* [1693], 'Praefatio', in Patrick Riley (ed), *Leibniz – Political Writings* (2nd edn, CUP 2006) 165–76.

[40] Samuel von Pufendorf, *De Jure Naturae et Gentium*, II [1672] C.H. Oldfather and W.A. Oldfather (eds) (Clarendon 1934) 12–13; Christian Wolff, *Jus Gentium Methodo Scientifica Pertractatum*, II [1749] Joseph H. Drake (ed) (Clarendon Press 1934) 20.

[41] Jouannet, *Liberal-Welfarist* (n 16) 112.

[42] John Westlake, *Chapters on the Principles of International Law*, I (CUP 1894) 5.

[43] Parlett, *Individual* (n 2) 11–13.

from States' interests, or at least no interests that cannot be pursued in the international sphere by the State; and States have the exclusive and discretionary right to establish membership criteria in international society, and thus to accept, deny or exclude other subjects from international society. This led to what can be qualified as the *Golem moment* in international law: from social creations, States became the creators and dominant players of the international legal sphere, which absorbed and represented private actors both in domestic and in international affairs, which implied that private actors were excluded from the international sphere. In this sense, international law followed the matrix of a patriarchal system, where only the father (ie the State) is responsible for the family constituents (ie individuals) and his sole voice is relevant in decision-making processes.

Curiously, however, such a system of a law between nations was very keen to subject individuals to a prohibition of piracy, since outlawing piracy was, and ought to be, a primary aim of a State-centric law of nations. A definition of piracy can be found in Blackstone:

> [T]he crime of piracy … is an offence against the universal law of society; a pirate being … *hosti humani generis*. As therefore he has renounced all the benefits of society and government, and has reduced himself afresh to the savage state of nature, by declaring war against all mankind, all mankind must declare war against him[44]

This is not a particularly authoritative writing on piracy, but embodies some of the most important features of repression of piracy at that time, when the State as a structure and legal person was being shaped: the high seas were conceived as a place outside society and civilisation, if not a place of anti-civilisation;[45] 'Law' being a social artefact, piracy was apparently carried out outside the province of law also; by nature, piracy was a statement against the States' system, for it assumed an alternative, Stateless form of organisation of life in a state of nature;[46] therefore, it was necessarily a realm of private violence (ie of individuals), the employment of State-sponsored force being the necessary means to eliminate piracy and promote trade and navigation. The emergence of the State following a claim to the monopoly of the use of legitimate force and the 'absorption' of individuals subject to their authority was not easy to reconcile with a concurrent claim to the use of force (employed against States and private vessels flying their flags) and to non-subjection to the States' system. Because piratical acts were so abhorrent to the new-born State, the international legal order sought to protect itself and deter concurrent claims to the legitimate use of force, since the building of the States' system presupposed binding individuals to a duty not to act outside the province of law and civilisation, not to

[44] William Blackstone, *The Commentaries on the Laws of England* [1753], in George Sharswood (ed), *The Commentaries on the Laws of England* (Liberty Fund 2004) 71.
[45] Philip Steinberg, *The Social Construction of the Ocean* (CUP 2001) 112.
[46] ibid 131.

pronounce against the system of the law of nations,[47] and especially not to reject State authority.[48]

1.2.2. The Ongoing Erosion of the Vattelian Premise

The Vattelian premise has survived until the twenty-first century, although subject to an ongoing, ever more intense process of erosion. The current state of the art is not exactly the same: States remain the lords of international law, but private actors are conquering autonomy vis-à-vis States in the international legal system. The de-Vattellisation of international law has been the result of conceiving private actors as objects of protection with autonomous interests, of conceiving private actors as beneficiaries of international law, and of the emergence of private actors as rights-holders in special domains of international law.

In fact, conceiving individuals as objects of protection was a particular consequence of the Vattelian premise, since transforming former subjects of law into objects of protection was key to their absorption at the international level. That protection was obtained by means of diplomatic or flag State protection, which operates at the level of secondary norms. But conceiving private actors as objects of protection is also evidence of the autonomy of their interests vis-à-vis States. In fact, as a social artefact, international law is concerned with human beings:[49] as the International Criminal Tribunal for the former Yugoslavia (ICTY) pointed out, '*hominum causa omne jus constitutum est*'.[50] The object matrix does not imply equipping private actors with rights and duties, but it entails affording protection to them at the level of primary norms also. For instance, awareness that the marine environment is unfriendly to human beings – 'It's no fish ye're buying, it's men's lives',[51] said Scott's character – explains the adoption of rules for the protection of seafarers and on the rescue of persons in distress at sea, a concern which is also visible in Article 98 of the LOSC and in the International Convention for the Safety of Life at Sea (SOLAS). In these cases, private actors are conceived of as objects of *special* protection, therefore imposing upon States obligations of conduct to protect human interests. This implies that international law assumes that States' interests might not be equivalent to human beings' interests but prioritises these

[47] *Lotus* [1927] 'Dissenting Opinion by Judge Moore', 70.

[48] William Hall, *A Treatise on International Law* (8th edn, OUP 1924) 310–11.

[49] See inter alia Gerhard Hafner, 'Some Thoughts on the State-Oriented and Individual-Oriented Approaches in International Law' (2009) 14 *Austrian Review of International and European Law* 27, 28; Antônio Augusto Cançado Trindade, *The Access of Individuals to International Justice* (OUP 2011) 13.

[50] *Prosecutor v Duško Tadić* [Decision, 2 October 1995] ICTY Case No. IT-94-1-A, § 97.

[51] Walter Scott, *The Antiquary* [1816] (Adam and Charles Black 1886) 108.

latter interests.[52] As mentioned by Meron, the 'humanization' of international law took place largely outside the subjects matrix.[53]

On the other hand, at the end of the nineteenth century, the concern with the status of private actors raised two seminal questions of international law: can treaties directly confer rights and duties on private actors within domestic legal systems? If so, what is the interplay between rules of domestic and international law? At first, scholars were reluctant to accept that a treaty could confer rights or impose duties upon private actors within the domestic legal system. The scenario changed, in the twentieth century, when international courts argued that States could commit themselves vis-à-vis other States in order to confer rights or impose duties upon private actors.[54] Wide support for direct effect was voiced, implying that treaties can be the direct source of private actors' rights and duties as enforced in the domestic legal order. More important, direct effect entails that international rules favour private actors within domestic law. For instance, maritime activities as regulated in the LOSC are apparently framed in terms of inter-State relations, but their ultimate beneficiaries can be private actors:[55] for example, under Article 116 of the LOSC 'All States have the right for their nationals to engage in fishing on the high seas'. Reflex protection of private actors under the direct effect of international rules is formally consistent with the tenets of the Vattelian premise, for it still works upon States' rights and duties, and not private actors' entitlements. However, it assumes that the nominal veil of statehood is artificial, as international rules, after mediation of the State, are addressed at private actors. Finally, the most blatant example of the erosion of the Vattelian premise has been the option under some international law domains to equip private actors with rights or duties at the very international level – a trend that is particularly visible under human rights law, investment law and criminal law, although the subjects matrix can be seen in most realms of international law.

'If there is a sense of reality, there must also be a sense of possibility'.[56] Therefore, if international law has evolved as an autotelic narrative based upon the totemic position of States – in contrast with private actors' status as bystanders – that ought not to preclude an enhanced position of private actors,

[52] Gerhard Hafner, 'The Emancipation of the Individual from the State under International Law' (2011) 358 *Collected Courses of the Hague Academy of International Law* 263, 319–20.

[53] Theodor Meron, *The Humanization of International Law* (Martinus Nijhoff 2006).

[54] *Jurisdiction of the Courts of Danzig (Pecuniary Claims of Danzig Railway Officials Who have Passed into the Polish Service, against the Polish Railways Administration)* [Advisory Opinion, 3 March 1928] PCIJ Series B, No. 75, 17–18.

[55] eg Jan Klabbers, 'Setting the Scene', in Jan Klabbers, Anne Peters and Geir Ulfstein (eds), *The Constitutionalization of International Law* (OUP 2009) 1, 16–17; Papanicolopulu, 'Human Rights' (n 20) 517, and *International Law* (n 20) 43; Vukas, 'Droit de la mer' (n 20) 71–72.

[56] Robert Musil, *The Man Without Qualities* [*Der Mann ohne Eigenschaften*: 1930–43] (Picador 2017) 10.

and especially it ought not to contaminate the reader of international law rules. In fact, from history one can conclude that the exclusion of private actors from the international legal order is not a dogma of faith, but rather a historical formula of contingency of international law: States have in fact become the dominant players in the international legal system, and the Vattellian premise is largely still in force. Nonetheless, there is no rule impairing private actors from holding rights and duties under the current rules of international law;[57] and international law has in fact evolved from a 'monoglossia' narrative based upon the heroic depiction of States into a 'heteroglossia' narrative where private actors, in the face of the gradual 'dethronement of States in modern international society',[58] have gained an enhanced participation.

1.3. Private Actors' Participation through Interpretation

The claim of this book is that an ordinary rule of international law can assign rights and duties to private actors. The major obstacle to recognising them as subjects of law with rights and duties under international law (ie as recipients of its rules) is a prevailing narrative (or *conception*) of international law as a domain of States-only jural relations, which leads to an implicit interpretative bias against assigning rights and duties to entities other than States, thus including private actors. Awareness of such bias, combined with an interpretation that is neutral but open to private actors, might help to unveil rights and duties of private actors under treaty provisions. The claim of this book is not that the assignment of rights and duties to private actors is benign or preferable: my claim is that, in some cases, private actors are already recipients of rights and duties, but an implicit bias against their membership in international law affects the interpreter of treaty provisions. To evidence this implicit interpretative bias, this book uses examples from the law of the sea, since this is a classic field of international law, ingrained in a State-centred conception, but where it is possible to find rights and duties assigned to private actors.

The claim of this book, therefore, is that private actors' participation can be obtained by means of treaty interpretation, namely if interpretation is neutral but open to private actors. Nonetheless, this book is *not* about treaty interpretation. The role of the interpretation of legal rules is to establish canons that assist the interpreter of a particular legal rule. In international law, Articles 31–33 of the VCLT establish a set of rules on treaty interpretation which are applicable by default and in principle to all treaties, even if

[57] eg Hersch Lauterpacht, *International Law and Human Rights* (Stevens and Sons 1950) 4.

[58] Antonio Cassese, 'States: Rise and Decline of the Primary Subjects of the International Community', in Bardo Fassbender and Anne Peters (eds), *The Oxford Handbook of International Law* (OUP 2014) 49, 65 ff.

their parties are not parties to the VCLT also.[59] The elements mentioned in Articles 31–33 of the VCLT are responsive to the specificities of international law and treaty interpretation, but they echo what was devised by legal scholarship, civil codes and other statutory norms in domestic legal systems. According to those provisions, treaties 'shall be interpreted in good faith', taking into account the 'ordinary meaning' of the terms used and the 'context' and 'object and purpose' of the treaty.[60] In addition, because international law is a system, systemic interpretation is required, although carefully designed with a reference to other treaties binding upon the same parties.[61] Preparatory works and other supplementary means of interpretation can also be used in order to confirm or to rule out one particular interpretation.[62] Finally, there is a special mention of the interpretation of treaties authenticated in two or more languages.[63] Even though the 'intention of the parties' and the 'spirit of the treaty' are not explicitly mentioned in Articles 31–33 of the VCLT, they are intuitive to lawyers trained at any domestic legal system, and therefore the ICJ stated that treaty provisions must be interpreted 'in accordance with the intentions of its authors as reflected by the text of the treaty and the other relevant factors in terms of interpretation'.[64] In a nutshell, this is the legal regime established in the VCLT, which largely reflects the customary international law.[65]

The claim of this book is not that any of these rules on treaty interpretation should be revisited, but rather that, hand in hand with them, the interpreter needs to be aware of the role of the biases that may affect the result of his interpretative effort. In fact, the canons on treaty interpretation (as reflected in Articles 31–33 of the VCLT) assist the interpreter in how to read a provision and its environment, but not in how to read the interpreter himself; they were not built, and are not supposed to deal with, the role of one's biases in the interpretative process. Irrespective of one's adherence to an objective, subjective or teleological approach, Articles 31–33 of the VCLT refer to the normative elements of the legal system, which are exogenous to the interpreter, whereas biases are intrinsic to every human being. As such, two different readers may follow the exact same interpretative protocol under Articles 31–33 of the VCLT (for example by sharing the same understanding of the 'ordinary means', 'context' and 'object and purpose' of that provision, and taking into account the same preparatory works and system of international law), but end up with different conclusions regarding who is the recipient of the same provision: that who follows a States-only conception of international law concludes that only

[59] Richard Gardiner, *Treaty Interpretation* (2nd edn, OUP 2017) 7.

[60] Article 31(1) of the VCLT.

[61] Article 31(3) of the VCLT.

[62] Article 31 of the VCLT.

[63] Article 33 of the VCLT.

[64] *Dispute regarding Navigational and Related Rights (Costa Rica v Nicaragua)* [Judgment, 13 July 2009] ICJ Rep 214, § 48.

[65] *Legal Consequences of the Construction of a Wall in the Occupied Palestinian Territory* [Advisory Opinion, 9 July 2004] ICJ Rep 136, § 94.

States (can) hold rights and duties under that provision, whereas who follows a formal conception of international legal personality assumes that private actors may also derive rights and duties from the same provision. The difference in the readings is not explained by a misuse of any of the canons set out in Articles 31–33 of the VCLT, or the adherence to a different approach, but rather on the biases that are inherent in all human beings.

Therefore, my claim is not that one should use different tools to read treaty provisions and their environment, but rather that the interpreter of those provisions and their environment may be affected by a bias against private membership in international law, which eventually affects the reading of those provisions. Biases may impact the very notion of international legal personality,[66] but of special concern for me are the interpretative biases that, even though not affecting one's conception of international legal personality, still have a reductive impact on the reading of international law rules and their environment. Such biases are inherent, in the sense that all interpretation involve presuppositions, conceptions and prior understandings of what one expects to find.[67] There is nothing dramatic about this, but one should be aware of the potential reductive effect of interpretative biases: first, by excluding private actors' rights or duties in face of an ambiguous wording; second, by excluding or reducing private actors' rights or duties despite the clear wording; finally, by not taking systemic interpretation seriously.

2. SCHEME OF THE BOOK

Chapter 2 aims, first, to evidence that international law is agnostic with respect to State or private membership (ie it is neutral but open to State and private participation). To that end, Chapter 2 establishes what could be 'international legal personality'. The traditional view is that private actors, in exceptional cases, can be viewed as international legal persons under a specific regime if they hold rights or duties under specific international law provisions and, according to some authors, have the means to enforce such rights and duties. This, however, is a fragmented view which is not shared in this book. First, because it would be tantamount to transposing into the legal system the Schrödinger's cat paradox: depending on a given legal domain, private actors would be and not be international legal persons at the same time. Moreover, it would be the same as depicting a private actor as someone affected by some kind of multiple personality disorder, by allowing the same entity to add an entirely new international legal personality to its domestic one. Both assumptions are counterfactual, methodologically inaccurate, and in fact an instrument for disenfranchisement

[66] Roland Portmann, *Legal Personality in International Law* (CUP 2010).
[67] Hans-Georg Gadamer, *Truth and Method*, (2nd edn, Bloomsbury 1989) 299–300.

of private actors from international law. Therefore, Chapter 2 assumes that there is no such thing as an *international* legal personality, since private actors have a *single* legal personality, which, as an epistemological tool, is prior to any given legal order and valid *ipso facto* under all legal orders, including international law. The immediate effect is that, if private actors are *ipso facto* potential addressees of rules from any legal system (including international law), then all legal systems are neutral but open to private actors.

Chapter 3 deals with the first *modus operandi* of the interpretative bias against private actors' participation in international law: the exclusion of private entitlements in the face of an ambiguous wording. More particularly, it analyses the navigational entitlements set out in the LOSC, with a particular mention of the detailed legal regimes of the right of innocent passage and the right to compensation. These entitlements are assigned to ships instead of States or private actors, but the analysis of their structure and the *ex ante* and *ex post* responsibility points to private actors being the holders of navigational entitlements directly under the LOSC. As such, they evidence the effects of interpretative biases in international law: the exclusion of possible, alternative interpretations of a specific legal rule, not because that rule cannot accommodate such interpretation, but rather because the interpreter shares an ontologically reduced reading of international legal rules and a dogmatic bias against private entities.

Chapter 3 refers to cases where the wording of the given provision is clear in assigning rights and duties to private actors, but still an interpretative bias has a reductive effect. That is the case of the status of private miners in the legal regime of the Area (Part XI of the LOSC) and of private applicants in the proceedings for the prompt release of vessels and crew members. In the case of private miners, their status is governed directly under the LOSC and other relevant international law instruments, which assign property rights to private miners as the exclusive rights of exploration for and exploitation of resources, and the ownership rights over the collected minerals. Nonetheless, the analysis of the position of private miners is still contaminated by a suspicion of private membership in international law. An example of such reluctance to accept the proper consequences of an explicit status under international law refers to the position of the sponsoring State, as shared by the ITLOS in the Advisory Opinion. If one looks carefully at the wording and the rationale of the legal regime of Part XI of the LOSC, one concludes that the sponsoring State was created in order to help the Authority in the exercise of its public function of resource governance. However, the ITLOS promoted the role of the sponsoring State in the performance of the resource exploitation activity, but at the expense of the private miner, and not of the Authority. A second case is the submission of applications for the prompt release of vessels and crew members, which can be submitted on behalf of the flag State. Article 292 of the LOSC is open to an interpretation according to which private actors can ignite a prompt release proceeding, despite the nominal participation of the flag State, but this provision has been interpreted in terms of a genuine State-to-State matrix. In other words, the effect of the interpretative bias is not reductive of the legal status of private applicants under Article 292 of the LOSC, but actually their exclusion *tout court*.

Finally, Chapter 4 refers to systemic interpretation. Considering the law of the sea and human rights law, this chapter assesses how the interaction between the European Convention on Human Rights (ECHR) and the LOSC uncovers new private actors' rights. This should not be surprising, but awareness of both fragmentation and cross-regime interaction is relatively new in the law of the sea: having been crafted as an exceptional regime for activities taking place outside the 'normal' province of law, the law of the sea evolved as a special domain of international law that would barely interact with general international law or with other special domains. This explains why the protection of life and the prohibition of slavery were included in the LOSC but detached from the homonym provisions from human rights law. However, if both domains share a common genetic code, then human rights treaties apply at sea and the LOSC and human rights treaties should be interpreted in conjunction. If this latter exercise is taken seriously, ie setting aside interpretative biases, one conclusion follows: if under LOSC some norms refer to States' sovereign powers, cross-regime interaction has the potential of transforming such powers into States' obligations towards private actors.

2

Participation of Private Actors as Subjects of Law

THE TOPIC OF this book is the status of private actors as rights-holders under the international legal order – ie *cases where they are the addressees of rules of international law, and therefore rights-holders under such rules* – with particular reference to the law of the sea. An inquest on the so-called 'international' legal personality of private actors is therefore instrumental for this book.

One could assume that this is a well-established concept, or at least that differences in scholarship and case law are negligible – but the notion of legal subjectivity is still unsettled in international law and was relatively overlooked for a long period: even in the wake of the human rights movement in the twentieth century only limited enthusiasm was devoted to legal personality under international law;[1] and attention paid to this doctrine declined after the ICJ's advisory opinion in the *Reparation for Injuries* case,[2] since most scholars took its definition as an authoritative starting point even if they considered it controversial.[3]

In fact, when reading a textbook or the syllabus of courses on public international law, one feels tempted to say that *there are* international legal subjects; that this concept is *autonomous* from legal subjectivity known in domestic legal systems; and that States are the *template* of full international legal subjectivity – in contrast to other entities (as private actors) who only have limited access to the international legal order, and therefore hold limited international legal subjectivity, if at all.[4] Yet these ideas are all but clear …

In addition, the reading of the same documents would lead to the conclusion that the criterion to assess the international legal personality of private

[1] Astrid Kjeldgaard-Pedersen, *The International Legal Personality of the Individual* (1st edn, OUP 2018) 2; Christian Tomuschat, 'International Law: Ensuring the Survival of Mankind on the Eve of a New Century – General Course on Public International Law' (1999) 281 *Collected Courses of the Hague Academy of International Law* 9, 149.

[2] Janne Nijman, *The Concept of International Legal Personality* (TMC Asser Press 2004) 4.

[3] eg see Ian Brownlie and James Crawford, *Brownlie's Principles of Public International Law* (9th edn, OUP 2019) 105; Kjeldgaard-Pedersen, *International* (n 1) 2.

[4] This 'narrow' subjectivity in international law is based on the argument that some rights can never be held by private actors, such as the right to wage war. See Anne Peters, *Beyond Human Rights – The Legal Status of the Individual in International Law* (CUP 2016) 42.

actors is simple, although composite: following the ICJ's *Reparation for Injuries* opinion, one would say that private actors are international legal subjects when States have intended to create an autonomous international legal entity; the new legal subject can act with actual autonomy from States;[5] and the entity concerned holds rights and duties conferred, or imposed, by an international rule (i), which might be enforced through international remedies, namely an international body, court or tribunal (ii).[6] Nonetheless, besides being a circular definition of what it means, for private actors, to be an international legal subject,[7] the very existence of an 'international' legal personality is all but evident, at least as an autonomous doctrine of international law.

In this framework, the first task of this chapter is to establish the epistemological relevance of the concept of international legal personality for the purpose of this study (Section 1). This doctrine can have several functions, but of my concern only is its methodological function as a means to determine relevance within the legal system. Section 2 explains what it means to be a legal person in general theory of law so that a more robust definition of 'international' legal person might be drafted. Section 3 explains why the idea of *States*' international legal personality results from a historical redundancy that influenced the drafting of the different concept(ion)s of international legal personality. Section 4 suggests the criteria that, in my view, are fit to assess the (one) legal personality of private actors, so that one might be in a better position to explain that the misconception referred to in Section 2 was the result of mixing concepts of legal personality and capacities (Section 5).

1. THE EPISTEMOLOGICAL FUNCTION OF LEGAL PERSONALITY

If there is a *function* assigned to international legal personality it is to identify 'those social entities relevant to the international legal system and those excluded from it';[8] those who can have rights and duties under international law and those who cannot.[9] In this sense, the usefulness of the concept of international legal subjectivity is epistemological: it is not an end in itself, neither does it have an inner life – it is rather a purposeful epistemological tool assigned with the function of identifying what entities can hold rights and duties under

[5] *Reparation for Injuries* [1949] 179; *Legality of the Use by a State of Nuclear Weapons in Armed Conflict* [Advisory Opinion, 8 July 1996] ICJ Rep 66, 75.

[6] *Reparation for Injuries* [1949] 178; *Western Sahara* [Advisory Opinion, 16 October 1975] ICJ Rep 12, § 148.

[7] As the ICJ acknowledged, this definition 'give[s] rise to controversy'. *Reparation for Injuries* [1949] 178.

[8] Roland Portmann, *Legal Personality in International Law* (CUP 2010) 1 and 5.

[9] eg Gerhard Hafner, 'The Emancipation of the Individual from the State under International Law' (2011) 358 *Collected Courses of the Hague Academy of International Law* 263, 282; Kjeldgaard-Pedersen, *International* (n 1) 1; Nijman, *Concept* (n 2) 3; Peters, *Beyond* (n 4) 41; Malcolm Shaw, *International Law* (CUP 2017) 155.

international law. As such, it is an objective and binary (yes–no) measure of relevance for the legal system – of determining what entities 'the legal system has cast to appear on the stage of the law'[10] as the 'actors of the play', and what entities 'participate in the production and overall performance' but are not vested with the 'privilege of making an appearance on stage'.[11]

This idea was challenged by the New Haven School, which claims that international legal theory has been held captive by the fruitless distinction between subjects and objects of international law, and thus disregards international legal subjectivity as a valuable tool.[12] Alternatively, authors from this school prefer resorting to an undefined concept of *participants* in the international decision-making structures,[13] coupled with a presumption of relevance in favour of any entity that *de facto* intervenes in international decision-making processes.[14] These scholars focus on the empirical evidence of entities that do participate in the international decision-making processes (regardless of their legal qualification) and on what behaviour is governed by international law rules.[15] Based on this evidence, they notice a system of 'democracy of access',[16] and end up concluding that private actors *are* participants in international law.[17]

The aim of the New Haven School is not to deny private actors' qualification as international legal persons, but to note the unhelpfulness of such qualification.[18] However, the main profit that can be taken from the New Haven School approach is that it makes clearer that private actors can act as *de facto* legal persons, even if not being formally recognised as such – but this is no help when dealing with specific legal issues, such as 'can a relevant actor be held responsible for a certain conduct?' The answer might be affirmative if that actor is the addressee of a legal norm, ie if that entity is a legal person; but the

[10] Bin Cheng, 'Introduction to Subjects of International Law', in Mohammed Bedjaoui (ed), *International Law: Achievements and Prospects* (Martinus Nijhoff 1991) 23, 24.

[11] Andrea Bianchi, 'The Fight for Inclusion: Non-State Actors and International Law', in Ulrich Fastenrath, Rudolf Geiger, Daniel-Erasmus Khan, Andreas Paulus, Sabine von Schorlemer and Christoph Vedder (eds), *From Bilateralism to Community Interest: Essays in Honour of Bruno Simma* (OUP 2011) 39, 40.

[12] eg Rosalyn Higgins, *Problems and Process – International Law and How We Use It* (Clarendon 1995) 49.

[13] ie the decision-making processes controlled by power, meaning attended by sanctions, Myres McDougal, 'International Law, Power, and Policy: A Contemporary Conception' (1953-I) 82 *Collected Courses of the Hague Academy of International Law* 133, 172, which are translated into a continuous flow of decisions taken by those who are expected to take them in accordance with criteria expected by the community, Myres McDougal, Harold Lasswell and Lung-chu Chen, *Human Rights and World Public Order* (Yale University Press 1980) 162.

[14] eg Higgins, *Problems* (n 12) 39–55.

[15] ibid 160–62. Lung-chu Chen, *An Introduction to Contemporary International Law – A Policy-Oriented Perspective* (3rd edn, OUP 2015) 94–95.

[16] Myres McDougal and Harold Lasswell, 'The Identification and Appraisal of Diverse Systems of Public Order' (1959) 53 *American Journal of International Law* 1, 18.

[17] Higgins, *Problems* (n 12) 50.

[18] ibid.

fact that it is a *relevant* participant means nothing, and helps nothing, in this task. Thus, the concept of international legal subjectivity is useful to provide some clarity and certainty to the legal system[19] and establishes with enhanced accuracy the pool of potential addressees of international law rules.[20] Being legal subjectivity 'participation plus some form of community acceptance',[21] participants (if relevant) should be legal persons; if they are socially relevant within the sphere of the international community, but are still deprived of legal personality, that fact per se is still meaningful for them.

A different, appealing idea is to shift attention to the concept of international legal relationship, ie a jural relation which is directly governed by an international law rule.[22] This shift makes clear that international legal subjectivity is not a concept from which one can deduce a certain number of qualities or capacities. It is rather an epistemological tool (a centre of allocation of rights and duties) used by a legal norm to equip specific entities with the capacities to promote their own interests. However, this approach is only slightly different from the legal personality approach, thus diverting attention to the other side of the same coin, with its specific, but symmetrical problems. Not surprisingly, it also loses in precision when determining an exact measure of private actors' relevance within the international legal order.

Therefore, my provisional option is to follow the concept of 'international' legal subjectivity, since this notion is useful to assess private actors' relevance under international law. As such, it is *the* criteria of relevance of actors, the boundary demarcating the territory of those entities that can hold rights and duties under the law, that might have the power of creating the law, and that are agents of action under the international legal system. Alternative options imply 'sailing in uncharted waters',[23] where clear insights and conclusions are scarce. As will be seen, what I use is actually the concept of legal capacity – but to understand that, some words on legal personality are necessary.

2. THE CONCEPT OF LEGAL PERSONALITY IN THE THEORY OF LAW

Resorting to the theory of law and to insights from municipal law to ascertain *what it means to be a legal person* is useful for several reasons. First, there is no concept of legal person in international law, no list of legal persons from which

[19] Anne Peters, 'Membership in the Global Constitutional Community', in Jan Klabbers, Anne Peters and Geir Ulfstein (eds), *The Constitutionalization of International Law* (OUP 2009) 153, 156.

[20] Nijman, *Concept* (n 2) 27; Peters, 'Membership' (n 19) 155.

[21] Shaw, *International Law* (n 9) 156.

[22] Christian Walter, 'Subjects of International Law', *Max Planck Encyclopedia of Public International Law*, §§ 30–31. For early assertions of such idea, see Hildebrando Accioly, *Tratado de Direito Internacional Público*, I (Imprensa Nacional 1933) 69; Paul Guggenheim, *Traité de droit international public*, I (Librairie de l'Université 1953) 171; or Alfred Verdross, *Völkerrecht* (5th edn, Springer 1964) 188.

[23] Bianchi, 'Fight' (n 11) 39–40.

one can infer the criteria of international legal subjectivity, and no established field of international law of persons.[24] In contrast, in domestic legal orders, the subjects of law (human individuals and juristic or fictitious entities) are clearly established.[25] The only apparently established rule is a presumption in favour of States' international legal personality.[26] Second, since international law was incubated, as *ius gentium*, under a truly monist system of law, international legal personality was crafted as a 'parasitic'[27] notion of legal personality in general. Third, the increased permeability between international and domestic legal orders also supports the legitimacy of a comparative law methodology in the absence of a specific concept in the international legal order. Finally, perhaps more importantly, it is not a task for a given legal order, but rather for the general theory of law, to define *what is* and *what it means to be* a legal subject, for this is a meta-legal concept.[28] This explains why the concept of legal personality common to domestic legal systems seems to have been automatically transposed into the international realm: being prior to the law province, the concept of legal subjectivity followed by domestic legal systems is sufficiently elastic to describe the phenomena of legal personality in all legal systems, including international law.

In contrast with domestic legal orders, however, in international law the discussion has never been whether juristic persons can be subjects of law: the historical evolution of the international legal system has made it as a law between juristic persons (ie States); the abnormal, *if* possible, would be the legal personality of human beings and other non-State entities. In this sense, discussions on international legal personality end up assuming that a State is genetically *the* subject of international law, whereas other entities might be qualified as such if the criteria for membership in the international community are fulfilled. But once admitted, a new subject of law is described through the same lenses of the theory of law as a centre of allocation of rights and duties as in domestic law.

In the theory of law, 'legal person' is a concept that surgically identifies *an entity that holds rights and/or duties deriving from norms of a specific legal order*.[29] In domestic legal orders, the thorough analysis of this category is the by-product of specific historical events that did not directly impact the international legal order, and the need to address societal problems that are not replicable in international law. However, being a *general concept of law*, it is

[24] Jan Klabbers, *International Law* (3rd edn, CUP 2021) 74; Peters, *Beyond* (n 4) 35; Portmann, *Legal Personality* (n 8) 5.

[25] Portmann, *Legal Personality* (n 8) 8.

[26] Alfred Verdross, *Die Verfassung der Völkerrechtsgemeinschaft* (Springer 1926) 156–63. Against, see Portmann, *Legal Personality* (n 8) 277.

[27] Mortimer Sellers, 'International Legal Personality' (2005) 11 *Just Gentium* 67, 67. See also Bianchi, 'Fight' (n 11) 40; Gerasimos Fourlanos, 'Subjectivity in International Law and the Position of the Individual' (1984) 53 *Nordisk Tidsskrift for International Ret* 9, 10.

[28] Portmann, *Legal Personality* (n 8) 10.

[29] Hans Kelsen, *Reine Rechtslehre* (2nd edn, Verlag Österreich, 2000) 172.

able to universalise and to apply in different legal contexts: that is the result of the common inception of *ius gentium* and private law, the fact that all jurists are born and trained in a particular domestic legal context (which explains the appeal of the legal tools they were taught as meta-positive), and the absence of a comprehensive study of legal personality in international law.[30]

This notion of legal personality is purely formal, meaning any entity with the abstract aptitude to hold rights or duties under the legal system – and *not* necessarily *to create* the law: this capacity, if it exists, is a plus, not a requirement. This is an important note since a historical misconception in international law is the idea that a (full) subject of international law is the entity possessing the capacity to *make* the law.[31] Nonetheless, for those following a formal conception of international subjectivity, the law-making capacity is not attached to this status:[32] international legal personality being a mere epistemological status, it is not coupled with a basic set of rights and duties, but rather refers to the ability to hold rights and duties of any nature under international law.[33]

The most disturbing conclusion from those who argue that law-making capacities are part of (full) international legal personality is the idea that being private-actor rule-takers, but not rule-makers, they cannot be (full) legal persons but only objects or beneficiaries of international law; or, alternatively, that they have a limited international legal subjectivity, as they have only limited access to downstream mechanisms of production of law (if such access is granted by a given treaty). However, in domestic law, private actors also do not have the right to make the law, but still they are proper and full legal subjects.[34] Moreover, private actors *de facto* have rights of participation in international processes and transnational governance, and take part in standard-setting processes.[35] To some extent, that is tokenism, since it is not the same thing to have actual

[30] On the migration of concepts and doctrines between domestic and international law, see Hersch Lauterpacht, *Private Law Sources and Analogies of International Law* (Longmans, Green, & Co 1927).

[31] eg see Dominique Carreau and Fabrizio Marrella, *Droit international* (11th edn, Pedone 2012) 368ff; Alexander Orakhelashvili, 'The Position of the Individual in International Law' (2001) 31 *California Western International Law Journal* 241, 256; Prosper Weil, 'Le droit international en quête de son identité – Cours générale de droit international public' (1992-VI) 237 *Collected Courses of the Hague Academy of International Law* 9, 118ff. As an alternative, some authors claim that a distinction should be made between members or active subjects (those who can create the law), and simple or passive subjects of law (those who are only recipients of legal norms). See inter alia Accioly, *Tratado*, I (n 22) 72; Robert Kolb, 'Nouvelle observation sur la détermination de la personnalité juridique internationale' (2002) 57 *Zeitschrift für öffentliches Recht* 229, 239; Alfred Verdross, 'Règles générales du droit international de la paix' (1929-V) 30 *Collected Courses of the Hague Academy of International Law* 275, 347; Verdross, *Völkerrecht* (n 22) 189.

[32] Peters, *Beyond* (n 4) 38; Portmann, *Legal Personality* (n 8) 173 and 274.

[33] Peters, *Beyond* (n 4) 41; Shaw, *International Law* (n 9) 208.

[34] Antônio Cançado Trindade, 'A consolidação da personalidade e da capacidade jurídicas do indivíduo como sujeito do direito internacional' (2003) 16 *Anuario Hispano-Luso-Americano de Derecho Internacional* 237, 247 and 284; Antônio Cançado Trindade, *International Law for Humankind: Towards a New Jus Gentium* (Martinus Nijhoff) 221.

[35] Peters, 'Membership' (n 19) 160; Cançado Trindade, 'A consolidação' (n 34) 247–49.

powers of law making or to have a participatory right, qualified or not, but at least it puts private actors somewhere halfway between merely possessing substantive rights and being able to shape the law that confers those rights.[36] In the end, there is no dogma against boosting the international legal personality of private actors: the nuances of history have successfully excluded private actors from international law making, but they do not preclude the development of a different framework in which private actors assume this function. The same way there is no rule establishing *who are* or *who can be* subject of international law, certainly 'there is no general legal rule impairing the individual from becoming a "subject of international law"',[37] let alone based on the absence of law-making capacities.

What can be said is that States hold the law-making competence;[38] some international organisations have the same competence granted by a specific provision of their (State-authored) constituent treaty, although limitedly; and other actors cannot create treaties or customs, even though they might have some kind of participation in the procedure prior to the adoption of a treaty. As said, the concept of legal person is useful to identify the relevant entities for the international legal system but is of very little assistance with regard to the specific capacities attached to it, namely the law-making competence.[39]

> The [common] mistake lies in the assumption that there is some prototype entity sitting away on a cloud somewhere for which the word 'person' stands, and which all entities pretending to 'personality' must imitate in their behaviour and characteristics if they are to pass the test of legal competence.[40]

This might have been correct in the past when only the State was equipped with international rights and duties; but it is no longer valid. Any suggestion that an entity is only an international legal subject when holding all the capacities historically defined for States (including the law-making competence) is misleading and implies being trapped in a contingent state of development of positive law.[41]

3. STATES' INTERNATIONAL LEGAL PERSONALITY: A HISTORICAL REDUNDANCY

3.1. States as the Centrepiece of International Law

In domestic legal orders, legal personality was originally granted or recognised as a result of the human condition. In international law, the analogy between

[36] Peters, 'Membership' (n 19) 160.
[37] Brownlie and Crawford, *Principles* (n 3) 111.
[38] Portmann, *Legal Personality* (n 8) 9.
[39] DP O'Connell, *International Law*, I (Stevens & Sons 1965) 89.
[40] ibid 89–90. See also Bianchi, 'Fight' (n 11) 41.
[41] Peters, *Beyond* (n 4) 41.

individuals and States was tempting already at an early stage, when the soul that gave life to States was the sovereign condition. In that period, State *sovereignty* was the key for international subjectivity and the sole requirement of membership in international law.

Under this conception, the sovereign State was conceived as the means through which the people of a territory could engage in the international arena, in a way regulated and facilitated by international law.[42] This meant that private actors were seen as if they were legally 'incapable' subjects in need of a legal representative to protect their interests at the international level, although these interests were transformed (after a formal process of legal novation) into States' interests.[43] Transposed into current lenses, this led to the belief that States are the typical and ordinary international legal subject, whereas other entities have a mere derived personality, in the sense that they are only created after an endowment from States acting as the gatekeepers of international law;[44] this conception of international law looks at other subjects as mere 'historical anomalies'.[45]

In early international legal scholarship,[46] States were compared to individuals: Hobbes compared man with the Commonwealth, and used an anthropomorphic image to match the political entity with specific parts of the human body;[47] Rachel, an early positivist, adopted the same metaphor;[48] and Wolff compared States to the individuals living in a state of nature.[49] The immediate result was that for some time the true subject of *ius gentium* was the person of the sovereign ruler – not the State-like community. This made possible the immediate translation of the idea of *individual* legal subjectivity into the international realm, even if the new legal subject was not a human being, but rather a fictitious entity known as 'State'. Even in the early twentieth century, scholars kept referring to the natural similarities between the State and individuals: some claimed that this analogy helped States to relate in the international legal sphere in the same way individuals do in the domestic legal sphere,[50] whilst others claimed that international law was addressed primarily to the human beings who are State agents or organs.[51]

[42] Timothy Endicott, 'The Logic of Freedom and Power', in Samantha Besson and John Tasioulas (eds), *The Philosophy of International Law* (OUP 2013) 245, 255.

[43] Emmanuel Roucounas, 'Facteurs privés et droit international public' (2002) 299 *Collected Courses of the Hague Academy of International Law* 9, 113.

[44] As identified also by Hafner, 'Emancipation' (n 9) 371; Tullio Treves, *Diritto internazionale – Problemi fondamentali* (Giuffrè 2005) 51.

[45] Paul de Visscher, 'Cours général de droit international public' (1972-II) 136 *Collected Courses of the Hague Academy of International Law* 1, 44–45.

[46] Early international legal scholars means, for this purpose, authors writing before 1758, the publication date of Vattel's treatise on the law of nations.

[47] Thomas Hobbes, *Leviathan*[1651] ed Richard Tuck (CUP 1996) 9–11.

[48] Samuel Rachel, *De Jure Naturae et Gentium Dissertationes* [1676] ed Ludwig von Bar (Carnegie Institute of Washington 1916) 157–58.

[49] Christian Wolff, *Jus Gentium Methodo Scientifica Pertractatum*, II [1749] (Clarendon 1934) 9–10.

[50] William Hall, *A Treatise on International Law* (8th edn, Clarendon 1924) 17.

[51] See inter alia Hugo Krabbe, *Die moderne Staats-Idee* (Martinus Nijhoff 1919) 272ff; Wilhelm Kaufmann, *Die Rechtskraft des Internationales Rechtes und das Verhältnis der Staatsgesetzgebungen und der Staatsorgane zu demselben* (Enke 1899) 1ff.

On the other hand, in a time when States would hardly act, in domestic affairs, as legal persons, it was easy to argue that international legal subjects were actually entities different from the ordinary domestic legal persons. As such, Wolff – the first author to refer to States as juristic persons (*personae morales*) – referred to States as *personae iure gentium*, and not just to *personae iure*, because he assumed that they could only be legal persons within the realm of *ius gentium*.[52] A century before, all authors that referred to a State-like entity in *ius gentium* – such as Leibniz (who introduced the expression *persona iure gentium*),[53] Althusius,[54] or Hobbes[55] – assumed that the entity acting in the international realm had no existence within the domestic sphere. Pufendorf also provided some flesh to the conception of the State as an artificial person, a moral person where 'supreme sovereignty … is found … and by which, as by the soul, it lives and is animated'.[56] But it would be with Vattel that it became established that States were *the* person who acts in international law, *the* entity that can hold rights and duties.[57]

As a result, the 'pragmatic answer' of international law to the problem of legal personality was to accept the State as the 'primary', if not the sole, subject of international law.[58] And one must concede that, despite the absence of specific rules regarding international legal personality, States are the normal addressees of the rules of international law.[59] This approach to international legal personality was based on the idea that only territorial entities could be subjects of international law; and even these entities had to comply with a very tight condition of *sovereign* membership. Afterwards, other entities claiming international legal subjectivity (as international organisations or private actors) had to face the same discomfort from States (but also from scholarship and case law) when it came to be recognised as such. The major outcome of this approach, shared even by those who acknowledge the existence of other subjects of international law, was the idea that States are the *lords* of international law[60] – meaning that they have the 'capacité nécessaire à la réalisation de l'idée du droit'[61] – whereas all other subjects owe their existence and international capacities to the treaties celebrated by States. This means, according to this view, that if a new legal

[52] Wolff, *Jus Gentium*, II (n 49) 9–10.

[53] Nijman, *Concept* (n 2) 29; JHW Verzijl, *International Law in Historical Perspective*, Part II, *International Persons* (AW Sijthoff 1969) 2–3.

[54] Johannes Althusius, *Politica – An Abridged Translation of Politics Methodically Set Forth and Illustrated with Sacred and Profane Examples* [1603] ed Frederick Carney (Liberty Fund 1995).

[55] *Thomas Hobbes, On the Citizen* [1642] ed Richard Tuck and Michael Silverthorne (CUP 1998).

[56] Samuel von Pufendorf, *De Jure Naturae et Gentium*, II [1672] (Clarendon 1934) 1000.

[57] Emer de Vattel, *The Law of Nations* [*Le droit des gens*: 1758] (Liberty Fund 2008) 67.

[58] Anthony Carty, *Philosophy of International Law* (Edinburgh University Press 2007) 81.

[59] Antonio Cassese, *International Law* (2nd edn, OUP 2005) 72.

[60] Angelika Emmerich-Fritsche, *Vom Völkerrecht zum Weltrecht* (Duncker & Humblot 2007) 104 ff.

[61] Hermann Mosler, 'Réflexions sur la personnalité juridique en droit international public', in *Mélanges offerts a Henri Rolin – Problèmes de droit des gens* (Pedone 1964) 228, 240.

subject emerges in international law, its subjectivity is bequeathed by the discretionary will of States, not per se or by the nature of the system.[62]

Nonetheless, other entities were ultimately recognised as international legal subjects. In reaction, some authors refer now to the State not as the *sole* or the *major* subject,[63] but rather as the *normal* international legal person[64] – meaning that States still control the international law making and enforcement, and that only States can have 'natural' access to the international legal sphere, whilst other entities are prima facie disenfranchised and have a mere accidental or abnormal international legal personality.

3.2. Reaffirming the Redundancy: States-only Conception of International Legal Personality

As mentioned, the State eventually became the primary, or even the sole, subject of international law. Of particular interest is its dogmatic offspring: the perception among scholars and adjudicators that States were also the *only* entities that *could be* subjects of international law.

It is true that nowadays one cannot say that States are the sole international legal persons, or even that they have the exclusive and absolute right to establish criteria and bestow personality on other legal entities.[65] Nevertheless, the impact of that understanding in the international legal thought was dramatic, since at some point the concepts and the *conceptions*[66] of international legal personality were purposively, although unconsciously, drafted to accommodate or exclude specific entities, in accordance with a previous conception of what *is* (or *should be*) international law. As with the *observer effect* in physics, here also the observer himself, through his act of observation and description, influenced the object of observation through the wording chosen to give flesh to the definition of international legal subjectivity. Accordingly, 'international law deliberately [displayed] a "self-protecting myopia" that [kept] other actors at the periphery'.[67] From a methodological standpoint, this myopia was the result of

[62] eg see Dionisio Anzilotti, *Corso di diritto internazionale*, I, *Introduzione – Teorie Generali* (Cedam 1955) 112; Cassese, *International Law* (n 59) 149; Patrick Daillier, Mathias Forteau, Alain Pellet and Ngyuen Quoc Dinh, *Droit international public* (8th edn, LGDJ 2009) 445; Orakhelashvili, 'Position' (n 31) 387.

[63] See Anne Peters, *Völkerrecht* (3rd edn, Schulthess 2012) 27, referring to the 'Hauptvölkerrechtssubjekte'.

[64] See *inter alia* Knut Ipsen, *Völkerrecht* (6th edn, CH Beck 2014) 49 ff; Hersch Lauterpacht, 'The Subjects of International Law', in E. Lauterpacht (ed), *International Law – Being the Collected Papers of Hersch Lauterpacht*, I (CUP 1970) 136, 136 [Subjects I]; Mosler, 'Réflexions' (n 61) 231 and 243; Verzijl, *International Law*, II (n 53) 5.

[65] Portmann, *Legal Personality* (n 8) 2–3.

[66] On this difference, see Ronald Dworkin, *Law's Empire* (Hart Publishing 1998) 70ff.

[67] Stephen Tully, *Corporations and International Lawmaking* (Martinus Nijhoff 2007) 5.

an interpretative bias, by assessing who could be the recipient of a rule of international law not according to the strict canons of interpretation of international law set out in the VCLT or in international customary law, but rather according to a restrictive reading of who are the subjects of international law, and therefore who could be the recipients of its rules.

This view of international law and the interpretative bias implicit in it was challenged in the first half of the twentieth century after the emergence of revisionist or individualist theories of international law, the statement of the Permanent Court of International Justice (PCIJ) in the *Danzig* case, and the drafting of some treaty provisions referring to rights or duties apparently conferred on private actors, which led some authors to reaffirm that only States could have legal subjectivity, whereas private actors could only be objects of protection of international norms. Among them, Triepel, Cavaglieri and Heilborn stood out, but the most prominent was certainly Anzilotti.[68] In his view, rules that apparently equip private actors with rights or duties are rather addressed at States, who should then confer that right, or repress that conduct, through domestic acts.[69] The immediate effect of this theory was that private actors could only enjoy that right after it was adopted by a domestic statute, and could not be punished for adopting a certain conduct before the adoption of the said statute.[70] When conferred, the right or duty in question would exist under domestic law and would be enforced through domestic remedies.[71]

But the reader should note that the need to explain why an *apparent* conferral of rights and duties is not actually a conferral of such rights and duties is already illustrative of the interpretative bias: it is not the case that the wording of those treaty law provisions could not accommodate a more ecumenical interpretation, but rather the interpreter could not conceive such interpretation as possible. Anzilotti himself acknowledged that his view, instead of proving that States were the only subjects of positive international law, took for granted that States were the only entities that could be subjects of international law.[72] In this sense, his argument was circular and presupposed infinite regression. A rule, if read with the lenses of a States-only conception, will determine a pure inter-State relation, whereas if read with different lenses will determine the existence of a right or duty held by private actors. By sharing an interpretative bias against private actors' relevance, these authors excluded other interpretations of international law rules, not because such rules cannot accommodate such alternative readings, but rather because the interpreter was clouded by an ontologically reduced reading of international law.[73]

[68] Anzilotti, *Corso* (n 62) 121.
[69] ibid 121.
[70] ibid 121.
[71] ibid 121.
[72] ibid 113.
[73] See *mutatis mutandis* Kjeldgaard-Pedersen, *International* (n 1) 3.

This leads to a question of interpretation that is not referred to in traditional studies on this topic: despite the efforts of the dogmatic project of Articles 31–33 of the VCLT, which aim at providing a certain objectivity and scientific character to the interpretation of treaties, this task is never entirely objective and depends on the specific prior understandings of the reader.[74] In this sense, the 'interpretative result' has no absolute value of itself; it is not a hidden treasure that any player can find provided that he follows a set of predetermined rules. Two readers using the same map will not find the same treasure: their interpretations of the same rule will differ as a result of their biases, presuppositions and conceptions. Accordingly, finding an objective, 'ordinary meaning' can be illusory: the prejudices one shares in favour of or against private membership will necessarily impact one's interpretation of a certain legal rule – including the definition of who holds rights and duties under that rule. There is nothing inherently dramatic about this, but it is important for all participants in the interpretative process to be aware of the potential reductive effect of such biases.

Furthermore, according to the legal methodology canons, one cannot interpret an international rule in terms of pure inter-State obligations because international law only binds States; only after interpreting the rule in question does one know if that norm binds States solely, or other entities also. For instance, pursuant to Article 17 of the LOSC, 'ships of all States … enjoy the right of innocent passage through the territorial sea'. This provision is studied in more detail in Chapter 3, but at this point it suffices to mention that if one follows a States-only conception of international legal personality, one will conclude that it is addressed at States, as if it read 'States enjoy the right of innocent passage'. However, what should be followed in terms of interpretative protocol is to assume that in theory other entities can be the recipients of this rule (including, hypothetically, a ship), and then enquire who is the actual recipient of the right of innocent passage. Moreover, under Article 137(2) of the LOSC 'All rights in the resources of the Area are vested in mankind as a whole'. Again, if one follows a States-only conception of international legal subjectivity, the conclusion could be that mankind means States; or, realising the difficulty of reconciling such view with the semantic element, that because States are not 'mankind as a whole', then resources in the Area are *res nullius* or *res communis*. In my view, again, one should be open-minded in terms of who could be the rights-holder under this provision – including, for instance, to ask if 'mankind' is the actual holder of such rights.

In addition, the States-only conception assumes that States are not a *creation* of law, but rather *the creator* of international law. This thought led to the remarkable conception of a fictitious legal order (international law) governing the relations between fictitious entities (States), in which the protection of

[74] Hans-Georg Gadamer, *Truth and Method* (2nd edn, Bloomsbury 1989) 299–300.

private actors' interests depended upon the performance of these fictions.[75] The problem, in my view, is that more than defining the legal status of private actors under this legal order, these scholars were defining what is international law.[76] In fact, by reducing international law to those entities that meet the criteria for statehood, a clear-cut boundary between domestic and international law is demarcated.[77] But if one defines this legal order by reference to its subjects governed by its set of rules, the most obvious outcome is to miss what is peculiar to each question, and provide a misleading answer to both.

3.3. The Advent of Private Actors: Individuals-only Conception of International Legal Personality

A States-only conception is hardly supported nowadays; its heyday ended as States started being conceived of as *pouvoirs contitués*, and not as the *pouvoir constituants* of international law.[78] Already on the eve and at the dawn of the twentieth century, authors such as Kaufmann, Lapradelle or Rehm claimed an opening of international law to private actors, but the most outstanding claims for enhancing the legal status of individuals were made in the 1920s and 1930s by authors such as Krabbe, Politis, Spiropoulos, Brierly, Kelsen, Scelle or Le Fur, who tried to move international law into a truly universal law.[79] These authors claimed that the State is a *legal fiction* and an *abstraction*, historically crafted in order to protect human interests. In order to protect such interests, international law should lift the veil of statehood and acknowledge that individuals are the ultimate subjects of international law and, as such, the ordinary recipients of international norms. These authors first claimed that the State is only a group of human beings connected by a link of nationality, not a metaphysical entity:[80] States are a mere legal fiction, not a person in a biological sense of the word.[81] As such, the actual members of the international community are States' nationals,[82] which implies that only individuals could be subjects of

[75] As mentioned by Roucounas, 'Facteurs privés' (n 43) 24.

[76] Kjeldgaard-Pedersen, *International* (n 1) 4.

[77] ibid 18.

[78] Peters, 'Membership' (n 19) 179–80.

[79] Nicolas Politis, *Les nouvelles tendances du droit international* (Hachette 1927) 55–93.

[80] Hans Kelsen, *Das Problem der Souvenatität und die Theorie des Völkerrechts* (Mohr Siebeck 1920) 16–18; Hans Kelsen, 'Les rapports de système entre le droit interne et le droit international public' (1926-IV) 14 *Collected Courses of the Hague Academy of International Law* 227, 242–43; Georges Scelle, *Précis de droit des gens – Principes et systématique*, I (Sirey 1932) 62.

[81] James Leslie Brierly, 'Règles générales du droit de la paix' (1936-IV) 58 *Collected Courses of the Hague Academy of International Law* 5, 47; James Leslie Brierly, *Law of Nations – An Introduction to the International Law of Peace* (6th edn, Clarendon 1963) 62–63; Scelle, *Précis*, I (n 80) 35.

[82] Georges Scelle, 'Règles générales du droit de la paix' (1933-IV) 46 *Collected Courses of the Hague Academy of International Law* 331, 343.

international law.[83] As a result, rules of international law are addressed to individuals and are binding upon them, within the municipal realm, without any need for an internal act of reception or transformation.

After World War II, the same path was followed by scholars such as Jessup[84] or Lauterpacht[85] – who claimed that nothing precludes private actors from being direct addressees of international law rules, and therefore from being subjects of international law.[86] In the 1960s, O'Connell touched the heart of the question when asked: 'Does it suffice to admit that the individuals' good is the ultimate end of the law but refuse the individual any capacity in the realisation of that good?'[87] Claiming that it is 'fallacious' to say that human beings are objects in the same way as 'stocks and shares and ships', he concluded that 'The common good of the community of men is the only intelligible end of international law'.[88] Hence, 'The individual as the end of community is a *member* of the community, and a member has a status: he is not an object'.[89] Apart from these authors, in the last 70 years scholars have upheld the idea that individuals are the ultimate subjects of international law,[90] or followed a Kantian, cosmopolitan view of international law, according to which the new societal paradigm of international life imposes enhanced forms of private actors' participation, but also a new conception of international law as a law governing mankind.[91] To delve into these authors' thought is beyond the scope of this book, but one aspect should be pointed out: what moved some of these authors was ideology and a belief in the benefits of upgrading the membership of individuals in the international arena. My view is not that such upgrade is necessary or beneficial, but rather that it may just be the result of an interpretative process that tries not to be contaminated with a bias against private membership in international law.

For its critics, this pro-individual view could only be seen as a radical school of thought. And in fact, one cannot actually say that private actors are the *sole* subjects of international law, even if the protection of their interests

[83] Brierly, 'Règles générales' (n 81) 47; Hans Kelsen, 'Théorie générale du droit international public – Problèmes choisis' (1932-IV) 42 *Collected Courses of the Hague Academy of International Law* 117, 145–46; Krabbe, *Die moderne* (n 51) 275–76; Scelle, *Précis*, I (n 80) 42; Scelle, 'Règles générales' (n 82) 366–67.

[84] Philip Jessup, *A Modern Law of Nations – An Introduction* (Macmillan 1950) 2 and 10.

[85] Hersch Lauterpacht, *International Law and Human Rights* (Stevens & Sons 1950) 69ff.

[86] Hersch Lauterpacht, 'The Grotian Tradition in International Law' (1946) 23 *British Yearbook of International Law* 1, 33–36.

[87] O'Connell, *International*, I (n 39) 107.

[88] ibid 92.

[89] ibid 118.

[90] eg Tomuschat, 'International' (n 1) 23.

[91] eg Rafael Domingo, *The New Global Law* (CUP 2010); Emmerich-Fritsche, *Vom Völkerrecht* (n 60) 338ff, esp. 338; CW Jenks, *The Common Law of Mankind* (Stevens 1958); Theodor Meron, *The Humanization of International Law* (Martinus Nijhoff 2006); John Rawls, *The Law of Peoples* (Harvard University Press 1999); Ruti Teitel, *Humanity's Law* (OUP 2011); or Cançado Trindade, *Humankind* (n 34).

is the ultimate end of international law. At least, it would be bizarre if States were the major international law-makers but were deprived of legal personality or capacities under international law. At most, what can be said is that beneath the veil of statehood there are individual human beings. In any case, the advent of individualism made possible the acknowledgment of private actors as international legal subjects, and the conclusion that 'there are no *a priori* international persons'.[92] This status is only acquired as a result of a discretionary option of an international norm (if not prior to the system itself, as explained below) when it takes a specific entity as the addressee of rights and duties.[93] This implies, nonetheless, that the international legal system is not a safe haven for any entity, apart from individuals in those very specific situations, although it is hard to imagine the abolition of the State as an (international) legal person.

4. CRITERIA FOR ASSESSING THE INTERNATIONAL LEGAL PERSONALITY OF PRIVATE ACTORS

A list of international legal persons is always displayed in international law textbooks. But apart from its pedagogic usefulness, no other consequence can be drawn from this enunciation, and in particular one cannot take such list as authoritative to determine who are the recipients of international legal norms. In fact, the method must be the opposite: first, to assess who are conceived by the international rule as the reference point for allocation of rights and duties; afterwards, based on that evidence, to recognise who the international legal persons are.[94] Therefore, the absence of a rule establishing who the international legal persons are is irrelevant from a methodological standpoint. What is critical, however, is to avoid any interpretative bias when identifying the addressees of international law rules.

4.1. The Criteria Adopted by the ICJ

Although referring to international organisations, the ICJ referred to a composite criteria to qualify international legal persons in general: (1) there is a new

[92] Against, see Frédéric Sudre, *Droit européen et international des droits de l'homme* (14th edn, Presses Universitaires de France 2019) 86, according to whom the international legal personality of private actors is precarious, because it presupposes a prior act of States conferring a right or a duty and the enforcement means, and since States can always denounce the treaty that conferred these rights and means (see Article 58 of the ECHR and Article 78 of the American Convention on Human Rights (ACHR)). However, considering that these treaties only *recognise*, and not *create*, new rights, if States denounce or revoke a human rights treaty, they will be depriving individuals of the institutional guarantees covered by that instrument, but not abrogating the substantive human rights in question.

[93] Mosler, 'Réflexions' (n 61) 244; Portmann, *Legal Personality* (n 8) 3.

[94] Bianchi, 'Fight' (n 11) 43.

international legal subject when States intended to create an autonomous entity; (2) when the new legal person can act with actual autonomy from States;[95] and (3) when the entity concerned holds rights and duties conferred or imposed on it by an international rule (i), which can be enforced through international remedies, namely a court, a tribunal, or a committee (ii).[96] This was not the most insightful formula articulated by the ICJ, but it is still the most authoritative formula regarding international legal personality.

Elements (1) and (2) of the criteria are not particularly relevant for assessing the legal subjectivity of private actors. For instance, with respect to the requirement (1) outlined by the ICJ, its assessment is based on treaty interpretation,[97] but only very exceptionally do constituent treaties of international organisations refer to its international legal personality, and no treaty-based provision explicitly refers to private actors' international legal personality.

4.2. A Composite Concept of International Legal Personality of Private Actors

Based on the ICJ's advisory opinion, a first approach to assert the international legal personality of private actors is what can be called a *composite* approach (coupling substantive and procedural requirements), according to which a private actor can only be qualified as an international legal person when holding a right or duty conferred on it by an international norm, coupled with an international remedy, ie the chance of enforcing that right or duty through international mechanisms, adversarial or not.[98] By implication, if private actors are deprived of remedies open to them in the international legal order, they are not subjects of international law, for they will inevitably depend on domestic remedies. For instance, Article 137(3) of the LOSC admits the allocation of property rights to the entities engaged in the exploitation of the Area's resources (including private actors), but this provision per se is not sufficient to qualify these entities as subjects of international law. However, private actors' subjectivity can be inferred from this provision coupled with the enforcement rights set out in Article 187(c) of the LOSC.

[95] *Reparation for Injuries* [1949] 179; *Legality of the Use of Nuclear Weapons* [1996] 75.

[96] *Reparation for Injuries* [1949] 178; *Western Sahara* [1975] § 148.

[97] Walter, 'Subjects' (n 22) § 5.

[98] See inter alia Brownlie and Crawford, *Principles* (n 3) 111; Daillier et al, *Droit* (n 62) 716 ff; Pierre-Marie Dupuy and Yann Kerbrat, *Droit international public* (13th edn, Dalloz 2016) 26 and 237; Guggenheim, *Traité*, I (n 22) 171; Hafner, 'Emancipation' (n 9) 321–22; Mosler, 'Réflexions' (n 61) 244–45; Carl Nørgaard, *The Position of the Individual in International Law* (Munksgaard 1962) 26ff, 33; Orakhelashvili, 'Position' (n 31) 256; Alf Ross, *A Textbook of International Law* (Longmans 1947) 24 and 110; Roucounas, 'Facteurs privés' (n 43) 41; Sudre, *Droit* (n 92) 84–85; Tomuschat, 'International' (n 1) 150–51; Verdross, 'Règles générales' (n 31) 348; *Völkerrecht* (n 22) 221–22; Verzijl, *International Law*, II (n 53) 3–4; Visscher, 'Cours général' (n 45) 44.

What happens if an international norm confers, at least apparently, a right or a duty on a private actor but does not mention any international enforcement means? For instance, Article 110 of the LOSC sets out an obligation (binding upon the ship-owner and operator) to tolerate interferences with navigation in specific cases, but apart from self-enforcement by the intervening State, nothing else is set out in that provision. For this conception, the norm might refer to jural relations in which private actors take part, but these relations are ruled by municipal law. Apparently implied, also, is the idea that the rule's obligational scope is purely inter-State, and imposes upon States a reciprocal obligation to confer, within their national legal order, the rights or duties set out in the international norm. As a result, some authors conclude that the 'individualisation' of international norms is much more common than the international legal personality of private actors.[99] But the disturbing conclusion that should follow is that if, for example, a ship is suspected of being engaged in one of the proscribed activities listed in Article 110(1) of the LOSC, non-flag States can only exercise their competence under this provision if the LOSC has been incorporated within the domestic legal order of the flag State of that ship, since no enforcement mechanism is laid down in that provision. But this limitation to Article 110 of the LOSC is by no means logical or established in its wording or in State practice.

Two factors help to explain this school of thought: on the one hand, the genetic legacy of the nineteenth-century positivism and Austin's ideas of law as a command; on the other hand, the temptation to compare with municipal legal orders, where rights are normally coupled with a specific judicial remedy. But this approach fails to understand the dynamics of international legal personality and capacities within both international and domestic legal systems.

In fact, the idea of coupling the possession of an international right or duty with an international remedy fails on accuracy and excessively narrows the subjectivity of private actors into a notion of adversarial relations. This is the interpretative bias stretched to the extreme: even if the wording of a provision indicates that private actors hold rights or duties, the temptation is to seek a reason to exclude such interpretative result. The underlying idea is that in the absence of a specific remedy in the international legal order, the right or duty in question does not exist within this realm, because each right or duty should have a specific remedy. However, this idea cannot be reversed to mean that without a remedy there is no right; in the absence of an international remedy, one cannot infer *ipso facto* the non-existence of an international right or duty without infringing the rules of legal science.[100] It might just be the case that the protection granted by the system to that specific right and duty is imperfect,[101]

[99] eg Sudre, *Droit* (n 92) 85.
[100] Fourlanos, 'Subjectivity' (n 27) 21.
[101] ibid; Higgins, *Problems* (n 12) 99, with respect to social, economic, and cultural rights.

but enforceability of a right is a common consequence of possessing that right, not a prior requirement[102] or an operative fact of the substantive right.[103] Secondary norms that provide for a remedy do not influence the qualification of primary norms: '"*Jus*" can exist without "action" (or "*remedium*")'.[104] After all, in international law, secondary rights are often granted to States (eg under diplomatic or flag State protection) although the primary right is held by a private actor. This means that in all cases where private actors bear a substantive right, the international legal system actually established a specific remedy to enforce that right, even if that remedy is assigned to the home State. Rules on diplomatic or flag State protection evidence the limited legal standing of private actors but are unhelpful to characterise their substantive position.[105]

In addition, the international remedies conferred on private actors are always the result of the political convenience agreed among the parties to a treaty, meaning that options regarding the enforcement of its provisions do not necessarily reflect the substance of rights and duties agreed, but rather the possible compromise among the law-makers.[106] At best, this approach undervalues the role of domestic institutions to enforce international law.[107] In some cases, as with respect to human rights, they are actually conceived of by the international treaty not as the default forum, but the ordinary means of enforcement of treaty provisions.[108] The idea that private actors should only be qualified as subjects of international law if they can enforce that right or duty within the same international level is still embedded in an insular view of international law (ie the view of a legal order as separate and with limited connections with domestic legal orders): although 'rights are meaningful only if they confer entitlements and when there is a remedy', 'the remedy can take various forms' and can be enforced 'on different levels of governance, on the international and on the domestic level. And it does not necessarily require judicial action'.[109] This idea is particularly important in international law, where States are not subject to compulsory dispute settlement and where a rule of exhaustion of local remedies is valid.[110]

[102] Brownlie and Crawford, *Principles* (n 3) 105; Fourlanos, 'Subjectivity' (n 27) 19; Lauterpacht, *International Law* (n 85) 27, 48, 61, and 159–60; O'Connell, *International*, I (n 39) 109; Peters, *Beyond* (n 4) 45ff; Tomuschat, 'International' (n 1) 150; Philipp Wendel, *State Responsibility for Interferences with the Freedom of Navigation in Public International Law* (Springer 2007) 76–77.

[103] Andrew Clapham, *Human Rights Obligations of Non-State Actors* (OUP 2006) 74.

[104] Peters, *Beyond* (n 4) 47; Peters, 'Membership' (n 19) 162.

[105] Kjeldgaard-Pedersen, *International* (n 1) 68.

[106] Hersch Lauterpacht, 'The Subjects of International Law', in Elihu Lauterpacht (ed), *International Law – Being the Collected Papers of Hersch Lauterpacht*, vol I (Cambridge: Cambridge University Press, 1970) 279–307, 287 [Subjects II].

[107] Roucounas, 'Facteurs privés' (n 43) 49.

[108] See inter alia Article 13 of the ECHR or Article 25 of the ACHR, as well as Article 35(1) of the ECHR and Article 46(1)(a) of the ACHR, regarding prior exhaustion of domestic remedies as a criterion of admissibility of a complaint.

[109] Peters, 'Membership' (n 19) 162.

[110] See Peters, *Beyond* (n 4) 49; Peters, 'Membership' (n 19) 162.

On the other hand, the adoption of a composite approach is the result of mixing two different questions, namely whether (and in what circumstances) the right or duty in question is supposed to be valid and enforced in the international legal order, and why subjects must comply with an obligation if no international remedy to enforce it exists, and thus apparently no sanction attached to infringement exists.[111] By mixing both questions one easily concludes that, without a proper sanction from international law, private actors can only invoke, apply and enforce rights and duties within the domestic legal orders. But the initial question was blurred by intertwining the questions of the existence of rights and of their enforceability.[112] A better position is to recognise that procedural capacities of private actors are an *important*, *but autonomous* dimension of legal personality. Procedural rights stand for international legal scholars as the dark matter for experimental physicists: international substantive rights held by private actors are difficult to observe directly, but one can look at the gravitational effects around them. If it is not clear whether a specific international rule confers a substantive right on a private actor, the existence of an international remedy open to private actors entails that these latter hold a substantive international right, because one cannot conceive a remedy without a virtual substantive right applicable.[113] But even if deprived of procedural capacities to enforce a right or a duty, a legal person is still a *legal person*.[114]

With this in mind, I come to the last, structural argument against the composite approach. By framing the argument in these terms, what this approach admits is that international remedies are only assigned in order to enforce international rights and duties, and in this sense, they presuppose the (prior) existence of those rights and duties. But if rights or duties are created without an international remedy, this means that they are not international subjective rights or duties, for they presuppose a (prior) international remedy, which for its part presupposed the (prior) existence of the given right or duty … Only with infinite regression can one support this position.

4.3. A Procedural Concept of International Legal Personality

A procedural approach might be an alternative to ascertain private actors' international legal subjectivity. Here, the focus is limited to the international remedies that can be triggered by private actors – eg before an international court or tribunal, a committee or a panel. If remedies are the decisive criterion for assessing legal personality, private actors should be conceived of as subjects

[111] Lauterpacht, 'Subjects II' (n 106) 286–87.
[112] Lauterpacht, *International Law* (n 85) 27.
[113] Yet, this idea does not perforce apply to States, as they can hold a secondary right (eg diplomatic protection) detached from a primary right.
[114] Lauterpacht, 'Subjects II' (n 106) 286–87.

of international law provided that they can challenge another international legal person with regard to a presumptive right or duty. The ultimate test for this approach would be, for instance, a petition brought before an international body based on a right not covered by international law, or beyond the jurisdiction of that body. The case would be declared inadmissible on grounds of incompatibility with the provisions of the relevant treaty, abuse of the right of individual petition, or being manifestly ill-founded.[115] By doing so, the international body will say that this private actor should not have submitted his application; but will never say that he could not do it because he already did … I do not ignore the fact that enforcement mechanisms are meant to be substantively fulfilling, ie they potentially create an effective change in the legal sphere of the plaintiff. But third-party enforcement means (adversarial or not, judicial or not) have an additional, autonomous function of *protest*, meaning that they not only exert a dispute settlement function, but can also be used to promote societal changes and work as 'arenas where political and social movements agitate for, and communicate, their legal and political agenda':[116] submitting a case per se can be a catalyst for disseminating a particular message, or to exert pressure over a specific person or group.[117] Of course to submit a complaint with this sole purpose might be objectionable, perhaps an abuse of the right of complaint, and goes against the heart of what is understood as the role and function of courts in a legal community. I do not argue that the use of courts as a forum for protest is protected by the legal system, but rather highlighting that sociologically courts also play this function. This approach understands that remedies are the mechanism that confers dynamics on private actors' participation in the international legal order. Deprived of these remedies, private actors may be equipped with rights and duties conferred by international rules, but there is no visible difference between these rights and duties and those conferred by the domestic legislator.

This approach, nonetheless, is embedded in an adversarial notion of international legal personality, focused only on the moments of (actual or potential) infringement of international law, and disregards all the other moments of compliance with its norms in legal relations in which private actors take part. In addition, this approach reduces the international relevance of private actors, for they seem not to be full members of this legal order, but rather tourists who only seldom make an appearance on the international stage, if at all. Furthermore, the idea that international rights and duties are pointless if deprived of international remedies not only confines their analysis to the pathologic moments of non-compliance, but is also based on a false assumption that international and municipal legal orders are two separate planets, when domestic remedies are often the primary fora for infringements of international law, and thus are part

[115] eg Article 35(3)(a) and (4) of the ECHR.
[116] Jules Lobel, 'Courts as Forums for Protest' (2004) 52 *UCLA Law Review* 477, 479.
[117] ibid, 487.

of the same system of enforcement and compliance. Finally, this approach would be difficult to reconcile with the fact that, under international law, often secondary rights are assigned to States (eg under flag State or diplomatic protection rules), even if the primary right is kept in the legal sphere of the private actor.

4.4. A Formal Concept of International Legal Personality

In my view, one should only focus on what is, according to the theory of law, the sole requirement of legal personality: the aptitude to hold rights or duties (of primary or secondary nature) under the legal system, ie of being the addressees of an international norm.[118] Under this view, one cannot assume that an entity is a subject and then infer the rights and duties it holds, but rather assess who holds rights and duties and, based on that evidence, recognise its international legal subjectivity – and, at the same time, avoiding interpretative biases. This approach should be credited for circumventing the *magna quaestio* of the right's or duty's enforcement. Domestic courts, as the default judges of international law, can enforce that right or duty if in a better position. For instance, in the *LaGrand*[119] and the *Avena*[120] cases, the ICJ recognised the existence of these international rights, but accepted that they could be enforced at the domestic and/or the international level.

At this point, a Kierkegaardian question arises: if the only international feature of that right or duty is its source, can one qualify the private actor in question as a legal person under international law? In fact, in some cases private actors can be equipped with rights or duties afforded by international norms, but which are meant to be applied and/or enforced *only* or *mainly* in legal relations within domestic law. In these cases, it might be disputed whether the right itself is international in nature (ie if it is an *international* subjective right), or if it merely derives from an international source by a contingent accident on its generation. Posing this question explains why the enhancement of the legal status of private actors in international law has been 'obscured' by the limitedness of their procedural capacity.[121] But this reluctance is the by-product of the same methodological errors identified in Section 4.1.

[118] See inter alia Accioly, *Tratado*, I (n 22) 71; Brierly, 'Règles générales' (n 81) 44, by implication; Clapham, *Human Rights* (n 103) 74; Higgins, *Problems* (n 12) 47, by implication; Lauterpacht, *International Law* (n 85) 4–5; Lauterpacht, 'Subjects I' (n 64) 136 and 144–45; Robert McCorquodale, 'The Individual and the International Legal System', in Malcolm Evans (ed), *International Law* (5th edn, OUP 2018) 259, 267–68; Peters, *Beyond* (n 4) 37; Peters, 'Membership' (n 19) 161; Shaw, *International Law* (n 9) 208; Cançado Trindade, 'A consolidação' (n 34) 252–53; Cançado Trindade, *Humankind* (n 34) 222; Walter, 'Subjects' (n 22) §§ 1 and 29.

[119] *LaGrand (Germany v United States of America)* [Judgment, 27 June 2001], ICJ Rep 466, § 77.

[120] *Avena and Other Mexican Nationals (Mexico v United States of America)* [Judgment, 31 March 2004], ICJ Rep 12, § 40.

[121] Lauterpacht, 'Subjects I' (n 64) 143.

To address this question, I must take into account what is actually a more structural one. Take, for instance, the navigational rights and freedoms set forth in the LOSC: the absence of international remedies, coupled with the existence of municipal remedies, could imply that these jural relations are governed by municipal law only. In the end, if the international rule can only be invoked by private actors (1) if it possesses direct effect within municipal law and (2) before national authorities, this implies perforce that under international law such provision only binds the States parties. And if this reasoning is correct, then legal personality of private actors requires more than the apparent allocation of rights and duties.

Nonetheless, this argument is methodologically invalid. I will not challenge the fact that these jural relations are also governed by domestic law, or that the body of domestic law includes treaty provisions that have been incorporated or that possess direct effect. However, what *cannot* be said is that the subjection of a jural relation to domestic law precludes its subjection to other legal orders (as international law), or that the jural relation is governed by a given domestic law only. Instead, the scope of application of rules of international and domestic law might overlap. When this happens, subjection to one legal order does not imply *ipso facto* the exclusion from the other legal order: in most cases, the legal system will only establish a rule of conflicts to guide the law enforcers in the choice of one of the conflicting norms. As such, if an international rule can be invoked as part of a domestic legal system, that does not exclude that it might also be invoked as a valid rule of the international legal system, since the existence of an *international* right or duty (ie valid in the international legal order) encapsulated in a treaty provision is independent of its incorporation or direct effect in domestic legal orders. For their part, direct effect or incorporation of a treaty provision in domestic legal orders are only of limited relevance: they aim to fulfil the requirements of the rule of law and division of powers between national institutions;[122] to afford constitutional authority to domestic institutions to interpret, apply and enforce that norm; or, in cases where the treaty provision fails to determine its obligational elements, to characterise the rights and duties enshrined in that norm. Therefore, the subjection of a jural relation to municipal law does not entail the exclusion of international law to govern that jural relation also, since the right or duty in question can have a double life and be simultaneously valid within the domestic and the international legal systems.[123] If this is the case, the private actor who holds that right or duty is *ipso facto* conceived of by the international legal system as a legal subject.

Furthermore, the absence of a secondary norm (reaction against defection) does not necessarily mean the absence of a primary norm. Therefore, if remedies

[122] Lauterpacht, 'Subjects II' (n 106) 286.

[123] See, however, André Nollkaemper, *National Courts and the International Rule of Law* (OUP 2012) 133; André Nollkaemper, 'The Duality of Direct Effect of International Law' (2014) 25 *European Journal of International Law* 105, 115–17, according to whom direct effect (or, more precisely, the lack of it) has also a general function of a protective 'shield' of the domestic legal order against interferences from international law.

are not placed in a given legal system, that does not imply that those rights and duties are not assigned to private actors within that legal system: if there can be a primary norm without a secondary norm, *a fortioti ratione* there can also be a primary norm of international nature coupled with a secondary norm of domestic nature. In this case, the international rule is enforced by domestic courts, but that does not transform the international nature of the obligation: at most, it is evidence that, to the drafters of that treaty, domestic courts are better placed to enforce that obligation; *ad terrorem*, the lack of enforcement mechanisms would qualify the rule as *lex imperfecta.*[124] What often happens is that the primary right or duty entails a secondary claim, but – to cope with the limits of international institutions, and taking into account the *nouvelle ambience juridique* of the secondary norm – the international legal system (1) devolves to domestic courts the authority to enforce that norm, and/or (2) substitutes the private actor for his flag or home State on the international plane (procedural substitution).[125] When this happens, domestic courts are the 'first port of call'[126] to settle international law claims, ie disputes whose claims are in substance based upon international law.[127] Empowering domestic courts with this primary task is not an express or explicit option of the international legal system, but rather its default rule.

To avoid implicit interpretative bias, what is relevant is to assess whether the relevant right or duty is valid in the international legal system despite the absence of international remedies: ie if the norm establishes all the necessary obligational elements, and thus private actors might substantiate a legal claim solely on the international law rule. As such, what will be assessed in this book are the cases where a rule of international law confers upon private actors a right or freedom, ie an advantageous position of enjoyment, conferred or acknowledged by the legal system, which allows the rights-holder the use of a specific good (right *in rem*, attached to a claim valid against the world), or to seek from another subject the performance of a specific conduct (right *in personam*, attached to a claim against another legal subject). For example, implicit in Article 137(3) of the LOSC, and more explicitly in Article 1 of Protocol III to the LOSC, is a property right over the minerals recovered from the Area, whereas pursuant to Article 17 of the LOSC a right to innocent passage in the territorial sea is conferred, opposable to the coastal State. The international rule must be aimed at protecting an interest of the rights-holder and must establish a corresponding obligation (ie the imposition of a specific conduct from

[124] Fourlanos, 'Subjectivity' (n 27) 12.

[125] Roucounas, 'Facteurs privés' (n 43) 346–48. See also Peters, *Beyond* (n 4) 168.

[126] Nollkaemper, *National Courts* (n 123) 11–12.

[127] Chittharanjan Amerasinghe, *Jurisdiction of International Tribunals* (Kluwer 2003) 4–7; Nollkaemper, *National Courts* (n 123) 9–10; Anne Peters, 'International Dispute Settlement: A Network of Cooperational Duties' (2003) 14 *European Journal of International Law* 1, 3. Against, see JG Merrills, *International Dispute Settlement* (5th edn, CUP 2011) 1; Yuval Shany, *The Competing Jurisdiction of International Courts and Tribunals* (OUP 2003) 101.

a specific legal subject, prescribing or prohibiting that conduct) incumbent on the duty-bearer. At this point, the magic formula is 'sufficiently characterised obligation', referring to a duty created by an international norm and whose obligational elements are entirely established in that norm. The question of what happens in case of non-compliance, however, is only relevant for determining a secondary obligation.

5. THE SOURCE OF A MISCONCEPTION: LEGAL PERSONALITY AND LEGAL CAPACITY

As seen, legal personality (*Persönlichkeit*, *personnalité juridique*) is the quality of an entity that is a virtual recipient of legal rules and that as such can hold rights or duties. In the theory of law, this concept is both *qualitative* and *absolute*: one rather is, or is not, a legal person. In a Shakespearian fashion, the *magna quaestio* is to be or not to be a legal person. Thus, legal personality is not a gradual concept depending on the rights conferred on a given entity: it merely depicts the *abstract aptitude of an entity to hold rights or duties* – even if or when *de facto* deprived any right or duty.[128] This means, inter alia, that the concept of legal personality embodies a heterogeneous number of entities under a single, unified, undivided concept – which explains why a dichotomy between legal personality and legal subjectivity does not exist.[129]

In contrast, *legal capacity* (*Handlungs-*, *Rechtsfähigkeit*, *capacité juridique*) refers to the *quantitative* and *relative* feature of legal personality, meaning *the specific rights and duties a person can or actually holds under a specific system of norms*. As a result, whereas the concept of legal personality is geometrically rigid, the different capacity of legal persons provides elasticity to legal subjectivity, allowing the legal order to allocate certain rights or duties to specific categories of legal persons, or to prevent them from holding those rights or duties. Whereas legal personality per se says little about what it means, legal capacities shape differences between legal persons.[130] Not surprisingly, both concepts orbit each other, since legal personality needs legal capacities to be meaningful to its holder, whilst legal capacities presuppose a prior qualification of a given entity as a legal person.[131]

[128] See inter alia Julio Barberis, 'Nouvelles questions concernant la personnalité juridique international' (1983) 179 *Collected Courses of the Hague Academy of International Law* 145, 168, by implication; Kolb, 'Nouvelle observation' (n 31) 237–38; O'Connell, *International*, I (n 39) 91.

[129] Gaetano Arangio-Ruiz, 'Stati e altri enti (Soggettività internazionale)', in Antonio Azara and Ernesto Eula (eds), *Novissimo Digesto Italiano* (UTET 1971) 135–36; Cançado Trindade, 'A consolidação' (n 34) 249–50; Visscher, 'Cours général' (n 45) 56. On the theory of law, see inter alia Alf Ross, *On Law and Justice* (The Lawbook Exchange 2012) 181; Elsa Vaz de Sequeira, *Da Contitularidade de Direitos em Direito Civil – Contributo para a sua Análise Morfológica* (Universidade Católica Editora 2015) 441.

[130] O'Connell, *International*, I (n 39) 80.

[131] ibid 81; Sequeira, *Da Contitularidade* (n 129) 441; Visscher, 'Cours général' (n 45) 56; Walter, 'Subjects' (n 22) § 22.

5.1. The Ordeals of Private Actors' International Legal Personality

In international law, however, some misconceptions have prevailed. The first is that international legal personality, legal subjectivity, and legal capacity are often defined interchangeably,[132] when in fact this is where the misconception begins. In part, the reason why authors refer to both concepts as synonyms relies on the fact that the ICJ mixed concerns on legal personality and capacity in the *Reparation for Injuries* opinion.[133] Nonetheless, the concepts of international legal personality, on the one hand, and capacity, on the other, refer to different epistemological tools: the first is the aptitude of an entity to be a recipient of rights and duties; the second is the measure of the rights and duties that a given entity can hold, or does hold, under a specific system of law.

Furthermore, scholars often refer to the concepts of *full* and *limited* international legal personality, taking into account the distinctive measure of rights and duties held by States and other subjects of international law.[134] The idea is clear cut, for even an inexperienced observer soon realises that the role of States, international organisations or private actors in the international arena is very different. But this dichotomy is also inaccurate, for there is no reason to believe that there are two concepts or degrees of international legal personality, but rather different capacities under international law. The distinction between full and partial international legal personality was based on a paragraph from the ICJ's advisory opinion in the *Reparation for Injuries* case, where it stated that the 'subjects of law in any legal system are not necessarily identical in their nature or in the extent of their rights'.[135] Under this distinction, States' personality would be the prototype of full international legal personality. Hence, some subjects (as States) could hold the lion's share of international rights and duties (even in the absence of an express norm conferring that right or duty), whereas others (as private actors) could only hold specific rights or duties resulting directly from the international rule.[136] Thus, in contrast with States, other entities would only have limited, partial or low-density international legal personality.

This idea was developed with respect to international organisations, where a comparison with domestic legal persons is tantalising: the same way, in domestic legal spheres, an individual is the model of full legal personality and juristic persons can only hold the rights and duties compatible with their fictitious nature, the template of international legal personality would be the State, and international organisations would only hold the rights and

[132] Sometimes one concept is even used precisely to define the other: eg Carreau and Marrella, *Droit* (n 31) 367.

[133] Peters, *Beyond* (n 4) 36.

[134] eg Cassese, *International Law* (n 59) 72.

[135] *Reparation for Injuries* [1949] 178.

[136] Bianchi, 'Fight' (n 11) 41; Kolb, 'Nouvelle observation' (n 31) 120–21; Visscher, 'Cours général' (n 45) 46; Walter, 'Subjects' (n 22) § 23.

duties compatible with their nature and that are granted by States. Moreover, another analogy with domestic legal systems was eye-catching: the same way juristic persons, in the domestic legal order, can only pursue the specific ends of their constituent document (in contrast with individuals, who can pursue any lawful end), international organisations can only pursue the specific goals set out in their constituent treaty (in contrast with the State, which can pursue any lawful end).

Finally, even if considered as international legal persons, private actors would always have *fragmented* legal personality – eg under the microcosm of human rights law, or under investment law, but not necessarily under general international law.[137] By overvaluing fragmentation over interaction of international regimes, legal scholars translated into the theory of international law the Schrödinger's cat paradox: depending on a given international legal domain, private actors would *be* and *not be* international legal subjects at the same time, ie would be subjects of human rights law, but not subjects of the law of the sea.[138]

The ultimate result of this distinction is the exclusion of private actors from the category of international legal persons, with the argument that, possessing only limited rights or duties under international law, they are not proper members of the international legal system, but rather visitors (even if regular) to the international legal system. However, one cannot say that those not possessing full personality are not actual legal persons. As said, the fact that States can make the international law means only that they are the recipients of an international rule conferring on them such capacity, not that other entities lack legal personality under international law.

Furthermore, this dichotomy, although visual and appealing, is misleading and technically incorrect: States do not possess, even virtually, all rights conferred by international norms, as can be illustrated by the rights to life or to physical integrity, covered by Articles 2 and 3 of the ECHR or Articles 4 and 5 of the ACHR, which are held by individuals.[139] Against this view, the reader could argue that States 'may refer to the [European Court of Human Rights – ECtHR] any alleged breach of the provisions of the [ECHR] by another [State]',[140] which would suggest that States are also human rights-holders; or that States can always claim their citizens' rights under diplomatic protection rules. This particular aspect of the Vattelian fiction has been eroded since the *Chorzów* case, where it was established that one act of a State can

[137] See inter alia Bianchi, 'Fight' (n 11) 39; Cassese, *International Law* (n 59) 72.

[138] This paradox is further fuelled by those who claim that, in contrast with international organisations, private actors' legal personality is relative and valid only before the States bound by the rule that equips them with a right or duty: Orakhelashvili, 'Position' (n 31) 255; Shaw, *International Law* (n 9) 206–07. Thus, private actors would be subjects of human rights law before Portugal but would not be subjects of international law before a dystopian State.

[139] Scelle, 'Règles générales' (n 82) 363–64. More recently, see Peters, *Beyond* (n 4) 42–43.

[140] Article 33 of the ECHR. See also Article 45 of the ACHR.

infringe, at the same time, the rights of another State and of this State's citizens.[141] This implies, to begin with, that separate – even if 'fundamentally identical'[142] – rights of the State and the private actor exist. Moreover, implied in this *dictum* is a fictitious separation of primary and secondary rights, which has been preserved as the basis of diplomatic protection rules.[143] This implies a system of separate 'ownership of the claim at the levels of primary and secondary law between two different subjects',[144] according to which, in case of infringement of an individual's right, States can be the exclusive holders of a secondary right (eg right of flag State or diplomatic protection, right of action before international bodies), but the individual remains the holder of the primary right (ie the substantive right itself):[145] at the secondary level States act solely as the 'legal representatives'[146] of private actors. This 'collective' representation (or *replacement*)[147] of the rights-holder at the level of secondary norms enables the system to accommodate two different concerns: the imbalance in the jural relations between States and private actors, which could undermine compliance and enforcement of private actors' rights; and the exiguity of compliance and enforcement mechanisms in international law, which requires limited participation in the processes governed by secondary norms. What it does not mean is that States hold the primary right also: diplomatic and flag State protection are a compensation for private actors' exclusion from international dispute settlement, not from international law.[148]

In this sense, subjects of international law (States and private actors) can only hold the rights and duties that are compatible with their nature. As a result, if capacity implies personality, personality in international law refers always to limited capacity to hold specific rights and duties.[149] In the end, all entities in international law have only partial or limited legal personality.[150]

[141] *Case concerning the Factory at Chorzów (Claim for Indemnity) (Merits)* [Judgment, 13 September 1928] PCIJ Series A, No. 17, 27–28.

[142] *Case concerning the Payment of Various Serbian Loans Issued in France / Case concerning the Payment in Gold of the Brazilian Federal Loans Issued in France* [Judgment, 12 July 1929] PCIJ Series A, Nos. 20/21, 18.

[143] Peters, *Beyond* (n 4) 190.

[144] Peters, *Beyond* (n 4) 171–72. See also James Crawford, *State Responsibility – The General Part* (CUP 2013) 77; Roucounas, 'Facteurs privés' (n 43) 347–48.

[145] *Ahmadou Sadio Diallo (Republic of Guinea v Democratic Republic of the Congo) (Preliminary Objections)* [Judgment, 24 May 2007] ICJ Rep 582, § 39.

[146] Roucounas, 'Facteurs privés' (n 43) 113.

[147] ibid 347.

[148] See inter alia Hafner, 'Emancipation' (n 9) 374. As referred in the *Eritrea v Yemen* case, '[t]hat legal fiction served the purpose of allowing diplomatic representation (where the representing State so chose) in a world in which individuals had no opportunities to advance their own rights': see *In the Matter of an Arbitration pursuant to an Agreement to Arbitrate Dated 3 October 1996, between Eritrea and Yemen (Maritime Delimitation) (Award of the Arbitral Tribunal in the Second Stage of the Proceedings)* [Award, 17 December 1999] PCA Case no. 1996-04, § 101.

[149] O'Connell, *International*, I (n 39) 91; Peters, *Beyond* (n 4) 43.

[150] Clapham, *Human Rights* (n 103) 68; Jessup, *Modern* (n 84) 16; Philip Jessup, 'The Subjects of a Modern Law of Nations' (1947) 45 *Michigan Law Review* 383, 393; Peters, *Beyond* (n 4) 43.

The functional comparison pointed out above (between domestic juristic persons and international organisations) helps to explain the idea of limited international legal personality, especially if one bears in mind that under domestic law a juristic person (as the individual) is not a partial or *limited* legal person, but rather a full person with *limited capacities*, since all subjects can only bear the rights and duties that are compatible with their human or fictitious nature.

5.2. Single (Not Multiple) Legal Personality

Not only is the concept of legal personality the same as the homonym used in domestic legal orders, but also the legal personality itself (the epistemological tool used) is the same: ie a morphologically distinct personality in international law does not exist. In fact, the contrast between domestic and international legal personality of an entity is whimsical, as if both legal personalities were two different concepts, ie as if that entity suffered from some kind of multiple legal personality disorder. Moreover, according to some scholars, not only are these two different concepts, but also the possession of one does not necessarily imply the possession of the other. Therefore, an international organisation might be an international legal person, but be deprived of domestic legal personality; and private actors might be domestic legal persons but fail to possess legal personality under international law. When both legal personalities overlap, the entity concerned would be subject to a process of transmogrification when crossing the boundaries between international and domestic law.[151] In the end, this is a means of disenfranchisement of private actors from international law.

This idea of a multiple, overlapping personality is deceptive. The fact that for a long time legal scholars have focused on autonomous concepts – such as 'international legal personality' or 'membership in the international community or society' – has led them to miss the crux of the issue: international law and international society, as social artefacts, are not separate planets from domestic laws and societies. When person A holds rights or duties under Portuguese law and under the German law, he or she is always the same legal person acting under different legal systems. The same is true when person A holds a right under an international norm: that entity is exactly the same legal person, whose legal sphere was enlarged with the allocation of specific rights or duties under international law. When having legal personality, an entity might not have the capacity to act under a specific domestic law; or might have the capacity to act under some or all domestic legal orders. Structurally, it is exactly the same with respect to relations between domestic legal orders (eg recognition of personality and capacities of a German company in the Italian legal system), and domestic

[151] eg, see Jean Combacau and Serge Sur, *Droit international public* (12th edition, LGDJ 2012) 316.

and international legal orders (eg recognition of an international organisation within a national legal order, or of a Spanish company within the international legal order). To some extent, this is just the other side of the ICJ's *dictum* in the *Barcelona Traction* case:

> [I]nternational law is called upon to recognize institutions of municipal law that have an important and extensive role in the international field. This does not imply drawing any analogy between its own institutions and those of municipal law, nor does it amount to making rules of international law dependent upon categories of municipal law. All it means is that international law has to recognize the corporate entity as an institution created by States in a domain essentially within their domestic jurisdiction.[152]

As a result, private actors (as all legal persons) are *not* international legal persons, but rather legal persons *tout court*: if and when relevant for the international legal system, it is the same legal person that is equipped with domestic and international rights and duties. Thus, private actors can be subjects of law relevant under multiple legal orders including international law. This 'porosity' of the legal systems has meant, inter alia, that a single legal order can govern relations from separate social orders; as well as that a single social order might be subjected to a regulation from different legal orders.[153] This means that the legal status of a private actor can be affected by rules from different legal orders, but does not mean that the legal personality of such entity is different when acting in the domestic or the international arena, for the legal capacities (ie the substantive and/or procedural rights and duties) might be different, but the legal personality itself is the same. And this is not just a technicality: under this view, private membership in the international community is not a conquest, but rather implicit in private legal personality.

5.3. Legal Personality as a Status Prior to a Given Legal Order

To some extent, this misconception is rooted in the idea that legal personality voices a relation between an entity and *a given* legal order.[154] Nonetheless, legal subjectivity is a specific status of an entity bestowed by the 'legal system' itself;[155] and when a subject of law acts under so-called 'different' legal personalities, it is

[152] *Barcelona Traction, Light and Power Company Limited (Belgium v Spain) (2nd Phase)* [Judgment, 5 February 1970] ICJ Rep 3, § 38.

[153] Emmanuelle Jouannet, *A Short Introduction to International Law* [*Le droit international*: 2013] (CUP 2014) 32–33.

[154] eg Anzilotti, *Corso* (n 62) 112; Combacau and Sur, *Droit* (n 151) 314.

[155] Rolando Quadri, *Corso di diritto internazionale pubblico* (Libreria Scientifica) 391; Rolando Quadri, 'Cours général de droit international public' (1964-III) 113 *Collected Courses of the Hague Academy of International Law* 237, 376.

actually the same legal person with different capacities added to its legal status. Hence, to be a legal person virtually connects that individual or juristic person with all legal orders; the actual link between the entity concerned and a specific legal system derives from the rights and duties assigned to that entity by this legal system.

This implies that subjectivity cannot be deduced from the norms of one specific legal system.[156] Legal norms (including from international law) merely identify those who are the *relevant* legal persons within a given legal system, ie those who hold rights and duties under the norms of the system in question. Thus the notion and the list of legal persons is 'unitary'[157] and prior to a given system: the legal norm that confers rights or duties on an entity is creating a new capacity to a subject that exists – and not creating subjectivity. In the case of international law, it would be bizarre if States, being a creation of individuals (as domestic legal persons), were at the same time the creators of the same individuals (as international legal persons). Yet, since being the recipient of norms implies the possession of a prior legal personality, the allocation of specific rights and duties under a system of law is sufficient evidence of the possession, by a given entity, of this legal status.

Thus, when one refers to the legal person as a centre of allocation of rights and duties, this centre was 'created' prior to the system itself and is presupposed by the international norm when allocating rights and duties.[158] The autonomy of the international legal system, therefore, is not dependent on the discretionary decision of creating new subjects, but rather on allocating them capacities. The openness and autonomy of the international legal system means that, reacting to stimulus or provocations from elements exogenous to the international *legal* order, international law internalises these elements and adjusts them into its own grammar; it observes its environment through its own lenses, with its own categories of assessment and interpretation; and if relevant, international law equips a (prior) legal person with new capacities. As a result, the *magna quaestio* of whether States can exclude the legal personality of private actors should have a negative answer, for their subjectivity is not dependent upon States' benediction.

In Section 1, I stated provisionally that legal personality is the measure of relevance within international law. That assertion seems to be at odds with this idea of a single legal personality, for, in fact, it is more accurate to contend that the measure of relevance rather lies with the *international* legal *capacities*. But this is only apparently contradictory and does not imply a deviation from that original work plan for this study: to enquire whether, and in what

[156] Robert Kolb, 'Une observation sur la détermination de la subjectivité internationale' (1997) 52 *Zeitschrift für öffentliches Recht* 115, 115.
[157] ibid; Quadri, 'Cours général' (n 155) 424.
[158] Kolb, 'Une observation' (n 156) 116.

circumstances, private actors are rights-holders under international law is to consider their single legal personality and assess if, in that quality, they are equipped with international rights or duties.

5.4. An Open and Empty Concept(ion)

As said, the notion of legal personality is prior to the international legal system, and the legal persons themselves (as centres of allocation of rights and duties conferred by norms, whatever their origin) are the same entities when engaging in jural relations governed by international law, domestic law or any other legal system. Therefore, the autonomy of the international legal system resides not in the idea of *different subjects*, but rather of *different capacities* conferred on the *same subjects*. In the end, however, legal personality does not entail any specific entitlement under international law, but a legal person deprived of any right or duty under a specific legal system is not legally relevant to that legal system.[159]

Therefore, both the concept and the conception of legal personality under international law followed in this book are empty of meaningful content,[160] whereas the States-only, the individuals-only and even the recognition conceptions would give some substantive content to this concept. The conception of legal personality followed in this book is purely formal and describes only the abstract aptitude of an entity to be the recipient of legal norms, and thus to hold rights and duties. But to possess legal personality says little about what it entails,[161] and therefore it is normal that legal subjects possess a differentiated international capacity.[162] This emptiness of the notion of legal personality is the immediate outcome of the enlargement of the concept in order to cover other entities apart from States. In fact, after this enlargement, it became hardly possible to identify a sociological denominator common to all of them or to deduce from their status a minimum common capacity within the international legal order, however limited it might be.[163]

5.5. An Inclusive Concept(ion)

A final consequence of adopting a formal and open concept (and conception) of legal subjectivity under international law is that it ends up assuming that

[159] See *mutatis mutandis* Peters, *Beyond* (n 4) 58–59.
[160] See inter alia Kate Parlett, *The Individual in the International Legal System – Continuity and Change in International Law* (CUP 2011) 38; O'Connell, *International*, I (n 39) 80.
[161] See inter alia Clapham, *Human Rights* (n 103) 71; Fourlanos, 'Subjectivity' (n 27) 18.
[162] Barberis, 'Nouvelles questions' (n 128) 169–70; Mosler, 'Réflexions' (n 61) 240, but referring to legal capacity as a synonym of legal personality.
[163] Mosler, 'Réflexions' (n 61) 241.

there is no *numerus clausus* in international law – which means that, with respect to membership, international law is a liberal system.[164] The result is that, deprived of any prior presumption in favour of or against inclusion (except a possible one in favour of States' membership), not only should the past experience of tectonic subjective transformation of the international legal system not be surprising, but also new tectonic movements might occur in the future. Awareness of this agnosticism towards membership implies a duty to avoid any interpretative bias with respect to who holds rights or duties under international law rules.

A possible consequence of this position is to render unnecessary the claims of global or international constitutionalism to an individual's international right to have international legal personality. The urge of these claims is based on the thoughts of Arendt,[165] and the idea that legal personality is the 'right to have rights', to be integrated into a political community, which should be the paramount right in a society based on human dignity. In contrast, my claim is that it is not possible to preclude private actors from membership of a legal system that was crafted to pursue human (despite collective) goals and values. If one argues that 'international' legal personality is a mere follow-up of legal personality in general, and that being a legal person under a specific set of norms entails virtually, but necessarily, legal personality under all systems of law, then the only relevant interpretation of the 'right to have rights' is not to ensure that private actors are bestowed with 'international' legal personality, but rather that they are equipped with the relevant international rights and duties for the promotion of their legitimate goals.

6. CONCLUSION

As this book is about private actors as rights-holders under international law, a chapter on legal personality and capacity under international law was necessary to set the scenario on which this study is performed.

My claim is that private actors are *not* international legal persons, but rather legal persons *tout court*: such qualification ('international') refers to the rights and duties conferred on private actors, not to their legal personality. Private actors have a *single* legal personality, which, as an epistemological tool, is prior to any given legal order and valid *ipso facto* under all legal orders, including international law. Thus, the binary instruments to measure relevance under international law are the concepts of rights and duties, which entails that private actors are legal persons with international legal capacities whenever they are the recipients of an international legal rule, of rather primary or secondary nature.

[164] Peters, *Beyond* (n 4) 35. See also Portmann, *Legal Personality* (n 8) 276.
[165] Hannah Arendt, '"The Rights of Man": What Are They?' (1949) 3 *Modern Review* 24.

If the relevance of private actors in international law relies solely on the fact that these entities are the addressees of an international rule, to measure their relevance should be just a matter of treaty interpretation. But, as mentioned before, implicit interpretative biases can affect this simple task and even lead the interpreter to exclude the possibility of assigning rights or duties to private actors as a result of a prior and unconscious conception of who can be the recipients of international law rules. Interference of such bias is visible when the reader of a treaty provision excludes private actors' entitlements in light of an ambiguous wording (navigational entitlements – Chapter 3), or excludes or limits private actors' participation in spite of a clear wording (deep seabed private mining or submission of application for the prompt release of vessels and crew members on behalf of the flag State – Chapter 4), or when the reader of that treaty provision does not consider cross-regime interaction in a proper manner (Chapter 5).

3

Unveiling Private Actors' Entitlements

One of the claims of this book is that interpretative bias may lead to a reading of a rule of international law that excludes private actors from being rights-holders or duty-bearers. Such exclusion is not the mere result of following the canons of interpretation of treaty-based rules set out in Articles 31–33 of the VCLT, but rather of a prejudice that clouds the interpreter. In the law of the sea, this can be viewed with respect to navigational entitlements.

In fact, freedom of navigation originally was crafted as an individual's entitlement (or, at most, of communities conceived of as a collection of individuals) and grounded on private interests. However, the process of States' appropriation of the seas obfuscated private actors' entitlements and led to a reading that excludes them from being navigational rights-holders. But this State-to-State reading is only the result of an interpretative bias: if one sets aside such orthodox conception of international law, a dormant life of private actors' entitlements can be uncovered.

To assess if private actors can hold any navigational rights and freedoms, Section 1 assesses the different entitlements deriving from freedom of navigation and the conditions for the full enjoyment of navigational entitlements. Based on the dissection of the structure of these entitlements, Sections 2 and 3 can explain the references to ships as rights-holders in the LOSC and the assignment of these navigational entitlements to States *and* private actors. With that in mind, Section 4 assesses the interaction between ship-owners and flag States in the exercise of navigational entitlements. Finally, Section 5 briefly analyses the right to compensation (a guarantee of freedom of navigation), as it also sheds light on the question of who the navigational rights-holders are.

1. ENTITLEMENTS DERIVING FROM FREEDOM OF NAVIGATION

The major entitlement is *freedom of navigation stricto sensu*, ie the right to move a ship from points A to B at sea without any external interference with the ship's motion. To guarantee the principle of freedom of navigation, flag States enjoy primary enforcement jurisdiction,[1] which entails not only its authority over all events and persons on board irrespective of their nationality,[2] but also that governance and legal order on the high seas are primarily enforced by flag States, who are required to exercise effective control and jurisdiction on certain issues.[3]

However, legal principles are not boundless and have to adjust to other values, rules and principles of the legal system.[4] Therefore, far from being an 'immutable theological dogma', freedom of navigation has several levels of implementation and must be balanced with other interests and values of the legal system.[5] In fact, limitations regarding geography, activities, and participants have confined the scope of the freedom of the seas: it has been transformed from a freedom of the seas into a freedom of the *high* seas;[6] some activities have been outlawed, and the permissible ones must have a peaceful purpose and need to be balanced with other values and activities; not all subjects of law may use the seas and expect full protection from the legal order (eg those carrying out activities proscribed by the LOSC); and freedom of navigation has been impacted by the activity of international organisations such as the UN Security Council or the International Maritime Organization (IMO). But the variable geometry of navigational rights and freedoms is mostly the result of the distinctive balance of interests and values on each maritime zone: the closer a foreign ship is to the coast, the weaker its navigational entitlement is.[7] Following Tanaka, who engineered an insightful categorisation of the navigational entitlements on the different maritime spaces, these entitlements can be grouped according to Table 3.1[8]

This categorisation corresponds *grosso modo* to the major navigational entitlements established in the LOSC (others, such as rights to non-discrimination or to information, are accessory to these). Nevertheless, my major concern is not to analyse the opposite cases – ie the broad navigational rights and freedoms and the exceptional entitlements on internal waters – but rather the right of

[1] Article 92(1) of the LOSC.

[2] *M/V 'Saiga' (No. 2) (Saint Vincent and the Grenadines v Guinea)* [Judgment, 1 July 1999] ITLOS Rep 10, 106.

[3] Article 94 of the LOSC.

[4] António Cortês, *Jurisprudência dos Princípios – Estudo sobre os Fundamentos da Decisão Jurisdicional* (Universidade Católica Editora 2010) 127ff. With respect to the freedom of the seas in particular, see David Anderson, 'Freedoms of the High Seas in the Modern Law of the Sea', in David Freestone, Richard Barnes and David Ong (eds), *The Law of the Sea – Progress and Prospects* (OUP 2006) 327, 332.

[5] Tullio Scovazzi, 'The Evolution of International Law of the Sea: New Issues, New Challenges' (2000) 286 *Collected Courses of the Hague Academy of International Law* 39, 228–29.

[6] eg Rosemary Rayfuse, *Non-Flag State Enforcement in the High Seas Fisheries* (Brill 2004) 20; or Jean Combacau and Serge Sur, *Droit international public* (12th edn, LGDJ 2016) 461.

[7] See generally Robin Churchill and Vaughan Lowe, *The Law of the Sea* (3rd edn, Manchester University Press 1999) 264; DP O'Connell, *The International Law of the Sea*, II (Clarendon 1988) 733.

[8] Yoshifumi Tanaka, 'Navigational Rights and Freedoms', in Donald Rothwell, Alex Oude Elferink, Karen Scott and Tim Stephens (eds), *The Oxford Handbook of the Law of the Sea* (OUP 2015) 538.

Table 3.1 Navigational rights and freedoms of foreign vessels under the LOSC

Maritime spaces under territorial sovereignty of coastal States	
Internal waters	Only exceptional navigational rights or freedoms
Territorial sea	Right of innocent passage
International straits	Right of transit and right of non-suspendable innocent passage
Archipelagic waters	Right of innocent passage and right of archipelagic sea lane passage
Maritime zones under the jurisdiction of coastal States	
Exclusive economic zone	Freedom of navigation
Continental shelf	Freedom of navigation in the superjacent waters (which are not part of the continental shelf)
Maritime zones beyond national jurisdiction	
High seas	Freedom of navigation
The Area	Freedom of navigation in the superjacent waters

innocent passage: whereas in the first two cases a balance in favour of freedom or authority is relatively clear, with respect to the right of innocent passage (as well as its *alter egos* on the archipelagic waters and international straits) this balance is more contentious, which explains its detailed legal regime. But providing such detail is also an opportunity for itemising the different rights and duties encompassed by it, and thereby for assessing its structure. This assessment, for its part, is central for determining who is entitled to innocent passage.

1.1. The Right of Innocent Passage

As said, to balance the conflicting interests of flag and coastal States on the territorial sea, the *right of innocent passage* is subject to a detailed legal regime.

Despite prior references by Gentili and Grotius to the *transitus innoxium*, Vattel was decisive on this point, stating that 'These parts of the sea, thus subject to a nation, are comprehended in [its] *territory*;'[9] but further added that 'it is a duty incumbent on every proprietor to allow to strangers a free passage … when it can be done without damage or danger'.[10] In this sense, Vattel – like his immediate followers, who worked on early conceptions of the territorial sea as *dominium* (ownership) of the coastal State – referred to innocent passage

[9] Emer de Vattel, *The Law of Nations* [*Le droit des gens*: 1758] (Liberty Fund 2008) 253, emphasis added.

[10] ibid.

as *permitted* by coastal States,[11] which was the result of transposing into the law of the sea the Roman property law concept of servitude and the need for reinforcing the sovereign's authority over adjacent waters. But from the mid-nineteenth century onwards (when the right of innocent passage was established as a customary international law rule),[12] innocent passage was framed in terms of a right not subject to the coastal State's authorisation.[13] This conception of innocent passage as a right – which was only possible due to the view of sovereignty and jurisdiction as different epistemological tools, and thus that the sovereignty of the coastal State does not perforce preclude the jurisdiction of the flag State[14] – was adopted by Articles 14ff of the Territorial Sea Convention (TSC) and later Articles 17ff of the LOSC. As such, implicit in the LOSC is a conception of coastal States' sovereignty in the territorial sea as the same as exercised over their internal waters, but whose jurisdiction *rationae loci* is limited by the right of innocent passage.[15]

According to Article 17 of the LOSC, 'ships of all States, whether coastal or land-locked, enjoy the right of innocent passage through the territorial sea'. The right of innocent passage entails a right of 'traversing the territorial sea without entering the internal waters or calling at a roadstead or port facility outside internal waters',[16] and the right of 'proceeding to or from internal waters or a call at such roadstead or port facility'[17] when a right to enter into the internal waters is conferred. The corresponding duty is laid down in Article 24 of the LOSC, according to which 'The coastal State shall not hamper the innocent passage of foreign ships through the territorial sea',[18] and shall 'give appropriate publicity of any danger to navigation, of its knowledge, within its territorial sea',[19] as well as of its lighthouses, rescue facilities or other basic navigational services.[20] From this provision flows a duty to provide information, which means that a corresponding *right to information* also exists under Article 24(2) of the LOSC.

[11] DP O'Connell, *The International Law of the Sea*, I (Clarendon 1982) 60 and 261–62.

[12] ibid 275; Yoshifumi Tanaka, *The International Law of the Sea* (3rd edn, CUP 2019) 104; Tanaka, 'Navigational' (n 8) 540.

[13] eg Gabriel Massé, *Le Droit commercial dans ses rapports avec le droits de la gens et le droit civil*, I (Guillaumin 1844) 112; Carlos Calvo, *Derecho internacional teórico y práctico de Europa y América*, 1 (Amyot 1868) 570ff.

[14] Jean Combacau, *Le droit international de la mer* (Presses Universitaires de France 1985)) 22; Ivan Shearer, 'Problems of Jurisdiction and Law Enforcement against Delinquent Vessels' (1986) 35 *ICLQ* 320, 321. Against, see Jean-Paul Pancracio, *Droit de la mer* (1st edn, Dalloz 2010) 23.

[15] See generally Antonio Cassese, *International Law* (2nd edn, OUP 2005) 85; Jan Klabbers, *International Law* (3rd edn, CUP 2021) 262.

[16] Article 18(1)(a) of the LOSC.

[17] Article 18(1)(b) of the LOSC. The ICJ stated that this provision 'does no more than codify customary international law on this point', *Military and Paramilitary Activities in and against Nicaragua (Nicaragua v United States of America) (Merits)* [1986] ICJ Rep 14, § 214.

[18] Article 24(1) of the LOSC.

[19] Article 24(2) of the LOSC. See also *Corfu Channel (United Kingdom v Albania)* [Judgment, 9 April 1949] ICJ Rep 4, 22.

[20] Churchill and Lowe, *Law of the Sea* (n 7) 100.

The right of innocent passage is of limited scope: the LOSC requires passage to be continuous and expeditious, even though it might entail a right of stopping and anchoring in cases where it is incidental or necessary to render assistance to persons, ships or aircraft in danger or distress;[21] submarines and other underwater vehicles are required to navigate on the surface and show their flag;[22] foreign ships must comply with all generally accepted international regulations relating to the prevention of collisions at sea;[23] coastal States might require foreign ships to exercise the right of innocent passage through sea lanes and traffic separation schemes adopted to foster safety of navigation;[24] and coastal States can adopt laws and regulations in respect of several topics, such as the safety of navigation, the conservation of living marine resources, or the prevention of the infringement of its customs, fiscal, sanitary, or immigration laws and regulations.[25] In case of breach of any of these laws and regulations, the passage is not deprived of its innocent character unless the violation might be of such intensity as to be prejudicial under Article 19 of the LOSC, or otherwise Article 21 of the LOSC would be meaningless.[26] As such, the right of innocent passage kept its composite nature: following the principle *ubi commoda ibi incommoda*, those who enjoy the benefits of innocent passage are bound by the duties that limit and are attached to its exercise.

If passage is not innocent, the right ceases to exist: technically, there is no restriction to the right; rather the 'right' has no legal force. For a long time, the concept of *innocent* passage was unclear. The ICJ referred to it in the *Corfu Channel* case and considered the *manner* of the passage to be the quintessential element for determining the innocence of the passage.[27] The *Draft Articles on the Law of the Sea* expressed a clear preference for determining innocence according to acts, and not the manner of the passage,[28] but the relevant draft article was not accepted during the negotiations under the UNCLOS I: Article 14(4) of the TSC adopted a negative wording to qualify passage as

[21] Article 18(2) of the LOSC. As such innocent *non*-passage activities, such as trade, fishing, hovering or cruising, are outside the scope of this provision. The purpose of defining 'passage' (in Article 18) autonomously from innocence (in Article 19) is to protect coastal States' authority against claims to non-passage activities. Richard Barnes, 'Article 18', in Alexander Proelß (ed), *United Nations Convention on the Law of the Sea – A Commentary* (CH Beck 2017) 181, 182; O'Connell, *Law of the Sea*, I (n 11) 269.

[22] Article 20 of the LOSC.

[23] Article 21(4) of the LOSC. Eg see the 1972 Convention on the International Regulations for Preventing Collisions at Sea, regardless of being the coastal State party to this convention and regulations.

[24] Article 22(1) of the LOSC.

[25] Article 21 of the LOSC.

[26] Carlos Espaliú Berdud, *Le passage inoffensive des navires de guerre étrangers dans la mer territoriale – Portée du régime contenu dans la Convention des Nations Unies sur le droit de la mer* (Bruylant 2006) 54; Patricia Birnie, Alan Boyle and Catherine Redgwell, *International Law and Environment* (3rd edn, CUP 2009) 417; Churchill and Lowe, *Law of the Sea* (n 7) 84; Tanaka, 'Navigational' (n 8) 543; Tanaka, *Law of the Sea* (n 12) 107.

[27] *Corfu Channel* [1949] 30–31.

[28] ILC, 'Report of the ILC on the Work of its Eighth Session' (4 July 1956) UN Doc. A/CN.4/104, 272.

non-innocent and did not refer to the violation of a specific coastal State's law, or the commission of a specific act.

Although the LOSC follows the same approach by focusing on the activities that are prejudicial to coastal States, the definition of innocent passage was substantially amended in the UNCLOS III. Pursuant to Article 19(1) of the LOSC, 'Passage is innocent so long as it is not prejudicial to the peace, good order or security of the coastal State'. Then, Article 19(2) – with the aim of confining coastal States' discretion in this regard[29] – establishes a non-exhaustive list of activities that are presumed to be prejudicial to coastal States. The fact that this provision lists activities suggests that a presumption emerges when specific acts are undertaken (the 'manner in which the passage was carried out'), and not necessarily when a specific ship enters into the territorial sea.[30] However, the different wording of Article 19(1) and (2), and the absence of a reference to 'activities' in paragraph 1, suggests that coastal States might invoke Article 19(1) autonomously in order to consider that the passage of a specific ship per se is not innocent, or otherwise paragraph 1 would be superfluous in the face of paragraph 2.[31] Moreover, the wording of Article 19(2)(a) of the LOSC is wide enough to include threats directed not only to the coastal State in whose waters the right of innocent passage is being exercised, but also threats against other States.[32] What seems undisputed is that the violation of coastal States' laws does not deprive *ipso facto* passage of its innocence,[33] or otherwise, Article 17 of the LOSC would not be a self-executing international law rule, but rather a mere guideline to domestic authorities.[34] Finally, and contrary to what a literal interpretation of this provision could suggest, not only activities, but also other facts can deprive passage of its innocence.[35]

Where a ship is engaged in any of these activities or another fact prejudicial to coastal States, these latter can take the appropriate measures to prevent or repress it,[36] which include requesting the ship to stop its activities, to leave the territorial waters, or even stopping and boarding the ship.[37] Where State

[29] See generally Berdud, *Le passage* (n 26) 49; Churchill and Lowe, *Law of the Sea* (n 7) 85.

[30] Churchill and Lowe, *Law of the Sea* (n 7) 85; Kari Hakapää, *Marine Pollution in International Law – Material Obligations and Jurisdiction* (Suomalainen Tiedeakatemia 1981) 184; Erik Jaap Molenaar, *Coastal State Jurisdiction over Vessel-Source Pollution* (Wolters Kluwer 1998) 197; Tanaka, 'Navigational' (n 8) 542. See also *Corfu Channel* [1949] 30.

[31] Lindy Johnson, *Coastal State Regulation of International Shipping* (Oceana 2004) 64–66; Molenaar, *Coastal State* (n 30) 196–67; Tanaka, 'Navigational' (n 8) 542; Tanaka, *Law of the Sea* (n 12) 107. See *mutatis mutandis* Berdud, *Le passage* (n 26) 41.

[32] Churchill and Lowe, *Law of the Sea* (n 7) 85.

[33] Richard Barnes, 'Article 19', in Proelß (ed), *UN Convention* (n 21) 186, 191; Churchill and Lowe, *Law of the Sea* (n 7) 84. With respect to violations of 'passive requirements', see Molenaar, *Coastal State* (n 30) 197.

[34] *See mutatis mutandis* Barnes, 'Article 19' (n 33).

[35] Molenaar, *Coastal State* (n 30) 196; Haijiang Yang, *Jurisdiction of the Coastal State over Foreign Merchant Ships in Internal Waters and the Territorial Sea* (Springer 2006) 162.

[36] Article 25(1) of the LOSC.

[37] Richard Barnes, 'Article 25', in Proelß (ed), *UN Convention* (n 21) 222, 224–25; Pancracio, *Droit* (n 14) 166; Donald Rothwell and Tim Stephens, *The International Law of the Sea* (2nd edn, Hart Publishing 2016) 233; Shearer, 'Problems' (n 14) 326–27; Tanaka, 'Navigational' (n 8) 544; Tanaka, *Law of the Sea* (n 12) 114.

authorities suspect a ship is not complying with environmental laws and regulations, they are entitled to inspect the ship and, if there is enough evidence, institute proceedings or seize the ship.[38] In other words, this means that ships that have stepped outside the scope of the right of innocent passage are subject to full jurisdictional powers of coastal States.[39]

Finally, the right of innocent passage might be suspended by coastal States on grounds of being necessary for their security, provided that suspension is temporary and confined to a demarcated area.[40] Since this provision requires specific grounds for the suspension of the right of innocent passage, as well as that suspension must not be discriminatory, rights to *legitimate grounds*, to *non-discrimination* and to *publicity* are implicit in this provision. Suspension might only derive from the fact that passage of *any* ship (regardless of its flag) might be prejudicial to the coastal State's interests.[41] Therefore, the simple threat of damage to the coastal State by a ship does not imply *ipso facto* the loss of the innocent manner of the passage.[42]

Coastal States have prescriptive jurisdiction over ships exercising the right of innocent passage[43] – although the laws and regulations adopted 'shall not apply to the design, construction, manning or equipment of foreign ships unless they are giving effect to generally accepted international rules or standards'[44] – but coastal States must give due publicity to such laws and regulations.[45] In addition, foreign ships must comply with 'all generally accepted international regulations to the prevention of collisions at sea',[46] regardless of the flag and/or the coastal States being parties to the conventions where these regulations are laid down.[47] To guarantee freedom of navigation, coastal States cannot levy charges,[48] and the laws and regulations enacted by coastal States cannot hamper the right of innocent passage.[49] Of course all laws and regulations adopted by coastal States have the potential

[38] Article 220(2) of the LOSC.

[39] Churchill and Lowe, *Law of the Sea* (n 7) 87.

[40] Article 25(3) of the LOSC.

[41] Barnes, 'Article 25' (n 37) 226; Churchill and Lowe, *Law of the Sea* (n 7) 87; Pancracio, *Droit* (n 14) 167.

[42] Hakapää, *Marine Pollution* (n 30) 185; Molenaar, *Coastal State* (n 30) 197.

[43] Article 21 of the LOSC.

[44] Article 21(2) of the LOSC.

[45] Article 21(3) of the LOSC.

[46] Article 21(4) of the LOSC.

[47] Churchill and Lowe, *Law of the Sea* (n 7) 95.

[48] Article 26 of the LOSC. However, coastal States can charge non-discriminatory taxes for specific services provided to ships exercising the right of innocent passage (eg rescue or pilotage): Ian Brownlie and James Crawford, *Brownlie's Principles of Public International Law* (8th edn, OUP 2012) 301; Churchill and Lowe, *Law of the Sea* (n 7) 95; Malcolm Shaw, *International Law* (8th edn, CUP 2017) 424; Yang, *Jurisdiction* (n 35) 179. Non-payment does not imply *ipso facto* the non-innocence of passage: Richard Barnes, 'Article 26', in Proelß (ed), *UN Convention* (n 21) 226, 229.

[49] Article 24(1) of the LOSC. This has been recognised as being also a customary international law rule. See *Maritime Delimitation and Territorial Questions between Qatar and Bahrain (Qatar v Bahrain) (Merits)* [Judgment, 16 March 2001] ICJ Rep 40, § 253.

to hamper innocent passage, which means that per se hampering navigation is not forbidden but only if sufficiently characterised: the relevant test is one of proportionality between the interests protected by the coastal State's laws and regulations, on the one hand, and the actual restriction to innocent passage, on the other.[50] Nonetheless, laws and regulations – enacted to achieve legitimate aims of coastal States (eg regarding the safety of navigation or the preservation and protection of the marine environment), but which in fact are intended to deny or impair innocent passage (ie *détournement du pouvoir*) – are forbidden.[51] However, if ships have stepped outside the scope of the right of innocent passage, they are subject to coastal States' full prescriptive and enforcement jurisdiction.[52]

1.2. The Role of Nationality of a Vessel as a Condition for the Enjoyment of Navigational Entitlements

Describing the right of innocent passage is relevant to assess who holds such right. But before making such assessment, one needs to bear in mind that the enjoyment of navigational entitlements set out in the LOSC depends upon meeting certain conditions. An obvious condition for the enjoyment of freedom of navigation is the ship's possession of seaworthiness. Ultimately, if a ship fails absolutely to meet the most basic seaworthiness conditions (eg it is not apt to float or navigate), one may ask if it can be qualified as a 'ship' for the purposes of the law of the sea treaties.[53] In any case, one can claim that it is 'obvious' in the interest of all the community – including of ship-owners, seafarers, flag and coastal States – that maritime navigation should be as safe as possible.[54] Consistently, States are required to adopt the necessary measures so that ships flying their flag have the appropriate seaworthiness conditions,[55]

[50] Richard Barnes, 'Article 24', in Proelß (ed), *UN Convention* (n 21) 217, 220; Molenaar, *Coastal State* (n 30) 202, although referring to reasonableness. Before the LOSC, Myres McDougal and William Burke, *The Public Order of the Oceans – A Contemporary International Law of the Sea* (Martinus Nijhoff 1987) 255, but on broader terms.

[51] Molenaar, *Coastal State* (n 30) 202; John Norton Moore, Myron Nordquist, Satya Nandan and Shabtai Rosenne (eds), *United Nations Convention on the Law of the Sea – A Commentary 1982*, III (Martinus Nijhoff 1995) 226.

[52] Churchill and Lowe, *Law of the Sea* (n 7) 95; Johnson, *Coastal State* (n 31) 62–63 and 83; O'Connell, *Law of the Sea*, II (n 7) 953; Yang, *Jurisdiction* (n 35) 151.

[53] On the notion of 'ship', see Richard Barnes, 'Article 17', in Proelß (ed), *UN Convention* (n 21) 176, 180; Vaughan Lowe, 'Ships', in Nerina Boschiero, Tullio Scovazzi, Cesare Pitea and Chiara Ragni (eds), *International Courts and the Development of International Law – Essays in Honour of Tullio Treves* (Springer 2013) 291; Tullio Treves, 'Navigation', in René-Jean Dupuy and Daniel Vignes (eds), *A Handbook on the New Law of the Sea*, II (Martinus Nijhoff 1991) 835, 841ff; Yang, *Jurisdiction* (n 35) 7ff.

[54] Churchill and Lowe, *Law of the Sea* (n 7) 264.

[55] Article 94(2)–(4) of the LOSC.

which, for practical and governance reasons, follow the internationally accepted standards.

For the purpose of determining who is the holder of navigational entitlements, most relevant is the possession of nationality as a condition for the full enjoyment of navigational entitlements. In fact, even though Stateless ships are not afforded full protection from the legal order – eg under Article 110(1)(d) of the LOSC interference with navigation of Stateless ships on the high seas is *ipso facto* justified – in the current law of the sea there is no explicit prohibition of Stateless navigation on the high seas.[56] And even in areas under their spatial jurisdiction, coastal States can authorise the navigation of Stateless ships. However, the international legal system has a deep suspicion of Stateless ships, which at this point can only be compared to ships engaged in piracy – not that the conduct is comparable, but Stateless ships also embody a claim against the system of States governance. As such, full enjoyment of navigational entitlements depends upon the conferral of *nationality* by a State. For that reason, some brief words on the nationality of a ship are necessary, especially if one bears in mind that nationality will play an important role in the distribution of responsibilities between the players (ie rights-holders and duty-bearers) engaged in maritime navigation.

But what is the nationality of a ship? One can start by explaining what it is *not*: the same doctrine as that of the nationality of individuals, which refers to membership in a political community.[57] And it is also not the same doctrine as the nationality of corporations, which are a natural extension of individuals' activities. However, as with individuals and corporations, the nationality of a ship establishes a relationship with a particular State, namely one of jurisdiction of the flag State over the ship. In this sense, the *core function of nationality* is to determine what State has primary prescriptive and enforcement jurisdiction over persons and events on board, in order to establish a unified authority – and not that it appertains to the flag State,[58] or that it is a floating piece of its territory. For that reason, whereas States' jurisdiction

[56] Against, see inter alia Edward D Brown, *The International Law of the Sea*, I (Dartmouth 1994) 291–92.

[57] See inter alia Andrew Anderson, 'Jurisdiction over Stateless Vessels on the High Seas: An Appraisal under Domestic and International Law' (1982) 13 *Journal of Maritime Law & Commerce* 323, 338; Vincent Cogliati-Bantz, 'Disentangling the "Genuine Link": Enquiries in Sea, Air and Space Law' (2010) 79 *Nordic Journal of International Law* 383, 387; Maurice Kamto, 'La nationalité des navires en droit international', in Daniel-Heywood Anderson, Vincent Bantz, Geneviéve Bastid-Burdeau, Mohammed Bedjaoui and Josette Beer-Gabel (eds), *La mer et son droit – Mélanges offerts à Laurent Lucchini et Jean-Pierre Quéneudec* (Pedone 2003) 343, 344–45; Doris König, 'Flag of Ships', in *Max Planck Encyclopedia of Public International Law*, § 17; Myres McDougal, William Burke and Ivan Vlasic, 'The Maintenance of Public Order at Sea and the Nationality of Ships' (1960) 54 *American Journal of International Law* 25, 40; Moore et al (eds), *UN Convention*, III (n 51) 106.

[58] In contrast, see David Attard and Patricia Mallia, 'The High Seas', in David Joseph Attard, Malgosia Fitzmaurice and Norman A Martínez Gutiérrez (eds), *The IMLI Manual on International Maritime Law*, I, *The Law of the Sea* (OUP 2014) 246–47.

over individuals and juristic persons is based on the nationality principle, over ships it is determined in spatial terms,[59] ie it includes all persons and events on board the ship. Ultimately whereas jural relations of individuals and juristic persons could be governed without conferring a nationality on them, the nationality of a ship is the means to subject all ships and persons/events on board to a legal system.[60]

In that sense, the nationality of a ship is pivotal in the law of the sea: it is the hinge between the ship and the province of law, the criterion for determining the rights and obligations that 'ship' bears, as well as for determining what State has primary jurisdiction over that ship, can exert flag State protection, and account for acts or omissions of the ship that, according to rules of international law, may be attributed to the State.[61] Not surprisingly, thus, a ship flying two or more flags may be assimilated to a ship without nationality;[62] and in the absence of a nationality, some rights and freedoms enshrined in the LOSC might not be enjoyed.

Although jurisdiction over a ship (as a unit) is determined in spatial terms, one cannot say, as the PCIJ does, that the ship 'is assimilated to the territory of the State the flag of which it flies'.[63] A better explanation is found in the principles of freedom of navigation and the submission of the high seas to law,[64] in conjunction with a presumption that the flag State is better suited to enforce the legal system over ships of its nationality. But the primacy of flag State jurisdiction does not mean that States do not have a title to exert jurisdiction over a foreign ship – otherwise, Stateless ships would be immune from interference by any State; it only establishes a presumption on the high seas in favour of flag State jurisdiction, which can only be rebutted by a permissive international law rule.[65]

[59] For a similar approach, comparing the generic nature of flag State jurisdiction with territorial jurisdiction, see Urfan Khaliq, 'Jurisdiction, Ships and Human Rights Treaties', in Henrik Ringbom (ed), *Jurisdiction over Ships* (Brill Nijhoff 2015) 324, 330; Irini Papanicolopulu, *International Law and the Protection of People at Sea* (1st edn, OUP 2018) 132.

[60] Benedetto Conforti, *Il regime giuridico dei mari* (Casa Editrice Dott. Eugenio Jovene 1957) 83–86; Momtaz Djamchid, 'The High Seas', in Dupuy and Vignes (eds), *Handbook* (n 53) 383, 401.

[61] Attard and Mallia, 'High Seas' (n 58) 246; Churchill and Lowe, *Law of the Sea* (n 7) 257; König, 'Flag' (n 57) § 16; Tanaka, *Law of the Sea* (n 12) 193–94.

[62] Article 92(2) of the LOSC. The spatial regulatory purpose of the nationality explains why, unlike individuals, ships can have one nationality only: Douglas Guilfoyle, 'The High Seas', in Rothwell et al (eds), *Handbook* (n 8) 203, 216.

[63] *The Case of the SS 'Lotus'* [Judgment, 7 September 1927] PCIJ Series A, No. 10, 25.

[64] Djamchid, 'High Seas' (n 60) 400–01; Paul Fauchille, *Traité de droit international public*, I (Rousseau 1925) 46; Gilbert Gidel, *Le droit international public de la mer – Les temps de paix*, I, *Introduction – La haute mer* [1932] (Topos Verlag/Librairie Edouard Duchemim 1981) 225; Guilfoyle, 'High Seas' (n 62) 203, 210; Tanaka, *Law of the Sea* (n 12) 190; Tanaka, 'Navigational' (n 8) 556.

[65] Rayfuse, *Non-Flag State* (n 6) 22.

2. THE PUZZLING REFERENCE TO SHIPS

2.1. Ships as Apparent Rights-holders

Having determined the structure and obligational scope of entitlements deriving from freedom of navigation, and the pivotal role of assigning nationality to a ship, one can turn to the assessment of the holder(s) of those navigational entitlements. In this context, a disturbing formula adopted by the LOSC and other treaties is the allocation of navigational entitlements to ships, suggesting not only that the entity who actually bears the right or freedom in question is the ship, but also that ships (far from being an object of protection) are a subject of law, enjoying specific international capacities under law of the sea treaties.

In fact, Article 18 of the LOSC establishes that 'ships of all States ... enjoy the right of innocent passage through the territorial sea';[66] Article 21(4) and Articles 22 and 23 of the LOSC explicitly refer to 'ships exercising the right of innocent passage' in the territorial sea; Article 24, when framing the corresponding duty of the coastal State, provides that this latter 'shall not hamper the innocent passage of foreign ships ...', and further provides for specific duties towards ships,[67] as if the entities in the jural relation were the State and the ship; Article 26 of the LOSC, in coherence with this relational framework, refers to the charges that might or might not be levied upon ships; Article 21(4) and Article 30 of the LOSC refer to ships and warships that do not comply with the laws and regulations of the coastal State (ie as if the duties were imposed upon it); Article 32 of the LOSC refers to the 'immunities of warships and other government ships operated for non-commercial purposes', as if the ship itself were granted immunity, not the flag State. As such, 'an entitlement of the "ship" does not seem to be foreign to the [LOSC] and the drafting of [these provisions] cannot be merely erroneous'.[68] Other treaties also explicitly assign navigational rights and freedoms to ships: eg Article II of the SOLAS Convention states that this treaty 'shall apply to ships entitled to fly the flag of States ...', whilst Article 17(3) of the 1988 United Nations Convention against Illicit Traffic in Narcotic Drugs and Psychotropic Substances refers to 'a vessel exercising freedom of navigation'.

[66] The preposition 'of' should not be interpreted as a by-word for 'ownership', but rather as meaning 'flagged ships': Barnes, 'Article 18' (n 21) 180; Myron Nordquist, Satya N Nandan, Shabtai Rosenne and Neal Grandy (eds), *United Nations Convention on the Law of the Sea 1982 – A Commentary*, II (Martinus Nijhoff 1993) 156.

[67] See Article 24(1)(a) and (b) of the LOSC.

[68] Philipp Wendel, *State Responsibility for Interferences with the Freedom of Navigation in Public International Law* (Springer 2007) 70.

On a different level, several provisions of law of the sea treaties have referred to ships as being entitled to compensation in case of interference with navigation: that is the case of Article 22(3) of the HSC and its successor Article 110(3) of the LOSC, Article 111(8) of the LOSC, or Article 9(2) of the Migrant Smuggling Protocol. Other provisions refer to the acts committed by ships and the responsibility of flag States for unlawful interference with their navigation, such as Article 21(18) of the 1995 Fish Stocks Agreement, or Article 8*bis*(10) of the 2005 Protocol to the Convention for the Suppression of Unlawful Acts against the Safety of Maritime Navigation (SUA) Convention. Before the adoption of the LOSC, and regarding port State jurisdiction, some provisions refer to the same right to compensation enjoyed by the ship, such as Article 7(2) of the International Convention for the Prevention of Pollution from Ships (MARPOL) Convention, or Chapter XI-2, Regulation 9, no. 3.5 of the SOLAS Convention.

Nonetheless, it is argued that rights and obligations enshrined in the LOSC and other treaties cannot be enjoyed by, or imposed upon, *ships* since these are deprived of international legal personality,[69] but it is hardly questioned whether ships possess legal personality under domestic law, and thus whether they can derive the exact same rights and duties from the State whose flag they fly.[70] Nevertheless, with respect to the claims to compensation for unlawful interference with navigation on the high seas, some judges[71] and scholars[72] do claim that the LOSC confers the right on the ship itself.

A possible explanation for this puzzling reference to ships made by the LOSC and law of the sea treaties can be that ships are legal persons holding specific international legal rights and duties. Legal personality being a purely epistemological tool, in the abstract there is no obstacle to viewing ships as legal persons, ie an autonomous centre for the allocation of rights and duties, whose will would be exercised through legal representatives. If corporations and States – which have no physical existence in nature – can possess legal personality, why could a ship not possess it also? Moreover, several domestic systems confer legal personality (although with limited capacities) on things and estates that have a certain level of autonomy vis-à-vis their potential owners (eg the estate of a deceased person). Considering that the foundational dichotomy opposing things (or *res*) to persons (or *persona*) has been gradually eroded, ships could fit somewhere in between the seemingly porous border between persons and things. At least, recognising ships' legal personality would

[69] Churchill and Lowe, *Law of the Sea* (n 7) 257; Djamchid, 'High Seas' (n 60) 401.

[70] Churchill and Lowe, *Law of the Sea* (n 7) 257 and 263–64.

[71] *M/V 'Saiga' (No. 2)* [1999] 'Separate Opinion of Judge C. Rao', § 14. See also *Corfu* [1949] 'Separate Opinion of Judge Alvarez', 46.

[72] Barnes, 'Article 17' (n 53) 179; Erik Molenaar, 'Multilateral Hot Pursuit and Illegal Fishing in the Southern Ocean: The Pursuits of the *Viarsa 1* and the *South Tomi*' (2004) 19 *International Journal of Marine and Coastal Law* 19, 37.

have some correspondence with the 'ordinary meaning' of the LOSC, and thus comply with Article 31(1) of the VCLT.[73]

Nonetheless, the semantic element is far from being the definitive element of treaty interpretation.[74] The acid test is to look at the procedural rules meant to enforce or guarantee the entitlements derived from freedom of navigation – although, as seen in Chapter 2, the absence of remedies cannot be regarded as the absence of a substantive right. In particular, prompt release proceedings admit entities other than States and are meant to provide protection to freedom of navigation. As such, if a ship is seized in breach of the LOSC provisions, and if ships were acknowledged as legal persons, they could be referred to in Article 292(2) of the LOSC or Article 110 of the ITLOS Rules (which aim at enlarging the circle of procedural rights-holders) and enjoy a right of igniting prompt release proceedings. However, under these provisions States and private actors can institute prompt release procedures before the ITLOS, but ships cannot do so; and private actors are entitled to submit a prompt release proceeding on behalf of the State – but not on behalf of the ship, acting as its legal representative. This could mean only that there is a deficiency in the legal system, but the silence of the international treaties (compared with liberal references to entities other than States) rather suggests that ships are not seen as legal persons and do not hold navigational rights and freedoms.

Another argument is the contextual reading of the LOSC's provisions regarding the navigational rights and freedoms, including the references to ships. It is disturbing that ships are equipped only with navigational entitlements in areas under national spatial jurisdiction, whereas on the high seas no reference is made, except to a possible right to compensation. Considering that the further off coast a vessel is, the broader the scope of navigational entitlements is, it would be odd that no right or freedom would be assigned to ships on the high seas.[75] Per se, this is not a final argument, but it strongly suggests that the intention of the drafters might not have been to confer an entitlement on ships. Moreover, if the right were assigned to the ship as a legal person, the identity of the entity in physical control of the ship would be irrelevant for the purpose of exercising the navigational entitlements on areas under State's sovereignty or jurisdiction. But this would imply, for instance, that if a ship were captured by a group of pirates, it would be entitled to a right of innocent passage provided they did not perform any of the activities prohibited under Article 19 of the LOSC. In short, it seems that little room exists to argue that ships are the addressees of the navigational entitlements described before

[73] See also Wendel, *State Responsibility* (n 68) 69.

[74] Articles 31–33 of the VCLT. See *Arbitral Award of 31 July 1989 (Guinea-Bissau v Senegal)* [Judgment, 12 November 1991] ICJ Rep 53, § 48. On this topic, see Richard Gardiner, *Treaty Interpretation* (2nd edn, OUP 2017) 181ff.

[75] Wendel, *State Responsibility* (n 68) 85.

(ie that they are legal persons) – although some room exists, if the law-makers so intend, to afford legal capacity to ships.[76]

2.2. The Pragmatic Reason for Assigning Rights to Ships

Ships are not legal persons – and certainly not the bearers of navigational entitlements – yet for some reason the LOSC and other treaties adopted an explicit reference to them. One explanation for that is the conception of the oceans as a 'transport surface' and a void between the land territories (ie between provinces of law and civilisation), which entailed that the sea itself would not require any particular regulation: such regulation should be directed at the authority claims of coastal States and the activity of ships.[77]

However, a better explanation is the discomfort with assigning rights to the State or other entity (including private actors): it was just more comfortable and less elliptical to refer to ships instead of 'States and other subjects when using a ship for the exercise of a navigational entitlement'. The same level of unease with assigning rights and duties to private actors (with the prima facie personification of the ship) is visible in Article 230(3) of the LOSC, where a reference is made to 'proceedings in respect of such violations committed by a foreign vessel' and the observance of the '[fundamental] rights of the accused'.[78] As such, references to ships ('une figure de rhétorique')[79] were just more convenient in terms of drafting and thus this should be interpreted broadly as a catch-all term intended to cover all possible entities holding navigational entitlements: by referring to ships, the LOSC and other treaties avoid referring to the holder of navigational entitlements.

3. STATES *AND* PRIVATE ACTORS NAVIGATIONAL RIGHTS-HOLDERS

3.1. States as Navigational Rights-holders

Under an orthodox view of international law (coupled with a bias in favour of States' participation in international law), the obvious candidate to be the recipient of these entitlements is the flag *State*. A good reason for that, but not final, could be that these entitlements are invoked against other States

[76] eg in theory, ships could hold procedural rights in substitution of the navigational rights-holders in proceedings before international institutions: eg they could fit in the category of those who can submit a prompt release proceeding 'on behalf' of the flag State.

[77] Philip E Steinberg, *The Social Construction of the Ocean* (CUP 2001) 14.

[78] Regarding the oddness of this wording, see Papanicolopulu, *International Law* (n 59) 85.

[79] Laurent Lucchini and Michel Vœlckel, *Droit de la mer*, I (Pedone 1990) 124.

(whether coastal, flag or port States) and embody a delicate balance between the interests of flag States, coastal States and the international community as a whole. In any case, the problem only arises with respect to foreign merchant vessels since navigational entitlements of warships or other governmental ships are by implication assigned to the State; and jural relations between merchant vessels and their flag State are governed by their domestic law, even if impacted by treaties.

In fact, some entitlements are worded as assigned to flag *States*: eg Article 58(3) of the LOSC provides that 'In exercising their rights and performing their duties, States shall have due regard to the rights and duties of the coastal States …'; Article 90 of the LOSC establishes that 'Every State, whether coastal or land-locked, has the right to sail ships flying its flag on the high seas'; Article 106 of the LOSC, concerning the right to compensation in case of unlawful interference with navigation, refers to the right of the flag State, although other provisions on the right to compensation refer to the ship.[80] In addition, land-locked States have a special mention in the LOSC, in order to be equipped with equal chances of access to the seas and of exploiting its resources. As such, Article 125(1) of the LOSC provides that 'Land-locked States shall have the right of access to and from the sea'; 'To this end, land-locked States shall enjoy freedom of transit through the territory of transit States'. Some of the rights mentioned here are clearly enjoyed by States only – such as the right to negotiate the establishment of free zones and other customs facilities in the ports and territory of coastal States.[81]

In this context, my view is that flag States enjoy navigational rights and freedoms enshrined in the LOSC and other treaties, but this only means that flag States have such rights and freedoms for their warships and publicly owned vessels, as well as being able to confer their nationality on privately owned vessels and exercise flag State protection with respect to any incident involving these latter flagged vessels. What it does not entail, in my view, is that the navigational entitlements of privately owned vessels are also assigned to flag States. In fact, if the LOSC and other law of the sea treaties intended to confer navigational rights and freedoms *only* on States, they could have said so where appropriate. Instead, the puzzling reference to ships in several treaties points to a different solution. As a result, the next task is to determine whether a more inclusive narrative of navigational entitlements is possible, allowing private actors to hold navigational entitlements.

[80] Drafters of the LOSC should have been aware of the different wording of Article 106, on the one hand, and Articles 110(3) and 111(8), on the other: Wendel, *State Responsibility* (n 68) 70. An explanation might be the fact that the private interests needing protection in the case of a seizure of pirate ships (Article 106) are minor if compared with the case of boarding and inspection of other vessels referred to in Articles 110(3) and 111(8) of the LOSC, ibid 70–71.

[81] Article 128 of the LOSC.

3.2. Private Actors as Navigational Rights-holders

In my view, *private actors are also recipients of the provisions of the LOSC and other treaties regarding navigational entitlements* – not because they are ultimate beneficiaries of these rights and freedoms, but because the structure and the obligational scope of such provisions and the remedies afforded suggest that private actors are, hand in hand with States, the direct recipients of the LOSC's provisions. The elliptical description of the 'right of flag States to sail the vessels flying their flag' already suggests that these entitlements might not be held by States solely, but concurrently with private actors.[82] At most, an alternative wording – similar to that adopted by Article 116 of the LOSC – would have been to establish that States hold this right 'for their nationals'.[83]

This claim is not new in scholarship. For instance, Accioly claimed that when a vessel is seized, the owner of the ship has rights under international law.[84] After analysing the structure of navigational entitlements, the corresponding obligations attached to its exercise, and the consequences of non-compliance, Accioly acknowledged that States hold entitlements deriving from freedom of navigation, but also claimed that ship-owners hold concurrent entitlements.[85] Lucchini and Vœlckel claimed that the freedoms of the high seas and the rights of passage are assigned to the relevant private actor, ie the ship-owner, operator or master.[86] And Wendel – although not referring solely to navigational rights and freedoms, but also to a right to compensation – affirmed that if current law of the sea treaties criminalise certain acts committed at sea by private actors (eg piracy), 'it seems logical to grant in return some rights to such entities if they are related to the individual criminal activity'.[87]

Furthermore, other entities have also recognised that navigational entitlements are also held by private actors: eg the European Committee on Crime Problems, when interpreting Article 26(2) of the European Agreement on Illicit Traffic by Sea,[88] assumed that both Article 22(3) of the HSC and Article 110(3) of the LOSC confer an entitlement on a private actor; and the ECJ stated that

> individuals are *in principle* not granted independent rights and freedoms by virtue of [the LOSC]. In particular, they *can enjoy the freedom of navigation* only if they establish a close connection between their ship and a State which grants its nationality to the ship and becomes the ship's flag State.

[82] *M/V 'Saiga' (No. 2)* [1999], 'Separate Opinion of Judge Wolfrum', §§ 51–52. See also Lucchini and Vœlckel, *Droit*, I (n 79) 124.

[83] *M/V 'Saiga' (No. 2)* [1999], 'Separate Opinion of Judge Wolfrum', § 53.

[84] Hildebrando Accioly, *Tratado de Direito Internacional Público*, I (Imprensa Nacional 1933) 72–73.

[85] ibid 73.

[86] Lucchini and Vœlckel, *Droit*, I (n 79) 124.

[87] Wendel, *State Responsibility* (n 68) 71. See also Karl Zemanek, 'Does the Prospect of Incurring Responsibility Improve the Observance of International Law?', in Maurizio Ragazzi (ed), *International Responsibility Today – Essays in Memory of Oscar Schachter* (Martinus Nijhoff 2005) 133.

[88] *Explanatory Report to the Agreement on Illicit Traffic by Sea, implementing Article 17 of the United Nations Convention against Illicit Traffic in Narcotic Drugs and Psychotropic Substances* (ETS No. 156), §§ 94–95.

'If the ship is not attached to a State, neither the ship *nor the persons on board enjoy the freedom of navigation*'.[89] Other international treaties seem to convey this same idea: eg Article III(1) of the 1969 International Convention on Civil Liability for Oil Pollution Damage provides that 'the owner of a ship … [is] liable for any pollution damage caused by oil which has escaped or been discharged from the ship' (which means that the conditions subjected to the exercise of navigational rights and freedoms in all maritime zones are addressed to private actors also), whereas Article 7(1) of the 2010 International Convention on Liability and Compensation for Damage in Connection with the Carriage of Hazardous and Noxious Substances by Sea provides that 'the owner at the time of an incident shall be liable for damage'.

Before discussing this topic further, I should mention that in this context the term 'private actors' encompasses several players, such as the ship-owner, the operator, the charterer or others. This taxonomy is not entirely relevant as all these different entities can ultimately hold the same entitlements. However, to determine who is the addressee of the norm, a useful concept could be the *beneficial owner*: according to the UN Conference on Trade and Development, 'The beneficial owner [of a ship] is the person, company or organisation which gains the pecuniary benefits from the shipping operations',[90] regardless of holding a right of ownership over the ship. Law of the sea treaties adopt the same comprehensive approach.[91] For the purpose of this work, I will refer broadly to the ship-owner as a catch-all term that can encompass any of these private actors.

3.2.1. *The Structure and Obligational Scope of the LOSC's Provisions*

To assess who holds the right of innocent passage (as an example of a navigational entitlement), the core issue is to consider the structure and obligational scope of Articles 17ff of the LOSC to see who can request performance of specific obligations and against whom.

The task now is to consider the primary obligations attached to the exercise of these rights and freedoms (ie the conditions laid down in the LOSC that constrain its exercise) and ascertain if these obligations are addressed to the flag State or the relevant private actor (ie the ship-owner or the master of the vessel acting as its agent). The wording of those provisions is far from clear, but one element seems evident: the ship-owner is the entity that can better (if not the

[89] Case C-308/06 *The Queen, on the Application of International Association of Independent Tanker Owners (Intertanko) and Others v Secretary of State for Transport* [2008] ECR I-04057, §§ 59–60, emphasis added.

[90] Report by the Secretariat of UNCTAD, in *Review of Maritime Transport 1978* (New York, 1981) 11.

[91] eg Article 1(3) of the 2001 International Convention on Civil Liability for Bunker Oil Pollution Damage, which includes in the notion of ship-owner 'the registered owner, bareboat charterer, manager and operator of the ship'.

only one that actually can) control the performance of such obligations, and of whom its performance will be requested. In other words, the ship-owner holds the *ex ante facto* responsibility for the performance of these obligations.

For illustrative purposes, Article 26 of the LOSC – limiting the taxes and charges that can be levied upon foreign ships exercising the right of innocent passage – is addressed to the ship-owner engaged in shipping activities: the charges that can be levied under Article 26(2) shall be paid by him, not the flag State (or otherwise a problem of State immunity would arise); and other taxes and charges, if not forbidden under paragraph 1 of this provision, would also be levied upon the ship-owner, not the flag State. Conditions for admission to ports, as laid down in Article 25(2) of the LOSC and Article 5 of MARPOL, are addressed to ship-owners, for only they can control that the vessel seeking to enter a port complies with the entrance conditions: if access is denied, the action taken refers to the ship not complying with those conditions, not to all ships flying the same flag. Likewise, Article 5 of MARPOL refers to the actions that can be taken by coastal States against the ship-owners in case of failure to comply with the obligation of sailing a ship carrying the appropriate certificates: notably, access to ports will be denied to a specific ship only, and not to all vessels flying the same flag. If a ship cannot leave the port (eg for failure to comply with seaworthiness conditions), ship-owners (not flag States) are asked to carry out the necessary operations. With respect to the exercise of the right of innocent passage, it seems clear that the obligations that constrain its exercise are addressed to ship-owners: eg ship-owners are asked to comply with the laws and regulations adopted by coastal States under Article 21(1) of the LOSC, or with the generally accepted international regulations relating to the prevention of collisions at sea referred to in Article 21(4) of the LOSC; and ship-owners are also responsible for respecting sea lanes and traffic separation schemes adopted under Article 22 of the LOSC. Finally, innocence of passage must be assured by the ship-owner, not the flag State. In all these cases, flag States can ask their nationals to comply with these obligations, but the only entity that can *de facto* perform the obligations laid down in the LOSC is the ship-owner: if coastal States intend to enforce these obligations, they will act against the ship-owner, not the flag State. With regard to the high seas, Articles 111(8) and 110(3) of the LOSC also indicate that navigational entitlements are held by private actors: since these provisions establish that, in the event of an infringement of the freedom of navigation, compensation must be paid, they presuppose 'the pre-existence of an internationally protected right whose violation gives rise to international responsibility', which 'indicate[s] that the freedom of navigation incorporates a right of natural or juridical persons, too'.[92]

[92] *M/V 'Saiga' (No. 2)* [1999], 'Separate Opinion of Judge Wolfrum', § 51.

According to the UN Consultative Group on Flag State Implementation, these *ex ante facto* obligations are held by flag States.[93] However, the artificial construction of the report is noticeable: at most, the consultative group identified cases where due diligence of the flag State ought to be exercised, implying that flag States may hold indirect responsibility to control the performance of an obligation by a private actor. Failure to understand this difference between direct and indirect attribution helps to explain the disappointing results of this consultative group work.

The acid test to identify the addressee of the LOSC's provisions is to assess who will be *ex post facto* accountable or responsible for not complying with them. The question to be answered is 'if duties imposed to navigation are not performed, who will be held responsible or accountable?' If a ship is sailing in breach of national laws and regulations of the coastal State regarding, eg, the protection and preservation of the marine environment, can the flag State be held responsible for that breach?

The 'conduct of the ship' is not directly or automatically attributable to the State under the rules of State responsibility. Where a ship fails to comply with a particular rule, there will be no attribution of its conduct to the flag State. States being fictitious legal entities with no psyche, 'Attribution is the process by which international law establishes whether the conduct of a natural person or other such intermediary can be considered an "act of state," and thus be capable of giving rise to state responsibility'.[94] Chapter II of the Articles on Responsibility of States for Internationally Wrongful Acts (ARSIWA)[95] sets out the circumstances that determine the attribution of conduct to States, establishing that attribution exists only, for the purpose of this section, with regard to the conduct of State organs and agents, or to the conduct of private actors who are empowered by domestic law to exercise acts of public authority, or who act on the instructions of, or under the direction or control of, the State:[96] since private navigation does not fit in any of these hypotheses, the conduct of the ship-owner is not directly attributable to its flag State.[97] At most, flag States

[93] Report of the Secretary-General, 'Oceans and the Law of the Sea. Consultative Group on Flag State Implementation' (5 March 2004) UN Doc. A/59/63, §§ 208–09.

[94] James Crawford, *State Responsibility – The General Part* (CUP 2013) 113.

[95] The ARSIWA is not a binding treaty of international law, but rather a document produced by the ILC. In any case, there is room to contend, as the ICJ did, that it 'is the state of customary international law;' it 'reflects' or 'express[es] present customary international law' (*Application of the Convention on the Prevention and Punishment of the Crime of Genocide (Bosnia and Herzegovina v Serbia and Montenegro)* [Judgment, 26 February 2007] ICJ Rep 43, §§ 385, 388, 401, 406, 407 and 414).

[96] Articles 4, 5 and 8 of the ARSIWA.

[97] *Request for an Advisory Opinion Submitted by the Sub-Regional Fisheries Commission (SRFC)* [Advisory Opinion, 2 April 2015] ITLOS Rep 4, § 146. See also Maria Gavouneli, *Functional Jurisdiction in the Law of the Sea* (Martinus Nijhoff 2007) 34; Khaliq, 'Jurisdiction' (n 59) 344; Yoshinobu Takei, 'Assessing Flag State Performance in Legal Terms: Clarifications of the Margin of Discretion' (2013) 28 *International Journal of Marine and Coastal Law* 97, 130.

can be internationally responsible for failure to comply with their due diligence obligations. But whereas direct attribution of conduct could imply that navigational entitlements were held by the flag State, indirect attribution of conduct (under the aegis of due diligence) suggests that the exercise of navigational entitlements is private. As such, in case of non-compliance with the limits laid down in the LOSC to the exercise of the right of innocent passage (as an example of navigational entitlements), the accountability for those acts lies only with the ship-owner.

This is evidence that the obligations attached to the exercise of the right of innocent passage are addressed to the ship-owner. Thus, the navigational right itself must also be assigned to the same legal entity. The most explicit evidence of such accountability of private actors is to be found in Article III(1) of the 1969 Liability for Oil Pollution Convention, which provides that 'the owner of a ship … [is] liable for any pollution damage caused by oil which has escaped or been discharged from the ship'.

At the level of secondary norms, one must also consider the existing remedies under the LOSC but bearing in mind that they are of limited value. In any case, remedies are evidence of the existence of a substantive right or duty. Thus, if ship-owners have remedies under the LOSC, this perforce means they hold the corresponding navigational entitlements. Nonetheless, this presumption only applies to private actors, since the contingent evolution of international law determines that States may hold secondary rights (eg under the umbrella of diplomatic or flag State protection) that do not necessarily correspond to a primary right. In this sense, the fact that the LOSC crafted an inter-State system of dispute settlement is not final, since States might hold remedies or procedural rights to protect their own rights, or procedurally in lieu of private actors. However, as mentioned before, flag State protection (judicial or not) is a compensation for private actors' exclusion from international dispute settlement, not from international law.

Nonetheless, a perfunctory analysis of Part XV of the LOSC suggests that there is more than meets the eye. In particular, Article 292(2) of the LOSC and Article 110(1) of the ITLOS Rules establish that, in prompt release proceedings (of ships and crew members), an application may be submitted 'on behalf' of the flag State, provided that it is duly authorised by the flag State. To avoid a redundant interpretation, if the LOSC uses the formula 'applications submitted by or on behalf of the flag State', it aims at introducing an alternative that would not exist if applications could only be submitted *by* States.[98] As will be discussed in Chapter 4, the only meaningful interpretation of this provision entails the submission of applications by private actors who are not a State's agents. But if private actors hold a procedural right before

[98] Bernard Oxman, 'Observations on Vessel Release under the United Nations Convention on the Law of the Sea' (1996) 11 *International Journal of Marine and Coastal Law* 201, 211.

the ITLOS, they necessarily hold a substantive entitlement also. One could ask whether this provision aims at protecting a navigational entitlement or a personal value (such as human life or integrity), but the urgency and broadness of that remedy indicate that it aims at protecting navigational entitlements of private actors also.

The absence of more (and more robust) private actors' remedies does not imply that they are deprived of any navigational right or freedom: it might just mean there is a flawed protection of their substantive position; or rather that the appropriate, open fora for private actors are domestic mechanisms acting as the ordinary enforcers of international law. In fact, since States hold immunity from enforcement jurisdiction under national law, Article 295 of the LOSC (which stipulates the need for the exhaustion of local remedies) entrusts national authorities with the task of enforcing navigational entitlements. If disputes regarding the interpretation and application of the LOSC were purely inter-State, this provision would be meaningless.[99] Thus, implicit in this provision is a substantive entitlement held by ship-owners, which is primarily enforced by domestic bodies and directly flows from the LOSC. If ship-owners are equipped with specific remedies under domestic law to enforce the rights and freedoms they hold *directly* under the LOSC, then the LOSC *implicitly* recognises that private actors are also the bearers of navigational entitlements.[100]

3.2.2. *Conferral of Rights Irrespective of Direct Effect*

It could be said that hypothetical navigational entitlements held by private actors would be invoked before domestic authorities – which would suggest they are not conferred on them under the LOSC, but rather through domestic mechanisms – and thus, that they are not enjoyed at the international level, but rather at the domestic level. This argument is often used as part of the arsenal that reinforces the interpretative bias against recognising rights and freedoms of private actors under international law. The vexed question here is the direct effect of the LOSC regarding navigational entitlements within domestic legal systems.

Since Article 292(2) of the LOSC and Article 110 of the ITLOS Rules admit the participation of private actors in prompt release proceedings, it is not true that only domestic bodies can enforce navigational entitlements of private actors. In any event, Article 295 of the LOSC, regarding exhaustion of local remedies, mandates domestic authorities, as the ordinary judges of international law, to enforce rights or duties held by private actors, since they are better

[99] *M/V 'Saiga' (No. 2)* [1999], 'Separate Opinion of Judge Wolfrum', § 51; *M/V 'Virginia G' (Panama v Guinea-Bissau)* [Judgment, 14 April 2014] ITLOS Rep 4, 'Joint Separate Opinion of Judges Cot and Kelly', § 14. Against, see *M/V 'Saiga' (No. 2)* [1999], §§ 97–98.

[100] *M/V 'Saiga' (No. 2)* [1999], 'Separate Opinion of Judge Wolfrum', § 51.

positioned to enforce the LOSC. In light of the current level of development of international dispute settlement means (and notably the voluntary jurisdiction of these bodies), it would just be naive to empower an international body (such as the ITLOS) with the task of settling *all* disputes regarding the enforcement of navigational entitlements.

The acid test is to consider a case where a coastal State has ratified the LOSC (and therefore is internationally bound by its terms) but the LOSC has no direct effect within its domestic legal order (eg because it failed to comply with constitutional requirements, such as publication in the official journal). In this case, national courts would apparently have no constitutional authority to settle that dispute based on the LOSC. However, the LOSC being valid in the international legal order, this implies (using the same wording of the LOSC) that a ship holding the flag of another State party holds the navigational rights and freedoms set out in this treaty. Therefore, it can invoke the right of innocent passage against another State party, based on Article 17 of the LOSC, even if the LOSC fails to have direct effect within this latter State's domestic legal order. In this case, the lack of domestic direct effect (as traditionally framed by international legal theory) would only impair the 'ship' from resorting to domestic authorities, not from the navigational entitlements themselves – and even that lack of domestic remedies is far from evident. As seen before, epistemologically the question whether international law rules have direct effect within domestic legal orders is radically different from the question of whether that rule creates private actors' rights and duties.[101]

Disputes concerning navigational entitlements of private actors would only be an issue of domestic law if the definition and limits of the maritime jurisdiction of States were also an issue of domestic law solely. However, maritime jurisdiction of States over portions of the sea is conferred and demarcated by the LOSC. Claims made by States are articulated pursuant to specific provisions of the law of the sea treaties, and not as original (or 'natural') rights of States: their competence is conferred by international law and cannot be derived from their territorial sovereignty.[102] That explains why navigational entitlements on the territorial sea, the archipelagic waters or international straits – which conflict with national sovereignty – are *not* permitted by States' authorities, but are rather a self-executing rule imposed upon coastal States. Until the twentieth century, portions of the seas were claimed by rulers as their property, 'grounded on the consideration of [their] guarding and protecting the seas from pirates and robbers'[103] or similar arguments. That meant that navigational entitlements depended on a specific permission from coastal

[101] Anne Peters, *Beyond Human Rights – The Legal Status of the Individual in International Law* (CUP 2016) 501.

[102] See *mutatis mutandis* Pancracio, *Droit* (n 14) 11.

[103] William Blackstone, *The Commentaries on the Laws of England* [1753], ed George Sharswood (Liberty Fund 2004) 290.

States, acting as the *original proprietor* of those waters. But under the LOSC the conception is the opposite: maritime jurisdiction of States is conferred by international law instruments; and navigational entitlements exist regardless of any coastal States' authorisation and are imposed upon States.[104]

But there is a deeper reason why navigational entitlements are held by private actors irrespective of any direct effect. This doctrine is the result of a discussion between monist and dualist views of the relations between international and domestic laws. In my view, however, both views ask the wrong questions and, not surprisingly, provide the wrong answers.

In fact, the doctrines of direct effect, monism and dualism are deeply embedded in an insular view of the way legal orders act and interact – a view according to which any legal order is a self-referential, isolated sociological phenomenon, which can control and filter how norms deriving from different islands can have any kind of legal relevance within its space. Moreover, they claim that legal orders can decide on how this interaction is to be performed, instead of realising that this is an empirical phenomenon of observation.

A true monism only existed before the full establishment of the Vattelian premise. After that, what Constitutions in general have largely proclaimed, and scholars supported, are different conceptions of what is technically dualism (ie the idea of different, self-referential, autonomous legal orders), with the following peculiarity: whereas the 'new' monism asserts that international legal rules can produce legal effects within domestic legal orders in that quality (ie of international legal rules), the hard dualists, shielded in a classical conception of sovereignty-freedom, claim that norms need to be somehow transformed and applied in the new quality of domestic law rule: under the first view, the LOSC is applied as a treaty; under the second view, as a domestic statutory law that incorporates the LOSC's provisions. This seems to lead to the conclusion that the new monism and the hard dualism are dramatically different, but in fact the only difference between both approaches lies in what they accept to be the impact of crossing the channel between the islands of international and domestic law: whereas under the new monism the international legal rule will have a safe journey and arrive apparently intact at its port of destination, under hard dualism a severe storm on arrival on the island of domestic law necessarily transforms the very nature and genetic code of that international legal rule. But the common problem of such doctrines is that they dismiss the *sole* relevant question: what is the authority of (international) law?

Before answering that, the reader should consider two reasons why a domestic legal order might need to decide to what extent international legal rules can be valid (ie authoritative) within the domestic legal system. First, but historically dated, is the idea that the subjects of international law would be different from the subjects of domestic law and would not include private actors.

[104] O'Connell, *Law of the Sea*, I (n 11) 261–62.

For that reason, when private actors are the beneficiaries of an international legal rule, States would have to provide the domestic means to establish and enforce the rights and duties binding upon them. This, however, is the result of mixing the questions of 'who are the subjects of international law' and 'where lies the boundary between international and domestic law'. The second reason is the principle of sovereignty-freedom, according to which the territorial State can claim exclusive territorial jurisdiction, therefore being the ultimate and sole authority within its own boundaries. But this reason is not valid either, because the exclusive territorial jurisdiction of States does not preclude the possibility of extraterritorial authority claims by different States (eg on grounds of the nationality principle or other criteria tested and valid under international law). It is surprising how national legal orders are liberal and comfortable with the authority of third States under their own rules of private international law (in a case where a clear clash of sovereigns exists), but suddenly are inclined to a more orthodox view when it comes to acknowledging the authority of international law (where no clash of sovereigns exists, and whose norms, notably treaty-based norms, were created by the same State organs who have domestic and international prescriptive authority). Now, if sovereignty is the key issue, then in my view there is no issue at all. As said before, a positivist answer to this question of the authority of law refers to the law as a commandment adopted by the will of a sovereign State, through its appropriate organs and decision-making processes. But if that holds true, then one must point out that treaties are adopted by the organs that, according to domestic rules (usually, of constitutional nature), are afforded that competence, which usually also happen to be equipped with the symmetrical competence to adopt domestic rules. In fact, the reason why international law binds States – and why the ideas of direct effect, monism or dualism are misleading – is because the 'authors' of that rule have the constitutional authority to adopt binding norms of domestic *and* international law; the reason why a State is internationally bound by a treaty is because it was concluded and ratified by that sovereign State's organs. It is thus sovereignty of that State that explains why it is bound by that treaty at the international *and* the domestic level.

This means in my view that what distinguishes domestic and international law is not the different nature of the legal orders nor the different institutions that adopt binding legal rules; nor even the source of authority of a specific binding legal rule (in both cases, it is the sovereignty of the State and the constitutional authority of an organ and decision-making process). The sole difference lies in the shared decision-making process adopted. But what does this entail? What is there so different in terms of structure of that process and authority of the players to justify the different chances of an individual claiming a right or a duty under a domestic or an international legal rule? In my view, nothing! The only difference lies in the scope *ratione loci* and *ratione personae* of the rule enacted after that process, in the sense that more persons will be bound by that treaty-based rule as a result of the intervention of more sovereign authorities in that process. In this sense, and herein lies the *heresy* of the view, treaties – because they express the will of a sovereign State as adopted by its appropriate organs and decision-making processes – are part of the law of the land: an international law rule is applicable *ipso facto* within the domestic legal order, and thus its provisions must be interpreted, applied and enforced by domestic courts: the obedience to their Constitution (their master) means that domestic courts need to interpret, apply and enforce the law of the land, which includes those norms adopted autonomously by processes of domestic law, and those norms adopted by shared processes of international law, provided that those norms have behind them the authority of the sovereign State's will: far from serving two masters, domestic courts are always serving the same sovereign will.

As a result, because there is no 'shield effect' that can be used by domestic legal orders, domestic courts must apply treaty-based rules ratified by the appropriate constitutional organs of their State, through the appropriate constitutional proceedings, at least in three cases: first, when a private actor invokes against the State a specific entitlement directly derived from that treaty (eg the right of innocent passage); second, where the treaty-based rule is not of self-executing character, when a private actor asks for compensation from the State for failure to implement its obligations under that treaty; and third, when two private actors, under their contractual freedom, expressly accept to rule themselves by that treaty. In all these cases, a treaty such as the LOSC can create entitlements of private actors irrespective of any direct effect.

4. INTERTWINING THE POSITION OF SHIP-OWNERS AND FLAG STATES

Having established that ship-owners hold navigational entitlements under the LOSC, the next question refers to the autonomy of their position with respect to the flag State. This task is of particular importance, because part of the interpretative bias against acknowledging rights and duties of private actors under international law is connected with the fact that States can ask for the protection of rights apparently held by private actors: for instance, if the flag State can ask for the protection of a flagged ship's right of innocent passage, should this not mean that the flag State holds that right of innocent passage? Confusion results from a lack of understanding of what is the dual ownership of the claim on the level of remedies (secondary norms) and the derivative nature of the substantive right held by the ship-owner (primary norms). A correct understanding of such factors, however, confirms that navigational entitlements are held by ship-owners.[105]

[105] *M/V 'Saiga' (No. 2)* [1999], 'Separate Opinion of Judge Wolfrum', § 53.

In fact, whereas ship-owners can only ask for the protection of their own navigational entitlements, flag States can ask for the protection of any right held by ships flying its flag (to resort again to the same wording of the LOSC). The reason for such difference is straightforward: under the legal regimes of diplomatic or flag State protection, at the level of secondary norms, States can ask for the protection of the primary rights of their nationals (individuals, juristic persons, or objects). But, as mentioned before, the replacement of the ship-owner by the flag State at the level of secondary norms only aims at compensating for its exclusion from international dispute settlement – it does not mean that ship-owners do not hold a right or a duty at the level of primary norms. The acid test is to assess whether the flag State is a primary creditor, ie if it could, for instance, waive its *and* the ship-owner's navigational entitlements. Prima facie there would be good reasons to consider so, since flag States can withdraw the nationality from the ship (and thus deprive the ship-owner of navigational entitlements) and can authorise third States to interfere with navigation of its ships on the high seas. However, the withdrawal of nationality means only that the enjoyment requirements are not met and the loss of its own flag State protection; and if it authorises non-flag State interferences with navigation on the high seas, it is not tolerating an interference with the navigational entitlement, but rather with its own right to primary jurisdiction over that ship.[106]

On the other hand, the full enjoyment of navigational entitlements of private actors on areas under national spatial jurisdiction are derived from the flag State nationality[107] – and this *derivative* nature is *the* source of difficulties when assessing the legal status of private actors. In fact, ship-owners can only invoke a fully fledged navigational entitlement against a coastal State if its ship flies a flag granted by another State: its navigational entitlements *exist only and because* the flag State granted its nationality to that vessel. To some extent, the derivative nature of navigational entitlements explains the narrow margin that coastal States have to assess the genuine link of the flag flown by a particular ship: if the conclusion was the absence of a genuine link, the consequence would be the deprivation of the entitlements to navigate in waters under national spatial jurisdiction.

Nonetheless, because the entitlements held by the ship-owner and its flag State overlap, there is room to generate a shared accountability between both of them. Considering the unsettled terminology in this domain, 'accountability' here refers to the *ex post facto* attribution of the consequences of the breach of an international legal rule.[108] For their part, 'international responsibility'

[106] See also Richard Barnes, 'Flag States', in Rothwell et al (eds), *Handbook* (n 8) 313.

[107] Brown, *Law of the Sea* (n 56) 286.

[108] For a similar definition, see Klabbers, *International Law* (n 15) 139, for whom accountability expresses the need to 'explain and justify their behavior to someone else'; André Nollkaemper and Dov Jacobs, 'Shared Responsibility in International Law: A Conceptual Framework' (2013) 34 *Michigan Journal of International Law* 359, 369.

and 'liability' are also used here as an *ex post facto* consequence of a breach of an international rule, but 'international responsibility' will be used as a broad term to identify the reaction of the legal system to cases of non-compliance with international obligations and purports to enforce legality in international law (as it is an instrument of reaction against *unlawful* outcomes),[109] damage *not* being an operative fact of international responsibility;[110] finally, the term liability will be used to refer to cases where the secondary obligation is established by reference to the damage (instrument of reaction against *harmful* outcomes).[111]

Before referring to the regime of accountability of the ship-owner and the flag State, the reader will allow me to come back to the nationality of a ship and the genuine link requirement, because its function in terms of ocean governance explains why flag States can hold indirect international responsibility linked to the conducts of flagged ships, but this is neutral regarding the assignment of navigational entitlements to ship-owners.

4.1. The Genuine Link Requirement

According to Article 91(1) of the LOSC, 'there must exist a genuine link between the State and the ship'. It is not a surprise that States cannot freely confer their nationality on any ship,[112] but what the genuine link rule does is to set out a positive duty of States to assess the existence of a strong connection between a ship and its domestic legal order, not only before conferring its nationality on any ship, but also thereafter. If nationality is pivotal to the promotion of order at sea, it cannot be limited to a negative side of excluding other States' jurisdiction over a ship but rather includes its positive side of effective exercise of jurisdiction powers. To know whether States comply or not with the obligation set out in those provisions, one has to ask 'what is a genuine link?' and 'what are the consequences in case of absence?' The answer to these questions has been the source of severe friction.

The *purpose* of the genuine link rule is to assure that flag State jurisdiction is effective.[113] However, the LOSC (like the HSC before it) failed to establish the

[109] Alain Pellet, 'The Definition of Responsibility in International Law', in James Crawford, Alain Pellet and Simon Olleson (eds), *The Law of International Responsibility* (OUP 2010) 3, 15.

[110] Nollkaemper and Jacobs, 'Shared Responsibility' (n 108) 402; Pellet, 'Definition' (n 109) 9–10.

[111] See, *mutatis mutandis*, Klabbers, *International Law* (n 15) 138; Nollkaemper and Jacobs, 'Shared Responsibility' (n 108) 369.

[112] eg Barnes, 'Flag States' (n 106) 304, 306–08; Cogliati-Bantz, 'Disentangling' (n 57) 401; König, 'Flag' (n 57) §§ 21–23; McDougal et al, 'Public Order at Sea' (n 57) 27–28.

[113] *'M/V Saiga' (No. 2)* [1999] § 83; *'Virginia G'* [2014] § 113, *in fine*. See also Cogliati-Bantz, 'Disentangling' (n 57); Oude Elferink, 'The Genuine Link Concept: Time for a *Post Mortem*?', in Ige Dekker and Harry Post (eds), *On the Foundations and Sources of International Law* (Asser Press 2003) 41, 47–48; König, 'Flag' (n 57) § 15; Rayfuse, *Non-Flag State* (n 6) 26; Rayfuse, 'The Anthropocene,

concept or criteria of genuine link; and to describe its purpose is helpful and should guide the interpreter, but ultimately says nothing about what it means. Resorting to the established means of treaty interpretation is also of limited help. For instance, the preparatory works[114] (which include the influential works of the ILC during the 1950s) only mention that 'there must be a minimum national element' for the ascription of nationality to their ships.[115] Afterwards, Article 5 of the HSC and Articles 91 and 94 of the LOSC,[116] following the *Nottebohm* judgment, included a reference to the genuine link and the effective exercise of jurisdiction rules.[117] This link is tempting but misleading: *Nottebohm* refers to nationality as membership of individuals in a political community, where a genuine link rule might be evidence of an individual's belonging to a particular community – but says nothing about the aptitude of a flag State to exercise effective jurisdiction over a ship:[118] eg if the flag State does not possess the necessary means to exercise jurisdiction and control over ships, this cannot be remedied by the most intimate link with a ship.[119]

But if the genuine link requirement were added to Article 91(1) of the LOSC, one could not read this latter provision as saying that it 'has no relevance at all to the grant of nationality'.[120] The wording of this provision is very strong, requiring a true or legitimate link (as opposed to an artificial link) between the State and the interests represented in the ship.[121] But one must note that, ultimately, any link between an object (the ship) and a legal fiction (the State) is always artificial; and the purpose of the genuine link is not to connect the interests represented in the ship to a particular State, but rather to assess who is best suited to exercise effective jurisdiction and control over that ship. In this sense, the wording of Article 91(1) of the LOSC is of very limited value.[122]

Autopoiesis and the Disingenuousness of the Genuine Link: Addressing Enforcement Gaps in the Legal Regime for Areas beyond National Jurisdiction', in Erik Jaap Molenaar and Alex Oude Elferink (eds), *The International Legal Regime of Areas beyond National Jurisdiction: Current and Future Developments* (Martinus Nijhoff 2010) 170–71; Rothwell and Stephens, *Law of the Sea* (n 37) 168.

[114] Article 32 of the VCLT, although framed as a supplementary means of interpretation.

[115] ILC, 'Report' (n 28) 278–79.

[116] The preparatory works of the LOSC are of no help in this regard, possibly because at that time the genuine link was on the agenda of the UN Conference for Trade and Development: Elferink, 'Genuine Link' (n 113) 48.

[117] See inter alia Anderson, 'Freedoms' (n 4) 333; Robin Churchill and Christopher Hedley, *The Meaning of the 'Genuine Link' Requirement in Relation to the Nationality of Ships: Project Report* (International Transport Workers' Federation 2000) 22; Churchill and Lowe, *Law of the Sea* (n 7) 258; König, 'Flag' (n 57) § 6; Rayfuse, *Non-Flag State* (n 6) 26; Rayfuse, 'Anthropocene' (n 113) 171; Tanaka, *Law of the Sea* (n 12) 194.

[118] See also McDougal and Burke, *Public Order* (n 50) 1030–33; McDougal et al, 'Public Order at Sea' (n 57) 39. In contrast, see inter alia Cogliati-Bantz, 'Disentangling' (n 57) 402.

[119] Cogliati-Bantz, 'Disentangling' (n 57) 403.

[120] *M/V 'Saiga' (No. 2)* [1999] 'Separate Opinion of Judge Anderson', 1. See also Anderson, 'Freedoms' (n 4) 338.

[121] Cogliati-Bantz, 'Disentangling' (n 57) 398; Kamto, 'La nationalité' (n 57) 343.

[122] Churchill and Hedley, *Meaning* (n 117) 45.

Furthermore, State practice is also of little help, since some States are known for ascribing their flag to ships owned by foreigners having no real connection with them, and States' courts and public authorities have refrained from lifting the veil of nationality in the case of foreign flags of convenience.[123] For its part, the ITLOS adopted a pragmatic case law. In the *Saiga (2)* case, it ruled that the 'Determination of the criteria and establishment of the procedures for granting and withdrawing nationality to ships are matters within the exclusive jurisdiction of the flag State'[124] – and this is not of minor importance, as I will explain soon. In the '*Virginia G*' case, it argued that Article 91(1) of the LOSC, 'requiring a genuine link between the flag State and the ship should not be read as establishing prerequisites or conditions to be satisfied for the exercise of the right of the flag State to grant its nationality to ships'.[125] As such, the ITLOS set forth an empty notion of genuine link:

> once a ship is registered, the flag State is required, under article 94 of the [LOSC], to exercise effective jurisdiction and control over that ship in order to ensure that it operates in accordance with generally accepted international regulations, procedures and practices. This is the meaning of 'genuine link'.[126]

This *dictum* of the ITLOS fits with a trend of shifting the focus from the concept or evidence of genuine link to the effective exercise of jurisdiction over ships flying the State's flag.[127] But technically this assertion is not particularly fortunate, since the duty to exercise effective jurisdiction *is not* what the natural reading of this provision would entail:[128] one thing is the relationship between a ship and a flag State that is strong enough to allow the flag State to effectively exercise authority; another is the actual employment of competences to prescribe and/or enforce the law. They are related, but they are not synonymous.

Being an undetermined concept, the genuine link rule brought with it the difficulty of knowing what exactly its meaning and scope is, when there is a violation of this requirement, and what the consequences thereof are. In my view, two actors-based models of interpretation and enforcement of the genuine link rule are possible. The first is the *international* model, under which international institutions (eg the ITLOS or an international organisation) or non-flag States can assess the link between ships and their flag States. The second is the *domestic* model, under which the flag State is responsible for this assessment.

[123] Churchill and Lowe, *Law of the Sea* (n 7) 261.
[124] *M/V 'Saiga' (No. 2)* [1999] § 65.
[125] '*Virginia G*' [2014] § 110.
[126] ibid § 113.
[127] eg König, 'Flag' (n 57) § 10; Rayfuse, *Non-Flag State* (n 6) 26; 'Anthropocene' (n 113) 172; Tullio Treves, 'Flags of Convenience before the Law of the Sea Tribunal' (2004–5) 6 *San Diego International Law Journal* 179, 187.
[128] Cogliati-Bantz, 'Disentangling' (n 57) 403; Robin Churchill, 'Dispute Settlement in the Law of the Sea: Survey for 2014' (2015) 30 *International Journal of Marine and Coastal Law* 585, 593.

If policy oriented towards improving compliance with the genuine link, the first model is clearly better, or otherwise the genuine link rule will in practice have no substantive meaning apart from place of registration. Nonetheless, in face of such a vague concept, any unilateral discretionary act of States denying the nationality of ships on grounds of absence of an undetermined notion of genuine link would be open to abuse and thereby would endanger the freedom and governance of the seas.[129] In this sense, a domestic model is a price worth paying to guarantee access of all States to navigation and the oceans' resources.[130] In addition, the relationship between a ship and a flag State cannot be directly assessed through the usual terms, eg in terms of nationality of the ship-owner, or the connection of the interests represented in the ship with the flag State. At most, what can be said is that indirectly, because the nationality of the ship-owner might be relevant for the flag State to exercise its jurisdictional competence (eg freezing assets of the ship-owner), it is indicative of a genuine link. In the end, however, it only diverts attention from the vagueness of the genuine link to the concepts of nationality or residence, which can also be manipulated by ship-owners and flag States: more important than these criteria are the powers that the flag State can actually employ.[131]

The risk of abuse reflects a deeper question. In my view, the genuine link rule is more of a guideline than a hard rule: it is goal oriented to ensure effective jurisdiction, not an end in itself. As said, it reflects a relationship between a ship and its flag State, one that from a legal standpoint assures that the flag State has the means to exercise effective jurisdiction and control over the ship. The splitting of the genuine link and the effective jurisdiction rules into two provisions does not mean that they are unrelated, but rather that failure by a flag State to ensure effective jurisdiction and control cannot be seen as evidence of the absence of a genuine link:[132] it might just be the case that flag State authorities are unwilling to exercise their competence under international law. In the end, Article 91(1) of the LOSC confers upon flag States the competence to assess what ships have such a relation as to be subject to their effective exercise jurisdiction and control, although stressing also that conferral of nationality on a ship cannot be reduced to a mere administrative formality. What this provision could not do (and international law cannot either) is to replace the flag State in its assessment of the existence of a link strong enough to ensure effective jurisdiction and control over a specific ship, for only the flag State is aware of the capacity of its machinery to exercise effective jurisdiction and control over particular ships. This is another case where the relationship between international and domestic legal orders is not one of conflict, but rather of cooperation: the international rule asks flag States to complement the concept

[129] Anderson, 'Freedoms' (n 4) 336; McDougal et al, 'Public Order at Sea' (n 57) 40–42.
[130] McDougal et al, 'Public Order at Sea' (n 57) 40.
[131] Djamchid, 'High Seas' (n 60) 406.
[132] Anderson, 'Freedoms' (n 4) 334–35; Brown, *Law of the Sea* (n 56) 289.

of genuine link and as such to protect at the domestic level the interests of all States, of ocean governance and of mankind as a whole. In the end, the interest of the international community is not to ensure that there is a genuine link between the ship and its flag State, but rather that the latter exercises effective jurisdiction and control over the former. What seems clear is that even if no genuine link exists, the ship-owner is entitled to rely on the lawfulness of the conferred nationality and cannot be accountable for the flag State's failure to effectively exercise jurisdiction and control over the ship.[133]

Despite this minimalistic content, the genuine link rule 'is neither useless nor redundant: it reminds States of the fundamental consequences that go with the conferral of their nationality on ships',[134] notably of their duty to ensure effective jurisdiction and control over ships. And this is particularly important, not only because it entails flag State responsibility for conducts of ship-owners, but also because, if not properly understood, the genuine link requirement can be viewed as evidence that the position of the ship and the ship-owner is a matter of domestic law – not of international law.

4.2. The Indirect Responsibility of the Flag State

Returning to the topic of this section, I mentioned before that the conduct of 'ships' is directly attributed to the ship-owner only. However, accountability might arise from the infringement of *direct obligations*, as well as from the violation of *indirect obligations* (ie those whose primary addressee is not necessarily the accountable entity). In particular, flag States can be *indirectly* responsible if they fail to exercise the competences they are afforded by the LOSC.[135] The major problem, however, is how both accountabilities interact with one another where the exercise of a navigational entitlement entails an unlawful or harmful event.

The crux of the issue is the obligational scope underlying the notion of 'flag State jurisdiction'. Pursuant to Article 92(1) of the LOSC, ships 'shall be subject to its [flag State] exclusive jurisdiction on the high seas', with some exceptions laid down in treaties; in other maritime areas, flag State jurisdiction is concurrent with coastal States' jurisdiction, but flag States hold primary jurisdiction

[133] Churchill and Hedley, *Meaning* (n 117) 51; Rüdiger Wolfrum, 'Reflagging and Escort Operations in the Persian Gulf: An International Law Perspective' (1989) 29 *Virginia Journal of International Law* 387, 392.

[134] Cogliati-Bantz, 'Disentangling' (n 57) 413. See also *M/V 'Saiga' (No. 2)* [1999] 'Separate Opinion of Vice-President Wolfrum', § 19; *'Virginia G'* [2014] 'Dissenting Opinion of Judge Jesus', § 47; Robin Geiß and Christian Tams, 'Non-Flag States as Guardians of the Maritime Order: Creeping Jurisdiction of a Different Kind?', in Ringbom (ed), *Jurisdiction* (n 59) 19, 24. On these *ex ante* responsibilities, before the entering into force of the LOSC, see Nagendra Singh, 'Maritime Flag and State Responsibility', in Jerzy Makarczyk (ed), *Essays in Honour of Judge Manfred Lachs* (Martinus Nijhoff 1984) 657.

[135] See, regarding illegal, unlawful or unreported fishing activities, *SRFC* [2015] § 146.

over persons and events on board their ships. For its part, Article 94(1) of the LOSC provides that 'Every [flag] State shall effectively exercise its jurisdiction and control in administrative, technical and social matters over ships flying its flag'. Afterwards paragraphs 2, 3 and 4 of the same provision set out a non-exhaustive list of cases where the effective exercise of jurisdiction is particularly important.[136] The vexed question is whether the flag State has the duty to effectively exercise jurisdiction under Articles 92 and 94 of the LOSC.

As a starting point,

> sovereignty cannot limit itself to its negative side, i.e. to excluding the activities of other States; for it serves to divide between nations the space upon which human activities are employed, in order to assure them at all points the minimum of protection of which international law is the guardian.[137]

This implies an important distinction between competences that are conferred on States so that they might pursue their own interests as a collectivity (and therefore their exercise is discretionary) and other powers that are assigned to States to protect interests transcendent and autonomous to them (eg seaworthiness conditions are established in the interest of other States, whose exercise is mandatory).

With regard to Articles 92 and 94 of the LOSC, the interests protected by these provisions can fall into both categories, which entails that an effective exercise of jurisdiction might be required under international law if the interests at stake are transcendent and autonomous vis-à-vis the flag State. The semantic element of Article 94(1) ('shall effectively exercise its jurisdiction') is particularly illustrative, as well as the wording of paragraph 6 of the same provision.[138] Furthermore, other treaties also establish an explicit duty of exercising flag State jurisdiction, as is the case under Article 18(2) and (3) of the 1995 Fish Stocks Agreement.

Accordingly, the competences conferred by the LOSC have a corresponding side of responsibility *ex ante facto*:[139] they are only purposeful and meaningful if goal oriented to the protection of specific social-legal interests. In the case of flag State jurisdiction, if its main justification is the promotion of public order at sea, then it implies not only the negative character of non-interference from non-flag States, but also a positive character of effective exercise of jurisdiction by the flag State, or otherwise no such public order is attainable. As such, flag States

[136] *SRFC* [2015] § 117.

[137] *Island of Palmas (Netherlands v USA)* [Arbitral Award, 4 April 1928] RIAA, II, 829, 839.

[138] *SRFC* [2015] § 118, concluding as to the existence of an 'obligation to inform the reporting State about the action taken'.

[139] See generally Attard and Mallia, 'High Seas' (n 58) 256–57; Barnes, 'Flag States' (n 106) 314ff; Rayfuse, *Non-Flag State* (n 6) 28; Henrik Ringbom, 'Ship-Source Marine Pollution', in André Nollkaemper, Ilias Plakokefalos and Jessica Schechinger (eds), *The Practice of Shared Responsibility in International Law* (CUP 2017) 265, 268; Takei, 'Assessing' (n 97) 100ff; Tanaka, *Law of the Sea* (n 12) 191–92.

have the competence *and* the obligation to exercise the jurisdiction conferred on them under the LOSC when these competences are suitable to protect transcendent and autonomous interests.[140] This includes, inter alia, a duty of a flag State to effectively demand from flagged ships compliance with rules on shipping or maritime law, seafarers' rights or seaworthiness conditions.[141]

Exercising effective authority over ships can be a daunting task. However, flag States can always deter their ships on the high seas, ask the ship to route to its ports, or ask third States to perform the necessary measures (eg inspection and reporting). Since the genuine link should refer to a strong link between the ship-owner and the flag State, other mechanisms of domestic law might be relevant to exert pressure over the ship-owner, such as periodic penalty payments. Moreover, flag States are not obliged to grant their flag to a ship and can confer it on their own terms. If they know they will not be able to exercise effective jurisdiction, they ought not to grant their flag.[142] Here the *ubi commoda ibi incommoda* principle is critical: if flag States want to benefit from ascribing their nationality to ships, they ought to bear its burdens also. As seen, nationality of ships has more than the protective nature of citizenship, for it also identifies which State has primary jurisdiction over persons and events on the ship, and thus is responsible for the ship under international law. In this sense, if a flag State has jurisdiction over a ship, it has to deploy the possible means available to enforce the law, even if the means *de facto* available are meagre; what it cannot show is an absolute indifference towards compliance with law.

If flag State jurisdiction is not an optional exercise, this means that flag States have to ensure compliance with the international rules and standards whose performance can be requested by other States during the exercise of any navigational right or freedom (eg seaworthiness conditions). As the ITLOS stated, 'This mechanism consists in the creation of obligations which States Parties must fulfil by exercising their power over entities of their nationality and under their control'.[143] It applies to cases where 'it is … not considered satisfactory to rely on mere application of the principle that the conduct of private persons or entities is not attributable to the State under international law';[144] and requires flag States to adopt 'enforcement mechanisms to monitor and secure compliance with these laws and regulations'.[145] As seen,

> [i]n the view of the [ITLOS], once a ship is registered, the flag State is required, under article 94 of the [LOSC], to exercise effective jurisdiction and control over that ship in order to ensure that it operates in accordance with generally accepted

[140] *SRFC* [2015] §§ 119 and 137.
[141] Rothwell and Stephens, *Law of the Sea* (n 37) 169.
[142] Rayfuse, 'Anthropocene' (n 113) 188.
[143] *Responsibilities and Obligations of States Sponsoring Persons and Entities with Respect to Activities in the Area* [Advisory Opinion, 1 February 2011] ITLOS Rep 10, § 108; *SRFC* [2015] § 138.
[144] ibid § 112.
[145] *SRFC* [2015] § 138.

> international regulations, procedures and practices. This [for the ITLOS] is the meaning of 'genuine link'.[146]

This is not, in my view, what the genuine link actually means, but ascribing nationality entails at least the correlative presumption that flag States can and have to ensure compliance with these international standards by 'ships' of their nationality.[147] If the nationality of ships is a criterion for determining what State has primary jurisdiction over a ship, then when a State grants its nationality to that ship (after discretionally establishing its own terms) it assumes by implication that it has the means to exercise effective jurisdiction.

4.3. The Obligation of Due Diligence

In particular, 'responsibility to ensure', as upheld by the ITLOS, implies a *duty of due diligence* with respect to private actors' conduct under their jurisdiction, meaning

> an obligation which entails not only the adoption of appropriate rules and measures, but also a certain level of vigilance in their enforcement and the exercise of administrative control applicable to public and private operators, such as to monitor the activities undertaken by such operators, or to safeguard the rights of the other party.[148]

In this case, the accountable entity is not the addressee of the obligation whose violation originated the unlawful conduct, but rather an entity that held the obligation to prevent the unlawful conduct if it had ensured compliance with international law.[149] As such, the conduct attributed to the flag State is not the unlawful or harmful conduct of the ship-owner – because it fails to meet the standards enshrined in the ARSIWA – but rather its omission of a conduct to ensure compliance.[150] This means that accountability of the ship-owner (enforced before domestic bodies) and of the flag State (enforced before international bodies) are *autonomous and individual, and not shared*.[151]

The next question is to determine 'in what circumstances do due diligence obligations arise?' One of the difficulties of this topic derives from the lack of a unified regime of due diligence in international law, since it is rather

[146] *'Virginia G'* [2014] § 113.

[147] See *mutatis mutandis* Rayfuse, 'Anthropocene' (n 113) 172–73.

[148] *Pulp Mills on the River Uruguay (Argentina v Uruguay)* [Judgment, 20 April 2010] ICJ Rep 14, § 197.

[149] Barnes, 'Flag States' (n 106) 323; Vincent Chetail, 'The Legal Personality of Multinational Corporations, State Responsibility and Due Diligence: The Way Forward', in Denis Alland, Vincent Chetail, Olivier de Frouville and Jorge Viñuales (eds), *Unity and Diversity of International Law – Essays in Honour of Professor Pierre-Marie Dupuy* (Martinus Nijhoff 2014) 105, 125; Joanna Kulesza, *Due Diligence in International Law* (Brill Nijhoff 2016) 136–37 and 266.

[150] *Responsibilities and Obligations of Sponsoring States* [2011] § 109.

[151] Ringbom, 'Ship-Source' (n 139) 287–89.

fragmented in rules from its different fields, often identified not in a treaty regime but rather by the case law. This is further complicated by the fact that courts, tribunals, bodies and practitioners working in each field of international law resort to their own lenses (ie a bias derived from their perspective of the legal system and their primary concerns) when establishing their own views on due diligence. The result is that what is established as valid under environmental law (eg a duty to monitor activities performed by private actors to prevent an unlawful or harmful event) is not necessarily responsive to the needs of the law of the sea, and for sure will not match with the intricacies of human rights or criminal law (where monitoring private actors clearly falls short of what is entailed by rules from these domains, and the actual employment of means to ensure a desirable event might be required). Not surprisingly, despite the attempts to universalise a legal regime on State due diligence, the foundations of such legal regime are still to be crafted. But probably the biggest difficulty is to understand what is the ultimate purpose of due diligence, namely if it points to a problem of agency which requires some kind of 'affirmative action' regarding the exercise of sovereignty, or if it is rather conceived of as a means of compensation or counter-balancing the decommissioning of some activities to private actors (in which case it actually reinforces the Vattelian narrative of international law): in the first case, sovereignty itself needs to be rethought, whereas in the second case only a problem of shared (*ex ante* and *ex post*) responsibility is raised.

For the purposes of this book, it suffices to mention that due diligence obligations arise in particular circumstances, namely when: international law equips States with the competence to perform a specific conduct; international law establishes that States have the duty to perform that conduct: eg instead of being a permissive rule aimed at protecting States' interests, it encompasses 'a comprehensive duty of protection incumbent upon the State'[152] aimed at protecting other values of the legal system; and finally the conduct, if duly performed, must be apt to prevent an unlawful or harmful event – which implies that the obligation binding upon the State is one of conduct (ie 'to deploy adequate means, to exercise best possible efforts, to do the utmost, to obtain this result'[153]) and not of result.[154] Nevertheless, 'due' diligence is a necessarily flexible notion that must be assessed in light of the unique circumstances of each case, here including the effectiveness of State control, social and economic factors, or the predictability of the unlawful or harmful event:[155] the competences that are due in a case where a flagged ship is anchored in a flag State's port are extensive, but not if the same ship is anchored in the port of any other State.

[152] Peters, *Beyond* (n 101) 69.

[153] *Responsibilities and Obligations of Sponsoring States* [2011] § 110.

[154] Chetail, 'Legal Personality' (n 149) 125; Kulesza, *Due Diligence* (n 149) 266; Ringbom, 'Ship-Source' (n 139) 267; Takei, 'Assessing' (n 97) 125.

[155] *Responsibilities and Obligations of Sponsoring States* [2011] § 117. See also Chetail, 'Legal Personality' (n 149) 125; Kulesza, *Due Diligence* (n 149) 141, 161 and 263–64; Takei, 'Assessing' (n 97) 125.

At this point the reader could expect the conclusion that, for instance, in the case of marine environmental damage whose cause is a ship's lack of seaworthiness conditions, or in the case of illegal, unreported or unregulated fishing activities, the lack of due diligence from flag States entails their international responsibility. However, that is far from being evident. In fact, flag States' international responsibility for the infringement of due diligence obligations can only be established after a demanding process of evidence; and the fact that ships are beyond the spatial jurisdiction of their flag States poses a difficulty for the enforcement of international rules by flag States under the aegis of due diligence obligations. Even if for the sake of the argument the omniscient reader could know that causation actually exists, it would be a *probatio diabolica* to establish before any judicial authority that the non-performance of a due diligence obligation caused the unlawful or harmful event, or that this event could have been prevented had the State exercised its competences under the LOSC or any law of the sea treaty.

In the domains of international criminal law and human rights law, a looser test of 'overall control' may be enough to attribute to a State the conducts of private actors.[156] Yet in the *Genocide* case, the ICJ rejected this approach as suitable for international law in general, for it 'stretches too far, almost to breaking point, the connection which must exist between the conduct of a State's organs and its international responsibility'.[157] In the law of the sea, it would also be excessive to hold flag States internationally responsible for any conduct of ships of their nationality on grounds that their jurisdiction confers on them an 'overall control' over the conduct of ship-owners. Little room exists to contend that responsibility should (or even could) be shared between the ship-owner and the flag State. In theory, this attribution could exist, but in practice only in specific cases does the breach of direct obligations incumbent on ship-owners trigger the international responsibility of flag States for failure to comply with due diligence standards.

Nevertheless, breach of due diligence obligations exists not when an unlawful or harmful event occurs: even if no such event exists, if the flag State does not perform the tasks it is mandated and asked to, it is *ipso facto* not complying with a primary international obligation,[158] even if a secondary obligation (eg liability, international responsibility) will not follow. The reader might claim that, if it is difficult to imagine how a flag State can be held responsible for failure to comply with due diligence standards in single cases (except if it clearly

[156] eg *Prosecutor v Duško Tadić* [Judgment, 15 July 1999] ICTY Case No. IT-94-1-A, §§ 120–22.
[157] *Convention on the Crime of Genocide* [2007] §§ 404 and 406.
[158] Crawford, *State Responsibility* (n 94) 227; Rüdiger Wolfrum, 'Obligation of Result Versus Obligation of Conduct: Some Thoughts About the Implementation of International Obligations', in Mahnoush Arsanjani, Jacob Katz Cogan, Robert Sloane and Siegfried Wiessner (eds), *Looking to the Future – Essays on International Law in Honor of W. Michael Reisman* (Martinus Nijhoff 2011) 363, 375.

evidences that it is not willing to comply with its due diligence duties),[159] it is even more difficult to see how it could be held responsible in the absence of an unlawful or harmful conduct of the 'ship'. However, flag States can be internationally responsible for failure to comply with due diligence standards, irrespective of the conduct of their flagged 'ships', if non-compliance is persistent,[160] eg if flag States often receive reports on non-compliance with international rules by their ships and blatantly ignore those reports.[161] When this is the case, the persistent absence of any conduct from State organs is sufficient to give rise to a characterised non-compliance with international law obligations that entails that State's international responsibility. At this point, the public and objective nature of international responsibility is evident. All treaties (including the LOSC) create more than bilateral (although plural) jural relations: compliance with the law is in the interest of the entire international community, and ergo of all participants who can ask for compliance with the terms of the treaty. This means that, in the case of persistent non-compliance with international law, any State party to the LOSC or other treaty can ask the flag State to perform its obligations under international law, irrespective of any unlawful or harmful conduct of 'ships' of their nationality.[162]

To conclude that indirect responsibility (after non-compliance with due diligence obligations) may arise is, to some extent, comparable to assigning States a competence to exercise flag State protection: it evidences that international law relies on States to promote the rule of law within the international legal system, and that States are asked to compensate for failures of private action. The interpretative bias could be that, if States are responsible for such failures regarding international navigation, then they also hold such navigational rights and freedoms exclusively. Stressing that this international responsibility is indirect helps to keep such bias at bay.

5. RIGHT TO COMPENSATION

Contrary to what a literal reading of Article 92(1) of the LOSC suggests, flag State jurisdiction is not exclusive, for non-flag States may have titles to jurisdiction over foreign ships in the circumstances defined in international law. In this respect, the solution drawn by the LOSC (and other treaty-based or customary law rules) was to establish a general rule of ordinary flag State jurisdiction and

[159] Takei, 'Assessing' (n 97) 131.

[160] Barnes, 'Flag States' (n 106) 323–24; Takei, 'Assessing' (n 97) 131–32.

[161] Article 228(1) of the LOSC provides an example of a sanction (the pre-emptive jurisdiction of the coastal State) against a flag State that 'has *repeatedly* [ie when there is a pattern] disregarded its obligation to enforce effectively the applicable international rules and standards': Anderson, 'Freedoms' (n 4) 336.

[162] Rayfuse, 'Anthropocene' (n 113) 172–73.

of its primacy over concurrent titles to jurisdiction over ships flying its flag – entailing that non-flag States can only interfere with navigation of a foreign-flagged ship when duly authorised by the flag State.[163] However, this primacy is not absolute, for there are cases where non-flag States may – in accordance with the law of the sea rules – interfere with navigation of a foreign-flagged ship on the high seas irrespective of any authorisation from the flag State.

Just as with flag State jurisdiction, the rationale for non-flag State jurisdiction on the high seas is the promotion of public order at sea, notably in cases of failure of the system of flag State jurisdiction (eg Stateless vessels, or flag States who are unwilling to or incapable of coping with a particular situation), or of particularly heinous conducts. However, to protect freedom of navigation, non-flag State jurisdiction on the high seas is exceptional and thus can only be exercised in the specific circumstances defined by a permissive treaty-based or customary rule. These rules often embody the following elements: interference is justified by specific grounds; the non-flag State is *de facto* better positioned to pursue the public order reasons that justify interference with navigation on the high seas;[164] as such, the non-flag State is vested with the competence to interfere with the navigation of a foreign ship. At this point, *interference* with navigation should be read as encompassing several acts that impact the normal navigation of a foreign vessel, including to pursue, intercept, stop, board, visit, inspect, report or seize the ship (and its cargo), and/or arrest, try and sentence the crew members. Each permissive rule lists the acts and the procedures that can be lawfully performed by the interfering State. With respect to these acts, and in order to prevent abusive non-flag State interferences, a right to compensation under a regime of strict liability is seldom enshrined if interference is ungrounded. A final word on the right to compensation is necessary, since this can shed some light on who is the navigational rights-holder.

5.1. The Grounds for Lawful Interference with Navigation

Being an exceptional rule, non-flag State interference can only occur when there is a particular suspicion defined in the permissive international rule: when this happens, non-flag States have the authority to intercept, stop, board or visit the foreign ship. If such suspicion is confirmed, then they may also have the authority, depending on the facts and the applicable rule, to seize the ship and cargo, and arrest, try and sentence its crew members. In most cases set out in law of the sea rules, interference with navigation is lawful provided that there are reasonable grounds to find that a proscribed activity is being performed

[163] *Lotus* [1927] 25.

[164] Otherwise, it would amount to a claim incompatible with Article 89 of the LOSC. See *mutatis mutandis* Natalie Klein, *Maritime Security and the Law of the Sea* (OUP 2012) 106.

with or in that ship. Accordingly, to justify interference, it is not necessary that the ship is actually engaged in an outlawed activity, but only that there is a *reasonable* suspicion. None of the relevant treaties defines what reasonable grounds or suspicion mean, and thus non-flag States hold a certain margin of interpretation of the facts and their legal framework. What can be said as being established is that an ad hoc and objective analysis of the facts is required; a mere suspicion is not sufficient to justify interference; but actual evidence is not also a requirement for interference.[165]

An exhaustive assessment of the grounds for non-flag State interference on the high seas is beyond the scope of this book. It suffices to mention that the cases of non-flag State interference that may entail a right to compensation include the repression of piracy,[166] repression of slavery,[167] illegal broadcasting,[168] statelessness of the ship,[169] when the interfering State has reasonable grounds to believe that a prima facie foreign ship rather holds its own nationality,[170] other detrimental conducts against navigation,[171] drugs trafficking,[172] human trafficking,[173] the exercise of the right of hot pursuit,[174] illegal, unregulated or unreported fishing,[175] and the protection of the marine environment.[176] In all these cases, the ship 'shall be compensated for any loss or damage that may have been sustained', 'If the suspicions prove to be unfounded, and provided that the ship boarded has not committed any act justifying them'.[177] But if a ship suspected of being involved in piracy is seized by a non-flag State under Article 105 of the LOSC 'without adequate grounds', the interfering State 'shall be liable' to the flag State.[178]

[165] Robin Geiß and Anna Petrig, *Piracy and Armed Robbery at Sea – The Legal Framework for Counter-Piracy Operations in Somalia and the Gulf of Aden* (OUP 2011) 56; Klein, *Maritime Security* (n 164) 116; Eftthymios Papastavridis, *The Interception of Vessels on the High Seas – Contemporary Challenges to the Legal Order of the Oceans* (Hart Publishing 2014) 62; Anna Petrig, 'Piracy', in Rothwell et al (eds), *Handbook* (n 8) 852; Robert Reuland, 'Interference with Non-National Ships on the High Seas: Peacetime Exceptions to the Exclusivity Rule of Flag-State Jurisdiction' (1989) 22 *Vanderbilt Journal of Transnational Law* 1161, 1172.

[166] Articles 105 and 110(1)(a) of the LOSC.

[167] Article 110(1)(b) of the LOSC.

[168] Article 110(1)(c) of the LOSC.

[169] Article 110(1)(d) of the LOSC.

[170] Article 110(1)(e) of the LOSC.

[171] Articles 3, 3*bis*, 3*ter* and 3*quater* of the SUA Convention, as well as Articles 2, 2*bis* and 2*ter* of the 2005 Protocol to the SUA Convention.

[172] Article 9 of the 1995 Agreement on Illicit Traffic by Sea.

[173] Article 8(2) of the Migrant Smuggling Protocol.

[174] Article 111 of the LOSC.

[175] Article 21 of the 1995 Fish Stocks Agreement.

[176] Article I(1) of the 1969 Intervention Convention.

[177] Article 110(3) of the LOSC. See also Article 8*bis*(10)(b) of the SUA Convention, Article 26 of the 1995 Agreement on Illicit Traffic by Sea, Article 9(2) of the Migrant Smuggling Protocol, Article 21(18) of the 1995 Fish Stocks Agreement, and Article VI of the 1969 Intervention Convention.

[178] Article 106 of the LOSC.

5.2. The Holder of the Right to Compensation

As said, the duty to pay compensation will arise whenever the suspicion on which interference was based is not verified. In such case, it is not discussed if interference was legitimate or lawful, but rather if compensation should be paid. Compensation is provided for cases of lawful but unfounded interferences with navigation[179] – except in the case of Article 111(8) of the LOSC, where compensation is due in the case of illegal hot pursuit, or of unreasonableness of the means employed.[180] This should not be read as meaning that no right to compensation exists in the case of unlawful interference with navigation, as this by its nature entails a right to compensation if damage occurs; but with respect to lawful interferences the legal system had to define if a right to compensation should follow or not.

When a right to compensation emerges as a result of non-flag State interference with navigation, the relevant treaty provisions promote a transfer in the risk of damage to the interfering State to encourage control over the acts, intensity and duration of interference.[181] However, flag States can also be responsible for the same damage. The typical case for shared responsibility would be the damage caused after a request or an authorisation of the flag State for interference. In this second case, shared responsibility exists but the causal link between damage and the flag State conduct is weak. But if the flag State requests interference by non-flag States, one must ask whether the conduct of these latter organs and agents is not attributable to the flag State under the rules on State responsibility. Under Article 26(3) of the 1995 Agreement on Illicit Traffic by Sea, a regime of shared responsibility is also established where the flag State asks a third State to interfere with the navigation of its own ships: to protect the holder of the right to compensation, this provision sets out that liability rests with the flag State, which afterwards might seek compensation from the interfering State.

With respect to the damage covered by the right to compensation, it is curious that rules do not follow the same wording. For instance, Articles 110(3) and 111(8) of the LOSC, although in the context of the same treaty, refer to 'any loss or damage that may have been sustained' and 'any loss that may have been *thereby* sustained':[182] a perfunctory reading would suggest that, under Article 110(3) of the LOSC, compensation covers any damage or loss, irrespective of any causation, in contrast with Article 111(8) of the LOSC. The curious wording of Article 110(3) of the LOSC is even more puzzling if compared with

[179] Treves, 'Navigation' (n 53) 850; Wendel, *State Responsibility* (n 68) 113.

[180] Robert Reuland, 'The Customary Right of Hot Pursuit onto the High Seas. Annotation to Article 111 of the Law of the Sea Convention' (1993) 33 *Virginia Journal of International Law* 557, 587; Wendel, *State Responsibility* (n 68) 116.

[181] Wendel, *State Responsibility* (n 68) 55.

[182] Emphasis added.

Article 21(18) of the Fish Stocks Agreement, Article 8*bis*(10)(b) of the SUA Convention, Article VI of the 1969 Intervention Convention, Article 26(1) and (2) of the 1995 Agreement on Illicit Traffic by Sea, or Article 9(2) of the 2000 Migrant Smuggling Protocol, which refer to a link of causation. Yet in my view the different wording of these provisions is not meaningful: as a rule of general international law, responsibility or liability of States is always limited by rules of causation,[183] and thus only covers the damage that was intended or resulted from negligence during interference.[184]

Two forms of damage are relevant to determine the interfering State's accountability: damage caused to the interests represented in the ship as a result of interference; and damage caused to the flag State entitlement to primary jurisdiction over that ship. This second type of damage is not referred to explicitly in the LOSC but derives from the rules on State responsibility and is less controversial: the interfering State bears responsibility, and a simple admission of the wrongfulness of the act might be sufficient to repair the damage caused.[185] With respect to the first type of damage, compensation should include all material damage that typically arises from the acts performed by the interfering State (eg the value of the ship or its cargo), injuries to persons on board, or economic damage such as loss of profits, interest, contractual penalties, or delay[186] – but excludes remote damage.[187]

With regard to the holder of the right to compensation, the LOSC and other treaties apparently assign the entitlement to the *ship*, which would mean that ships are legal persons and recipients of a right to compensation: this is the case, for example, for Articles 110(3) and 111(8) of the LOSC, or (more explicitly) for Article 9(2) of the Migrant Smuggling Protocol. Not surprisingly, some scholars consider the ship the recipient of a right to compensation.[188] Nonetheless, the same arguments analysed before can be replicable here: in light of the complex web of entities that can be involved in these jural relations, references to ships work out as a catch-all formula meant to avoid complexity, and should not be read as evidence of the ship's legal personality.

For its part, Article 106 of the LOSC – when referring to the seizure of ships suspected of being engaged in piracy – assigns to the flag State the right to compensation for any loss or damage suffered as a result of the interference, if the seizure was effected 'without adequate grounds'. The *travaux préparatoires* of Article 106 of the LOSC and Article VI of the Intervention

[183] Article 2(a) of the ARSIWA.

[184] Wendel, *State Responsibility* (n 68) 170–72.

[185] *M/V 'Saiga' (No. 2)* [1999] § 176. See also Douglas Guilfoyle, *Shipping Interdiction and the Law of the* Sea (CUP 2011) 330.

[186] ILC, 'Report' (n 28) 284. See also Douglas Guilfoyle, 'Article 106', in Alexander Proelß (ed), *UN Convention* (n 21) 753, 755; Guilfoyle, '*Shipping Interdiction* (n 185) 329–30; Wendel, *State Responsibility* (n 68) 173 and 179ff.

[187] Guilfoyle, *Shipping Interdiction* (n 185) 329; Wendel, *State Responsibility* (n 68) 171–72.

[188] Molenaar, 'Multilateral Hot Pursuit' (n 72) 37.

Convention are also clear in suggesting that the drafters wanted to confer the right to compensation on the flag State. The different wording of Articles 106 and 110(3) of the LOSC is not explained in the preparatory works, which led some authors to contend that the holder of the right to compensation should be the same under both provisions, and that assigning the right to the ship(-owner) is more consistent with general international law.[189] If one keeps in mind the aforementioned difference between the two types of damage, one realises that Articles 106 of the LOSC and VI of the Intervention Convention (which rule on cases of severe interference with flag State jurisdiction) articulate the idea that only under general international law should an interference with the flag State's right to primary jurisdiction over ships of its nationality be compensated. As a result, compensation to flag States does not cover all damage identified before.

In fact, the creditor of the right to compensation can be an individual on board, the ship-owner or the charterer (but not the cargo owner, who can seek compensation under the terms of the contract).[190] Some arguments can be adduced for this purpose. To begin with, if private actors hold navigational entitlements under the LOSC, it would be strange if the right to compensation for interferences with the same navigation were assigned to a different entity. I should note that the right to compensation enshrined in these provisions is not meant to provide protection to private property only, or even primarily.[191] If that was the case, there would be no distinction between cases of verified or unverified grounds for interference: if property were the sole interest to be protected, then damage caused as a result of *any* interference should be compensated. However, the semantic element of these provisions is clear when stating that compensation is only due when the grounds for suspicion are not verified. This suggests that, side by side with the property interests, compensation is meant to discourage interferences with navigation, thereby providing a further buttress to navigational entitlements. But if this is true, then the holder of navigational entitlements must also be the creditor of the right to compensation when his property rights are infringed. Moreover, a good place to pinpoint the creditor of the right to compensation is in the dispute settlement system. If the State is the holder of the right to compensation, then remedies provided for in case of interference with navigation must be available for States only. Remedies here are also delegated to the domestic level, where they are open to ship-owners or ships (in case of proceedings *in rem*). But if the ship-owner (or the ship, in procedural replacement) has a remedy to seek compensation, this

[189] Guilfoyle, 'Article 106' (n 186) 755; Douglas Guilfoyle, 'Article 110', in Proelß (ed), *UN Convention* (n 21) 767, 771.

[190] *M/V 'Saiga' (No. 2)* [1999] §§ 106–07. See also Klein, *Maritime Security* (n 164) 116; Guilfoyle, *Shipping Interdiction* (n 185) 325–26; Guilfoyle, 'Article 110' (n 189) 771; Wendel, *State Responsibility* (n 68) 111.

[191] See against Wendel, *State Responsibility* (n 68) 88–91, by implication.

means that private actors are the actual creditors of the right to compensation. Finally, in terms of policy, if private actors are the recipients of an international norm repressing and outlawing some activities – thus bearing a duty not to engage in activities such as piracy, slave trade, unauthorised broadcasting or migrant smuggling – it would just be logical that at least they could have some rights in case of unjustified interference.[192] More than logical, in my view, one can no longer accept that private actors might bear duties deriving from legal norms that criminalise some activities if they do not also have the rights meant to afford protection against ungrounded, unlawful, disproportionate or illegitimate interferences.

If before I could contend that flag States and ship-owners are concurrent holders of navigational entitlements, the same broad assertion cannot be made in the context of the right to compensation. This does not mean that flag States play no role in this context, since rules on diplomatic and flag State protection also apply here,[193] which means that at the level of secondary rights States can ask for compensation on behalf of the ship-owner, the charterer or the individuals on board.[194] Yet the LOSC does not establish a specific judicial mechanism to seek compensation, and thus it must be sought through the domestic courts of the interfering State.

6. CONCLUSION

The curious thing about navigational entitlements is that they were originally crafted in the international legal order as rights held by private actors (eg Vitoria, Gentili or Grotius), but were eventually transformed into rights and freedoms held by flag States only. At least, this is the orthodox interpretation of the provisions of the LOSC and other law of the sea treaties, in line with the prevailing State-centred conception of international law.

However, the purpose of this chapter is to evidence that this orthodox reading is mostly the result of an interpretative bias. In other words, if one sets aside the idea that only States can be the recipients of international law and is open to more ecumenical readings of international law rules, one will uncover entitlements held by private actors under the already *existing* rules of international law – *in casu*, navigational entitlements in general, including the right to compensation which was crafted as its shield. This implies, thus, that fostering the status of private actors in international law does not perforce require the making of new rules, for it can also be achieved under an unbiased reading of already existing rules of international law: hidden in the wording of these provisions can be entitlements of private actors. This is illustrative of how bias

[192] Wendel, *State Responsibility* (n 68) 71; Zemanek, 'Does the Prospect?' (n 87) 133.
[193] Article 18 of the Draft Articles on Diplomatic Protection.
[194] Guilfoyle, *Shipping Interdiction* (n 185) 329.

interferes with treaty interpretation beyond what is set out in Articles 31–33 of the VCLT, and therefore that unbiased interpretation is a powerful means to boost private emancipation and participation under international law. In any event, this unbiased reading of existing rules of international law entails also the other side of participation: if private actors are the recipients of navigational entitlements, they also bear the duties attached to the exercise of the same entitlements, since empowerment is not only about powers, but also about responsibility.

4

The Narrow Reading of Explicit Private Actors' Entitlements

NAVIGATIONAL ENTITLEMENTS ARE a good example of how interpretative bias can affect the reading of a rule of international law, namely in cases of a particularly foggy wording. But in some cases, the wording of a treaty-based rule is sufficiently clear and explicit in assigning a right or a duty to private actors and interpretative biases still impact the reading of such rules. For instance, private miners can engage in deep seabed mining, holding the complex of rights and duties set out in Part XI of the LOSC (substantive and procedural). And Article 292(2) of the LOSC entitles private actors to submit a prompt release application on behalf of a flag State. Nonetheless, such conferral of rights and duties under the LOSC was only possible by connecting the international legal status of private miners to their sponsor State, in the first case, and by linking private applicants to the flag State, in the second case. To some extent, these links explain why some scholars, courts and tribunals share a reading and practice of such rules that confines the role of private actors as subjects of law with rights and duties directly derived from Part XI and Article 292(2) of the LOSC. In both cases, the bias against private participation in international law interferes with treaty interpretation and is responsible for limiting the role of private miners and for excluding private applicants from the LOSC, in spite of its clear wording.

Section 1 is devoted to the exploration for and the exploitation of the Area by private miners, including a proper understanding of the role of, and the interaction with, the Authority and the sponsoring State. The analysis of the legal regime explains how private miners have a pivotal role in deep seabed mining, but the emergence of due diligence obligations in the case law eventually placed the sponsoring State at the centre of deep seabed mining activities. Additionally, Section 1 deals with property rights over collected minerals, since it is a notorious example of a right directly derived from the LOSC, in spite of the absence of a sophisticated international machinery. Finally, Section 1 provides a general overview of the *locus standi* of private miners in disputes regarding deep seabed mining, and thus refers to the possible avenues for the access of private miners to international dispute settlement. However, these procedural rights need to be balanced with the sponsoring State prerogatives that can only be explained by an orthodox conception of international law. Section 2 refers to the submission of prompt release applications on behalf of the flag State, which is a case where private applicants have access to the ITLOS. Since the proceeding is nominally between States, some have adopted a view that excludes private applications to the ITLOS. But even if a liberal reading is adopted (in line with its wording), the guarantees provided to the flag State may end up constraining (if not excluding) the procedural rights of private applicants.

1. RIGHTS EMERGING FROM THE ACTIVITIES IN THE AREA

For a long time, the seas were conceived as *res communis iuris gentium*, meaning that they could not be possessed by any State. Eventually, States successfully claimed jurisdiction over adjacent waters, but the willingness to possess marine resources did not include the inaccessible deep seabed. Only the discovery of polymetallic nodules and the prospect that in the future they would be an attractive investment triggered international attention. Because the adjacency criterion is of no help in defining a regime of exploration for and exploitation of marine mineral resources lying in areas beyond the continental slope, a new international legal regime needed to be devised: that regime is laid down in Part XI of the LOSC, which is specifically devoted to the Area, ie 'the sea-bed and ocean-floor and subsoil thereof, beyond the limits of national jurisdiction'.[1]

Being *res communis iuris gentium* meant that the deep seabed was governed by a rule of freedom of access, meaning that technologically developed States were in a better position to exploit and exhaust resources. As the 'first come, first served' rule was in conflict with the interest of developing States, an impressive achievement of the LOSC was the proclamation in Part XI of the LOSC of the common heritage of mankind as the pivotal principle governing the activities in the Area,[2] which entails the subjection of the Area and its resources to the rules of non-appropriation,[3] international management of resources,[4] peaceful use,[5] equitable sharing of the benefits from the exploitation of resources,[6] and protection and preservation of resources for future generations.[7] Despite its weak legal foundations under the LOSC, the common heritage of mankind

[1] Article 1(1)(1) of the LOSC.
[2] See Articles 136, 137(2), 140(1), 155(2) and 311(6) of the LOSC, as well as § 6 of its Preamble.
[3] Article 137 of the LOSC.
[4] Articles 156ff of the LOSC.
[5] Articles 141 and 143 of the LOSC.
[6] Article 140(2) of the LOSC.
[7] See generally Kemal Baslar, *The Concept of the Common Heritage of Mankind in International Law* (Martinus Nijhoff 1998) 246; Helmut Tuerk, *Reflections on the Contemporary Law of the Sea* (Martinus Nijhoff 2012) 35; Helmut Tuerk, 'The International Seabed Area', in David Joseph Attard, Malgosia Fitzmaurice and Norman A Martínez Gutiérrez (eds), *The IMLI Manual on International Maritime Law*, I, *The Law of the Sea* (OUP 2014) 276, 284; Silja Vöneky and Anja Höfelmeier, 'Article 136', in Alexander Proelß (ed), *United Nations Convention on the Law of the Sea – A Commentary* (CH Beck 2017) 949, 954.

principle 'brings new viewpoints beyond the State-to-State perspective in the law of the sea'[8] and overrides the view according to which States are the *arche* or the underlying substance of international law. As it requires a supranational, non-State authority to perform the task of public governance and increases the room for private participation in deep seabed mining, the common heritage of mankind principle is evidence that a State-to-State narrative can no longer work as a 'theory of everything' under international law.

1.1. The Ontological Function of the (State-like) Authority

In the legal regime of the Area (which includes Part XI of the LOSC, its Annex III, and the Implementation Agreement), the Authority is the *pouvoir constitué* responsible for the international management of the Area's resources. This means that the LOSC followed a paradigm of jural relations between one Authority and miners engaged in activities in the Area that mirrors their position of subjection before States at the domestic level but assigned that State-like position to the Authority, as if the Area was a politically enclosed portion of the Earth governed by the Authority's organs. In particular, the Authority is vested with the function of promoting and enforcing the legal regime regarding the exploration for and the exploitation of resources in the Area and is equipped with the prescriptive and enforcement tools to exercise this function[9] plus 'such incidental powers, consistent with the [LOSC], as are implicit in, and necessary for, the exercise of those powers and functions with respect to activities in the Area'.[10]

To some extent, the assignment of prescriptive and enforcement jurisdiction to the Authority is mimetic of the relation between States and private actors within domestic legal systems, even though the Authority is not a sovereign authority in the Austinian tradition. As a result, with respect to activities in the Area, there is an important twist in the traditional rules of States' jurisdiction at sea: here, the nationality of the ship engaged in the activities, as well as the nationality of the corporations and individuals involved in the same activities,

[8] Yoshifumi Tanaka, *The International Law of the Sea* (3rd edn, CUP 2019) 186.

[9] The most critical competence is the inspection of installations used by the contractor. As some installations are apt to move at sea and some devices might be used interchangeably as vessels or fixed installations, the boundary between both devices is not particularly sharp. Section 14 of the Standard Clauses annexed to the Cobalt, the Sulphides, and the Nodules Regulations, and Regulation 96 of the Draft Exploitation Regulations confer on the Authority the competence to inspect vessels used by the contractor. However, this inspection power is exceptional since only vessels used in the activities can be inspected (ownership or title are not sufficient), and inspection powers can only be exerted to control compliance with the legal regime of the Area, and not with any other rule.

[10] Article 157(2) of the LOSC and Section 1, paragraph 1 of the Annex to the Implementation Agreement, which articulates the theory of the implied powers.

has little relevance. In contrast, being the primary source of regulation conferred on the Authority, including the regulation of the activities in the Area and the conduct of all involved in these activities, some of its decisions are directly addressed to private actors, for the Authority's competence is exercised not only over other States, but also over private actors engaged in activities in the Area.

There is an ontological reason behind the legal status of the Authority, which explains why it was crafted as a State-like entity. The rationale of Part XI of the LOSC is to promote interests that are transcendent and autonomous to States, and the pursuit of these interests does not need to be assigned to States. Moreover, in the new template of deep seabed governance drafted by the LOSC, one can identify the emergence of *quasi*-Stateless relations of international law with private miners. However, the promotion of legal order at sea (like the promotion of legal order in general) presupposes the existence of vertical integration: whatever the justification for authority in society, a certain level of order and centralised authority is necessary for human existence. Thus, if the LOSC aimed at bypassing States in the governance of the Area, it ought to find an alternative institutional power to perform and centralise this function because an institutional machinery responsible for administering the Area is necessary to provide a framework of exclusive rights for exploration and exploitation of resources.[11]

In this sense, the existence of the Authority as a State-like entity is not accidental in Part XI of the LOSC: it is rather an ontological predicate for drafting a legal regime goal-oriented to the protection of future generations and for the emergence of *quasi*-Stateless jural relations of international law. Ultimately, since seabed mining under Part XI of the LOSC is at the frontiers of international law, assigning to the Authority the role of public governance of the Area was key to improving the participation of private miners as rights-holders and duty-bearers under the law of the sea.

1.2. The Participation of Private Miners in Activities in the Area

With a new international legal regime aimed at providing for a rational exploration for and exploitation of the Area's resources and establishing a ring-fence against States' claims of exclusive jurisdiction or sovereignty, the LOSC could innovate and assign mining rights to private miners, directly conferred by the Authority and directly governed by international law.

Subject to the legal regime of the Area – thus, object of mining rights of private miners – are 'all solid, liquid or gaseous mineral resources *in situ* in the Area at or beneath the seabed, including polymetallic nodules'. '[W]hen recovered

[11] Satya Nandan, 'Administering the Mineral Resources of the Deep Seabed', in David Freestone, Richard Barnes and David Ong (eds), *The Law of the Sea – Progress and Prospects* (OUP 2006) 75, 79.

from the Area, [these resources] are referred to as minerals'. According to Article 1(1)(3) of the LOSC, activities in the Area '[means] all activities of exploration for, and exploitation of, the resources of the Area'.[12] In this vein, the activities performed by private miners include 'the recovery of minerals from the seabed and their lifting to the water surface'[13] and the 'Activities directly connected' with these latter, namely 'the evacuation of water from the minerals and the preliminary separation of materials of no commercial interest, including their disposal at sea',[14] and the transportation within the part of the high seas/Area where the contractor operates.[15]

The original version of the LOSC adopted the so-called parallel system, which was the compromise formula devised to overcome the differences between those who upheld that the activities should be conducted by the Authority and the Enterprise, and those who advocated the openness of the system to States and private miners. Under this system, the Enterprise was conceived as the 'mechanism for translating into reality, so to speak, the idea of common heritage of mankind'.[16] In this vein, being the operative arm of the Authority, the Enterprise would assume the leading role in the development of mining activities in the Area,[17] although other entities referred to in Article 153(2)(b) of the LOSC could also apply for a contract and carry out exploration and exploitation activities: these include States parties and State enterprises, and also natural or juristic persons holding the nationality of a State party, or being effectively controlled by a State party or its nationals, provided they are sponsored by their State of nationality or control.[18]

The legal regime was based on a prior definition of two areas: a 'reserved area', which should be primarily explored and exploited by the Enterprise; and an 'area subject to a contract', which should be explored and exploited by a contractor identified in Article 153(2)(b) of the LOSC. To that end, applicants should identify areas for commercial mining operations of equal value, one reserved for the Enterprise and another subject to a contract between the Authority and the applicant.[19] With respect to reserved areas, the contractor that contributed such an area to the Authority would have a right of first refusal

[12] Prospecting is excluded but might be subject to some rules applicable to the activities in the Area. (*Responsibilities and Obligations of States Sponsoring Persons and Entities with Respect to Activities in the Area* [Advisory Opinion, 1 February 2011] ITLOS Rep 10, § 98). However, entities interested in prospecting are exempted from sponsorship of their State of nationality or of control (ibid § 98).

[13] ibid § 94.

[14] ibid § 96.

[15] ibid § 95. However, transporting, processing, and marketing of minerals are outside the scope of application of the legal regime of the Area.

[16] LDM Nelson, 'The New Deep Sea-Bed Mining Regime' (1995) 10 *International Journal of Marine and Coastal Law* 189, 196.

[17] Article 170(1) of the LOSC and Article 1 of Annex IV.

[18] Article 153(2)(b) of the LOSC and Article 3(1) of Annex III.

[19] Article 8 of Annex III.

to enter into a joint venture with the Enterprise, as well as a preferential right of evaluation of its application for a plan of work for the same reserved area, in case the Enterprise did not submit its own plan of work for activities in that area within a period of 15 years.[20] Moreover, the cross-references to joint ventures between the participants suggest that this operational agreement was preferred by the drafters of the LOSC in order to assure that activities in both areas were integrated and that the transfer of technology was feasible.

Nonetheless, the adoption of the Implementation Agreement changed the original system by superseding the technology transfer clause and making substantive changes to the regime of participation in deep seabed mining. If, in the original version, the Enterprise would be the centrepiece of the system of exploration for and exploitation of the Area's resources, the Implementation Agreement established that the Enterprise must necessarily conduct its mining operations through joint ventures (eg with private miners);[21] superseded the obligation, pending upon the contractor, to finance mining activities of the Enterprise;[22] and, in any event, the very establishment of the Enterprise was postponed.[23]

With respect to private miners, Article 4 of Annex III sets out stringent criteria for their participation, including in terms of nationality and sponsorship. In a legal regime that is apparently so liberal with respect to private actors' mining rights, this is a first obstacle to full participation as subjects of law. In fact, under Article 4(1) of Annex III (following Article 153(2)(b) of the LOSC), contractors must be nationals of a State party, or at least must be under the effective control of a State party or its nationals; and must be sponsored by the State party of nationality or control.

If nationality and control are defined broadly, the assessment of sponsorship is more rigid – which explains why some readings of the position of private miners are biased against private miners. The reason for this apparent paradox lies in the fact that sponsoring States perform an important function as watchdogs of exploration and exploitation activities. In fact, whilst the Authority has limited means of action vis-à-vis contractors, States can effectively control the conduct of private miners of their nationality, and thus guarantee the enforcement of the legal regime of the Area. Article 4(4) of Annex III is clear that 'The sponsoring State shall … have the responsibility to ensure, within their legal systems, that a contractor so sponsored shall carry out activities in the Area in conformity with the terms of the contract and its obligations under [the LOSC]', notably through the adoption of the appropriate laws and regulations

[20] Section 2, paragraph 5 of the Annex to the Implementation Agreement.
[21] Section 2, paragraph 2 of the Annex to the Implementation Agreement.
[22] Section 2, paragraph 3 of the Annex to the Implementation Agreement.
[23] Section 2, paragraph 1 of the Annex to the Implementation Agreement.

and the necessary administrative measures. In this vein, it is not surprising that Article 4(3) of Annex III and the Regulations adopted by the Authority are particularly stringent with regard to cases of multiple nationalities: if the home State is better positioned to control the conduct of its nationals, in the case of international consortia all home States should be involved as sponsors. Ultimately, the sponsorship requirement is evidence that international law is concerned with its comparative lack of sophistication, and as such is uncomfortable with the enhancement of the international legal status of private miners in the absence of the State machinery.

1.3. Entitlements of Private Miners

1.3.1. Pre-contractual Rights of the Applicants

The LOSC and the Implementation Agreement have scarce provisions regarding the procedure before the approval of a plan of work, the awarding of the contract, or the issuing of the authorisation. Most evident, there is no reference to a mandatory public tender or an open procedure prior to the selection of the contractor among the applicants. At most, what can be said is that an application for the approval of a plan of work is processed following the procedure established in Section 3, paragraph 11 of the Annex to the Implementation Agreement, and in the scarce mirror provisions of the Regulations adopted by the Authority (which are more concerned with the distribution of competences among the organs of the Authority). Moreover, under Section 1, paragraph 6(a) of the Annex to the Implementation Agreement, 'An application for approval of a plan of work shall be considered following the receipt of a recommendation on the application from the Legal and Technical Commission'.

The legal regime of the Area is also vague with respect to pre-contractual duties of the applicants, with two relevant exceptions. First, following a trend of privatisation adopted at a transnational level, the applicant must perform a prior assessment of the potential marine environmental damage and submit a description of a programme for oceanographic and baseline environmental studies.[24] Second, the applicant has to accept as enforceable and to be bound by Part XI and Annex III of the LOSC, the rules, regulations and procedures adopted by the Authority, the future terms of the contract, and the control of the Authority over the activities in the Area, and to provide a written assurance that it will fulfil its obligations in good faith.[25] The purpose of this rule is to foster compliance with the legal regime of the Area by asking the applicants, already in

[24] Section 1, paragraph 7 of the Annex to the Implementation Agreement, Regulation 18(1)(b), (c) and (d) of the Nodules Regulations, Regulations 20(1)(b), (c) and (d) of the Cobalts Regulations and of the Sulphides Regulations, and Annex IV to the Draft Exploitation Regulations.

[25] Article 4(6)(a)–(c) of Annex III.

the pre-contractual stage, to be voluntarily bound by the possible future content of the contract.[26]

1.3.1.1. Selection of the Contractor. Right to the Approval of the Plan of Work

Under Article 6(3) of Annex III, the Authority must periodically examine the proposals submitted by the applicants in the order of submission, and provided that the mandatory (and non-discretionary) requirements are satisfied, the proposed plan of work will normally be approved, the contract awarded and the authorisation issued. As this procedure only aims to assess if the conditions are met, under this provision private applicants hold a right to the approval of the plan of work.

Nonetheless, the right to the approval of the plan of work is not a by-word for the right to be awarded the contract or the authorisation. In cases where a selection among applications is made pursuant to Article 7(2) of Annex III, the Authority must adopt an objective and non-discriminatory procedure prior to the award of a contract and the issuing of an authorisation. In this case, some applicants have a right to priority pursuant to Article 7(3) of Annex III, notably those who 'give better assurance of performance', 'provide earlier prospective financial benefits to the Authority', 'have already invested the most resources and effort in prospecting or exploration',[27] have not been selected in a previous selection procedure,[28] or have already been awarded a contract for exploration only.[29] In cases where selection among applicants is not required, then a right to be awarded the contract and to the issuing of the authorisation can be derived from Article 7(1) of Annex III.

1.3.1.2. Procedural Entitlements of the Applicants

The LOSC and the Implementation Agreement outline limited procedural rights held by applicants, including private miners. One of these few provisions is Article 152(1) of the LOSC, which states that 'The Authority shall avoid discrimination in the exercise of its powers and functions, including the granting of opportunities for activities in the Area'. From this provision, a right to non-discrimination can be derived, although special attention shall be given to developing, land-locked and geographically disadvantaged States.[30] Although the LOSC and the regulations adopted by the Authority only have a few rules on

[26] Francisco Orrego Vicuña, 'The Régime for the Exploration and Exploitation of Sea-Bed Mineral Resources', in René-Jean Dupuy and Daniel Vignes (eds), *A Handbook on the New Law of the Sea* (Martinus Nijhoff 1991) 635, 657.

[27] Article 7(3)(a)–(c) of Annex III.

[28] Article 7(4) of Annex III.

[29] Article 10 of Annex III.

[30] Article 152(2) of the LOSC.

the procedural entitlements of the applicants, the rules that have been devised under the umbrella of global administrative law are applicable to the procedure prior to the selection of a contractor, the approval of the plan of work, and the awarding of the contract.

In fact, the emergence of global administrative law as a new scientific domain was the result of a transfer of normative and administrative tasks to international organisations and other bodies, and the resulting high degree of institutionalisation of these rules, principles and procedures.[31] Such transfer is particularly visible in the domains where the coordination role of private entities is essential for the regulation of activities and behaviours, as is the case of the management of natural resources. The activity of these international bodies is similar to that which, under domestic legal systems, is qualified as administrative action: rule-making, non-judicial adjudication between competing or conflicting interests, or the management of international or common resources.[32] The decisions taken and the actions performed by these international bodies may intend to regulate the behaviour of private actors, and thus might ultimately be addressed to them.

One of the outcomes of this shift from domestic to global regulation was the need to enhance instruments of governance that could subject these international bodies to specific rules and principles of administrative law as developed under domestic systems to provide a level of protection of States' and private actors' rights comparable to the protection granted under domestic legal systems.[33] When their decisions impact the legal status of private actors directly, the need to armour the latter with guarantees is even more pressing. In the context of mining activities in the Area, where private miners engage in direct relations with the Authority, the need for these sound rules and principles is self-explanatory. The sociology of legal education (based on the learning of domestic legal systems) and the similarities between the jural relation between the State and its citizens, on the one hand, and the (State-like) Authority and private actors, on the other, explain why scholars and practitioners transpose into international law the procedural and substantive rules identified and developed under domestic legal systems. As a result, developments in the field of global administrative law are of immediate relevance to identify rules applicable in the relation between the Authority and private miners. In fact the relation between the Authority and private miners is comparable to the relations governed at the domestic level by administrative law, since the

[31] eg Eyal Benvenisti, 'The Interplay between Actors as a Determinant of the Evolution of Administrative Law in International Institutions' (2005) 68 *Law & Contemporary Problems* 319, 320; Benedict Kingsbury, Nico Krisch and Richard Stewart, 'The Emergence of Global Administrative Law' (2005) 68 *Law & Contemporary Problems* 15, 16.

[32] Kingsbury, Krisch and Stewart, 'Emergence' (n 31) 17.

[33] eg Sabino Cassese, 'Administrative Law without the State? The Challenge of Global Regulation' (2007) 35 *International Law & Politics* 663, 694.

management of scarce or valuable resources that cannot be appropriated by any entity commonly corresponds, in domestic legal systems, to an administrative activity of resources management, promoted under the legal regimes of public domain, and performed by the State or an infra-State public entity. In this sense, the task performed by the Authority of resource management in the Area can be qualified as an international administration activity, subject to the rules and principles forged under global administrative law.

In that context, the effort made to spot rules and principles common to domestic legal systems, or uniformly applicable to different international organisations, ultimately identified an *acquis* that includes the rights to notice-and-comment, to prior hearing,[34] to reasoned decisions, to procedural transparency and access to information,[35] to a review of the decision,[36] to compliance with binding norms and with proportionality standards, and to the protection of expectations. One might question why there is this focus on the insights from global administrative law, instead of relying on the LOSC and its Annex III, the Implementation Agreement, or the Regulations adopted by the Authority. The reason is simple. These latter instruments are detailed in respect of several topics but evasive with respect to the applicants' procedural rights; and even if they were exhaustive in this regard, the set of entitlements of private applicants and miners would derive from the discretionary decision-making capacity of States or the Authority, whereas the principles of global administrative law, if perceived as general principles of law, including for the purposes of Article 38(1)(c) of the ICJ Statute, provide for entitlements that are per se binding upon the Authority irrespective of any provision in the positive legal regime of the Area. The immediate consequence of this view is that because these entitlements are not the product of a discretionary decision they cannot be revoked discretionally by States or the Authority.

1.3.2. Contractual Entitlements of Private Miners

Activities in the Area must be carried out in accordance with a formal written plan of work, which must be drafted in accordance with the LOSC and other relevant instruments and approved by the Council after being reviewed by the Legal and Technical Commission.[37] If the contractor is a State party or a private actor, the written plan of work will take the form of a contract concluded between the Authority and the applicant(s).[38] The contract will assume a function of

[34] WTO, *United States: Import Prohibition of Certain Shrimp and Shrimp Products* (12 October 1998) WT/DS58/AB/R, §§ 180ff.

[35] eg Aarhus Compliance Committee, ECE/MP.PP/2005/13/Add.1 (11 March 2005) §§ 2–3.

[36] eg *Shrimp-Turtle* [1998] §§ 180–81.

[37] Article 153(3) of the LOSC. See also Section 2, paragraph 4 of the Annex to the Implementation Agreement.

[38] Article 153(3) of the LOSC and Article 3(5) of Annex III. See also Section 2, paragraph 4 of the Annex to the Implementation Agreement.

normative instrument applicable inter partes, and thus will be the 'solemn legal expression of the rights and obligations of the parties'.[39]

The plan of work is valid for a period of 15 years (exploration contracts)[40] or at most 30 years (exploitation contracts),[41] but before the expiration of this period the contractor shall rather apply for an extension of the plan of work or the approval of work for exploitation.[42] Contractors might reasonably expect to keep the exclusive rights of exploration or exploitation for that fixed period of time, and therefore the contract provides for security of tenure[43] as it cannot be revised, suspended or terminated except if in the terms established in the LOSC (notably, in Articles 18 and 19 of Annex III) or in the contract itself.[44] Furthermore, the contract cannot be revised without the consent of the parties,[45] except if circumstances arise that 'would render the contract inequitable or make it impracticable or impossible to achieve the objectives set out in the contract or in Part XI [of the LOSC]' (*rebus sic stantibus* clause).[46]

Once the contract is awarded, the Authority shall issue an authorisation for deep seabed mining operations. This authorisation is a likely, but not a necessary element of the contract. Under Article 151(2)(e) of the LOSC, the authorisation should preferably be included in the plan of work and in the original contract. However, since the approval of the plan of work and the production of the authorisation follow different procedures, the contract might include only the plan of work approved. In this case, the Authority will later issue an additional and separate title (the authorisation itself), which will enable the contractor to start deep seabed mining activities. In any event, the plan of work for exploitation approved by the Authority must already establish an anticipated production schedule and the maximum limits of exploitation for each year.[47]

One of the most sensitive problems that the LOSC had to deal with was the choice of law applicable to the relations between the Authority and the contractor. According to Article 21 of Annex III, the exploration and/or the exploration contract is governed only by the terms of the contract, the rules, regulations and procedures adopted by the Authority, Part XI of the LOSC,

[39] Vicuña, 'Régime' (n 26) 683.

[40] Section 1, paragraph 9 of the Annex to the Implementation Agreement, Regulation 26(1) of the Nodules Regulations, and Regulations 28(1) of the Cobalts Regulations and of the Sulphides Regulations.

[41] Regulation 20(1) of the Draft Exploitation Regulations.

[42] Section 1, paragraph 9 of the Annex to the Implementation Agreement, Regulation 26(2) of the Nodules Regulations, Regulations 28(2) of the Cobalts Regulations and of the Sulphides Regulations, and Regulation 20(2) of the Draft Exploitation Regulations.

[43] Article 153(6) of the LOSC and Article 16 of Annex III. See also Regulations 18(4) of the Draft Exploitation Regulations.

[44] Article 153(6) of the LOSC.

[45] Article 19(2) of Annex III.

[46] Article 19(1) of Annex III.

[47] Section 6, paragraph 1 (e), of the Annex to the Implementation Agreement, Regulation 18 of the Nodules Regulations, Regulations 20 of the Cobalt Regulations and of the Sulphides Regulations, and Annex II (f) to the Draft Exploitation Regulations.

and other relevant instruments of international law. In this sense, the jural relation between the Authority and the contractor is governed by international law only. However, parties can subject collateral details of their jural relation (eg specific financial arrangements such as bank guarantees or deposits) to the laws applicable within a specific domestic legal system, provided that the primacy of the rules, regulations and procedures adopted by the Authority, Part XI of the LOSC, and other relevant instruments of international law is preserved. In this regard, a general principle of law for the purposes of Article 38(1)(c) of the ICJ Statute is that a contract can be governed by the law chosen by its parties. Moreover, under Article 188(2)(c) of the LOSC, in the absence of a provision in the contract on the arbitration procedure to be applied in the dispute, an arbitration shall be conducted in accordance with the UNCITRAL Rules or such other arbitration rules as may be prescribed in the rules, regulations and procedures of the Authority, unless the parties to the dispute otherwise agree. If a dispute arises concerning the interpretation or enforcement of the contract, the means available are those established in the LOSC only. However, bearing in mind that the jural relation could not be totally independent from domestic jurisdictions and that the enforcement of some final decisions (eg when establishing compensation or a penalty) would be more efficient in the territory of the State of nationality, Article 21(2) of Annex III establishes that the decisions of any dispute settlement body established by Part XI of the LOSC or its Annexes possess *exequatur*, and therefore are valid and enforceable in the territory of all States parties.

For the contractor, an important incentive is the right to exclusive exploration for and exploitation of specific Area resources, located in a demarcated area and for a particular period of time, which is protected under Article 16 of Annex III.[48] As such, although the contract has an inter partes binding force, the authorisation issued by the Authority can be invoked against the world (*erga omnes* binding force) and confers a property right on the contractor. As a first guarantee, the plan of work included in the contract shall identify the resources object of the contract, the area where deep seabed mining is to be performed, the production limits of mineral harvesting (annual and total), and the period of time during which the contractor has the exclusive exploration and/or exploitation right. As a set-off for the exclusive right of deep seabed mining, the contractor is bound to make specific payments to the Authority as established in Article 13 of Annex III.

Once extracted, collected minerals become the object of a property right under Article 137(3) of the LOSC and Article 1 of Annex III. This solution seems straightforward, but it is remarkable how the LOSC (despite its unease

[48] See also Regulation 24(1) of the Nodules Regulations, Regulations 26(1) of the Cobalt Regulations and of the Sulphides Regulations, and Regulation 18(1)–(3) of the Draft Exploitation Regulations.

with the role of private actors) assigned property rights to private miners in the absence of a sophisticated international institutional machinery to protect property: ie more than providing protection to property rights of private miners, the LOSC is the very source of that property right. It is pointless to define a property right (even the LOSC refers to 'rights' and 'titles' but refrains from referring to 'property' or 'ownership'), but being a property right valid against the entire world (*erga omnes* nature), physical and legal excludability are inherent in it, and therefore it needs the authority of law behind it to provide protection against others,[49] since most intrinsic to a property right is the entitlement to exclude someone from interfering with one's possessions.[50] Whereas domestic legal systems afford a high level of institutional protection to property rights, international law cannot. Nonetheless, there were good arguments to take the LOSC as the source of the private miners' property rights: on the one hand, claims to property over the Area's resources are not made in a legal vacuum, but rather within the framework of the LOSC, its Annex III, the Implementation Agreement, the terms of a contract awarded to the contractor, and the authorisation issued by the Authority; on the other hand, the *potestas* of law behind a title to property is especially relevant when competing claims exist, but they are more likely to arise on land rather than in the deep seabed, where few entities have the means of exploitation and where only one contractor will be entitled to lawfully undertake mining activities; and finally, because *apprehensio* is the most original method of acquisition of property, recognised since Roman law and in most of the domestic legal systems, adverse reactions from States were not foreseeable. Thus, the simple act of taking possession of the resource, as a result of the mining activity authorised and in accordance with the plan of work outlined in the contract, suffices to vest the private contractor with a right in the resources extracted from the deep seabed and/or its subsoil.[51]

This, in a nutshell, is the complex web of rights and duties held by private miners engaged in the activities in the Area. The detailed analysis of the pre-contractual and contractual rights and duties of private miners is evidence of a case where international law specifically considers private actors as direct recipients of its rules. The room for interpretative bias is very limited, but still the

[49] Richard Barnes, *Property Rights and Natural Resources* (Hart Publishing 2009) 24–25; Richard Barnes, 'Entitlement to Marine Living Resources in Areas beyond National Jurisdiction', in Erik Jaap Molenaar and Alex Oude Elferink (eds), *The International Legal Regime of Areas beyond National Jurisdiction: Current and Future Developments* (Martinus Nijhoff 2010) 95.

[50] Jeremy Waldron, *The Right to Private Property* (Clarendon 1990) 89ff.

[51] Since the Area's resources are not *res nullius*, their harvesting without appropriate authorisation cannot confer a title to ownership. From a policy-oriented perspective, nullity and non-recognition of ownership should be seen as the immediate consequence of unauthorised harvesting of minerals (perhaps the sole consequence apart from punitive damages), since this will be the only deterrence and sanction against wrongdoings: Silja Vöneky and Anja Höfelmeier, 'Article 137', in Proelß (ed), *UN Convention* (n 7) 957, 959.

analysis of the different responsibility (*ex ante* and *ex post facto*) of the Authority, private miners, and sponsor States is also evidence of how a prejudice against private membership in the international legal order can confine the legal status of private actors under international law. This is the topic of the next section.

1.3.3. The Locus Standi *of Private Miners in Disputes Arising Out of Deep Seabed Mining*

As seen, the exploration for and exploitation of minerals in the Area is carried out according to an intricate legal regime in which private miners are equipped with substantive rights and duties and enter into a contract with the Authority. In this framework, no domestic court would have a title to jurisdiction *ratione materiae* in disputes between the Authority and private miners regarding the performance of a contract or a plan of work, or with respect to claims based on the infringement of any right. Moreover, no domestic judicial machinery would have jurisdiction *ratione personae*, since the Authority is immune before domestic authorities.[52] Therefore, Part XI, Section 5 of the LOSC guarantees that private miners have standing in the same international proceedings as the Authority.

To that end, the system outlined in Part XI, Section 5 of the LOSC is automatically binding upon all States parties to the LOSC, which means not only that no declaration under Article 287 is required, but also that States cannot contract out.[53] Moreover, instead of creating a special body (ie independent from the ITLOS) to deal with the specificities of deep seabed mining, the LOSC created the SDC as a special chamber in the ITLOS, with exclusive and compulsory jurisdiction over all disputes concerning resources exploration and exploitation in the Area. Having exclusive jurisdiction over all disputes regarding deep seabed mining means that the compulsory jurisdiction of the SDC is extended to all private miners involved in activities in the Area, including prospective and current contractors. This solution is unique in international dispute settlement, since it means that, pursuant to Article 187 of the LOSC, the jurisdiction *ratione personae* of the SDC includes disputes involving States, international organisations and private actors. In fact, among other competences, the SDC has jurisdiction over disputes between parties to a contract (here including private miners referred to in Article 153(2)(b) of the LOSC), regarding not only the contract but also the plan of work approved, although this dispute may be submitted to binding commercial arbitration according to Article 188(2) of

[52] Articles 177ff of the LOSC.

[53] Mahdi El-Baghdadi, 'The Binding Nature of the Disputes Settlement Procedure in the Third U.N. Convention on the Law of the Sea: The International Seabed Authority' (1990–1) 6 *Journal of Mineral Law & Policy* 173, 180; Michael Lodge, 'The Deep Seabed', in Donald Rothwell, Alex Oude Elferink, Karen Scott and Tim Stephens (eds), *The Oxford Handbook of the Law of the Sea* (OUP 2015) 226, 249.

the LOSC.[54] The SDC also has jurisdiction over disputes between the Authority and a prospective contractor[55] where compliance with procedural rules of an administrative nature is questioned, or where the contract has been refused despite the meeting of the appropriate qualification standards[56] and the payment of the requisite fee.[57] In addition, the SDC has jurisdiction over disputes between the Authority and a State party, a State enterprise or a private miner where it is alleged that the Authority has incurred liability as provided in Article 22 of Annex III, notably for the exercise of the right of recourse.[58]

Accordingly, with respect to private deep seabed mining, the SDC has a broad jurisdiction over pre-contractual, contractual and tortious liability disputes, the interpretation and application of contracts, the refusal of a contract, or any legal issue arising in the negotiations or enforcement of the contract.[59] With this unique liberal regime of access to dispute settlement under Part XI of the LOSC, coupled with the possibility of joining cases set out in Article 47 of the ITLOS Rules, an efficient means is afforded to address problems of parallel accountability of the Authority, private miners and sponsoring States, without prejudice to the *Monetary Gold* principle.[60]

The jurisdiction of the SDC is limited by the possible submission of the case before a commercial arbitral tribunal.[61] Submission of these disputes to binding commercial arbitration might be desirable due to the nature of the rules to be interpreted and applied. In fact, in the absence of rules or principles of international law governing the relation between the parties, it would be normal if the parties chose the law applicable discretionally. By default, Article 188(2)(c) of the LOSC establishes that the UNCITRAL is applicable, but parties can also choose to submit the contract to another instrument. In these cases, international commercial arbitral tribunals are likely to be better placed than the SDC to render an award on the dispute, since one can presume they are more familiar with the relevant case law and practice regarding these bodies of rules. For that reason, under Article 188(2) of the LOSC, the international commercial arbitral tribunal has mandatory jurisdiction if the applicant *or* the respondent

[54] Article 187(c) of the LOSC.

[55] Article 187(d) of the LOSC.

[56] See Article 4(6) of Annex III to the LOSC, and Section 5(2) of the Annex to the Implementation Agreement.

[57] See Article 13(2) of Annex III to the LOSC, and Section 8(3) of the Annex to the Implementation Agreement.

[58] Article 187(e) of the LOSC.

[59] Francisco Orrego Vicuña, 'Individuals and Non-State Entities before International Courts and Tribunals' (2001) 5 *Max-Planck Yearbook of United Nations Law* 53, 58; Francisco Orrego Vicuña, *International Dispute Settlement in an Evolving Global Society – Constitutionalization, Accessibility, Privatization* (CUP 2006) 81.

[60] Ilias Plakokefalos, 'Environmental Protection of the Deep Seabed', in André Nollkaemper, Ilias Plakokefalos and Jessica Schechinger (eds), *The Practice of Shared Responsibility in International Law* (CUP 2017) 380, 395.

[61] Article 188(2)(a) of the LOSC.

so requests.[62] However, binding commercial arbitration is confined to the interpretation or application of the contract (eg financial arrangements), the plan of work, or other agreements between the parties, thereby excluding the assessment of acts or omissions of the parties.[63] Furthermore, the LOSC establishes that the arbitral tribunal is not competent to interpret or apply the LOSC. As such, a Gnostic-Manichaean conception of the dispute was adopted by the LOSC, according to which disputes regarding the interpretation or application of the contract or the plan of work can be tied off the interpretation or application of the LOSC itself. However, these contracts and plans of works are governed by international law, which means that the commercial arbitral tribunal will have to apply also rules of international law, including the LOSC. Therefore, in cases where only the interpretation or application of the contract or plan of work is necessary, the dispute might be submitted to a commercial arbitral tribunal with no further restraint; in cases where the interpretation of the LOSC is relevant, the question shall be referred to the SDC for a ruling, and the commercial arbitral tribunal will have to necessarily follow its *dictum*.[64] The purpose of the regime of mandatory referral is twofold: to ensure the monopoly of the SDC in the interpretation of Part XI of the LOSC, being authoritative judicial decisions regarding the interpretation or application of Part XI of the LOSC delivered by the SDC only; considering that arbitrators are freely chosen by the parties to the dispute, binding jurisdiction of the SDC is a means to ensure that the interpreters of the LOSC are familiarised with the law of the sea.[65]

Having established that private actors have *locus standi* before the SDC, Article 190 of the LOSC had to deal with particular issues arising from this innovative solution. Once tested, this provision will be key to assessing the possible impact of interpretative bias. To begin with, paragraph 1 of this provision establishes that if a private miner is party to a dispute before the SDC, the sponsoring State has the right to intervene in the proceedings and to submit written and oral statements. This solution is in line with other treaties that confer procedural rights on private actors coupled with diplomatic protection intervention,[66] but it is not consistent with international proceedings on investment or commercial disputes.[67] It is evidence that States were not comfortable with outlining an international proceeding where no State would have standing, and therefore

[62] ED Brown, *Sea-Bed Energy and Minerals: The International Legal Regime*, vol 2, *Sea-Bed Mining* (Martinus Nijhoff 2001) 370.

[63] Myron Nordquist, Shabtai Rosenne and Alexander Yankov (eds), *United Nations Convention on the Law of the Sea 1982 – A Commentary*, IV (Martinus Nijhoff 1991) 626.

[64] Article 188(2)(a) and (b) of the LOSC.

[65] James Harrison, *Making the Law of the Sea – A Study in the Development of International Law* (CUP 2011) 148.

[66] eg Article 36(1) of the ECHR.

[67] Niels-J Seeberg-Elverfeldt, *The Settlement of Disputes in Deep Seabed Mining* (Nomos 1998) 143.

admitted that the sponsoring State could intervene, although not as a party in the proceedings.[68] There seems to be one good reason to admit the intervention of the sponsoring State: since it has an obligation of due diligence with respect to the activities in the Area carried out by the sponsored entity, it has a legitimate interest in the course of the proceedings and in its final decision. Therefore, the intervention of the sponsoring State is meant not to work as a by-product of diplomatic protection of the private miner, but rather (or also) as a guarantee of the interests of the sponsoring State.[69]

Furthermore, pursuant to paragraph 2 of that provision, if an action is brought against a State by a private miner under Article 187(c) of the LOSC (therefore excluding other proceedings), the respondent State has the right to request the sponsoring State to intervene in the proceedings on behalf of the private actor – as if sponsoring meant more than what is actually set out in Part XI of the LOSC. This will happen in case of consortia, when the respondent State prefers to have an inter-State dispute.[70] If the sponsoring State does not intervene in the proceedings, the respondent State might decide to be represented by a legal person of its nationality. This solution voices a Vattelian conception of international law, in which a State can refuse to answer to private actors in the international legal arena, and therewith veto the establishment of the proceedings with a private actor.[71] However, this solution is not in line with the fact that one of the aims of Part XI, Section 5 of the LOSC is precisely to provide private actors with liberal access to the SDC.[72]

1.4. The Responsibility of Private Miners, the Authority and Sponsoring States

Human activity entails risk, and the visible side of risk is the production of damage. If private miners engage in activities in the Area, this means that their conduct is likely to produce damage. As a result, the LOSC and the Implementation Agreement set out a regime of accountability applicable to private miners, the Authority and the sponsoring State. But the reading adopted by the SDC unveils another side of interpretative bias: instead of excluding private miners from the activities in the Area, it seems to confine private miners to a minor role in deep seabed mining.

[68] This implies, eg, that the sponsoring State cannot make autonomous claims, as well as that the proceedings can be concluded even in the absence of the sponsoring State's intervention.

[69] See *mutatis mutandis* Seeberg-Everfeldt, *Settlement of Disputes* (n 67) 143–44.

[70] Nordquist et al (eds), *UN Convention*, IV (n 63) 638.

[71] Gerhard Hafner, 'The Emancipation of the Individual from the State under International Law' (2011) 358 *Collected Courses of the Hague Academy of International Law* 263, 371.

[72] Seeberg-Everfeldt, *Settlement of Disputes* (n 67) 145.

1.4.1. *The Accountability of Private Miners and the Authority*

The core provision to characterise private miners' accountability is Article 22(1) of Annex III, which provides that private miners are liable 'for any damage arising out of wrongful acts in the conduct of its operations, account being taken of contributory acts or omissions by the Authority'. Under this provision, liability derives only from wrongful and harmful conducts, including those of subcontractors, but excluding strict liability.[73] According to the standard clauses for exploration contracts, annexed to the Cobalt, the Sulphides, and the Nodules Regulations, private miners are

> liable for the actual amount of any damage, including damage to the marine environment, arising out of its wrongful acts or omissions, ... including the costs of reasonable measures to prevent or limit damage to the marine environment, account being taken to any contributory acts or omissions of the Authority.[74]

Then, Section 16(2) and (4) of the same standard clauses[75] set out an apparent regime of joint and several liability between the private miner and the Authority, grounded on the will of the parties to the future exploration contract, which is a practical remedy for the shortcomings of dispute settlement: eg being liability shared between the Authority and the private miner, there would be no domestic or international body where both entities have simultaneous legal standing as defendants.

Article 22 of Annex III captures the quasi-stateless nature of this jural relation and refers to its core players: the Authority (which exerts exclusively a State-like function in the legal regime of the Area) and the private miner (who is subject to the primary jurisdiction of the Authority under the international legal regime of the Area). In this sense, this provision implies that primary liability for wrongful and harmful acts in the Area should rest with the Authority and the contractor.

Nevertheless, the LOSC requires the sponsorship of the private miner by its State of nationality in order to assist the Authority in assuring compliance with the legal system. What is dismaying at this point is that, despite the absence of

[73] *Responsibilities and Obligations of Sponsoring States* [2001] § 189. See David Freestone, 'Responsibilities and Obligations of States Sponsoring Persons and Entities with Respect to Activities in the Area' (2011) 105 *American Journal of International Law* 755, 759; Rosemary Rayfuse, 'Differentiating the Commons? The Responsibilities and Obligations of States Sponsoring Deep Seabed Mining Activities in the Area' (2011) 54 *German Yearbook of International Law* 459, 483; Donald Rothwell and Tim Stephens, *The International Law of the Sea* (2nd edn, Hart Publishing 2016) 147; Yoshifumi Tanaka, 'Obligations and Liability of Sponsoring States concerning Activities in the Area: Reflections on the ITLOS Advisory Opinion of 1 February 2011' (2013) 60 *Netherlands International Law Review* 205, 220; Tanaka, *Law of the Sea* (n 8) 226; Silja Vöneky and Anja Höfelmeier, 'Article 139', in Proelß (ed), *UN Convention* (n 7) 968, 972.

[74] Section 16(1). A similar wording is used in Section 7(1) of the standard clauses for exploitation contracts, under Annex X to the Draft Exploitation Regulations.

[75] As well as Section 7(2)–(4) of the standard clauses for exploitation contracts.

any reference to the sponsoring State in Article 22(1) of Annex III, Article 139(2) of the LOSC and the advisory opinion rendered by the SDC in 2011 emphasise the sponsoring State's accountability. It could be just curious that the general rule on the shared liability of private miners and the Authority is 'hidden' in Annex III, whereas the rule on the liability of sponsoring States is set forth in Article 139 of the LOSC. But it is evidence of how international law is uneasy with private actors' participation.

1.4.2. The Accountability of Sponsoring States

In Chapter 3, Section 4, a general overview of the topic of interaction between the accountability of private actors and States was already adumbrated in the framework of flag State responsibility. Such overview is also applicable in the context of deep seabed mining, which means, for instance, that the conduct of the private miner is not automatically attributable to its sponsor State under the rules on State responsibility. Accordingly, private miners are autonomously liable for damage arising from their mining activities, and the sponsoring State only indirectly bears responsibility for such damage, particularly if it fails to comply with their due diligence obligations.[76]

In this regard, the core provision is Article 139 of the LOSC. Pursuant to this provision, the sponsoring State is responsible for ensuring that activities in the Area are carried out in accordance with Part XI of the LOSC when performed by private miners of their nationality, or effectively controlled by them or their nationals.[77] Afterwards, Article 4(4) of Annex III sets forth that the sponsoring State has the duty to ensure that private miners carry out activities in the Area in conformity with the terms of the contract and the LOSC – but such control must be performed within their domestic legal systems, since within the international legal order this competence is assigned only to the Authority. This solution is also surprising: being activities carried out beyond the spatial jurisdiction of States and under the primary, if not exclusive, competence of the Authority, it is a challenge for the sponsoring State to assume this function within its domestic legal order. But the aim of this provision is to guarantee that States do not decommission activities in the Area with the aim of bypassing the obligations set out in the LOSC. Moreover, States can always exert control over legal persons of their nationality on other bases – but one must keep in mind that the scope of the *ex ante* responsibility of the sponsoring State under this provision is limited by nature: pursuant to Part XI of the LOSC, its Annex III, and the Regulations adopted, only the Authority can inter alia inspect the

[76] *Responsibilities and Obligations of Sponsoring States* [2001] §§ 109ff. See also, generally, Brown, *Sea-Bed Energy* (n 62) 76; Seeberg-Elverfeldt, *Settlement of Disputes* (n 67) 77; Hui Zhang, 'The Sponsoring State's "Obligation to Ensure" in the Development of the International Seabed Area' (2013) 29 *International Journal of Marine and Coastal Law* 681, 685–86.

[77] Paragraph (1).

contractor's facilities in the Area, apply contractual penalties or control the performance by the contractor.[78] In its advisory opinion, the SDC adopted a policy-oriented approach and identified several direct obligations of the sponsoring State[79] (ie to assist the Authority in controlling activities in the Area, as required by Article 153(4) of the LOSC, to adopt a precautionary approach, to adopt best environmental practices, to provide guarantees in the event of an emergency order by the Authority for the protection of the marine environment, to conduct environmental impact assessments, to provide the means for servants to protect their labour rights, or to ensure the availability of recourse for compensation in respect of damage caused by pollution), but the confinement of the sponsoring State's responsibility to the means provided within its domestic legal order, and the fact that the international jural relation is established between the Authority and the private miner, would seem to confine the scope of these obligations.

Nonetheless, to point out the limited nature of the due diligence obligation of the sponsoring State is not the same as stating that no obligations exist. What one has to ask is 'what is sponsorship in the context of the legal regime of the Area?' For sure, it does not mean co-involvement in or financing of the operations, the nationality of the private miner (although it is predicated on nationality), or a genuine link between the private miner and its State of nationality. But it should also not be read as a letter of comfort certifying the aptitude of a private actor to conduct deep seabed mining. Sponsorship is rather an explicit assumption by a State that it will exercise effective jurisdiction within its domestic legal order over a particular private miner.[80] Therefore, the purpose of sponsorship is to ensure the rule of law in the Area and that private miners comply with the duties deriving from international law and binding upon States parties.[81] This explains, for example, why multiple sponsorship is necessary if a private miner has the nationality of one State but is effectively controlled by another State or its nationals.[82]

In such context, Article 139(1) of the LOSC is not a permissive international law rule. Conversely, it is innovative since it is based upon sponsorship (not upon nationality) and assigns competence to the State of nationality of the private miner, but further adding that the exercise of this jurisdiction is limited (it has to be reconciled with the competence of the Authority) but mandatory, since the interests protected under this provision are autonomous and transcendent to States.[83]

[78] Zhang, 'Obligation to Ensure' (n 76) 688.

[79] *Responsibilities and Obligations of Sponsoring States* [2001] §§ 121ff.

[80] See Regulations 11(3)(f) of the Colbalt, the Sulphides, and the Nodules Regulations, and Regulation 6 of the Draft Exploitation Regulations.

[81] *Responsibilities and Obligations of Sponsoring States* [2001] § 75. See generally Lodge, 'Deep Seabed' (n 53) 248; Tanaka, *Law of the Sea* (n 8) 225–26; Tanaka, 'Obligations and Liability' (n 73) 208.

[82] Article 4(3) of Annex III.

[83] *Responsibilities and Obligations of Sponsoring States* [2001] § 76.

The assumption of competence by the sponsoring State impacts its responsibility. In the context of navigation, we saw that flag States' responsibility derives from their jurisdiction over flagged ships, but only arises in case of systemic non-compliance. But this is certainly not the case for activities in the Area, where *ex ante* responsibility of sponsoring States rather arises in individual cases and derives from the act of sponsoring, and not from the nationality of private miners. Since there is no obligation to sponsor,[84] by issuing a certificate of sponsorship, States are binding themselves to the duty of exercising jurisdiction over a particular private miner in the performance of a particular activity,[85] which implies that *ex post* responsibility of sponsoring States also arises in individual cases.[86] In this vein, the Cobalt, the Sulphides, and the Nodules Regulations, and the Draft Exploitation Regulations require from the applicant to identify its place of registration and of business,[87] in order to assess the strength of the link with the sponsoring State – but not to recognise or refuse the nationality of the private miner.

Therefore, even though the means available at the domestic level are meagre, the sponsoring State has the duty to establish 'reasonably appropriate' measures, according to the specificities of each legal system.[88] For instance, where a private miner uses ships of its nationality, the flag State can interfere with their navigation to inspect whether private miners are complying with the terms of the contract and the authorisation (eg controlling the amount and nature of the minerals collected), thus overcoming the limits of the inspecting powers of the Authority. Moreover, considering the Authority's scarce institutional machinery, the sponsoring State can establish compulsory insurance schemes or compensation funds, the mechanisms for seizing moveable and immovable goods of the private miner, and the institutional means for third parties seeking compensation or for the Authority to exert its right of recourse.[89] Implicit, therein, is the assignment of extraterritorial jurisdiction to sponsoring States as a means to assist the Authority. In any case, the sponsoring State jurisdiction is limited to the adoption of 'laws and regulations' and 'administrative measures' that are 'reasonably appropriate' under its domestic law.[90]

[84] ibid § 78.

[85] See *mutatis mutandis* Gwénaëlle Le Gurun, 'Annex III, Article 4', in Proelß (ed), *UN Convention* (n 7) 2135, 2141.

[86] The responsibility of sponsoring States for systemic non-compliance with due diligence obligations, even in the absence of damage, cannot be derived directly from Article 139 of the LOSC, but results from its implied reference to general international law (the 'without prejudice' clause).

[87] Regulation 10(3)(b) of the Cobalt, the Suphides, and the Nodules Regulations, and Regulation 5(3)(b) of the Draft Exploitation Regulations. According to some authors, this should guide the interpreter as to the meaning of 'effective control': Lodge, 'Deep Seabed' (n 53) 248.

[88] Myron Nordquist, Satya Nandan, Shabtai Rosenne and Michael Lodge (eds), *United Nations Convention on the Law of the Sea 1982 – A Commentary*, VI (Martinus Nijhoff 2003) 127; Rayfuse, 'Differentiating the Commons?' (n 73) 486; Vöneky and Höfelmeier, 'Article 139' (n 73) 970.

[89] See *mutatis mutandis Responsibilities and Obligations of Sponsoring States* [2001] § 139.

[90] Article 4(4) of Annex III. See also *Responsibilities and Obligations of Sponsoring States* [2001] § 119, although the SDC failed to provide some flesh to the notion of 'reasonably appropriate' measures. (See also Zhang, 'Obligation to Ensure' (n 76) 689.)

In this context, Article 139(2) of the LOSC lays down that private miners are liable for any damage caused by their conduct, whereas sponsoring States are only responsible if they fail to take all necessary and appropriate measures to secure effective compliance with the legal regime of the Area. The same rule is set out in Article 4(4) of Annex III. As a result, these provisions set out that the *ex ante* responsibility of sponsoring States is confined to a due diligence obligation (which means that it is also one of conduct, not of result);[91] the *ex post* responsibility of sponsoring States arises in individual cases of non-performance of a due diligence obligation; the sponsoring State cannot be responsible for the failure of the private miner to meet its own obligations;[92] and the responsibility of the sponsoring State is limited to the harmful events that could have been prevented had it performed its competences under domestic law, if a causal link is established:[93] all other damages (ie which could not have been prevented by the duly exercise of States' jurisdiction under domestic law) do not entail its liability.[94] This implies that the liability of the sponsoring State in the legal regime of the Area 'exist[s] in parallel':[95] the liability of the private miner has first to be established; afterwards, one can assess if the damage not covered can be compensated by the sponsoring State. Considering the interplay between the liability of private miners and of the Authority, there is room to contend that the sponsoring State is only responsible for damages not covered by both entities' liability, which implies also that the responsibilities of the private miner and the sponsoring State are autonomous,[96] and as a result, that no regime of joint (and several) liability between the private miner and the sponsoring State exists.

With this solution, the LOSC sought a rational model of distribution of responsibility between private miners, the Authority and the sponsoring State. Yet the legal regime set out in Part XI of the LOSC and Annex III has some significant gaps. For instance, from a substantive perspective it leaves outside its scope cases such as if the sponsoring State adopted 'reasonably appropriate'

[91] *Responsibilities and Obligations of Sponsoring States* [2001] § 110. See also Robin Churchill, 'Dispute Settlement in the Law of the Sea: Survey for 2011' (2012) 27 *International Journal of Marine and Coastal Law* 517, 528; Freestone, 'Responsibilities' (n 73) 757–58; Ilias Plakokefalos, 'Seabed Disputes Chamber of the International Tribunal for the Law of the Sea: Responsibilities and Obligations of States Sponsoring Persons and Entities with respect to Activities in the Area' (2012) 24 *Journal of Environmental Law* 133, 136; Rayfuse, 'Differentiating the Commons?' (n 73) 476; Tanaka, *Law of the Sea* (n 8) 225–26; Tanaka, 'Obligations and Liability' (n 73) 209; Rüdiger Wolfrum, 'Obligation of Result Versus Obligation of Conduct: Some Thoughts About the Implementation of International Obligations', in Mahnoush Arsanjani, Jacob Katz Cogan, Robert Sloane and Siegfried Wiessner (eds), *Looking to the Future – Essays on International Law in Honor of W. Michael Reisman* (Martinus Nijhoff 2011) 363, 379; Zhang, 'Obligation to Ensure' (n 76) 685.

[92] *Responsibilities and Obligations of Sponsoring States* [2001] §§ 172 and 182.

[93] ibid §§ 181–84.

[94] ibid § 119.

[95] ibid §§ 203–04.

[96] ibid § 201.

measures, but the private miner is unable to compensate for the damage caused; if both the sponsoring State and the private miner complied with their primary obligations, but damage arises nevertheless; or if the sponsoring State failed to comply with its due diligence obligations, but no harm arises, or the causal link is not established.[97] With regard to procedural needs, the legal regime of the Area fails to grasp the polygonal nature of jural relations: if damage is produced and impacts the legal sphere of non-contractual parties (eg a coastal State or its nationals, or a private miner that holds a title to explore or exploit resources in an adjacent area), the SDC and the commercial arbitral tribunal referred to in Article 188(2) of the LOSC have no jurisdiction to settle the dispute.

So far, the practice of deep seabed mining is scarce and confined only to resources' exploration, which explains why little attention has been paid to the legal regime of the Area. The only case where an issue regarding the role of private miners was raised at the international level was the advisory opinion delivered by the SDC, where a clear State-centric view was adopted by the SDC. That was the result of adopting a policy-oriented approach aimed at ensuring that sponsoring States would need to have a highly sophisticated legal system and machinery to assist the Authority, but also of the fact that the jurisdiction of the SDC was limited by the request made by the Council of the Authority – which asked about the role of sponsoring States, not that of the Authority or private miners. But what is still impressive is the latitude given by the SDC to the sponsoring State's due diligence obligation, suggesting that, in the view of the SDC, a complete subjection of private miners to their sponsoring State is possible and desirable, and that the range and means of monitoring and vigilance by the sponsoring State are able to curb most of the risk arising from deep seabed mining. The result was the delivery of an advisory opinion where the pivotal role in deep seabed mining is given to the sponsoring State, and not the private miner, as if the sponsoring State was the boundary between the private miner and the international legal system. In light of the semantic element of Part XI of the LOSC and the other instruments regarding the legal regime of the Area, an interpretative bias could not exclude private miners from being direct recipients of rights and duties under international law, but was able to influence the view of the SDC on the role of the sponsoring State role and, as a result, on the role of private miners in deep seabed mining. A good example is the view regarding the precautionary approach, which requires sponsoring States 'to take all appropriate measures to prevent damage that might result

[97] See generally Donald Anton, 'The Principle of Residual Liability in the Seabed Disputes Chamber of the International Tribunal for the Law of the Sea: The Advisory Opinion on Responsibility and Liability for International Seabed Mining (ITLOS Case No. 17)' (2012) 7 *McGill International Journal of Sustainable Development Law & Policy* 241, 250; Plakokefalos, 'Seabed Disputes Chamber' (n 91) 141; Rayfuse, 'Differentiating the Commons?' (n 73) 484; Rothwell and Stephens, *Law of the Sea* (n 73) 147; Tanaka, *Law of the Sea* (n 8) 226; Tanaka, 'Obligations and Liability' (n 73) 221–22; Vöneky and Höfelmeier, 'Article 139' (n 73) 975.

from the activities of contractors that they sponsor', bearing in mind all 'plausible indications of potential risks'. But how can the SDC establish such a high bar for the sponsoring State if it is not directly involved in the operations, and its extraterritorial jurisdiction meets important international law limits? Only an interpretative bias explains such an iconic conception of the sponsoring State role in deep seabed mining.

2. THE *LOCUS STANDI* OF PRIVATE ACTORS IN PROMPT RELEASE APPLICATIONS

2.1. The Function of Prompt Release Proceedings in the Framework of the LOSC

Rules on the release of a vessel and its crew upon the posting of a bond or other financial security are common in several domestic legal systems and in law of the sea treaties. The LOSC itself introduced new obligations for the release of vessels and crews conditional upon the posting of a bond or other financial security[98] as a trade-off for the enlargement of coastal States' enforcement jurisdiction.[99] But the most impressive novelty of the LOSC was the introduction of a special judicial proceeding for the prompt release of vessels and crews, with respect to which the ITLOS has subsidiary but compulsory jurisdiction. Nine out of 29 cases brought before the ITLOS since its inauguration involved prompt release proceedings, which could evidence its dominance in the ITLOS docket and its significance in the law of the sea dispute settlement. However, a dismaying fact is the visible decline of prompt release proceedings submitted to the ITLOS and the lack of enthusiasm that practitioners share for this institution.

The purpose of Article 292 of the LOSC is to protect three types of interests: human freedom and the financial interests of the ship-owner or operator, which are of immediate relevance for private actors;[100] the economic and

[98] In order to provide some fluidity, hereinafter I will refer only to the 'posting of a bond', but always implicit in the text is a reference to 'the posting of other financial security'.

[99] *'Camouco' (Panama v France)* [Judgment, 7 February 2000] ITLOS Rep 10, 'Dissenting Opinion of Judge Wolfrum', § 7. See also Myron Nordquist, Shabtai Rosenne and Louis Sohn (eds), *United Nations Convention on the Law of the Sea 1982 – A Commentary*, V (Martinus Nijhoff 1989) 768.

[100] *'Camouco'* [2000] 'Declaration of Judge Laing', 2; ibid, 'Separate Opinion of Vice-President Nelson', 1. See also Igor Karaman, *Dispute Resolution in the Law of the Sea* (Martinus Nijhoff 2012) 25; Heiki Lindpere, 'Prompt Release of Detained Foreign Vessels and Crews in Matters of Marine Environmental Protection' (2005) 33 *International Journal of Legal Information* 240, 240–41; John Noyes, 'The International Tribunal for the Law of the Sea' (1998) 32 *Cornell International Law Journal* 109, 146; Louis Sohn, 'Settlement of Law of the Sea Disputes' (1995) 10 *International Journal of Marine and Coastal Law* 205, 208; Tullio Treves, 'The Proceedings Concerning Prompt Release of Vessels and Crews before the International Tribunal for the Law of the Sea' (1996) 11 *International Journal of Marine and Coastal Law* 179, 180; Tullio Treves, 'Article 292', in Proelß (ed), *UN Convention* (n 7) 1881, 1882; Budislav Vukas, 'Droit de la mer et droits de l'homme', in *The Law of the Sea – Selected Writings* (Martinus Nijhoff 2004) 71, 76; Florian Wegelein, 'The Rules of the Tribunal in the Light of Prompt Release of Vessels' (1999) 30 *Ocean Development & International Law* 255, 265–66.

humanitarian interests of flag States,[101] not only as the representatives in the international legal sphere of private interests, but also as advocates of their collective interests as States; and the interest of the detaining State to guarantee that a penalty or compensation will be paid at the end of the proceedings pending before domestic courts,[102] and that the crew-members, the ship-owner or the ship-operator will be presented before the competent domestic court.[103] In this sense, the ultimate goal of the LOSC is to protect private actors' and flag States' interests against excessive interference with navigation on waters under the spatial enforcement jurisdiction of coastal States.

Article 292 of the LOSC states:

> Where the authorities of a State Party have detained a vessel flying the flag of another State Party and it is alleged that the detaining State has not complied with the provisions of [the LOSC] for the prompt release of the vessel or its crew upon the posting of a reasonable bond or other financial security, the question of release from detention may be submitted to any court or tribunal agreed upon by the parties.

This provision is applicable to cases where the LOSC equips coastal States with the power to detain a vessel and its crew but obliges them to release the detained vessel and crew upon the posting of a reasonable bond. In the practice of the ITLOS, the concept of detention is broad and encompasses, for instance, cases where the passport of the master or other crew-members is seized by coastal States authorities.[104] Because it would be of no help to translate into a universal treaty the legal terminology from different languages and cultures, the term detention must be interpreted broadly as meaning any case in which the physical movement of the vessel or the crew is impaired by an act of the coastal State's authority.[105]

[101] Natalie Klein, *Dispute Settlement in the UN Convention on the Law of the Sea* (CUP 2005) 118; Rainer Lagoni, 'The Prompt Release of Vessels and Crews before the International Tribunal for the Law of the Sea: A Preparatory Report' (1996) 11 *International Journal of Marine and Coastal Law* 147, 148; Bernard Oxman, 'Observations on Vessel Release under the United Nations Convention on the Law of the Sea' (1996) 11 *International Journal of Marine and Coastal Law* 201, 202–04; Donald Rothwell and Tim Stephens, 'Illegal Southern Ocean Fishing and Prompt Release' (2004) 53 *ICLQ* 171, 171; *Law of the Sea* (n 73) 490; Yoshifumi Tanaka, 'Prompt Release in the United Nations Convention on the Law of the Sea: Some Reflections on the ITLOS Jurisprudence' (2004) 51 *Netherlands International Law Review* 237, 240; Tanaka, *Law of the Sea* (n 8) 530–31.

[102] *'Monte Confurco' (Seychelles v France)* [Judgment, 18 December 2000] ITLOS Rep 86, §§ 70–71; *'Volga' (Russian Federation v Australia)* [Judgment, 23 December 2002] ITLOS Rep 10, 65; *'Hoshinmaru' (Japan v Russian Federation)* [Judgment, 6 August 2007] ITLOS Rep 18, § 82; *'Tomimaru'* [2007] § 74. See also Oxman, 'Observations' (n 101) 204; Rothwell and Stephens, 'Illegal' (n 101) 171.

[103] Tanaka, *Law of the Sea* (n 8) 530–31; Tanaka, 'Prompt Release' (n 101) 240.

[104] *'Camouco'* [2000] § 71; *'Monte Confurco'* [2000] § 90; *'Juno Trader' (Saint Vincent and the Grenadines v Guinea-Bissau)* [Judgment, 18 December 2004] ITLOS Rep 17, § 78.

[105] Treves, 'Proceedings' (n 100) 182. For a similar position, see Myron Nordquist, Satya Nandan, Shabtai Rosenne and Neal Grandy (eds), *United Nations Convention on the Law of the Sea 1982 – A Commentary*, II (Martinus Nijhoff 1993) 795. See also Lagoni, 'Prompt Release' (n 101) 158.

A difficult task is the identification of the set of provisions of the LOSC whose violation entails the possible submission of an application for prompt release. This list of provisions is non-restrictive,[106] but the wording of Article 292 of the LOSC only gives room for the institution of prompt release proceedings if certain conditions are met. First, it must be a case where a power of qualified interference (ie detention) is conferred on coastal States by the LOSC – which means that the detention is lawful and squares with coastal States' enforcement jurisdiction.[107] Second, it must be a case where the LOSC explicitly enshrines a right to be released, conditional solely upon the posting of a bond.[108] Third, it must be a case where the coastal State has failed to comply with an obligation enshrined in the LOSC to post a (reasonable) bond, or to release the vessel and its crew, since the critical act is not the detention itself but the non-compliance with an international obligation of posting a bond and releasing.[109] If these conditions are met, the ITLOS can enforce the relevant provision of the LOSC by solely observing the existence of the breach and ordering the posting of a bond, or the release of the vessel and/or its crew.

This is a 'unique procedure – a special case of interference with the coastal State's judicial authorities',[110] which explains why, more than the balance of interests between coastal and flag States, this provision seeks to balance the role of domestic courts and the ITLOS, as well as to protect domestic authorities against excessive interferences from the international judiciary. In this vein, the scope of application of Article 292 of the LOSC is limited to cases where no discretion is conferred on the ITLOS.[111] Thus, beyond the scope of Article 292 of the LOSC are cases where the release of the vessel or its crew is conditional upon other factors apart from posting a bond; where the ITLOS has to assess topics other than the reasonableness of a bond or the release of the ship and its crew; or where it is asked if the laws and regulations enacted by a coastal State under its prescriptive jurisdiction comply with the LOSC.[112]

[106] Gudmundur Eiriksson, *The International Tribunal for the Law of the Sea* (Martinus Nijhoff 2000) 120. Contending that the list of provisions is restrictive, see *'M/V Saiga' (No. 1) (Saint Vincent and the Grenadines v Guinea)* [Judgment, 4 December 1997] ITLOS Rep 16, 'Collective Dissenting Opinion of Judges Park, Nelson, Chandrasekhara Rao, Vukas and Ndiaye' §§ 22–25.

[107] *M/V 'Saiga' (No. 1)* [1997] § 63. See also Karaman, *Dispute Resolution* (n 100) 29–30; Lindpere, 'Prompt Release' (n 100) 241–42. In this sense, 'Nothing pejorative or even critical of detaining State is implied in Article 292' (*'Camouco'* [2000] 'Declaration of Judge Laing', 1).

[108] *'Camouco'* [2000] § 59; *'Monte Confurco'* [2000] § 63; *'Volga'* [2002] § 59.

[109] *'Volga'* [2002] § 83; *'Grand Prince' (Belize v France)* [Judgment, 20 April 2001] ITLOS Rep 17, 'Separate Opinion of Judge Treves', 1.

[110] *M/V 'Saiga' (No. 1)* [1997] 'Collective Dissenting Opinion of Vice-President Wolfrum and Judge Yamamoto', § 16.

[111] Joseph Akl, 'Jurisprudence of the International Tribunal for the Law of the Sea in Prompt Release Proceedings', in Holger Hestermeyer, Doris König, Nele Matz-Lück, Volker Röben, Anja Seibert-Fohr, Peter-Tobias Stoll and Silja Vöneky (eds), *Coexistence, Cooperation and Solidarity – Liber Amicorum Rüdiger Wolfrum*, II (Nijhoff 2012) 1591, 1596; Oxman, 'Observations' (n 101) 208; Rothwell and Stephens, 'Illegal' (n 101) 185; Wegelein, 'Rules of the Tribunal' (n 100) 262.

[112] Rothwell and Stephens, 'Illegal' (n 101) 176; Treves, 'Proceedings' (n 100) 181.

This does not mean that other aspects of the detention of a vessel and its crew are irrelevant for international law. For instance, the force used in detention and the guarantees of domestic procedures must comply with international standards, which can be assessed by human rights bodies or under different proceedings established in Part XV of the LOSC.[113] However, Article 292 of the LOSC cannot be used to enforce these rights and provisions, since its sole function in international law is to provide for an urgent proceeding for the release of vessels and crews in the specific cases set out in the LOSC where strict requirements are met.[114]

In this context, three cases stand out in which a prompt release proceeding may be instituted under Article 292 of the LOSC:[115] if a bond has been paid, in accordance with Articles 73, 220(6) and 226(1)(b) of the LOSC, but the vessel and its crew have not been released as these provisions require; if the bond was requested by the detaining State under such provisions, but its amount is disputed on grounds of unreasonableness; if the detaining State has not requested the posting of a bond under such provisions, for example for lack of a domestic rule in that regard. All three cases are critical, but only the first is unlawful pursuant to the LOSC.

One goal of Article 292 of the LOSC is to create an independent and international remedy open to some players engaged in international navigation. Considering that important values might be at risk in the case of detention of vessels and crews (ie human freedom and freedom of navigation), the core goal of Article 292 of the LOSC is to provide the players with an urgent proceeding suitable to protect these values in a short period. Urgency, thus, is *the* rationale behind Article 292 of the LOSC.

[113] Robin Churchill, 'Dispute Settlement under the UN Convention on the Law of the Sea: Survey for 2007' (2008) 23 *International Journal of Marine and Coastal Law* 601, 613. See, for example, *Guyana v Suriname* [Award, 17 September 2007] PCA Case No. 2004-04, §§ 405–06.

[114] *M/V 'Saiga' (No. 1)* [1997] § 62; *'Volga'* [2002] §§ 81–83. See also Andrea Cannone, *Il Tribunale Internazionale del Diritto del Mare* (Cacucci 1991) 125; Thomas Mensah, 'The Tribunal and the Prompt Release of Vessels' (2007) 22 *International Journal of Marine and Coastal Law* 425, 438; Oxman, 'Observations' (n 101) 208–09.

[115] *M/V 'Saiga' (No. 1)* [1997] § 52. See also Akl, 'Jurisprudence' (n 111) 1596; David Anderson, 'Investigation, Detention and Release of Foreign Vessels under the UN Convention on the Law of the Sea of 1982 and Other International Agreements' (1996) 11 *International Journal of Marine and Coastal Law* 165, 169 and 170–76; Cannone, *Il Tribunale* (n 114) 121; Robin Churchill, 'Some Reflections on the Operation of the Dispute Settlement System of the UN Convention on the Law of the Sea During Its First Decade', in Freestone et al (eds), *The Law of the Sea* (n 11) 388, 393; Karaman, *Dispute Resolution* (n 100) 28; Klein, *Dispute Settlement* (n 101) 86; Noyes, 'International Tribunal' (n 100) 134; Treves, 'Proceedings' (n 100) 182–85; Treves, 'Article 292' (n 100) 1885; Tanaka, *Law of the Sea* (n 8) 532; Tanaka, 'Prompt Release' (n 101) 241; Seline Trevisanut, 'The Exercise of Administrative Functions by ITLOS: A Comment on Prompt Release Cases', in Nerina Boschiero, Tullio Scovazzi, Cesare Pitea and Chiara Ragni (eds), *International Courts and the Development of International Law – Essays in Honour of Tullio Treves* (Springer 2013) 311, 311–12; Wegelein, 'Rules of the Tribunal' (n 100) 271–73; Rüdiger Wolfrum, 'The Settlement of Disputes before the International Tribunal for the Law of the Sea – A Progressive Development of International Law or Relying on Traditional Mechanisms?' (2008) 51 *Japanese Yearbook of International Law* 140, 149.

With that in mind, the LOSC establishes that 'the question of release from detention may be submitted to any court or tribunal agreed upon by the parties or, failing such agreement within 10 days from the time of detention, to a court or tribunal accepted by the detaining State under [Article 287 of the LOSC] or to the [ITLOS], unless the parties otherwise agree'.[116] Thus, the LOSC held on to the principle of free choice of means, but dropped out the rule of subsidiarity of international remedies vis-à-vis domestic bodies, implying that remedies of the detaining State do not need to be exhausted beforehand.[117] Moreover, the (free) choice of means ought to be exercised within a very short time limit of 10 days, so that the alleged wrongdoing might be redressed in a very short time also. Finally, the jurisdiction of the ITLOS (or other body, if that is the case) is compulsory, and thus the flag State can ignite the proceedings irrespective of the agreement of the detaining State.

Once instituted, the proceedings are construed in order to achieve an expeditious decision without prejudice to the guarantees of a fair trial. To ensure an expeditious (but not perfunctory) decision, Article 111(1) of the ITLOS Rules requires the applicant to submit to the ITLOS only a 'succinct statement of facts and legal grounds upon which the application is based'. Then, Article 292(3) of the LOSC establishes that 'The court or tribunal shall deal without delay with the application for release'. With that in mind, Article 112(1) of the ITLOS Rules further states that applications for prompt release of vessels and crews 'shall [have] priority … over all other proceedings before the [ITLOS]'. Plus, if the applicant has so requested and the detaining State concurs with it, the application shall be dealt with by the ITLOS's Chamber of Summary Procedure.[118] Finally, it is established that the judgment shall be delivered as soon as possible.[119]

If the requirements are met, the ITLOS shall deliver a judgment[120] whose *dictum* consists of an order to release the vessel and/or crew members, conditional upon the posting of a bond, unless it has already been posted. As said, three cases are more likely to be brought before the ITLOS: if the bond has been posted, but the vessel and its crew have not been released; if the bond has been requested, but its amount is considered unreasonable; and if the bond has not been requested by the detaining State. In the first case, the decision of the ITLOS will limit itself to declaring that the requirements for the prompt release are met, and thus the detaining State has a positive obligation, under the LOSC, to release the vessel and/or its crew. In the second case, the ITLOS shall decide on the reasonableness and exact amount of the bond. In the third case, the ITLOS

[116] Article 292(1) of the LOSC.

[117] See *Draft Rules of the International Tribunal for the Law of the Sea*: Doc. LOS/PCN/SCN.4/L.10/add.1, § 31 (14 August 1989). See also *'Camouco'* [2000] §§ 57–58; *'Camouco'* [2000] 'Dissenting Opinion of Judge Vukas', § 4.

[118] Article 112(1) of the ITLOS Rules.

[119] Article 112(4) of the ITLOS Rules.

[120] Article 112(4) of the ITLOS Rules.

shall fix the exact amount of a reasonable bond. Hence, the ITLOS has variable powers in face of the different situations brought before it, but one aspect seems clear: the ITLOS will not consider the detaining State 'guilty' of any wrongdoing and neither will it be formally 'condemned'; at most, the ITLOS 'orders',[121] or 'determines that the State shall comply',[122] with the obligations needed for the enforcement of the judgment under Article 292(4) of the LOSC. This is consistent with the object of the proceeding – ie the release of the vessel and/or its crew members, not the punishment of the detaining State. This might seem of minor importance, but in fact it improves the room for private actors' participation, since it limits interference from the international judiciary in the legal sphere of the detaining State.

Once delivered, the judgment must be promptly complied with by the detaining State,[123] whereas the flag State has the onus of paying the bond determined by the ITLOS if it wants to make sure the judgment is binding upon the detaining State[124] (although a special rule exists with respect to applications submitted on behalf of the flag State, as will be seen below). Once the judgment is delivered, domestic courts have to comply with it 'as far as the release of the vessel and the bond or other security are concerned', but 'are not bound by any findings of fact or law that the [ITLOS] may have made in order to reach its conclusions'.[125] To improve the enforcement of the judgment and the release of the vessel and its crew, some scholars consider that States should confer on the judgment of the ITLOS the same *exequatur* that is conferred by Article 21(2) of Annex III on the decisions of dispute settlement bodies deciding on Part XI of the LOSC,[126] at least since the moment the ITLOS is notified that the bond or other financial security has been posted. This solution would be reasonable because the release of the vessel and its crew (ie compliance of the ITLOS judgment) depends only upon domestic authorities. However, this solution was not transposed into the LOSC.

2.2. The Submission of Applications on Behalf of the Flag State

At first sight, it appears that prompt release proceedings have been conceived as inter-State cases, following the matrix of dispute settlement in the LOSC. However, Article 292(2) of the LOSC establishes that the application for release might be made by the flag State itself, or on its behalf.[127] The meaning of this

[121] *'Camouco'* [2000] § 78(3).
[122] *M/V 'Saiga' (No. 1)* [1997] § 86(2); *'Monte Confurco'* [2000] § 96(5); *'Volga'* [2002] § 95(4); *'Juno Trader'* [2004] § 104(4); *'Hoshinmaru'* [2007] § 102(4).
[123] Article 296(1) of the LOSC.
[124] Treves, 'Proceedings' (n 100) 193.
[125] *M/V 'Saiga' (No. 1)* [1997] § 49.
[126] Treves, 'Proceedings' (n 100) 199.
[127] See also Article 110(1) of the ITLOS Rules.

reference 'on behalf of flag States' is disputed. In any event, to hold on to the semantic element, two ideas seem clear: other legal persons apart from flag States can submit an application for the prompt release of vessels or crews; but these persons must still be acting *on behalf* of the flag State. Prima facie, that seems to be the case of a State agent with a functional link to that State but who does not need to submit the powers of attorney. The apparent enlargement of the circle resonates well with Article 20 of the ITLOS Statute, which prescribes that (apart from the exceptional cases relating to Part XI of the LOSC or a special agreement conferring jurisdiction on the ITLOS) only States can be parties in proceedings before this court.

In this vein, two readings of this provision are possible: a water-tanked reading, according to which an application for the prompt release of vessels and crews can only be submitted by those who act in a specific public-like category; and a liberal reading, according to which private actors can submit the said applications.

Under the first reading, only flag States (and international organisations parties to the LOSC) can submit an application for the prompt release of vessels and crews. Thus, even if the economic interest at stake is private, States will be admitted to the proceedings in the interest of the ship-owner or other private actors under the aegis of flag State protection.[128] For their part, private actors can only submit claims before domestic fora.[129] In this vein, the possibility enshrined in Article 292(2) of the LOSC would be explained as a guarantee of the urgency of the procedure, and should not be read as a formulation aimed at enhancing participation of private actors. This reading of Article 292(2) of the LOSC should not be surprising: if the only link between a private actor and the law of the sea is the nationality of the vessel, then the only protection needed would be the flag State protection:[130] the flag State is the sole representative in the international arena of the vessel's and ship-owner's interests, even in cases where their participation is more nominal than real, as with vessels flying a flag of convenience.[131] Thus, it would seem that under Article 292 of the LOSC only flag States are equipped with a right of action.[132] But when submitting an application before an international body, States are free to choose their own representatives, agents and counsel, who might act on their behalf before that body. Often these individuals are not State officials, but rather private attorneys, hired ad hoc for a specific case, and whose selection and fees can be made and

[128] ED Brown, 'The *M/V 'Saiga'* Case on Prompt Release of Detained Vessels – The First Judgment of the International Tribunal for the Law of the Sea' (1998) 22 *Marine Policy* 307, 310; Treves, 'Proceedings' (n 100) 180.

[129] Lagoni, 'Prompt Release' (n 101) 161.

[130] *M/V 'Saiga' (No. 2)* [1999] § 106; *M/V 'Virginia G' (Panama v Guinea-Bissau)* [Judgment, 14 April 2014] ITLOS Rep 4, §§ 126–27.

[131] Klein, *Dispute Settlement* (n 101) 88; Vicuña, 'Individuals' (n 59) 58,; Vicuña, *Dispute Settlement* (n 59) 82.

[132] Eiriksson, *International Tribunal* (n 106) 118.

paid by the ship-owner or operator. These private attorneys 'play an irreplaceable role before international tribunals in aiding the administration of justice',[133] and they can submit applications for prompt release of vessels and crews on behalf of the flag State, for they fit in a broad category of State agents.[134] In the practice of the ITLOS most applications for prompt release were submitted by private attorneys on behalf of the flag State.[135]

At first sight, Article 110(2) of the ITLOS Rules confirms this line of thought when it provides that

> [a] State Party may … notify the [ITLOS] of: *(a)* the State authorities competent to authorize persons to make applications on its behalf under article 292 of the Convention; *(b)* the name and address of any person who is authorized to make an application on its behalf.

This provision aims to ensure that applications submitted on behalf of a flag State are actually made on behalf of it.[136] Even though the ITLOS Rules cannot supersede the text of the LOSC, it suggests that the practice of the ITLOS is to admit applications submitted not by any private actor, but rather by those who have a special power of representation of the flag State.

A different reading of this provision (which I follow) considers that applications submitted under Article 292(2) of the LOSC are not limited to those submitted by State agents or officials, but include also a private actor *lato sensu*, provided that it is authorised by the flag State.[137] In this case, only two requirements need to be met: the flag State must have authorised submissions on its behalf; and the vessel must fly the flag of the applicant State.[138] However, the ship-owner or operator may have a different nationality.[139]

[133] *'Grand Prince'* [2001] 'Declaration of Judge ad hoc Cot', § 9.

[134] Lagoni, 'Prompt Release' (n 101) 161; Chandrasekhara Rao, 'The International Tribunal for the Law of the Sea: An Evaluation', in Nisuke Ando, Edward McWhinner and Rüdiger Wolfrum (eds), *Liber Amicorum Judge Shigeru Oda* (Kluwer 2002) 667, 673; Jean-Pierre Cot, 'Appearing "for" or "on behalf of" a State: The Role of Private Counsel before International Tribunals', in Ando et al (eds), ibid 835, 840.

[135] *M/V 'Saiga' (No. 1)* [1997] §§ 41 and 44; *'Camouco'* [2000] § 1; *'Monte Confurco'* [2000] § 1 (together with a law professor); *'Grand Prince'* [2001] §§ 1 and 6; *'Chaisiri Reefer 2' (Panama v Yemen)* [Order, 13 July 2001] ITLOS Rep 82, § 3; *'Juno Trader'* [2004] § 1 (private corporations were advisers of the flag State). In *M/V 'Saiga' (No. 2)* [1999], the flag State was also represented by a private attorney. The other cases were submitted by (and not on behalf of) the flag States: *'Volga'* [2002] § 1, in which the agents of the flag State had to be authorised to represent it according to the same procedure as the private attorneys who act on behalf of it; *'Hoshinmaru'* [2007] § 1; *'Tomimaru'* [2007] § 1.

[136] Eiriksson, *International Tribunal* (n 106) 207.

[137] Matthew Drenan, 'Gone Overboard: Why the Arctic Sunrise Case Signals an Over-Expansion of the Ship-as-a-Unit Concept in the Diplomatic Protection Context' (2014) 54 *California Western ILJ* 109, 125–26; Klein, *Dispute Settlement* (n 101) 88; Noyes, 'International Tribunal' (n 100) 132; Sohn, 'Settlement' (n 100) 209; Tanaka, *Law of the Sea* (n 8) 531, & 'Prompt Release' (n 101) 251; Treves, 'Proceedings' (n 100) 188, & 'Article 292' (n 13) 1890; Wegelein, 'Rules of the Tribunal' (n 100) 260; Wolfrum, 'Settlement of Disputes' (n 115) 145.

[138] Tanaka, *Law of the Sea* (n 8) 531; 'Prompt Release' (n 101) 251.

[139] Trevisanut, 'Exercise' (n 115) 315.

In fact, Article 292 of the LOSC is the only provision in this treaty that uses the expression 'on behalf of' as opposed to 'by'.[140] As a general rule of interpretation, if a meaningful and valuable interpretation of a rule is to be achieved, 'Redundancy should not be presumed'.[141] As a result, one should avoid a reading that leads to the conclusion that two words that are used as being alternative or opposing have actually the same meaning. In this sense, Oxman is correct when mentioning that the LOSC uses the formula 'applications submitted by or on behalf of the flag State' to introduce an alternative that would not exist if applications were submitted *by* States only.[142] If an interpretation of Article 292 of the LOSC leads to a result where the categories of persons who can submit an application by *or* on behalf of the flag State are the same, then that reading should not be considered since it is hindered by general rules on interpretation: when Article 292(2) of the LOSC uses the expression 'or on behalf of the flag State', it aims at encompassing realities that would not be included under the formula 'by the flag State'. Therefore, an important obstacle to the narrow reading of Article 292 of the LOSC is that it leads to redundancy: if the interpretation of this provision is to include solely those private attorneys that might act as representatives, agents or counsel, one is depriving this provision of an autonomous content, for these persons could always participate in the proceedings in an application submitted *by* the flag State:[143] the newly added information would perhaps be limited to excusing these persons from submitting their powers of attorney or of representation. To confine the reading of Article 292(2) of the LOSC to the admission of applications submitted by private attorneys on behalf of the flag State is only possible if the reader is clouded by an interpretative bias that leads him to a reading in accordance with his prior prejudices regarding private access to international dispute settlement. Even if not consciously, the driver of this interpretation of Article 292(2) of the LOSC was the need to find a reading of the terms 'on behalf of' that would not include private applicants.

In the second place, it would be strange if the aim of Article 292 of the LOSC (as of Article 110 of the ITLOS Rules) was to exclude private actors from submitting applications for the prompt release of vessels and crews with a certain degree of freedom from the flag State, or otherwise the urgency of the proceeding would not be explained. If the sole interests protected by Article 292 of the LOSC were the flag State's interests, there would be no need for such an expeditious procedure: the existing remedies, including provisional measures, would be suitable to protect the flag State's navigational interests. However, urgency exists because 'The economic interest underlying the dispute

[140] Oxman, 'Observations' (n 101) 211.
[141] ibid. See also Alf Ross, *On Law and Justice* (Lawbook Exchange 2012) 132–33.
[142] Noyes, 'International Tribunal' (n 100) 147; Oxman, 'Observations' (n 101) 211.
[143] Oxman, 'Observations' (n 101) 211 and 212.

is … a private one'.[144] Moreover, if urgency itself cannot be understood in a context of pure inter-State disputes, one would have to ask why the same solution (submission of applications on behalf of a State by its attorneys) should not be extended to all other procedures before the ITLOS. This argument per se is not solid enough to establish a liberal reading of Article 292 of the LOSC, but it shows that this liberal understanding squares much better with the *telos* of this provision.

In the third place, liberal access of private actors in prompt release proceedings echoes the drafting history of the LOSC, including of this provision. The US delegation sought to introduce innovative provisions entitling certain private actors to international disputes: they were successful in deep seabed mining proceedings, and on establishing that the ITLOS might be open to entities other than States.[145] Yet in prompt release proceedings, the compromise formula was to establish formally an inter-State dispute, in which private actors could have some participation.[146] As an argument, this is a double-edged sword, for it also suggests that the drafters of the LOSC considered and ruled out a liberal access to the ITLOS. However, from the preparatory works of the LOSC, it seems reasonable to argue that the formula adopted in the final version of this article was meant not to compromise with a specific reading. Therefore, the wording of Article 292(2) of the LOSC was an ingenious solution to allow participation of private actors in prompt release proceedings without lifting the veil of Statehood.[147] By creating a proceeding where the flag State is nominally present, Article 292(2) of the LOSC is ingrained with a bias against private participation in international dispute settlement.

As a result, a broad interpretation of Article 292(2) of the LOSC is more in line with the interpretative canons set out in Articles 31–33 VCLT and entails that other applicants (such as private actors and other States)[148] may submit an application on behalf of the flag State. Nonetheless, this liberal reading of Article 292(2) of the LOSC has its own limits. The fact that private actors must submit their applications on behalf of the *flag* State implies that their participation in prompt release proceedings is still constrained by the action of flag States. To begin with, it is still required that the flag State authorises private

[144] Treves, 'Proceedings' (n 100) 180.

[145] Anderson, 'Investigation' (n 115) 167; Oxman, 'Observations' (n 101) 212.

[146] Oxman, 'Observations' (n 101) 212–13.

[147] Treves, 'Proceedings' (n 100) 188.

[148] According to Article 18 of the *Draft Articles on Diplomatic Protection*, the State of nationality of a crew member can exercise diplomatic protection and therefore can have standing in the dispute settlement procedures established in the LOSC if the requirement of flag State intervention is not specifically mentioned. In the case of Article 292 of the LOSC, the wording is clear and only the flag State (or someone on behalf of it) may submit applications for the prompt release of vessels and crew members. However, the flag State can also authorise its intervention under Article 292(2) of the LOSC.

actors to submit an application for the prompt release of vessels and crews. The most pragmatic option would be for the flag State to submit in advance a list of persons – by name or category (eg the ship-owners or operators, shipping associations, or trade unions)[149] – who are entitled to submit an application on its behalf, being the flag State free to change or withdraw this list.[150] Domestic decision-making procedures can be slow and bureaucratic (in some cases, intervention of parliaments might be required), and as such the urgency of instituting the proceedings might be hampered if ad hoc authorisations are to be given on a regular basis.[151] If this is the case, that does not mean that other persons are excluded from submitting an application on behalf of the flag State, but rather that they need an ad hoc authorisation from the flag State.[152] In the first case, the right of private applicants has a self-executing character; in the second case, it has not. This solution fits well with the text of Article 110(2) of the ITLOS Rules. As a result, even if in practice some private actors might have a liberal access to the ITLOS in prompt release proceedings, they need the flag State to act as the gatekeeper to their participation (which is further evidence of a bias against private membership in international law). One advantage of this interpretation is that it gives room for flag States not to involve themselves too much (including their financial and human resources) without prejudice to allowing the prompt release application to be submitted.[153] In this case, it is up to the private actor to balance the pros and cons of posting a bond and submitting an application.[154]

In this framework, Article 292 of the LOSC is, in fact, an heir of a Vattelian narrative of international law, under which States are the sole or major representatives of the relevant interests at the international level, including the interests of private actors. The proceeding is still formally inter-State,[155] and the flag State is not overridden as the primary legal subject in the quarrel.[156] In the end, the right to submit applications on behalf of the flag State is not primarily aimed at voicing the acknowledgment of the position of private actors in the law of the sea, but mostly to guarantee the urgent nature of the prompt release procedure – as those supporting the narrow reading of this provision contend.

[149] Joseph Akl, 'Article 110', in Chandrasekhara Rao and Phillipe Gautier (eds), *The Rules of the International Tribunal for the Law of the Sea* (Martinus Nijhoff 2006) 309; Oxman, 'Observations' (n 101) 212; Treves, 'Proceedings' (n 100) 188; Wegelein, 'Rules of the Tribunal' (n 100) 260–61.

[150] Oxman, 'Observations' (n 101) 212.

[151] Treves, 'Proceedings' (n 100) 189.

[152] Oxman, 'Observations' (n 101) 212.

[153] Karaman, *Dispute Resolution* (n 100) 44; Tullio Treves, 'Flags of Convenience before the Law of the Sea Tribunal' (2004) 6 *San Diego International Law Journal* 179, 185.

[154] Oxman, 'Observations' (n 101) 212.

[155] See generally Cot, 'Appearing' (n 134) 844; Trevisanut, 'Exercise' (n 115) 316. In the *Grand Prince* case, the ITLOS stated that the flag State is the only entity with *locus standi* in prompt release proceedings. Yet, this reference was specifically made to explain why the applicant State, not being the flag State, could not be party in the proceedings ('*Grand Prince*' [2001] §§ 66 and 93).

[156] Wegelein, 'Rules of the Tribunal' (n 100) 261.

To understand this apparent paradox, an analogy with the case of deep seabed mining operators is helpful. To undertake activities in the Area, these entities need the sponsoring of their State of nationality. Yet their access to international dispute settlement is more liberal, since in their case there is a direct, contractual jural relation with the Authority, and the sponsoring of the State of nationality is already required during the performance of the exploration or exploitation contract. But even in this case, the Vattelian conception of international law led the drafters of the LOSC to include the right of the sponsoring State of participation in the proceedings,[157] as well as the right of a respondent State to require the participation of the sponsoring State in the proceedings.[158] In prompt release proceedings, where no such direct relation with the Authority exists, a more liberal approach would not be acceptable for the drafters of the LOSC. The option, thus, was between allowing direct access to private actors, unless the flag and the detaining State object, or allowing an indirect access, in case the flag State so accords:[159] a clear choice for the second model was made, in order to respect the sensitivity of the issue and of the respondent State.

In any event, implicit in Article 292(2) of the LOSC is a procedural right of private actors:[160] when duly authorised by the flag State, they can freely submit before the ITLOS applications for the prompt release of vessels and crews. This right is conditional upon the flag State's initial authorisation to submit applications. As a result, in some cases this right will have a self-executing character, whilst in other cases it will lack this nature. But that does not preclude, on the one hand, a procedural right from being assigned to private actors under this provision, in procedural replacement of the flag State, and, on the other hand, the erosion of the fiction of the espousal of a claim by the flag State, by 'translat[ing] the material rights at the center of the dispute into procedural rights'.[161]

One final point to mention is that the autonomy (although limited) of the procedural right held by private actors has important consequences: as authorisation and control do not mean conduct of the proceedings by the flag State, this latter cannot be held responsible for the conducts of private actors acting on its behalf, or for its outcomes – particularly under Article 8 of the ARSIWA. In fact, decommissioning justice to private actors has its consequences. With respect to private attorneys, one has to agree with Judge *ad hoc* Cot, who stated that 'the lawyer-agent is not necessarily in close contact with the authorities of the flag State'.[162] His major concern was with 'credibility and reliability' of

[157] Article 190(1) of the LOSC.
[158] Article 190(2) of the LOSC.
[159] Oxman, 'Observations' (n 101) 213.
[160] Cot, 'Appearing' (n 134) 846; Wegelein, 'Rules of the Tribunal' (n 100) 266. By implication, see '*Grand Prince*' [2001] 'Declaration of Judge *ad hoc* Cot', § 11.
[161] Trevisanut, 'Exercise' (n 115) 316.
[162] '*Grand Prince*' [2001] 'Declaration of Judge *ad hoc* Cot', § 14.

information provided to the ITLOS, but the same concern can be voiced with respect to private applicants acting on behalf of the flag State.[163]

Three issues need to be tackled. If the proceedings are instituted in the absence of a bond posted by the coastal State, or challenging its reasonableness, the ITLOS will ask the coastal State to post it or to fix the amount of a reasonable bond. In both cases, the bond will be paid by the ship-owner or its insurance company,[164] but the flag State cannot be asked to pay the bond posted or to ensure, by whatever means provided for by international law, that the private actor posts the bond established. In fact, when submitted on behalf of the flag State, the interest and the risk of the proceedings are assumed by the private applicant, which means that the private applicant himself assumes that, if the claim is successful, he will post the bond required. Providing *exequatur* to the decisions of the ITLOS would help, for in this case the private applicant could be forced to post the bond (possibly under the domestic legal systems of the detaining State or even the flag State). Moreover, if the conduct of the private applicant acting on behalf of the flag State fails to meet certain standards (eg if it constitutes an abuse of the right of action, or an unreasonable litigation conduct), only he can be held accountable: that derives from the fact that, under the ARSIWA, the procedural conduct of the private actor cannot be attributed to the flag State. Finally, and for the same reason, if damage arises afterwards (eg because the ship is kept in a port for a failure attributable to the ship-owner or operator), only the private applicant (if the ship-owner or operator) can be held accountable.

This, however, leaves one question open for discussion: if the proceeding is submitted nominally on behalf of the flag State, can the State afterwards decide to intervene in the proceedings as a proper party (ie in lieu of the private applicant)? The silence of the LOSC and the ITLOS Rules should not be read as denying this possibility to the flag State, since nominally and formally it was for the flag State to institute proceedings. At most, this silence is a sign that the drafters did not consider this hypothesis. In fact, the triangular relation at the primary level should entail some resonance at the secondary level also. For example, pursuant to Article 34 of the ECHR, private actors can submit an application to the ECtHR. In this case, the home State of the applicant is entitled to submit written comments and to take part in the hearings under Article 36(1) of the ECHR. Of particular note, according to this provision, is the fact that participation of the home State is framed in terms of 'third-party intervention', which explains why the home State can submit alternative views but cannot substitute the private applicant in the proceedings. In this

[163] Cot, 'Appearing' (n 134) 842.
[164] Trevisanut, 'Exercise' (n 115) 316.

case, thus, the procedural level is mimetic of the trilateral nature of the jural relation established at the primary level. But the same, however, cannot be said with respect to the applications submitted under Article 292 of the LOSC on behalf of the flag State. In this case, a bilateral procedural relation is established (although artificial), which means that any intervention from the flag State would be made as the proper applicant, substituting the private actor who submitted the application. In my view, since the application is nominally and formally submitted by the flag State, it can intervene in the proceedings, thereby excluding private applicants. However, it cannot, for example, submit new or alternative views, replace the statement of facts, or provide new legal arguments: if it decides to intervene, it has to accept as its own the procedural acts of the private applicant, or otherwise the authorisation issued by the flag State would be meaningless, and the guarantees of the coastal State (ie the respondent State) would be jeopardised. Moreover, if it assumes the procedural conduct of the private applicant, it also becomes responsible for paying the bond fixed by the ITLOS. This is not the same thing as saying that Article 292(2) of the LOSC does not support private applications for the prompt release of vessels and crew members on behalf of the flag State, but ultimately it leads to a similar result since it enables the flag State to remove authorised private applicants from the international proceedings.

2.3. The Importance of Having Remedies

The slim practice regarding prompt release proceedings confirms a bias against private participation in international law. In fact, access to international remedies by private actors is only possible in specific international legal regimes and subject to certain conditions, which is the case for prompt release proceedings. The limited access to international dispute settlement and the interpretative bias against private access to international judicial proceedings may be explained by the function of remedies in the international legal system.

In fact, remedies play several functions in the legal system, including enlightening the reader of the international legal rule on the nature and structure of rights and duties conferred on private actors. In fact, one of the problems of the legal personality of a private actor under international law is that it is difficult to determine with surgical accuracy when he holds a primary or substantive right conferred by an international legal norm. For international legal scholars this problem equates to dark matter for experimental physicists: rights held by private actors are hard to observe directly, but one can look at the gravitational effects around them. In this sense, when in doubt whether a specific treaty rule confers a right on a private actor, the fact that coupled to that norm is a specific international remedy available to private actors makes it possible to ascertain that private actors hold that right under international law, for it is difficult to conceive a remedy without a virtual substantive right being applicable.[165] In this sense, the Roman principle *ubi jus, ibi remedium* can be reversed in order to mean that the same way every right *should* have a specific remedy, every remedy *is meant* to afford protection to a right. Thereby, remedies are not *the*, or even *a*, requirement of legal subjectivity, but rather an indicator: in the absence of other interpretative elements, the existence of an international remedy indicates that the primary right or duty enforced through that mechanism is valid within the international legal order; and per se, as a secondary right, it is direct evidence of international legal capacity. As such, in order to determine whether a legal person engages in processes of international law, remedies are *ipso facto* a form of engagement in this legal order under rules of secondary nature, and at the same time evidence of engagement in this legal order under rules of primary nature. To consider that private applicants can institute a prompt release procedure implies that they also hold primary rights under the LOSC (eg navigational entitlements).

Another function of remedies is to enable all subjects of law – including those who lack law-making capacity – to influence the downstream production of law through the impact of case law in the building of the legal system. This idea gives flesh to Lowe's binary function of international litigation: a private, retrospective function, aimed at settling the dispute; and a public, prospective function, aimed at future cases in which the same rules and reasoning might be applicable.[166] I do not challenge that the primary function of international courts, tribunals and other bodies is to settle legal disputes, and not to create new rules.[167] Therefore, Article 21 of Annex VI of the LOSC makes clear that, apart from an advisory competence of ITLOS, the natural function of this body is to settle legal disputes submitted before it. As an ultimate guarantee of judicial constraint, Article 33(2) of Annex VI of the LOSC establishes that judicial decisions have no binding effect except between the parties to the dispute.

My claim is not that Article 38(1)(d) of the ICJ Statute should be amended in order to qualify judicial decisions as a formal source of international law, or that a formal rule of precedent should be incorporated in international law; and I do not discuss whether, theoretically, judges can perform a law-making activity hand in hand with other authoritative institutions. My argument is only that the

[165] See inter alia Anne Peters, *Beyond Human Rights – The Legal Status of the Individual in International Law* (CUP 2016) 46. Nonetheless, this idea does not perforce apply to States, as they can hold a secondary right detached from a primary right, notably within the framework of diplomatic protection.

[166] Vaughan Lowe, 'The Function of Litigation in International Society' (2012) 61 *ICLQ* 209, 212. See *mutatis mutandis* Vaughan Lowe and Antonios Tzanakopoulos, 'The Development of the Law of the Sea by the International Court of Justice', in Christian Tams and James Sloan (eds), *The Development of International Law by the International Court of Justice* (OUP 2013) 177, 178.

[167] *Legality of the Threat or Use of Nuclear Weapons* [Advisory Opinion, 8 July 1996] ICJ Rep 226, § 18. See also, eg, Alan Boyle and Christine Chinkin, *The Making of International Law* (OUP 2007) 266; James Harrison, 'Judicial Law-Making and the Developing Order of the Oceans' (2007) 22 *International Journal of Marine and Coastal Law* 283, 284.

difference between upstream and downstream production of international law, as between making and applying the law, is more quantitative and procedural than qualitative.[168] To some extent, the actual content of legal norms depends upon its interpretation and application to specific cases, since only very rarely does a legal norm encompass one single meaning. Thus, in each process of interpretation and application of a treaty or customary rule, both redundancy and new information are added to the legal norm, enlightening the players in the legal system about the reading of that rule and what behaviour should be adopted to comply with it:[169] 'Judges ... are authors as well as critics. A judge deciding ... adds to the tradition he interprets; future judges confront a new tradition that includes what he has done'.[170] Thereby, irrespective of one's position regarding the role of courts in the legal systems, the fact is that they do play a role in the making of international law.[171] In the case of international law, as a result of the development of international adjudication in the last decades, judicial law-making is not a 'collateral effect' of adjudication,[172] but rather a natural effect.

Nonetheless, this does not mean that no hierarchy exists between making and applying the law, but rather that all moments of interpretation and application of a legal norm imply the breeding of new information that will be attached to the rule and the architecture of the legal system, and thus the nurturing of new norms for the legal system. In international law, accordingly, 'litigation [is not] simply a civilized alternative to the use of force. Cases make law'.[173] In fact, in the international legal system – where no central entity is responsible for the downstream production of norms, no authoritative law-making process exists, and customary law still holds a prominent role as a major source of law[174] – the role of the judicature is even more evident than in domestic legal systems: courts are responsible for illuminating the content of international rules and for providing consistency, stability, foreseeability and uniformity to the legal system.[175]

[168] Paul Stephan, 'Privatizing International Law' (2011) 97 *Virginia Law Review* 1573, 1587. As Dworkin affirmed, 'the distinction between author and interpreter [is] more a matter of different aspects of the same [mental] process': *Law's Empire* (Hart Publishing 1998) 229.

[169] Lowe, 'Function of Litigation' (n 166) 213.

[170] Dworkin, *Law's Empire* (n 168) 229.

[171] See generally Boyle and Chinkin, *Making* (n 167) 268; Eric De Brabandere, 'The Use of Precedent and External Case Law by the International Court of Justice and the International Tribunal for the Law of the Sea' (2016) 15 *The Law and Practice of International Courts & Tribunals* 24, 27–28; Geir Ulfstein, 'The International Judiciary', in Klabbers, Peters and Ulfstein (eds), *The Constitutionalization of International Law* (OUP 2009) 126, 127.

[172] Armin von Bogdandy and Ingo Venzke, 'Beyond Dispute: International Institutions as Lawmakers' (2011) 12 *German Law Journal* 979, 981.

[173] Lowe, 'Function of Litigation' (n 166) 214.

[174] Boyle and Chinkin, *Making* (n 167) 268; Harrison, 'Judicial Law-Making' (n 167) 284.

[175] Boyle and Chinkin, *Making* (167) 268.

In this context, because the ITLOS has a pivotal role in the dispute settlement system provided for under the LOSC, on the one hand, and has an accumulated experience with respect to law of the sea issues, on the other, decisions from the ITLOS regarding prompt release proceedings (although perfunctory) carry the necessary *auctoritas* to shape the provisions of the LOSC and to be significant to all players in the law of the sea, and not only to the parties in particular proceedings.[176] As such, procedural rights of private applicants can *de facto* compensate private actors for their lack of law-making capacities, and allow them to bring new topics before international institutions, therefore helping to shape the reading of the provisions of the LOSC. As a result, procedural rights are not only evidence of a primary right or a means to challenge States in the international arena; they can also help to change the reading of international law. Having in mind this *de facto* function of international litigation, it is hard to reconcile the access of private applicants to the ITLOS (although limited to the prompt release proceedings) with a State-to-State conception of international law. An implicit interpretative bias follows naturally and excludes a reading of Article 292(2) of the LOSC that allows the submission of private applications.

3. CONCLUSION

The purpose of this chapter is to provide the reader with examples of how the law of the sea has followed other domains of international law that equip private actors with explicit entitlements. That is the case, in the examples given, of the right of exclusive exploration for and/or exploitation of resources in the Area, the right of ownership over collected resources, the entitlements that are derivative and ancillary to the application and the development of the Area's activities, the procedural rights before the SDC, and the right to submit applications for the prompt release of vessels and/or crew-members on behalf of the flag State. Common to all these cases is the fact that the wording of the relevant provisions of the LOSC is not unclear: quite the opposite, the canons of treaty interpretation under Articles 31–33 of the VCLT validate that private actors enjoy rights and duties directly under those provisions.

Nonetheless, in the same way that interpretation can be a tool for enhancing private participation in the international legal system, it can also be used to disenfranchise or reduce the role of private actors within the international legal system. The practice with respect to activities in the Area and prompt release applications is very slim, but they confirm that the interpretative bias against private participation (based on prior conceptions of what is international law and who holds rights and duties under its rules) can impact the reading of the

[176] Harrison, 'Judicial Law-Making' (n 167) 284.

LOSC and other international treaties. In the case of the activities in the Area, the best example refers to the views shared by the SDC with respect to the role of the sponsoring State, where the SDC ultimately configured private mining as an activity centred not on the miner, but on its sponsoring State. With respect to the submission of prompt release applications on behalf of the flag State, the same interpretative bias has driven some to suggest that, despite the wording and *telos* of Article 292(2) of the LOSC, only flag States and their private attorneys have the right to submit those applications.

As with respect to navigational entitlements, the impact of an interpretative bias on the reading of provisions that explicitly confer rights and duties on private actors is evidence that the fight for inclusion ought to take place also at the interpretative level, hand in hand with the rules on treaty interpretation set out in Articles 31–33 of the VCLT, namely by raising awareness with regard to the impact of one's biases in favour of or against private participation in the international legal system.

5

Taking Systemic Interpretation Seriously

THE ARGUMENT OF this book is that just like Monsieur Jourdain (a character of Molière who was surprised to learn he had been speaking of prose all his life without knowing),[1] we have also been dealing with private actors' entitlements in the law of the sea, although we may have not been aware of it. In Chapters 3 and 4, entitlements deriving from the LOSC were studied to evidence how interpretative bias can drive the interpreter to exclude or limit the scope of private actors' entitlements under the LOSC. The last factor contributing to the apartheid of private actors from international law in general (and in the law of the sea in particular) is a failure to take systemic interpretation seriously, namely if the rules in need of systemic interpretation belong to different special regimes of international law.

In fact, the rules of any legal system need to be interpreted in light of its surrounding environment. In the case of international law, that task is an explicit commandment under Article 31(3)(c) of the VCLT. From the private actors' standpoint, the relevance of systemic interpretation is that it can also foster their participation by unveiling rights and duties. To assess if systemic interpretation may foster private participation under international law, the option of this book is to focus on human rights *qua tale* as derived from human rights treaties, or 'hidden' in the LOSC to evidence how 'new' rights and freedoms can be claimed by private actors engaged in maritime activities.

To that end, Section 1 assesses if cross-regime interpretation is possible between the law of the sea and human rights law, or if fragmentation and/or self-containment prevent systemic interpretation with respect to, and between, these special regimes of international law. Section 2 assesses how the application of human rights treaties is impacted by law of the sea rules, namely those referring to States' jurisdiction at sea. As will be said, human rights law was conceived for dry-land scenarios, and thus claims to human rights at sea meet important methodological difficulties deriving from the unique features of maritime jurisdiction. In particular, the lack of a proper understanding of how human rights jurisdiction is established at sea is an obstacle to human rights protection in the

[1] *Le Bourgeois gentilhomme*, Act II, Scene 4.

maritime environment. Finally, Section 3 assesses the impact of human rights in the reading of the LOSC, namely by analysing whether systemic interpretation helps to transform States' powers into States' duties towards individuals.

1. THE COMMON GENETIC CODE OF THE LAW OF THE SEA AND HUMAN RIGHTS LAW

Systemic interpretation is an intrinsic feature of any legal *system*, entailing that legal rules must be interpreted taking into account all other provisions from the same legal system. This is just the logical consequence of the necessary interaction between rules of the same system: that is the reason why it is called a *system*. Article 31(3)(c) of the VCLT works upon that idea and establishes that a treaty-based rule must be interpreted taking into account 'any relevant rules of international law applicable in the relations between the parties'. Among the different issues raised by this provision, my concern is to understand if systemic interpretation is impacted by the fragmentation of international law into several *lex specialis*, especially in light of the phenomenon of proliferation of international bodies. More particularly, in Chapter 2, I mentioned that the traditional view of 'international' legal personality is fragmented, meaning that private actors are recognised as such under the specific international law regimes that confer on them rights or duties. However, by downplaying the merits of systemic interpretation, fragmented views of 'international' legal personality reinforce a bias against private actors and prevent cross-regime readings that can accommodate private actors' rights or duties under international law.

Under the term *proliferation* of international courts, tribunals and non-compliance bodies, several presidents of the ICJ have referred to the perils of a fragmented international legal order, evolving without an 'overall plan',[2] and built upon a set of contradictory but equally authoritative decisions from different international bodies.[3] Evidence, however, does not support that concern:[4] eg the exquisite dispute settlement system adopted by the LOSC has allowed

[2] Robert Jennings, 'The Role of the International Court of Justice' (1997) 68 *British Yearbook of International Law* 1, 58.

[3] Gilbert Guillaume, 'The Future of International Judicial Institutions' (1995) 44 *ICLQ* 848, 862; Jennings, 'Role' (n 2) 58; Shigeru Oda, 'Dispute Settlement Prospects on the Law of the Sea' (1995) 44 *ICLQ* 863, 864. See also 'Address to the Plenary Session of the General Assembly of the United Nations by Judge Stephen M. Schwebel, President of the International Court of Justice', 26 October 1999; 'Address by H.E. Judge Gilbert Guillaume, President of the International Court of Justice, to the United Nations General Assembly', 26 October 2000; 'The Proliferation of International Judicial Bodies: The Outlook for the International Legal Order – Speech by H.E. Judge Gilbert Guillaume, President of the International Court of Justice, to the Sixth Committee of the General Assembly of the United Nations', 27 October 2000; 'Speech by H.E. Judge Gilbert Guillaume, President of the International Court of Justice, to the General Assembly of the United Nations', 30 October 2001.

[4] eg Boisson de Chazournes, 'Plurality in the Fabric of International Courts and Tribunals: The Threads for a Managerial Approach' (2017) 28 *European Journal of International Law* 13, 34.

different institutions (not horizontally or vertically integrated) to deliver equally authoritative decisions without damaging its integrity; and considering the topics developed by recent case law (eg maritime boundary delimitation), it is noticeable how judicial bodies have been able to adopt a convergent and consistent case law and a common methodology.[5]

Evidence also suggests that proliferation of international adjudicating bodies has not prevented dialogue between different international law realms. The plurality of international dispute settlement bodies has always existed and dispute settlement bodies are aware of such proliferation and try to reconcile their decisions.[6] It only requires courts and tribunals to act as a 'constellation' and to coordinate their methodologies and case law in order to 'prevent it from exploding into a multitude of small particles'.[7] Ultimately, if 'To each level of normative density, there corresponds a level of institutional density necessary to sustain the norms',[8] the proliferation of adjudicating bodies in international law is only the result of the maturing and ever-increasing complexity of international law. But proliferation *per se* does not preclude interaction between different realms of international law.

The same problem has also been dealt with under the concept of *fragmentation*, ie the atomisation of international law into autonomous fields as 'the product of conflicting but equally authoritative pronouncements on international law by courts and tribunals'.[9] Such fragmentation has the potential to create 'erratic blocks and elements' that interact and form an 'unorganised system',[10] a 'normative jungle'[11] or a 'kaleidoscopic reality',[12] full of intra-systemic tensions, contradictions and frictions. Fragmentation has become more visible in the second half of the twentieth century as a result of several factors, including the lack of a centralised system of upstream and downstream law-making, the creation of new international dispute settlement bodies (composed of judges

[5] Jonathan Charney, 'Is International Law Threatened by Multiple International Tribunals?' (1998) 271 *Collected Courses of the Hague Academy of International Law* 101, 348.

[6] Chazournes, 'Plurality' (n 4) 14.

[7] Georges Abi-Saab, 'Fragmentation or Unification: Some Concluding Remarks' (1999) 31 *New York University Journal of International Law & Politics* 919, 926.

[8] Georges Abi-Saab, 'Cours général de droit international public' (1987) 207 *Collected Courses of the Hague Academy of International Law* 9, 93; 'Fragmentation' (n 12) 925.

[9] James Crawford, 'Chance, Order, Change: The Course of International Law – General Course on Public International Law' (2013) 365 *Collected Courses of the Hague Academy of International Law* 9, 211–12.

[10] Gerhard Hafner, 'Pros and Cons Ensuing from Fragmentation of International Law' (2004) 25 *Michigan Journal of International Law* 849, 850; Karl Zemanek, 'The Legal Foundations of the International System – General Course on Public International Law' (1997) 266 *Collected Courses of the Hague Academy of International Law* 21, 62.

[11] Anja Lindroos, 'Addressing Norm Conflicts in a Fragmented Legal System: The Doctrine of *Lex Specialis*' (2005) 74 *Nordic Journal of International Law* 27, 31.

[12] Martti Koskenniemi and Päivi Leino, 'Fragmentation of International Law: Postmodern Anxieties' (2002) 15 *Leiden Journal of International Law* 553, 559.

with specialised legal training), and the widening, deepening and increasing regionalisation of international law. But fragmentation is also a problem of perspective: on the one hand, since its inception, international law has been a fragmented legal order[13] – only *awareness* of it was missing;[14] on the other hand, fragmentation logically presupposes 'some [prior] basic unity and integrity' of the system.[15] In fact, contradictions between regimes exist in all legal systems and are solved by resorting to the *lex specialis derrogat lex generalis* rule.[16] In international law, Article 55 of the *Draft Articles on Responsibility of States for Internationally Wrongful Acts* alluded to the existence of 'strong' and 'weak' cases of *lex specialis*.[17] And in domestic legal systems (where legal integration is stronger), special branches of law also gained autonomy without thwarting the unity of the legal system and the communication between different fields of law.

However, on its commentary to Article 55 of the *Draft Articles on Responsibility of States for Internationally Wrongful Acts*, the ILC alluded to the 'strong' cases of *lex specialis* in international law that constitute a *self-contained regime*, ie when a special domain of international law develops excessively by self-reference processes and ceases to interact with general international law,[18] ending up producing 'specialized rules and rule-systems that have no clear relationship to each other'.[19] This is the point where interaction between different regimes of international law must be discussed, for what needs to be questioned is not fragmentation per se, but rather whether a branch of international law is 'de-linked' from other domains, or does not fall back to the doctrines and rules of general international law.[20] If this is the case for the law of the sea and human rights law, it would mean that entitlements deriving from one field could not be relevant with respect to other fields of international law.

[13] ibid 576; Joost Pauwelyn, 'Fragmentation of International Law', in *Max-Planck Encyclopaedia of International Law*, § 7.

[14] Joost Pauwelyn, 'Bridging Fragmentation and Unity: International Law as a Universe of Inter-Connected Islands' (2004) 25 *Michigan Journal of International Law* 903, 904; Pauwelyn, 'Fragmentation' (n 13) § 11.

[15] Pemmaraju Sreenivasa Rao, 'Multiple International Judicial Forums: A Reflection of the Growing Strength of International Law or Its Fragmentation?' (2004) 25 *Michigan Journal of International Law* 929, 930. See also Christian Tomuschat, 'International Law as a Coherent System: Unity or Fragmentation?', in Mahnoush Arsanjani, Jacob Katz Cogan, Robert Sloane and Siegfried Wiessner (eds), *Looking to the Future – Essays on International Law in Honor of W. Michael Reisman* (Martinus Nijhoff 2011) 323, 323–24; Tullio Treves, 'Fragmentation of International Law: The Judicial Perspective' (2009) 27 *Agenda Internacional* 213, 214.

[16] Hafner, 'Pros and Cons' (n 10) 856.

[17] ILC, *Draft Articles on Responsibility of States for Internationally Wrongful Acts with Commentaries*, 140–41.

[18] Crawford, 'Chance' (n 9) 212; Pauwelyn, 'Bridging Fragmentation' (n 14) 904.

[19] ILC, 'Report of the Study Group of the International Law Commission, Finalized by Martti Koskenniemi: *Fragmentation of International Law: Difficulties arising from the Diversification and Expansion of International Law*' (13 April 2006) UN Doc. A/CN.4/L.682, § 483.

[20] Pauwelyn, 'Bridging Fragmentation' (n 14) 904.

From a substantive perspective, States are free to contract out by adopting rules of a special character vis-à-vis general international law. Accordingly, conflicts between special regimes '*must be accepted* as being in certain circumstances an *inevitable incident* of the growth' of international law.[21] From a procedural perspective, the emergence of 'functionally defined issue-areas'[22] of international law results from the fact that courts and tribunals may presume in favour of some degree of completeness of the treaty regime they are enforcing and under which they were created.[23] *The* danger of proliferation of courts, then, is 'the illusion of completely autonomous subsystems, each equipped with its own judicial or controlling system'[24] – a conduct followed by scholars and lawyers operating in the same field.[25] When judicial institutions try to follow a consistent case law of their own, they will consider special interests underlying the rules they are responsible for enforcing and adopt a specific linguistic code they conceive as a kind of 'global Esperanto'.[26] Furthermore, in general, the immediate object of a proceeding before a court or tribunal is confined to the norms enshrined in the specific treaty that constituted such body. That explains, eg, why the ITLOS in prompt release procedures only addresses specific law of the sea questions, and explicitly rejects the assessment of factors such as compliance with fair trial standards. In the end, a dispute settled by a judicial body of a special international law domain only settles the issues relating to that domain; other sources of quarrels ought to be addressed to the appropriate judicial bodies.[27] The result, as the ICTY sharply stated, is that 'In international law, every tribunal is a self-contained system (unless otherwise provided)'.[28] At this point, a problem may arise if mental shortcomings and automations are created, and end up (inadvertently) creating 'gnoseological, albeit not legal, barriers' to cross-regime interaction.[29]

[21] CW Jenks, 'Conflict of Law-Making Treaties' (1953) 30 *British Yearbook of International Law* 401, 405 (emphasis added).

[22] Pauwelyn, 'Fragmentation' (n 13) § 2.

[23] Bruno Simma and Dirk Pulkowski, 'Of Planets and the Universe: Self-Contained Regimes in International Law' (2006) 17 *European Journal of International Law* 483, 505.

[24] Pierre-Marie Dupuy, 'The Danger of Fragmentation or Unification of the International Legal System and the International Court of Justice' (1999) 31 *New York University Journal of International Law & Politics* 791, 796.

[25] Pierre-Marie Dupuy, 'L'unité de l'ordre juridique international' (2002) 297 *Collected Courses of the Hague Academy of International Law* 9, 436.

[26] Koskenniemi and Leino, 'Fragmentation' (n 12) 578. See also Rao, 'Multiple' (n 15) 945; Irini Papanicolopulu, *International Law and the Protection of People at Sea* (1st edn, OUP 208) 67; Tullio Treves, 'Human Rights and the Law of the Sea' (2010) 28 *Berkeley Journal of International Law* 1, 2.

[27] Hafner, 'Pros and Cons' (n 10) 858.

[28] *Prosecutor v Duško Tadić* [Decision, 2 October 1995] ICTY Case No. IT-94-I, Appeals Chamber, § 11.

[29] Irini Papanicolopulu, 'Human Rights and the Law of the Sea', in Attard Fitzmaurice and Martínez Gutiérrez (eds), *The IMLI Manual of International Maritime Law*, I, *The Law of the Sea* (OUP 2014) 509, 65–66.

Nonetheless, a certain interaction with other components of the same legal order can be observed: courts and tribunals normally consider not only the treaty whose interpretation or enforcement is being questioned, but also the entire set of legal norms that bind the parties in the dispute, as prescribed by Article 31(3) of the VCLT.[30] Therefore, 'As a legal system, international law is not a random collection of such norms',[31] and fragmentation 'does not signify the collapse of the system'.[32] Conversely, because consequences of fragmentation have become more visible, scholars, courts and tribunals have 'drawn closer together [the different branches of international law], not farther apart'.[33]

Moreover, evidence suggests that self-contained regimes do not completely contract out of general international law.[34] In his lecture to the Hague Academy, Charney illustrated how dispute settlement bodies in all fields of international law apply the VCLT with regard to questions of interpretation, reservations, or lawfulness of international treaties; resort to the same set of norms and international law sources; and share a common understanding of what is international law, which translates into the emergence of a coherent methodology and case law.[35] Hence, dispute settlement bodies of special regimes often refer to rules of general international law, and acknowledge that their treaties '[are] not to be read in clinical isolation from public international law'.[36]

Thus, despite the emergence of compartmentalised regimes, there is a common background that transforms international law in a unified legal order. Being part of international law means that these norms are not born in a vacuum, but rather have a common genetic code, and therefore are to be applied in a systemic manner, presupposing fall-back on norms of general international law. Article 311 of the LOSC is a good example of an explicit reference to fall-back processes with respect to interpretation, as it presupposes a systemic interpretation of its provisions; and Article 293 of the LOSC provides that 'A court or tribunal having jurisdiction shall apply [the LOSC] and other rules

[30] Abi-Saab, 'Fragmentation' (n 7) 926.

[31] ILC, 'Conclusions of the Work of the Study Group on the Fragmentation of International Law: Difficulties arising from the Diversification and Expansion of International Law' (18 July 2006) UN Doc. A/CN.4/L.702, § 14(1).

[32] Crawford, 'Chance' (n 9) 215.

[33] Pauwelyn, 'Fragmentation' (n 13) § 11. See also Irini Papanicolopulu, 'Human Rights and the Law of the Sea', in Nerina Boschiero, Tullio Scovazzi, Cesare Pitea and Chiara Ragni (eds), *International Courts and the Development of International Law – Essays in Honour of Tullio Treves* (Springer 2013) 535, 536.

[34] See inter alia Nele Matz-Lück, 'Norm Interpretation across International Regimes: Competences and Legitimacy', in Margaret Young (ed), *Regime Interaction in International Law – Facing Fragmentation* (CUP 2012) 201, 206–07; Yuval Shany, *The Competing Jurisdiction of International Courts and Tribunals* (OUP 2003) 99; Tomuschat, 'Unity or Fragmentation?' (n 15) 344ff; Treves, 'Fragmentation' (n 15) 220; Treves, 'Human Rights' (n 26) 1.

[35] Charney, 'Is International Law' (n 5) 347. See also Rosalyn Higgins, 'A Babel of Judicial Voices? Ruminations from the Bench' (2006) 55 *ICLQ* 791, 797–98.

[36] WTO, *United States: Standards for Reformulated and Conventional Gasoline* (20 May 1996) WT/DS2/AB/R, 17.

of international law not incompatible with [the LOSC]'. Resorting to fall-back mechanisms, as Articles 293 and 311 of the LOSC do, is a means of 'gene-therapy against excessive-fragmentation'[37] – it is a mechanism of self-balancing of the system to prevent one of its domains from becoming an independent legal order.

For the topic of this book, what matters is not to understand whether the ITLOS and the ECtHR can fall back on general international law, but rather if norms of the LOSC and the ECHR can interact with each other: if the ITLOS can only interpret and enforce the LOSC, and the ECtHR can only interpret and enforce the ECHR, then private actors cannot claim any entitlement deriving from one treaty before the dispute settlement body of another treaty, and regime interaction would be blocked. For a long time both fields were seen as different and isolated domains of international law:[38] academics and practitioners were hardly the same; the rules and principles applying in each field are different and hardly overlap; and the backbone of both domains (State-centred law of the sea vs individual-centred human rights law) hardly square with each other. Not surprisingly, the interaction between both domains was ignored for a long time.[39]

However, awareness of fragmentation lead scholars, courts and tribunals to ascertain that the law of the sea and human rights law 'are not separate planets rotating in different orbits. Instead, they meet in many situations'.[40] By pertaining to the same, unified legal order (although polycentric and polyhedral), a systemic reading of human rights or the law of the sea treaties requires that interpreters and enforcers consider all the existing international law and draw consequences from systemic unity. This means that the interpretation of a specific norm of the LOSC cannot be made in vacuum, but rather must take into account the entire legal system to which it pertains (which includes human rights instruments), and vice versa. Systemic interpretation is not only about relations between *lex generalis* and *lex specialis*, but also relations among different *lex specialis*.

Therefore, the legal status of private actors engaged in maritime activities is shaped by the LOSC and other law of the sea treaties – but is also deeply

[37] Pauwelyn, 'Fragmentation' (n 13) § 28.

[38] Treves, 'Human Rights' (n 26) 1.

[39] Bernard Oxman, 'Human Rights and the United Nations Convention on the Law of the Sea' (1998) 36 *Columbia Journal of Transnational Law* 399, 399–400.

[40] Treves, 'Human Rights' (n 26) 1. See also Papanicolopulu, 'Human Rights' (n 29) 511; Irini Papanicolopulu, 'A Missing Part of the Law of the Sea Convention: Addressing Issues of State Jurisdiction over Persons at Sea', in Clive Schofield, Seokwoo Lee and Moon-Sang Kwon (eds), *The Limits of Maritime Jurisdiction* (Martinus Nijhoff 2014) 387, 389; Efthymios Papastavridis, 'European Convention on Human Rights and the Law of the Sea: The Strasbourg Court in Unchartered Waters?', in Fitzmaurice and Merkouris (eds), *The Interpretation and Application of the European Convention on Human Rights – Legal and Practical Implications* (Martinus Nijhoff 2012) 115, 118; Budislav Vukas, 'Droit de la mer et droits de l'homme', in *The Law of the Sea – Selected Writings* (Martinus Nijhoff 2004) 71, 71.

impacted by human rights treaties. This explains why an enquiry into the position of private actors into the law of the sea cannot ignore how their legal status is fostered by the interaction of law of the sea and human rights instruments. In this chapter, this book will first explain how a proper understanding of human rights jurisdiction at sea could *ipso iure* unveil a myriad of human rights applicable to maritime activities – which is evidence of how a failure to take systemic interpretation seriously is a factor contributing to the biased exclusion of private actors from international law. After that, this book will turn its attention to how rules of the LOSC that confer powers on States eventually grant human rights to individuals if read together with human rights treaties.

2. THE APPLICATION OF HUMAN RIGHTS TREATIES AT SEA

Human rights aim to protect private actors against State's conducts that may affect values directly concerned with human dignity. By equipping individuals with rights and freedoms valid against the State, human rights law is the best example in international law of a primary right assigned to private actors, and thus evidence their international legal capacity. Although human rights were intended for dry-land scenarios, the necessary interaction between special regimes of international law and the cross-sectoral nature of private legal personality have the potential to enlarge the pool of rights and freedoms that individuals engaged in maritime activities can claim under international law.

An in-depth study of the nature of human rights law is beyond the scope of this book. What interests me is to assess whether human rights enshrined in international treaties are applicable at sea, therefore strengthening the legal status of private actors engaged in maritime activities. In particular, the focus will be not on the exact content of human rights, but rather on the way the scope of application of human rights treaties is shaped by the law of the sea rules, namely by establishing the *de iure* and *de facto* jurisdiction of coastal, port and flag States. To that end, my option is to analyse the ECHR as a case study, as such interplay is more conspicuous and the case law and other materials on the topic are more abundant, although this analysis is complemented with references from other treaties when they are evidence of a trans-system pattern. Once a State's human rights jurisdiction at sea is established, it is easier to understand what rights and freedoms are applicable to each case.

2.1. Jurisdiction as a Precondition of Human Rights Application

According to Article 1 of the ECHR, 'The High Contracting Parties shall secure to everyone within their jurisdiction the rights and freedoms defined in Section 1 of this Convention' – a wording similar to most human rights treaties.

Therefore, jurisdiction is the element that triggers the applicability of human rights treaties:

> The exercise of jurisdiction is a necessary condition for a Contracting State to be able to be held responsible for acts or omissions imputable to it which give rise to an allegation of the infringement of rights and freedoms set forth in the [ECHR].[41]

Jurisdiction, therefore, is key for defining the circle of beneficiaries of the entitlements set out in human rights treaties, and for establishing who is accountable for a human rights infringement and may be the defendant in a case submitted before a human rights body.

In the abstract, nothing prevents the application of human rights treaties to activities at sea, and there is no reason to differentiate between 'people at sea' (who would be deprived of such human rights) and 'people on land' (who would enjoy such human rights).[42] However, the application of human rights treaties at sea entails unique difficulties. On land, it is relatively easy to establish what State has to respect and ensure the human rights of an individual. But the special features of the marine environment pose specific problems for the establishment of States' jurisdiction at sea, which explains why States claim that human rights treaties are not applicable to all persons at sea.[43] Moreover, whereas jurisdiction on land is in principle exclusive, at sea multiple titles to jurisdiction exist (coastal, port and flag State jurisdiction) – titles that not only have different degrees of implementation (eg the spatial jurisdiction of coastal States varies according to the distance from the coast), but also often give rise to overlapping and conflicting jurisdiction of States over one individual.[44]

However, the special features of the marine environment do not preclude the application of human rights treaties and

> cannot justify an area outside the law where ships' crews are covered by no legal system capable of affording them enjoyment of the rights and guarantees protected

[41] *Ilaşcu and Others v Moldava and Russia* (App no. 48787/99) ECtHR 8 July 2004, § 311. See also *Issa and Others v Turkey* (App no. 31821/96) ECtHR 16 November 2004, § 66; *Solomou and Others v Turkey* (App no. 36832/97) ECtHR 24 June 2008, § 43; *Al-Jedda v United Kingdom* (App no. 27021/08) ECtHR [GC] 7 July 2011, § 74; *Hirsi Jamaa and Others v Italy* (App no. 27765/09) ECtHR [GC] 23 February 2012, § 70; *Nada v Switzerland* (App no. 10593/08) ECtHR 12 September 2012, § 118; *Lambi Longa v Netherlands* (App no. 33917/12) ECtHR 9 October 2012, § 61; *Catan and Others v Moldova and Russia* (App nos. 43370/04, 8252/05 and 18454/06) ECtHR [GC] 19 October 2012, § 103; *N.D. and N.T. v Spain* (Apps nos. 8675/15 and 8697/15) ECtHR 3 October 2017, § 49.

[42] Papanicolopulu, *International Law* (n 26) 4.

[43] *The Haitian Centre for Human Rights and Others v United States* (Case 10.675) ACmHR Report 51/96, 13 March 1997, § 119; *Hirsi Jamaa* [2012] § 65.

[44] Irini Papanicolopulu, 'La nozione di giurisdizione ai sensi dell'art. 1 della Convenzione Europea dei Diritti Umani nella recente giurisprudenza della Corte Europea dei Diritti Umani', in Tulio Scovazzi, Irini Papanicolopulu and Sabrina Urbinati (eds), *I diritti umani di fronte al giudice internazionale – Atti della giornata di studio in memoria di Carlo Russo* (Giuffrè 2009) 83, 120–21; Papanicolopulu, *International Law* (n 26) pp. 94–95.

by the [ECHR] which States have undertaken to secure to everyone within their jurisdiction, any more than it can provide offenders with a 'safe haven'.[45]

The enjoyment of human rights is not conditional upon a person being on land or at sea, or otherwise the universal vocation of human rights treaties would be at risk.[46] Hence, what is necessary is to identify the criteria to establish a link of jurisdiction for the purposes of Article 1 of the ECHR and the twin-clauses of other human rights treaties. Once that link is drawn, the pool of human rights and freedoms set out in the ECHR is theoretically applicable, although one must assess if limitations to such rights and freedoms are a natural consequence of the special nature of the marine environment: eg, right to privacy or freedom of movement cannot expectably be conceived of as widely as on land. Only an *in casu* assessment can determine what human rights and freedoms might be claimed by individuals engaged in maritime activities, *ergo* enlarging his status as rights-holder under international law.

2.2. Human Rights Jurisdiction at Sea

Jurisdiction and other linguistic variants are used at least since Roman law, and its chief problem actually derives from its widespread and polysemous use in different domains: jurisdiction has not *one* ordinary meaning, but rather *several* conflicting meanings.[47] In all cases, however, jurisdiction is used to describe the allocation of authority to an institution (here conceived of *lato sensu*, and encompassing a court, an organisation or the State), which is to be exercised free from external interference.[48]

In general international law, jurisdiction is also used to describe the competence of an international court or tribunal, but in most cases it is used to describe the power of a State, assigned by a permissive rule of international law, 'to regulate or otherwise impact upon people, property or circumstances'.[49] In this latter sense, jurisdiction 'is one of the most obvious forms of the exercise of sovereign power', crafted as a conceptual tool to demarcate the limits of States'

[45] *Medvedyev and Others v France* (App no. 3394/03) ECtHR [GC] 29 March 2010, § 81; *Hirsi Jamaa* [2012] § 178.

[46] Papanicolopulu, *International Law* (n 26) 24; Papanicolopulu, 'Human Rights' (n 29) 527.

[47] Marko Milanović, *Extraterritorial Application of Human Rights Treaties – Law, Principles, and Policy* (OUP 2011) 39.

[48] Vaughan Lowe and Christopher Staker, 'Jurisdiction', in Malcolm Evans (ed), *International Law* (5th edn, OUP 2018) 289, 290.

[49] Malcolm Shaw, *International Law* (CUP 2017) 483. See generally Ian Brownlie and James Crawford, *Brownlie's Principles of Public International Law* (8th edn, OUP 2012) 456; Antonio Cassese, *International Law* (2nd edn, OUP 2005) 49; Vaughan Lowe, *International Law* (OUP 2007) 170–71; Lowe and Staker, 'Jurisdiction' (n 48) 313; DP O'Connell, *International Law*, II (Stevens 1970) 599; 539; Cedric Ryngaert, *Jurisdiction in International Law* (OUP 2012) 42 and 47.

competences vis-à-vis each other:[50] it defines which State can lawfully prescribe and enforce rules over a specific territory or persons. In the case of human rights treaties, one can find references to the jurisdiction of the courts or bodies established for the enforcement of a treaty, but provisions such as Article 1 of the ECHR refer to States' jurisdiction.[51]

After the gradual enclosure of the territorial State since the sixteenth century, jurisdiction is mentioned by default as a power defined with respect to a territory:[52] as stated by the PCIJ, 'the first and foremost restriction imposed by international law upon a State is that – failing the existence of a permissive rule to the contrary – it may not exercise its power in any form in the territory of another State'.[53] But in an age of globalisation of social life, the *extraterritorial* jurisdiction of States is inevitable, and this phenomenon is noticeable in almost all aspects of daily life. As such, despite being primarily territorial, titles to *extraterritorial* jurisdiction are valid under international law, although enforcement jurisdiction in principle cannot be exercised outside the State's territory, unless supported by a permissive rule of international law.[54]

With respect to maritime jurisdiction, the LOSC does not explicitly mention States' jurisdiction over persons at sea,[55] but it still resorts to the conceptual toolbox of international law – not referenced in terms of the 'State' *tout court*, but rather of 'coastal', 'flag' or 'port' State, with different, but often overlapping, titles to jurisdiction.[56] As such, applied to the law of the sea, the general framework of States' jurisdiction is as shown in Table 5.1.

[50] *Legal Status of Eastern Greenland* [Judgment, 5 April 1933] PCIJ Series A/B, No. 53, 48. See, inter alia, Samantha Besson, 'The Extraterritoriality of the European Convention on Human Rights: Why Human Rights Depend on Jurisdiction and What Jurisdiction Amounts To' (2012) 25 *Leiden Journal of International Law* 857, 869; Brownlie and Crawford, *Principles* (n 49) 456; Michał Gondek, *The Reach of Human Rights in a Globalising World: Extraterritorial Application of Human Rights Treaties* (Intersentia 2009) 48–49; Rosalyn Higgins, *Problems and Process – International Law and How We Use It* (Clarendon 1995) 56; Kjetil Larsen, 'Territorial Non-Application of the European Convention on Human Rights' (2009) 78 *Nordic Journal of International Law* 73, 77–78; Lowe, *International Law* (n 49) 171; Lowe and Staker, 'Jurisdiction' (n 48) 313–14; Milanović, *Extraterritorial* (n 47) 23ff; Marko Milanović, 'From Compromise to Principle: Clarifying the Concept of State Jurisdiction in Human Rights Treaties' (2008) 8 *Human Rights Law Review* 411, 420; O'Connell, *International Law*, II (n 49) 599; Alexander Orakhelashvili, 'Restrictive Interpretation of Human Rights Treaties in the Recent Jurisprudence of the European Court of Human Rights' (2003) 14 *European Journal of International Law* 529, 539; Ryngaert, *Jurisdiction* (n 49) 5ff.

[51] Besson, 'Extraterritoriality' (n 50) 867; Milanović, *Extraterritorial* (n 47) 19; Milanović, 'From Compromise' (n 50) 415–16.

[52] Brownlie and Crawford, *Principles* (n 49) 456.

[53] *The Case of the SS 'Lotus'* [Judgment, 7 September 1927] PCIJ Series A, No. 10, 18.

[54] ibid 18–19.

[55] Papanicolopulu, 'Missing Part' (n 40) 394; Irini Papanicolopulu, 'The Law of the Sea Convention: No Place for Persons?' (2012) 27 *International Journal of Marine and Coastal Law* 867, 868–69.

[56] Maria Gavouneli, *Functional Jurisdiction in the Law of the Sea* (Martinus Nijhoff 2007) 33; Papanicolopulu, 'Human Rights' (n 29) 520.

Table 5.1 States' jurisdiction in the law of the sea

Territorial jurisdiction	Internal waters, territorial sea, and archipelagic waters: prescriptive and enforcement jurisdiction
Spatial-functional jurisdiction	Exclusive Economic Zone (EEZ), continental shelf: limited prescriptive and enforcement jurisdiction
Protective jurisdiction	Contiguous zone: limited enforcement jurisdiction
Active nationality – Flag State jurisdiction	High seas: limited prescriptive and enforcement jurisdiction
Port State jurisdiction	Limited enforcement jurisdiction
Universal jurisdiction	High seas: limited enforcement jurisdiction (eg piracy, cases under Article 110 of the LOSC)

Among the categories in Table 5.1, the spatial-functional jurisdiction of coastal States and the port State jurisdiction are unique to the law of the sea, but only a few notes are needed.

With regard to the EEZ and the continental shelf, because they lie outside their territory, coastal States' jurisdiction is extraterritorial.[57] Nevertheless, title to jurisdiction of coastal States is *spatial* (for these zones are determined by reference to an area measured from the States' baselines) and *functional* (for it refers to specific activities that can be performed by the coastal State).[58] In this respect, in the EEZ, coastal States have jurisdiction with respect to the exploration for and exploitation of living and non-living resources (energy included),[59] the establishment and use of artificial islands and structures,[60] including full civil and criminal jurisdiction over those located in the EEZ and in the continental shelf,[61] marine scientific research,[62] and the protection and preservation of the marine environment.[63] This implies, for example, that a coastal State has jurisdiction over a ship (and persons on board) engaged in fishing activities, but not over a ship (and persons on board) merely *en route*.[64] This is evidence of a core difficulty to assess jurisdiction at sea: in some cases, one needs not only to look to the place or the flag where a given fact occurs, but also to the activity being performed or regulated.[65]

[57] See Article 2(1) of the LOSC, *a contrario sensu*.

[58] See generally Robin Churchill and Vaughan Lowe, *The Law of the Sea* (3rd edn, MUP 1999); Gavouneli, *Functional* (n 56) 10, and 68–69; Lowe and Staker, 'Jurisdiction' (n 48) 321.

[59] Article 56(1)(a) of the LOSC.

[60] Article 56(1)(b)(i) of the LOSC.

[61] Articles 60 and 80 of the LOSC.

[62] Article 56(1)(b)(ii) of the LOSC.

[63] Article 56(1)(b)(iii) of the LOSC. Furthermore, pursuant to Articles 211 and 234 of the LOSC, coastal States have prescriptive jurisdiction regarding prevention and control of vessel-source pollution. Under Article 220 of the LOSC, enforcement jurisdiction is also conferred on the coastal State with respect to prevention of vessel-source pollution.

[64] Papanicolopulu, 'Missing Part' (n 40) 400.

[65] See generally Papanicolopulu, *International Law* (n 26) 116.

Moreover, an important innovation of the LOSC and the MARPOL Convention was the introduction of port State jurisdiction, a concept devised under the chapeau of the *aut dedere aut judicare* principle, referring to cases where States can exercise jurisdiction not as a representative, but in lieu of a flag or a coastal State.[66] In general, port State jurisdiction implies the assignment of *enforcement* authority to (coastal) State authorities to inspect and report compliance with specific international rules and standards by vessels that have entered its ports, or is meant to protect international values and interests (eg environment, illegal, unreported and unregulated fishing, labour conditions, or sanitary and health conditions).[67] Such enforcement competences are assigned to port States since interference with navigation by port State authorities is minimal (as entrance to ports is voluntary) and the exercise of enforcement powers is more likely to be effective in ports – whereas flag States often face difficulties in exercising authority over flagged vessels, and interference by coastal States can jeopardise freedom of navigation.

This, in a nutshell, is the so-called State's *de iure* jurisdiction. 'But what does this concept of jurisdiction from general international law has to do with the one found in human rights treaties? In short, precisely *nothing*', sharply asked and answered Milanović.[68]

Indeed, jurisdiction in general international law was crafted after inter-State relations – not after a jural relation between a State and a subordinate individual: whilst jurisdiction in general international law is a by-product of sovereignty and the non-interference principles, and is an epistemological tool to allocate competences, in human rights law it is a means to protect an individual in a position of subjection before a State; whilst in general international law it entails States' powers, in human rights law it entails States' obligations (negative and positive) vis-à-vis private actors (with corresponding rights). In the end, if jurisdiction under general international law and human rights law were not different doctrines, it would mean absurdly that States acting unlawfully under

[66] Gavouneli, *Functional* (n 56) 45.

[67] For a general overview, see Bevan Marten, 'Port State Jurisdiction, International Conventions and Extraterritoriality: An Expansive Interpretation', in Henrik Ringbom (ed), *Jurisdiction over Ships – Post-UNCLOS Developments in the Law of the Sea* (Brill Nijhoff 2015) 105; Erik Molenaar, 'Port State Jurisdiction: Towards Mandatory and Comprehensive Use', in David Freestone, Richard Barnes and David Ong (eds), *The Law of the Sea – Progress and Prospects* (OUP 2006) 192.

[68] Milanović, *Extraterritorial* (n 47) 26. See also Gondek, *Reach* (n 50) 56–57; Hugh King, 'The Extraterritorial Human Rights Obligations of States' (2009) 9 *Human Rights Law Review* 521, 536; Larsen, 'Territorial Non-Application' (n 50) 77–78; Milanović, 'From Compromise' (n 50) 417 and 429; Marko Milanović, '*Al-Skeini* and *Al-Jedda* in Strasbourg' (2012) 23 *European Journal of International Law* 121, 123; Sarah Miller, 'Revisiting Extraterritorial Jurisdiction: A Territorial Justification for Extraterritorial Jurisdiction under the European Convention' (2009) 20 *European Journal of International Law* 1223, 1231; Orakhelashvili, 'Restrictive Interpretation' (n 50) 540–42; Alexandra Rüth and Mirja Trilsch, 'Banković v. Belgium (Admissibility)' (2003) 97 *American Journal of International Law* 168 171; Ralph Wilde, 'Triggering State Obligations Extraterritorially: The Spatial Test in Certain Human Rights Treaties' (2007) 40 *Israel Law Review* 503, 513–14.

international law (for lacking a permissive rule ascribing jurisdiction) would not be subject to human rights standards.[69]

As such, *de iure* jurisdiction as crafted in general international law is a concept different from the one enshrined in Article 1 of the ECHR and other human rights treaties. In these latter, an autonomous concept of *de facto* jurisdiction is envisaged,[70] referring not to what acts States can practise under a permissive rule of international law, but rather to a factual relation between a State and an individual. In human rights treaties, jurisdiction is a tool for determining an actual physical subjection of an individual (question of fact)[71] – not the legal question of the lawfulness of States' prescriptive or enforcement measures:[72] if established, it does not entail the (un)lawfulness of States' acts, but only that one conduct 'stems from a necessarily lawfully organised institutional and constitutional framework, whether those institutions then act *ultra vires* or not'.[73] Evidence of this can be found in the semantic element of Article 1 of the ECHR and other human rights treaties, which do not refer to the title of a State over a territory,[74] or to the connection between the State and the facts it purports to regulate or to enforce its laws, but rather to the subjection of an individual to States' jurisdiction.[75] Moreover, the same *de facto* concept is visible in other treaties meant to protect individuals.[76]

As a result, if a warship engages in operations of interception of vessels on the high seas, a State might lack jurisdiction under international law (eg because it has no enforcement jurisdiction to do so under Articles 110 or 111 of the LOSC), but it may hold jurisdiction over the persons on board if it intercepts a ship under Article 1 of the ECHR. The existence or the absence of a permissive rule of international law to intercept that ship on the high seas might be relevant, but only subsequently (eg to determine whether precise and foreseeable legislation

[69] Gondek, *Reach* (n 50) 57; King, 'Extraterritorial' (n 68) 523; Wilde, 'Triggering' (n 68) 514.

[70] *Ilaşcu* [2004] 'Partly Dissenting Opinion of Judge Sir Nicolas Bratza Joined by Judges Rozakis, Hedigan, Thomassen and Panţîru', § 8, by implication.

[71] Loukis Loucaides, 'Determining the Extra-Territorial Effect of the European Convention: Facts, Jurisprudence and the *Banković* Case' (2006) 4 *European Human Rights Law Review* 391, 399; Milanović, *Extraterritorial* (n 47) 27, 32–33, 41, and 53; Milanović, 'From Compromise' (n 50) 417 and 423.

[72] *Loizidou v Turkey (Preliminary Objections)* (App no. 15318/89) ECtHR 23 March 1995, § 62; *Loizidou v Turkey* (App no. 15318/89) ECtHR 18 December 1996, § 52; *Cyprus v Turkey* (App no. 25781/94) ECtHR 10 May 2001, § 76. See also Gondek, *Reach* (n 50) 56; Larsen, 'Territorial Non-Application' (n 50) 78; Milanović, *Extraterritorial* (n 47) 41 and 60; Milanović, 'From Compromise' (n 50) 422–23; Papanicolopulu, 'Human Rights' (n 29) 522; Papastavridis, 'European Convention' (n 40) 123; Rüth and Trilsch, 'Banković v. Belgium' (n 68) 171; Wilde, 'Triggering' (n 68) 514.

[73] Besson, 'Extraterritoriality' (n 50) 865.

[74] Except Article 2(1) of the International Covenant on Civil and Political Rights (ICCPR), which clearly opposes the concepts of territory and jurisdiction.

[75] *Assanidze v Georgia* (App no. 71503/01) ECtHR 8 April 2004, 'Concurring Opinion of Judge Loucaides'; *Ilaşcu* [2004] 'Partly dissenting Opinion of Judge Loucaides'. See also Loucaides, 'Determining' (n 71) 399; Milanović, *Extraterritorial* (n 47) 8; Miller, 'Revisiting' (n 68) 1232.

[76] Milanović, *Extraterritorial* (n 47) 39; Milanović, 'From Compromise' (n 50) 434–35.

exists, pursuant to Article 5 of the ECHR). Accordingly, references to States' jurisdiction in human rights treaties cannot be read as a by-word for conferral of prescriptive or enforcement jurisdiction: whereas *de iure* jurisdiction empowers States, *de facto* jurisdiction under human rights treaties empowers individuals.

However, the difference between *de iure* and *de facto* jurisdiction is helpful, but not final: the notion of jurisdiction under human rights treaties refers to a *de facto* relation of subjection, but the existence of *de iure* jurisdiction may imply the existence of such *de facto* jurisdiction.[77] I do not ignore that, according to the ECtHR, 'the concept of "jurisdiction" for the purposes of Article 1 of the [ECHR] must be considered to reflect the term's meaning in public international law',[78] but in my view this assertion is incorrect, unclear and rests on a 'colossal *non sequitur*'.[79] What can still be said is that if a State holds *de iure* jurisdiction over a certain maritime area or vessel, one can presume (*iuris tantum*) that individuals in that area or vessel are *de facto* subject to its authority. Accordingly, whenever the LOSC confers *de iure* jurisdiction on flag, coastal or port States, one may legitimately presume that such State has *de facto* jurisdiction under Article 1 of the ECHR.[80]

Being a normative relation between a State and an individual, jurisdiction for the purpose of Article 1 of the ECHR could be devised in *spatial* or *personal terms*:[81] under the first model, one considers what areas are under the effective control of a State, whilst under the second model one considers when an individual is subject to a State's effective control. For the purposes of human rights treaties, jurisdiction is always a *personal* relation between an individual and a State:[82] that is the interpretation that best squares with the wording of this and similar provisions of human rights treaties; and the template implicitly adhered to by the ECtHR.[83] This implies, for instance, that if an individual or a ship is

[77] With a different view, see Papanicolopulu, *International Law* (n 26) 113.

[78] *Banković* [2001] §§ 59–60; *Gentilhomme, Schaff-Benhadji and Zerouki v France* (App nos. 48205/99, 48207/99 and 48209/99) ECtHR 14 May 2002, § 20; *Assanidze* [2004] § 137; *Ilaşcu* [2004] § 312; *Issa* [2004] § 67; *Nada* [2012] § 119; *Lambi Longa* [2012] § 69. A similar assumption was implied by the ICJ: *Legal Consequences of the Construction of a Wall in the Occupied Palestinian Territory* [Advisory Opinion, 9 July 2004] ICJ Rep 136, § 109.

[79] Milanović, *Extraterritorial* (n 47) 40; Milanović, 'From Compromise' (n 50) 419.

[80] Paul Tavernier, 'La Cour européenne des droits de l'homme et la mer', in Daniel-Heywood Anderson, Vincent Bantz, Geneviéve Bastid-Burdeau, Mohammed Bedjaoui and Josette Beer-Gabel (eds), *La mer et son droit – Mélanges offerts à Laurent Lucchini et Jean-Pierre Quéneudec* (Pedone 2003) 575, 577.

[81] Milanović, *Extraterritorial* (n 47) 119; Milanović, '*Al-Skeini*' (n 68) 122; Ralph Wilde, 'Legal "Black Hole"? Extraterritorial State Action and International Treaty Law on Civil and Political Rights' (2005) 26 *Michigan Journal of International Law* 739, 798.

[82] See also *Assanidze* [2004] 'Concurring Opinion of Judge Loucaides', 52, by implication. Apparently against, Milanović, *Extraterritorial* (n 47) 33; Milanović, 'From Compromise' (n 50) 429. However, what the author voices is his support for a spatial model to define the personal relation between an individual and a State, which is the view of this book also.

[83] *Issa* [2004] § 71; *Saddam Hussein v Albania et al* (App no. 23276/04) ECtHR (Decision) 14 March 2006; *Mansur Pad and Others v Turkey* (App no. 60167/00) ECtHR (Decision) 28 June 2007, §§ 53–54; *Solomou* [2008] §§ 44–45 and 51; *Al-Skeini and Others v United Kingdom* (App no. 55721/07)

physically detained by a State, he/it is automatically under that State's jurisdiction according to the personal model.[84]

A similar approach was upheld by Judge Bonello, who advocated that 'Jurisdiction means no less and no more than "authority over" and "control of". In relation to [ECHR] obligations, jurisdiction is neither territorial nor extraterritorial: it ought to be functional'.[85] As such, he concluded that 'Jurisdiction arises from the mere fact of having assumed those obligations *and from having the capability to fulfil them* (or not to fulfil them);'[86] If the perpetrators of an alleged human rights violation are within the authority and control of one of the Contracting Parties, it is to me totally consequential that their actions by virtue of that State's authority engage the jurisdiction of the Contracting Party'.[87] Thus,

> the one honest test, in *all* circumstances (including extraterritorially), is the following: did it the depend on the agents of the State whether the alleged violation would be committed or would not be committed? Was it within the power of the State to punish the perpetrators and to compensate the victims? If the answer is yes, self-evidently the facts fall squarely within the jurisdiction of the State.[88]

Despite the seductive thought of Judge Bonello, there are two main areas of confusion in his line of reasoning. First, he seems to merge jurisdiction with feasibility, or ability to protect human rights, and ergo goes too far in the definition of a link of jurisdiction – but only after establishing a link of jurisdiction as well as assessing the circumstances of the case can one determine what duties bind the State.[89] Additionally, his test seems to blend jurisdiction with attribution and responsibility, by stating that jurisdiction is only a matter of infringement, not of physical subjection. This is a common misunderstanding, but they are different concepts, attribution being a prerequisite of jurisdiction, and responsibility a possible outcome of jurisdiction.[90] But, to be fair to Judge Bonello, in some cases human rights infringements do not need the physical control or custody that the personal and the spatial models require: imagine, for instance, if the same State agents on a warship fatally shoot individuals on

ECtHR [GC] 7 July 2011, § 137; or *Medvedyev* [2010] § 64. See also Milanović, *Extraterritorial* (n 47) 191. UN treaty bodies have been enthusiastic proponents of a personal model of jurisdiction: *Sergio Euben Lopez Burgos v Uruguay* (Communication No. R.12/52) Human Rights Committee 29 July 1981, UN Doc. Supp. No. 40 (A/36/40), § 12.1–3; *Lilian Celiberti de Casariego v Uruguay* (Communication No. 59/1979) Human Rights Committee 29 July 1981, UN Doc. CCPR/C/OP/1, § 10.1–3. See also *Victor Saldaño v Argentina* [Decision, 11 March 1999] Inter-American Commission on Human Rights, Report No. 38/99, § 17.

[84] Milanović, *Extraterritorial* (n 47) 187.

[85] *Al-Skeini* [2011] 'Concurring Opinion of Judge Bonello', § 12.

[86] ibid § 13.

[87] ibid § 14.

[88] ibid § 16.

[89] Besson, 'Extraterritoriality' (n 50) 868.

[90] Gondek, *Reach* (n 50) 168–69; Milanović, *Extraterritorial* (n 47) 51–52.

another vessel. Only in these exceptional cases does the functional test of Judge Bonello seem appropriate.

Nonetheless, a model of jurisdiction based only on personal elements is not clear and tight enough, and risks encompassing situations in which clearly a State is not realistically able to respect or ensure human rights.[91] For that reason, the assessment of jurisdiction in a relation between an individual and a State must start with a spatial model, whereby jurisdiction is determined in terms of effective control over an area, ie jurisdiction exists over the persons in that particular area, regardless of the title that the State has over that space or of the lawfulness of the State's conduct.[92] Even if this method starts by assessing spatial elements, ultimately it is an indirect method of assessing personal control over individuals therein. Under this model, one can legitimately presume (*iuris tantum*) that persons on the territory of the State are within its jurisdiction (eg in the territorial sea);[93] extraterritorially, where actual control or authority over an area is exercised by a State, persons in that area are also presumed (*iuris tantum* also) to be subject to its jurisdiction (eg on board a flagged vessel); and a pure personal test should be relegated to cases where no spatial element is present, but physical control over a person or a vessel exists.[94] In this case, resorting to a purely spatial model – as the ECtHR did in the *Al-Saadoon* case – would lead to 'morally grotesque' results, where private actors were better protected if boarding a vessel occurs, rather than if it does not.[95] It is precisely because control over individuals or objects such as vessels 'is relatively easy' (ie they are particularly exposed at sea) that a simple control over them is the source of States' jurisdiction,[96] determined in light of the particular circumstances of each case.

In this light, it is important to note that there is no absolute presumption in favour of or against territoriality or extraterritoriality of jurisdiction in human rights treaties, although the existence of *de iure* jurisdiction is indicative of *de facto* jurisdiction. Being part of the States' *de iure* territory (eg territorial sea), or not (eg high seas), only matters for determining what can realistically be asked from the State, ie what rights and freedoms must be respected and ensured: States' obligations cannot be determined in the abstract, for they are dependent on 'the limits of realistic compliance',[97] and this depends on the actual circumstances of the States' control.[98] For that reason, a strict distinction

[91] King, 'Extraterritorial' (n 68) 537, by implication; Milanović, *Extraterritorial* (n 47) 207–09; Cedric Ryngaert, 'Clarifying the Extraterritorial Application of the European Convention on Human Rights' (2012) 28 *Merkourios* 57, 60.

[92] Milanović, *Extraterritorial* (n 47) 118.

[93] For a similar presumption, see *Assanidze* [2004] § 142; *Ilaşcu* [2004] § 312; *Al-Skeini* [2011] § 131.

[94] Milanović, *Extraterritorial* (n 47) 187.

[95] See, *mutatis mutandis*, Max Schaefer, '*Al-Skeini* and the Elusive Parameters of Extraterritorial Jurisdiction' (2011) 16 *European Human Rights Law Review* 566, 576.

[96] Milanović, *Extraterritorial* (n 47) 170.

[97] ibid 216.

[98] ibid 216–17. See also *Al-Skeini* [2011] § 137; *Hirsi Jamaa* [2012] § 74. See *mutatis mutandis* Besson, 'Extraterritoriality' (n 50) 878–79; King, 'Extraterritorial' (n 68) 539–42;

between positive and negative obligations is misleading,[99] for what needs to be considered is what kind of obligations depend only on the effectiveness of the control exercised by the State: whereas within its territory a coastal State must respect and ensure all human rights covered by the ECHR, when it intercepts a vessel on the high seas, it has to make sure that its agents' conduct does not infringe a human right (negative obligation); but if they do infringe, positive obligations (eg of investigating the occurrence) might flow from Articles 2 or 3 of the ECHR. However, some human rights obligations may not arise if they require a specific legal framework that presupposes States' *de iure* jurisdiction under general international law.[100] Furthermore, extraterritorially States also lack the machinery needed to comply with the sophisticated positive obligations unveiled by the ECtHR. But only an *in casu* assessment can determine whether a positive obligation arises or not. For that reason, in theory almost all human rights can be relevant when control over an area or a person is exercised, including on the high seas – but under a severability test, controlling States only have to respect and ensure the human rights they can realistically respect and ensure.

In the case law of the ECtHR, the method adopted has been to start assessing Article 1 of the ECHR in light of States' *de iure* jurisdiction, for it provides at least safe guidelines for establishing the subjection of a private actor to a State. Despite the shortcomings of the *de iure* concept of jurisdiction in human rights law, it can be a valid starting point provided that it is provisional and subject to validation.[101]

According to the ECtHR, indeed, jurisdiction under Article 1 of the ECHR is 'primarily' or 'essentially' territorial,[102] even though in the *Ilaşcu* case the ECtHR stated that 'jurisdiction is presumed to be exercised normally throughout the State's territory'.[103] This presumption, however, is limited and rebuttable[104]

Papanicolopulu, 'Human Rights' (n 29) 525; Papastavridis, 'European Convention' (n 40) 126. Against, see *Banković* [2001] § 75, where the ECtHR stated that the set of rights and freedoms established in the ECHR cannot be 'divided and tailored in accordance with the particular circumstances of the extraterritorial act'.

[99] Besson, 'Extraterritoriality' (n 50) 879. Against, see Milanović, *Extraterritorial* (n 47) 215–16.

[100] King, 'Extraterritorial' (n 68) 538 and 548; Erik Roxstrom, Mark Gibney and Terje Einarsen, 'The NATO Bombing Case (Banković et al. v. Belgium et al.) and the Limits of Western Human Rights Protection' (2005) 23 *Boston University International Law Review* 55, 88.

[101] Miller, 'Revisiting' (n 68) 1231; Orakhelashvili, 'Restrictive Interpretation' (n 50) 540–42; Armando Rocha, 'They Have Rights, Don't They? – As Fronteiras (da CEDH) Também Se Abatem' (2012) 144 *O Direito* 449, 456; Rüth and Trilsch, 'Banković v. Belgium' (n 68) 171.

[102] *Banković* [2001] §§ 59–61; *Gentilhomme* [2002] § 20; *Assanidze* [2004] § 137; *Ilaşcu* [2004] § 312; *Issa* [2004] § 67; *Maria Isaak and Others v Turkey* (App no. 44587/98) ECtHR (Decision) 28 September 2006, 19; *Solomou* [2008] § 43; *Al-Saadoon and Mufdhi v United Kingdom* (App no. 61498/08) ECtHR (Decision) 30 March 2009, § 84; *Rantsev v Cyprus and Russia* (App no. 25965/04) ECtHR 7 January 2010, § 205; *Al-Skeini* [2011] § 131; *Hirsi Jamaa* [2012] § 71; *Nada* [2012] 119; *Catan* [2012] § 104; *Lambi Longa* [2012] § 69; *N.D. and N.T.* [2017] § 50.

[103] *Ilaşcu* [2004] § 312; *Assanidze* [2004] §§ 138–39; *Al-Skeini* [2011] § 131; *Hirsi Jamaa* [2012] § 71; *Catan* [2012] § 104; *N.D. and N.T.* [2017] § 50.

[104] *Ilaşcu* [2004] §§ 333–35; *Assanidze* [2004] § 139. See also Pieter van Dijk, Fried van Hoof, Arjen van Rijn and Leo Zwaak (eds), *Theory and Practice of the European Convention on Human Rights*

'in exceptional circumstances, particularly when a State is prevented from exercising its authority in part of its territory'.[105] The exception adduced by the ECtHR is not meant to exclude a State's *de iure* jurisdiction over a portion of its territory, but to reduce its obligations under human rights treaties to what can realistically be asked from it, to condemn the indifference or contempt of the State before the amputation of authority over a portion of its territory, and the breach of the human rights of individuals therein.[106]

If an exception based on lack of realistic capabilities is possible, one can ask if this implies that flag States in principle lack *de facto* jurisdiction, considering how difficult it might be for them to exercise their competences: unless a flagged ship is in areas under its spatial jurisdiction, or nearby its warships, the flag State can only rely on self-compliance by the 'ship' or on non-flag States' intervention. However, the *Ilaşcu* decision is not meant to deal with cases where it is difficult to exert jurisdiction, or where the State refrains from exercising the competence assigned to it under international law: it aims at dealing with cases where States are unable to exercise competences as a result of an exogenous factor. With respect to flagged ships, difficulties in the exercise of flag State jurisdiction are documented, but the flag State can always exercise some control over flagged ships, even if limited.[107] As such, individuals on board a vessel are *ipso facto* subject to the *de facto* jurisdiction of the flag State,[108] and thus equipped with the human rights set out in the ECHR and other human rights treaties.

With respect to States' extraterritorial jurisdiction – of utmost importance for the law of the sea, where extraterritorial jurisdiction will be questioned more

(4th edn, Intersentia 2006) 14; King, 'Extraterritorial' (n 68) 547; Larsen, 'Territorial Non-Application' (n 50) 79; Bernardette Rainey, Elizabeth Wicks and Clare Ovey, *Jacobs, White, and Ovey: The European Convention on Human Rights* (7th edn, OUP 2017) 96.

[105] *Ilaşcu* [2004] § 312. See also *Cyprus v Turkey* [2001] § 78; *Catan* [2012] § 109; *Mozer v Moldova and Russia* (App no. 11138/10) ECtHR [GC] 23 February 2016, § 99; *Apcov v Moldova and Russia* (App no. 12463/07) ECtHR 30 May 2017, §§ 21–22; *Soyma v Moldova, Russia and Ukraine* (App no. 1203/05) ECtHR [GC] 30 May 2017, §§ 20–21; *Vardanean v Moldova and Russia* (App no. 22200/10) ECtHR 30 May 2017, §§ 20–21.

[106] Papanicolopulu, 'La nozione' (n 44) 93; Rocha, 'They Have Rights' (n 101) 460–61; Armando Rocha, *O Contencioso dos Direitos do Homem no Espaço Europeu* (Universidade Católica Editora 2010) 64; Frédéric Sudre, *Droit européen et international des droits de l'homme* (14th edn, PUF 2019) 322.

[107] A good example of how flag States can exercise their competence with regard to flagged ships in areas outside their spatial jurisdiction can be found in *Bakanova v Lithuania* (App 11167/12) ECtHR 31 May 2016, §§ 68–75.

[108] *Banković* [2001] § 73. See generally Stefan Kirchner, Katarzyna Geler-Noch and Vanessa Frese, 'Coastal State Obligations in the Context of Refugees at Sea under the European Convention on Human Rights' (2015) 20 *Ocean and Coastal Law Journal* 78. With respect to the ICCPR, see Urfan Khaliq, 'Jurisdiction, Ships and Human Rights Treaties', in Ringbom (ed), *Jurisdiction* (n 67) 324, 339ff. With a different view, but with the same conclusion, see Papanicolopulu, *International Law* (n 26) 152.

often than not – the magic formula drafted by the ECtHR is 'effective overall control'.[109] To support this view, the ECtHR mentioned that

> any other finding would result in a regrettable vacuum in the system of human rights protection in the territory in question by removing from individuals there the benefit of the [ECHR's] fundamental safeguards and their right to call a [State Part] to account for violation of their rights.[110]

Implied was the idea, following what the UN Human Rights Committee declared regarding the ICCPR, that 'it would be unconscionable to so interpret the responsibility under article 2 of the Covenant as to permit a State party to perpetrate violations of the Covenant on the territory of another State, which violations it could not perpetrate on its own territory':[111] such interpretation would 'lead to utterly absurd results'.[112] As such, the ECtHR affirmed that territoriality only means that, under general international law, a State's authority is in principle confined to its own territory, not that human rights standards apply only in that State's territory.[113]

In the *Banković* case, the *vexata quaestio* was the fact that the alleged victims were placed, and the wrongful act produced, not only outside the territory of the States concerned, but also outside the territories of the States parties to the ECHR (its 'espace juridique'). The ECtHR rejected the admissibility on grounds of lack of States' jurisdiction for three major reasons: the respondent States did not exercise effective overall control over the relevant area; thus, accepting jurisdiction in that circumstance would be 'tantamount to arguing that anyone adversely affected by an act imputable to a Contracting State, wherever in the world that act may have been committed or its consequences felt, [would be] thereby brought within the jurisdiction of that State for the purpose of Article 1 of the [ECHR]'; and that would be contrary to the intent of the drafters of the ECHR.[114] With regard to the law of the sea, this topic is crucial: apart from the territorial jurisdiction over internal waters, the territorial sea, or archipelagic waters, States' jurisdiction is always non-territorial and outside other States' territory also, ergo outside the improperly called 'territory of the ECHR'. For example, flag State jurisdiction on the high seas refers to the authority exercised over flagged vessels located in a zone where no State can formulate a sovereign claim.

[109] *Loizidou* [1996] § 56; *Cyprus v Turkey* [2001] §§ 76–77; *Ilaşcu* [2004] § 315; *Issa* [2004] § 70; *Al-Skeini* [2011] § 138; *Ivanţoc and Others v Moldova and Russia* (App no. 23687/05) ECtHR 15 November 2011, § 120; *Catan* [2012] § 106; *Braga v Republic of Moldova and Russia* (App no. 76957/01) ECtHR 17 October 2017, § 24; *Draci v Republic of Moldova and Russia* (App no. 5349/02) ECtHR 17 October 2017, § 28.

[110] *Cyprus v Turkey* [2001] § 78.

[111] *Lopez Burgos* [1981] § 12.3; *Celiberti de Casariego* [1981] § 10.3.

[112] ibid, 'Individual Opinion of Christian Tomuschat', paragraph 2.

[113] Loucaides, 'Determining' (n 71) 394.

[114] *Banković* [2001] § 75.

To some extent, *Banković* was a political decision of the ECtHR, and the result of it having to reconcile different policy options and still deliver a simple formula to keep the exceptional nature of States' extraterritorial jurisdiction.[115] The main point was that the ECtHR was institutionally inclined to preserve the ECHR's 'essentially regional vocation',[116] conscious that the system works efficiently precisely because it is regional, not universal. Furthermore, also implied in the reasoning of the ECtHR was the idea that a different *dictum* would be an imposition of European values upon different cultures, but the rationale of extraterritorial jurisdiction of human rights treaties is to prevent a vacuum in the system, ie to prevent individuals protected by the ECHR from being deprived of its institutional guarantees.[117]

With this, the ECtHR touched the crux of the issue: individuals who seek extraterritorial protection of human rights are *grosso modo* claiming the universality of the relevant human rights treaty.[118] This topic is beyond the scope of this book, but some notes are needed. The discussion regarding the regional or universal scope of human rights treaties is important for several purposes, but actually irrelevant for determining the extraterritorial jurisdiction of States parties: it is relevant, for example, for determining that Brazil is not bound by the ECHR; but it is irrelevant for determining that Portugal is bound by the ECHR wherever its conducts take place in the world. In this case, applying the ECHR to acts practised by Portuguese agents in a warship on the Antarctic Ocean is not a way of imposing European values upon different cultures, but rather upon a European State. 'Who is bound by the ECHR?' and 'where are their acts practised, or where are the effects of their acts produced?' are different questions that need a separate answer. From the standpoint of individuals, human rights either flow from their human condition *qua tale*, or do not, whereas from the standpoint of the respondent State, the ECHR 'provides a code of behaviour ... wherever they act in the exercise of their State authority with consequences for individuals'.[119] In this sense, the ECtHR correctly expressed its concern in preventing 'a regrettable vacuum in the system of human-rights protection',[120] but missed the point when it saw the issue from the perspective *only* of the holder of the right (someone who cannot be deprived of his human rights), and not *also* from the perspective of the bearer of the obligation (a State that cannot divest itself of its human rights duties): when States act extraterritorially, they carry with them the obligations under the ECHR. Moreover, nothing in the semantic element suggests a difference between acts practised in or outside the territory of the States parties to the ECHR taken collectively: 'The word

[115] Milanović, *Extraterritorial* (n 47) 55; Miller, 'Revisiting' (n 68) 1235–36.
[116] *Banković* [2001] § 80.
[117] ibid.
[118] Milanović, *Extraterritorial* (n 47) 55.
[119] *Assanidze* [2004] 'Concurring Opinion of Judge Loucaides', 52.
[120] *Cyprus v Turkey* [2001] § 78; *Banković* [2001] § 80.

"jurisdiction" either means "effective overall control of an area", or it does not. If it does, the legal status of the territory over which such control is exercised is irrelevant'.[121] And finally, the historical argument is incorrect,[122] and it should not pass unnoticed that the ECtHR did not substantiate its assertion.[123]

Right after *Banković*, the ECtHR stated in the *Issa* case that it '[did] not exclude the possibility that … [*in casu* Turkey] could be considered to have exercised, temporarily, effective overall control of a particular portion of the territory of [*in casu*] northern Iraq', even though Iraq 'is not a Contracting State and clearly does not fall within the legal space (*espace juridique*) of the Contracting States'.[124] Based on the *Lopez Burgos v Uruguay* decision, the ECtHR declared that 'Article 1 of the [ECHR] cannot be interpreted so as to allow a State party to perpetrate violations of the [ECHR] on the territory of another State, which it could not perpetrate on its own territory'.[125] Since this perspective was confirmed in several cases,[126] the established case law of the ECtHR is that a State's extraterritorial jurisdiction is not confined to the territory of the States parties to the ECHR: wherever a State exercises control over a territory, a person or a vessel, it holds *de facto* jurisdiction.

As seen, in all cases where a State holds *de iure* jurisdiction, it presumably holds *de facto* jurisdiction for the purposes of Article 1 of the ECHR. Translated into the law of the sea, this entails that whenever a coastal State has spatial jurisdiction – even if not sovereign or territorial – it is bound by the human rights and freedoms listed in the ECHR. This seems straightforward, but to set out human rights jurisdiction at sea is slightly harder. For example, human rights jurisdiction in the territorial sea must be reconciled with Article 27(5) of the LOSC, which comprises a wide limitation to coastal States' interferences with respect to foreign vessels in the exercise of a right of innocent passage.[127] This entails that any conduct by coastal States to ensure human rights should be confined to the limits imposed by this provision to the extent of coastal States' enforcement jurisdiction. The major hardship, however, is the fact the conceptual toolbox of human rights was crafted for dry-land scenarios, not for maritime spaces.[128]

[121] Milanović, *Extraterritorial* (n 47) 91.

[122] See, eg, Gondek, *Reach* (n 50) 75ff.

[123] Ralph Wilde, 'The "Legal Space" or "Espace Juridique" of the European Convention on Human Rights: Is It Relevant to Extraterritorial State Action?' (2005) 2 *European Human Rights Law Review* 115, 117.

[124] *Issa* [2004] § 74.

[125] ibid § 71.

[126] *Öcalan v Turkey* (App no. 46221/99) ECtHR [GC] 12 May 2005, § 90; *Saddam Hussein* [2006]; *Maria Isaak* [2006]; *Solomou* [2008] §§ 48–51; *Andreou v Turkey* (App no. 45653/99) ECtHR 27 October 2009, § 25; *Markovic and Others v Italy* (App no. 1398/03) ECtHR [GC] 14 December 2006, §§ 54–55; *Mansur Pad* [2007] §§ 53–54; *Al-Saadoon* [2009] §§ 86–89; *Al-Skeini* [2011] § 137; *Al-Jedda* [2011] §§ 85–86; *Hirsi Jamaa* [2012] § 81.

[127] For some authors, the only way to overcome this cogent limit is to conceive some human rights as *ius cogens* rules, which would prevail over Article 27(5) of the LOSC: Papanicolopulu, *International Law* (n 26) 140; Papanicolopulu, 'Human Rights' (n 29) 527.

[128] See generally Papanicolopulu, *International Law* (n 26) 112.

With respect to the EEZ and the continental shelf, functional *de iure* jurisdiction implies that coastal States can only adopt limited prescriptive and enforcement measures, which ought to comply with human rights standards.[129] The same can be said *mutatis mutandis* with respect to port State jurisdiction: vessels in a port are subject not only to coastal States' territorial jurisdiction, but also to specific authority powers assigned to the port State: when these are exerted, port States have to comply also with human rights instruments. With regard to artificial islands, structures and platforms in the EEZ, persons on board these objects are subject to the exclusive *de iure* jurisdiction of coastal States,[130] and thus presumably *de facto* under their human rights jurisdiction.[131] What is not clear is the exact extent of this functional link: for instance, if the coastal State has jurisdiction to regulate fishing activities on their EEZs, do they also have jurisdiction under human rights treaties to ensure protection against any form of slavery, servitude or forced labour? If these individuals kept as slaves are engaged in fishery activities, the answer would be positive, but would also lead to the curious situation in which slaves being transported or engaged in other activities apart from those listed in Article 56 of the LOSC would not be protected under the ECHR, unless one resorts to the doctrine of *ius cogens* to enlarge the *de iure* jurisdiction of coastal States.[132]

Nonetheless, even when coastal and port States act beyond the limits of their *de iure* functional jurisdiction at sea, they are still bound by the human rights and freedoms covered by the ECHR, provided that they exert *de facto* jurisdiction: the task of the ECtHR is not to assess whether coastal and port States act in accordance with the LOSC or another law of the sea treaty (since that task is primarily reserved for law of the sea adjudicating bodies), but rather whether these States comply with the ECHR when private actors are subject to their *de facto* authority. This should not be read as dismissing the relevance of States' *de iure* jurisdiction: if the coastal State exercised the competences it was assigned by the LOSC or other treaty, one must presume that it holds also *de facto* jurisdiction. Moreover, because the ECHR cannot be read in clinical isolation, the ECtHR should assess the conduct of the respondent State in light of the relevant treaty law, including the provisions that equipped it with authority to adopt certain acts. In the same way, in the event of lack of intra-territorial jurisdiction, the coastal or port State is only bound by the ECHR to a limited extent, whereas other States may *de facto* exert extraterritorial jurisdiction. That can be the case of States, acting in the context of repressing piracy or human smuggling, hold a joint operation on the territorial sea and EEZ of a third State: coastal States

[129] Papanicolopulu, 'Human Rights' (n 29) 526. See also *Federation of Offshore Workers' Trade Unions and Others v Norway* (App no. 38190/97) ECtHR (Decision) 27 June 2002, although declaring the petition inadmissible on different grounds.

[130] Article 60(2) of the LOSC.

[131] Papanicolopulu, *International Law* (n 26) 141; Papanicolopulu, 'Human Rights' (n 29) 527.

[132] See generally Papanicolopulu, *International Law* (n 26) 141–42.

may have a limited control over its maritime zones, but the flag States involved in the joint operation *de facto* exercise control over ships and persons therein.[133]

On the high seas, flag States hold primary *de iure* jurisdiction over persons and events on board flagged vessels,[134] even if technically the vessel is not part of the State's territory. The link is spatial and exclusive with respect to the vessel, but also limited insofar as it can only be exercised over a vessel flying its flag – not over the physical portion of the high seas where the vessel is located. As with the cases referred to earlier, *de iure* flag State jurisdiction is relevant under human rights law, meaning that facts occurring on board a vessel are presumed to be subject to the *de facto* flag State jurisdiction.[135] The immediate consequence is that individuals on board are entitled to the human rights listed in the ECHR and States are bound by the corresponding (positive and negative) obligations.[136]

This presumption is of utmost importance. I mentioned above that jurisdiction for human rights purposes means 'actual and factual authority' over persons. For that reason, I also claimed that jurisdiction in this context should refer to *de facto*, and not *de iure*, authority over persons. However, this conception of jurisdiction poses a specific problem with respect to vessels and persons aboard: although its authority is primary, the flag State may have difficulties with exerting any power over the vessels flying its flag, unless these latter come within its maritime spatial jurisdiction (ie in a place where the State can actually employ its physical authority). Moreover, non-flag States are barred from interfering with navigation of foreign ships, except in the specific cases where the LOSC or other treaty confers powers to do so. At most, it is possible that a ship will be subject to the limited port State jurisdiction. This implies, however, that it is likely that ships might be exempt from any States' *de facto* jurisdiction (especially, if the flag is of convenience), which would entail that no State has jurisdiction under Article 1 of the ECHR, and thus human rights protection would be non-existent with regard to ships on the high seas.[137] Therefore, the *de iure* concept of flag State jurisdiction is relevant for the protection of human rights of private actors on board ships on the high seas. Key to this question is

[133] Robin Geiß and Anna Petrig, *Piracy and Armed Robbery at Sea – The Legal Framework for Counter-Piracy Operations in Somalia and the Gulf of Aden* (OUP 2011) 108.

[134] Article 92(1) of the LOSC. See also *Al-Saadoon* [2009] § 85; *Al-Skeini* [2011] § 115; *Hirsi Jamaa* [2012] § 77.

[135] Douglas Guilfoyle, 'Human Rights Issues and Non-Flag State Boarding of Suspect Ships in International Waters', in Clive R Symmons (ed), *Selected Contemporary Issues in the Law of the Sea* (Martinus Nijhoff 2011) 83, 88.

[136] See *mutatis mutandis* Andreas Fischer-Lescano, Tillmann Löhr and Timo Tohidipur, 'Border Controls at Sea – Requirements under International Human Rights Law and Refugee Law' (2009) 21 *International Journal of Refugee Law* 256, 274–75; Douglas Guilfoyle, 'Counter-Piracy Law Enforcement and Human Rights' (2010) 59 *ICLQ* 141, 155; Papastavridis, 'European Convention' (n 40) 120.

[137] Papanicolopulu, *International Law* (n 26) 152–32; 'Human Rights' Papanicolopulu, (n 29) 526.

the existence of *de iure* jurisdiction, which carries with it a presumption *iuris tantum* of *de facto* jurisdiction. Moreover, under Articles 91 and 94 of the LOSC, conferral of nationality on ships is not mandatory but, if a State has conferred it, nationality of a ship implies for the flag State a set of positive and negative obligations, including human rights obligations. If a State is not realistically capable of controlling human rights protection on board its ships, it ought to be more measured when granting its nationality to ships.[138] For that reason, even if the exercise of effective flag State jurisdiction is more limited, there are always some powers that can be exerted; what the flag State cannot do is to use the limited extent of flag State competences to decline to ensure human rights with regard to flagged ships.[139] Other solutions would not be acceptable in terms of policy, for the rule of law and a State machinery are indispensable conditions for nurturing and protecting human rights.[140] Therefore, if the only State that presumably can exert jurisdiction over persons on board vessels is the flag State, this latter should be asked to *de facto* protect human rights on board vessels flying its flag.

The question that follows is 'what rights should be respected and protected by the flag State?' At this point, a test of feasibility (what can realistically be complied with) is needed, considering the features of the marine environment and the lack of a sufficiently characterised (*de facto*) control over the ship.

The key is the 'positive obligations' formula, a conceptual tool devised in the case law of the ECtHR to ensure the effectiveness of human rights protection.[141] In fact, 'the fulfilment of a duty under the [ECHR] on occasion necessitates some positive action on the part of the State; in such circumstances, the State cannot simply remain passive'.[142] The ECHR 'does not merely compel the State to abstain from such interference: in addition to this primarily negative undertaking, there may be positive obligations inherent [to each human right]',[143] which may include 'reasonable and appropriate measures to secure the applicant's rights'.[144] This case law was later consolidated in the *Ilaşcu* case, where the ECtHR stated:

> The undertakings given by a Contracting Party under Article 1 of the [ECHR] include, in addition to the duty to refrain from interfering with the enjoyment of the rights and freedoms guaranteed, positive obligations to take appropriate steps to ensure respect for those rights and freedoms within its territory.[145]

[138] Papanicolopulu, *International Law* (n 26) 154 and 196–97; Papanicolopulu, 'Human Rights' (n 29) 526.

[139] Oxman, 'Human Rights' (n 39) 399.

[140] ibid 402.

[141] Sudre, *Droit* (n 106) 244ff; Frédéric Sudre, 'Les "obligations positives" dans la jurisprudence européenne des droits de l'homme', in Paul Mahoney (ed), *Protection des droits de l'homme: La perspective européenne – Mélanges à la memoire de Rolv Ryssdal* (Carl Heymanns 2000) 1361.

[142] *Airey v Ireland* (App no. 6289/73) ECtHR 9 October 1979, § 25.

[143] *Marckx v Belgium* (App no. 6833/74) ECtHR 13 June 1979, § 31.

[144] *López Ostra v Spain* (App no. 16798/90) ECtHR 9 December 1994, § 51.

[145] *Ilaşcu* [2004] § 313.

'Those obligations', continued the ECtHR, 'remain even where the exercise of the State's authority is limited …, so that it has a duty to take all the appropriate measures *which it is still within its power to take*'.[146]

This idea of positive obligations has been transposed into the law of the sea.[147] For example, the LOSC voiced the interaction between jurisdiction and positive obligations by establishing that 'Every State shall effectively exercise its jurisdiction and control in administrative, technical and social matters over ships flying its flag'.[148] As seen in Chapter 3, this means that a flag State has to 'assume jurisdiction under its internal law over each ship flying its flag and its master, officers and crew in respect of administrative, technical and social matters concerning the ship'.[149] As such, the LOSC devised flag State jurisdiction not as an empty concept, but rather as a meaningful instrument entailing the actual employment of authority. Moreover, Article 98 of the LOSC includes positive obligations regarding saving lives at sea and organising search and rescue facilities, further extended under the SOLAS Convention and the International Convention on Maritime Search and Rescue (SAR Convention).

Although positive obligations are relevant under both domains, it is not clear whether compliance with the law of the sea requirements is enough to meet the bar of human rights bodies.[150] This was at stake in the *Hirsi Jamaa* case, but the ECtHR did not pay much attention to the duties deriving from the SAR Convention, perhaps because the respondent State was Italy, but the facts occurred within the Maltese search and rescue zone. The ECtHR being a treaty-based body, its primary task is to interpret and enforce its constitutive human rights treaty, not the LOSC. This does not mean that cross-fertilisation is not possible, or that the ECtHR should not take into account what is set forth in the LOSC. However, the requirements of the ECHR (like those of the LOSC) are autonomous. Therefore, if the law of the sea requirements are met, that does not mean that human rights requirements are met also (and vice versa). But when a petition is submitted to it, the ECtHR has to examine it only if those obligations enshrined in the ECHR have been complied with – and leave the law of the sea requirements for the appropriate fora.

As seen earlier, *de iure* flag State jurisdiction follows the ship – which entails that it often overlaps and concurs with coastal State jurisdiction, ie in the EEZ, the territorial sea or internal waters. Even on the high seas, in some cases States may have *de iure* jurisdiction over foreign vessels. When this happens, persons on board that vessel may be subject to concurring human rights jurisdiction.

In the *Drieman* case, the overlapping jurisdiction could have been discussed, for the facts referred to applicants on board a Dutch vessel, and dinghies

146 ibid (emphasis added).
147 Papanicolopulu, *International Law* (n 26) 171ff; Papanicolopulu, 'Human Rights' (n 29) 523.
148 Article 94(1) of the LOSC.
149 Article 94(2)(b) of the LOSC.
150 Papanicolopulu, 'Human Rights' (n 29) 523–24.

launched from it, within the Norwegian EEZ, claiming to be exercising their freedom of expression and association.[151] The ECtHR could have discussed whether Norway had *de iure* jurisdiction over that zone, or what the actual extent of flag State jurisdiction was in this case. However, it only stated that because Norway actually exercised the powers assigned to *de iure* jurisdiction of States with respect to the EEZ, it *de facto* held jurisdiction under Article 1 of the ECHR.[152] In this sense, it was still a form of intra-spatial (and quasi-territorial) State jurisdiction that *de facto* prevailed over flag State jurisdiction.

On a different level, warships and public-owned vessels might also have a limited, but still effective control over foreign vessels. This happens, for example, when States exercise the right of visit under Article 110 of the LOSC or other relevant law of the sea rule, search and rescue operations, interdiction operations or pollution control. When this is the case, Article 1 of the ECHR is immediately triggered, and States are bound by whichever human right might be infringed and whose protection can realistically be sought in that State: in most cases, that is the right to life, the prohibition of torture, the right to liberty or the *non-refoulement* principle, but there is room to contend that other human rights and freedoms may be questioned, as was freedom of expression in the *Women of Waves* case.[153] In the *Ali Samatar* and the *Hassan* cases, the ECtHR adjudicated on counter-piracy operations taking place off the coast of Somalia. Consistent with its prior case law, the ECtHR declared that the interception of a pirate vessel on the territorial sea of Somalia (*in casu*, duly authorised by the coastal State) entailed *ipso facto* the jurisdiction of the intercepting State as a result of the physical intervention of State agents.[154] Seen together, the *Drieman*, the *Ali Samatar*, and the *Hassan* cases were apparently decided differently: in the *Drieman* case, the ECtHR recognised the human rights jurisdiction of the coastal State; in the *Ali Samatar* and the *Hassan* cases, where the coastal State was non-European, it recognised the jurisdiction of the intercepting State. In their essence, however, these cases are cohesive and reflect the same idea already mentioned before: human rights jurisdiction is not to be recognised to a State that can lawfully exert authority under law of the sea rules, but rather to the State that has actually employed the physical force that entails effective control over a person. And considering the object of those cases, the ECtHR had to assess whether the respondent States held jurisdiction under Article 1 of the ECHR; what it did not say (and did not need to) is whether other States held a concurrent title to jurisdiction under general international law or a human rights treaty.

[151] *Drieman and Others v Norway* (App no. 33678/96) ECtHR (Decision) 4 May 2000, 2–3.
[152] ibid 7–8.
[153] *Women on Waves and Others v Portugal* (App no. 31276/05) ECtHR 3 February 2009.
[154] *Ali Samatar and Others v France* (App nos. 17110/10 and 17301/10) ECtHR 4 December 2014, § 31; *Hassan and Others v France* (App nos. 46695/10 and 54588/10) ECtHR 4 December 2014, § 39.

With regard to concurring jurisdiction on the high seas, the *Rigopoulos* was inaugural in the case law of the ECtHR, referring to the detention of crew members of a Panamanian vessel on the high seas by a Spanish vessel, but only after Panama's authorisation pursuant to Article 17(3) and (4) of the 1988 United Nations Convention against Illicit Traffic in Narcotic Drugs and Psychotropic Substances:[155] ie Spain could claim the exercise of *de iure* jurisdiction over a foreign vessel under law of the sea rules, even though the ECtHR did not discuss the lawfulness of this exercise of authority. Claimants argued that Article 5(3) of the ECHR had been violated, since they had not been submitted to a judge within a reasonable time after detention. Nonetheless, the ECtHR justified this delay with the fact that this provision could not have been enforced before due to the specific nature of the marine environment.[156] This suggests two ideas: first, the ECtHR accepted that the special features of the marine environment do not prevent the application of human rights at sea, although they pose delicate questions of feasibility of their enforcement;[157] second, the alleged infringement of the human right in question (the excessive time of detention) had occurred already on board the Spanish vessel (when individuals were already under *de iure* flag State jurisdiction of Spain), but the possible infringement of the human right was the result of a continuous conduct that began with the interception of the vessel and the detention of its crew members.

In the *Medvedyev* case, the applicants (crew members of the *Winner*, a Cambodian vessel intercepted by a French warship on the high seas) alleged that their human rights under Article 5 of the ECHR had been breached by an interception and subsequent detention on the high seas. The Cambodian authorities had authorised France to intercept the ship, which meant that France held *de iure* jurisdiction. During the operation, the French frigate pursued the *Winner* and, after several unsuccessful peaceful attempts, resorted to force to stop and board the *Winner*; finally, the *Winner* was towed to a port in France.[158] To assess jurisdiction, the ECtHR first referred to flag State jurisdiction, and seemed to be prepared to conclude that events were within France's jurisdiction, since it exercised flag State jurisdiction on board its warship.[159] However, it eventually explained France's jurisdiction with the fact that it 'exercised full and exclusive control over the *Winner* and its crew, at least *de facto*, from the time of its interception, in a continuous and uninterrupted manner until they were tried in France'.[160]

Both *Rigopoulos* and *Medvedyev* convey the idea that interception of a ship on the high seas entails jurisdiction of the intercepting State under Article 1

[155] *Rigopoulos v Spain* (App no. 37388/97) ECtHR (Decision) 12 January 1999, 2.
[156] ibid 9.
[157] See also *Ali Samatar* [2014] §§ 53–59; *Hassan* [2014] §§ 97–104.
[158] *Medvedyev* [2010] §§ 13–14.
[159] ibid §§ 65–66.
[160] ibid § 67.

of the ECHR, regardless of it being assessed as *de iure* or *de facto* jurisdiction. In both cases, the respondent States failed to contest that the applicants were subject to their jurisdiction, implicitly confirming that the employment of enforcement measures against a foreign vessel and crew is enough under such provision.[161] This same idea was implied in the *Vassis* case – where a Panamanian ship was intercepted by French authorities off the West coast of Africa – and no question of extraterritorial jurisdiction was raised.[162] Outside the Strasbourg system, the same idea was followed in the well-known *J.H.A. v Spain* case, decided by the UN Committee Against Torture, where persons on board the *Marine I* (a vessel that had capsized on the high seas) were considered to be within Spain's jurisdiction, not because of the flag of the vessel, but rather because it 'maintained control over the persons on board the *Marine I* from the time the vessel was rescued'.[163] As such, jurisdiction was determined as a result of physical and effective control over individuals, not the ship, possibly because, the vessel having capsized (thus, its instrumental function being hampered), the individual–State link was clearer.

In the case *Women on Waves*, a Dutch vessel was prohibited from entering the Portuguese territorial sea on grounds of non-innocent passage, since the crew members and the vessel were engaged in activities that were a felony under the Portuguese criminal law. Therefore, a warship prevented the Dutch vessel from entering into the territorial sea.[164] It is remarkable that the ECtHR did not explain under which test Portugal had jurisdiction over the applicants; it did not even assess if the *de iure* enforcement conduct of Portugal was derived from Article 19 of the LOSC – it assumed it was, and declared that the infringement of the applicants' freedoms of expression and association was a result of a disproportionate response of the Portuguese authorities to the actual threat posed by the applicants.[165] Therefore, implied in the reasoning of the ECtHR was the idea that a mere form of physical control is enough to establish a link of jurisdiction under Article 1 of the ECHR, even if physical control is not materialised in physical contact.[166] Contrary to *Rigopoulos* and *Medvedyev*, jurisdiction in the *Women on Waves* case was not the result of the interception of a vessel (ie stop and visit), but of a conduct of a warship able to interfere with the normal route or operation of a foreign vessel.[167]

Finally, in the *Hirsi Jamaa* case, the ECtHR had to decide on the alleged breach of human rights of Somali and Eritrean individuals who were rescued on

[161] Papanicolopulu, 'Human Rights' (n 29) 520.
[162] *Vassis and Others v France* (App no. 62736/09) ECtHR 27 June 2013, §§ 6–23.
[163] *J.H.A. v Spain*, CAT/C/41/D/323/2007, UN Committee Against Torture, 21 November 2008, § 8.2.
[164] *Women on Waves* [2009] §§ 7ff.
[165] ibid §§ 32ff.
[166] Milanović, *Extraterritorial* (n 47) 167; Papanicolopulu, *International Law* (n 26) 151; Papanicolopulu, 'Human Rights' (n 29) 522; Papastavridis, 'European Convention' (n 40) 122.
[167] Papanicolopulu, 'Human Rights' (n 29) 522.

the high seas (although in the Maltese Search and Rescue Region) by the Italian coastguard, transferred onto the Italian vessels, and returned to Libya.[168] With respect to jurisdiction, whereas the applicants and the third-party interveners clearly assumed Italy's jurisdiction over the applicants (respectively, on grounds of *de iure* flag State jurisdiction and *de facto* control over persons), Italy recognised that events took place on board its warships, but framed its intervention as a search and rescue, and not an interception for the purposes of the LOSC:[169] ie it claimed that *de iure* flag State jurisdiction did not amount to *de facto* human rights jurisdiction. However, the Italian submission was not entirely correct, since, as said before, the exercise of a search and rescue operation for the purposes of the SAR Convention is a form of spatial and flag State jurisdiction, although it entails a functionally limited responsibility for human rights protection. At most, Italy could claim that under the SAR Convention it was Malta, and not Italy, who was responsible for searching and rescuing, which would be evidence of the difficulties arising from the potential existence of multiple and overlapping titles to maritime jurisdiction. But once it intervened, regardless of the title or the source of obligation, Italy automatically had *de facto* control over ships and persons, and human rights jurisdiction arose.[170] In the end, faced with a problem of interaction of international regimes, Italy claimed that the application of the LOSC and the SAR Convention would preclude the application of human rights treaties. This position, however, is untenable. Being a human rights body, the ECtHR adopted an objective assessment test[171] and declared that *de iure* and *de facto* flag State jurisdiction entailed human rights jurisdiction of Italy over persons on board its warships, regardless of the motivations of the Italian operation; moreover, it declared that *de facto* control over a third vessel implies jurisdiction over the persons on board it.[172] For this purpose, the fact that the operations were of search and rescue per se was not relevant for hampering the emergence of a link of jurisdiction[173] and, not surprisingly, the ECtHR concluded that the applicants were *de iure* and *de facto* under the jurisdiction of Italy.[174]

From this case law, it seems clear that, for the ECtHR, *de iure* jurisdiction of flag States is enough to entail States' jurisdiction under Article 1 of the ECHR.

[168] *Hirsi Jamaa* [2012] §§ 9–14.

[169] ibid §§ 64–66.

[170] In general, see Guilfoyle, 'Counter-Piracy' (n 136) 155.

[171] Natalie Klein, 'A Case for Harmonizing Laws on Maritime Interceptions of Irregular Migrants' (2014) 63 *ICLQ* 787, 789 and 801; Irini Papanicolopulu, 'Hirsi Jamaa v. Italy' (2013) 107 *American Journal of International Law* 417, 420; Papanicolopulu, 'Human Rights' (n 29) 521–22, who highlights the benefits of the objective assessment of facts (not of intentions) in terms of rule of law and legal certainty.

[172] *Hirsi Jamaa* [2012] §§ 76–77. As such, the ECtHR apparently adopted a personal test of jurisdiction.

[173] ibid § 79.

[174] ibid § 81.

In this context, a curious example was the *Xhavara* decision, in which the ECtHR decided on a case wherein an Albanian boat had been sunk by an Italian warship 35 nautical miles off the Italian coast, with the resulting fatalities and injured persons[175] and applications submitted based on Articles 2 and 3 of the ECHR. The ECtHR first noted that only Italy (and not Albania) had jurisdiction under Article 1 of the ECHR, since according to the narrative submitted the boat had been sunk by the Italian warship[176] – which seems to convey a confusion between jurisdiction and attribution/responsibility, and thus a wide personal test for determining jurisdiction. However, this view seems to refer only to the lack of jurisdiction of Albania; Italy's jurisdiction, instead, seems to be implied as an extension of the *de iure* jurisdiction of the Italian courts, which had been discussing the same facts. However, the Italian courts' jurisdiction over the master of a ship in case of collision (under Article 97(1) of the LOSC) do not imply Italy's general jurisdiction over the persons on board that ship; such inference by synecdoche is methodologically incorrect. But the lesson from this and the previous cases is that the ECtHR is more comfortable with finding a basis of *de iure* jurisdiction of States to claim that individuals at sea can claim to be holders of human rights under the ECHR.

When the standard of jurisdiction enshrined in Article 1 of the ECHR is met, the entire set of human rights established in the ECHR is potentially applicable. Some entitlements are hardly applicable (eg right to marry, right to education, right to free elections, or equality between spouses); others will only be relevant in rare cases, such as freedom of religion, expression or association; and other rights and freedoms will often be relevant, such as the right to life, the right to physical integrity, criminal and fair trial guarantees, human freedom and the principle of *non-refoulement*. What cannot be said with respect to a particular right or freedom enshrined in the ECHR is that it will *never* be relevant in the context of States' human rights jurisdiction at sea. In the end, what is apposite is to assess what can realistically be asked of the flag State with respect to foreign vessels and persons aboard.[177]

3. HUMAN RIGHTS IN THE LOSC: PARTICULARLY, REPRESSION OF SLAVERY AND THE PROTECTION OF HUMAN LIFE

The LOSC is not a human rights treaty, but that does not mean that incidentally it cannot enshrine human rights. The 1963 Vienna Convention on Consular Relations is not a human rights treaty, but that did not prevent the ACtHR from

[175] *Xhavara and Others v Italy and Albania* (App no. 39473/98) ECtHR (Decision) 11 January 2001, 2–3.

[176] ibid 5.

[177] On this topic, see Papanicolopulu, *International Law* (n 26) 194ff.

qualifying the right of consular and diplomatic communication as a human right.[178] In the same way, a right of diplomatic and consular notification is also enshrined in Article 27(3) of the LOSC,[179] applicable when coastal States arrest crew members of a vessel in the exercise of the right of innocent passage, which is only established with respect to the exercise of coastal States' criminal jurisdiction, not civil jurisdiction. If one endorses the view of the ACtHR, then Article 27(3) of the LOSC enshrines a human right also.

Furthermore, several provisions of the LOSC articulate rights of private actors engaged in maritime activities, which are symmetrical to others nurtured under human rights law.[180] For instance, Article 73(3) of the LOSC establishes that coastal States cannot impose, as punishment for the infringement of their fisheries' laws and regulations on their EEZs, imprisonment (except if States concerned agree otherwise) or any form of corporal punishment. Under Article 73(4) of the LOSC, a right of communication with the flag State is enshrined where the vessel is arrested by the coastal State. Moreover, pursuant to Article 230 of the LOSC, monetary penalties can only be imposed in the specific cases of pollution set forth therein, and the 'recognized rights of the accused shall be observed'. Under this provision, not only the procedural guarantees under domestic law shall be observed, but also those guarantees that are established in human rights treaties, constituting a common minimum denominator on this topic, are incorporated by reference in Article 230 of the LOSC – which implies that coastal States are bound by these international fair trial standards even if they are not parties to the human rights treaty in question.[181] Furthermore, the structure of the prompt release procedure to some extent resembles the habeas corpus proceedings in domestic law. And finally, Article 227 of the LOSC establishes a right of non-discrimination (once more, apparently addressed to foreign *ships*) with respect to the exercise of coastal States' jurisdiction pursuant to Part XII of the LOSC. All these provisions are aimed at limiting coastal States' spatial jurisdiction in order to protect private actors' interests.[182]

In other law of the sea instruments, outlining possible human rights of private actors is also noticeable: that is the case, for example, for Articles 21(1) and 22(1) of the Fish Stocks Agreement, for Article 9(1) of the 2000 Protocol against the Smuggling of Migrants by Land, Sea and Air, for Article 17(5) of the 1988 UN Convention against the Illicit Traffic in Narcotic Drugs, or for Article 2*bis*(1) of the SUA Convention (which contains a non-prejudice clause concerning human rights in general). As a common element, these treaties contain a provision enabling the master, crew member or person on board to

[178] *The Right to Information on Consular Assistance in the Framework of the Guarantees of the Due Process of Law* [Advisory Opinion, 1 October 1999] ACtHR Series A, No. 16, § 124.

[179] See, *mutatis mutandis*, Papanicolopulu, *International Law* (n 26) 47 and 88.

[180] Treves, 'Human Rights' (n 26) 3.

[181] Oxman, 'Human Rights' (n 39) 426.

[182] Vukas, 'Droit de la mer' (n 40) 75.

contact the flag State or, in some cases, his State of nationality, in case of interference with navigation by a third State.[183]

In the case law, there are some examples of human rights activism also. In the *Arctic Sunrise* case, the arbitral tribunal constituted under Article 287 and Annex VII of the LOSC considered that the freedoms of expression and demonstration had been 'exercised in conjunction with the freedom of navigation'.[184] The arbitral tribunal refrained from explicitly deriving these human freedoms from the freedom of the high seas, or the freedom of navigation, but being a law of the sea body, its authority was to settle the dispute in accordance within the LOSC legal parameters. Thus, by referring to these human rights, the arbitral tribunal implicitly declared that freedoms of expression and demonstration are protected under the LOSC. In the context of the ITLOS, the key formula is 'considerations of humanity':[185] under this designation (ostensibly avoiding the expression human rights), the disproportionate use of force that endangers the right to life has been condemned,[186] and the value of human freedom upheld.[187] Moreover, in the '*Tomimaru*' and the '*Louisa*' cases, the ITLOS upheld the core value of the international standards of due process of law, in particular as developed under human rights law.[188] Nonetheless, so far considerations of humanity have been used by the ITLOS as an elastic tool aimed at delivering human-oriented decisions, but also neutral and empty of a clear and meaningful legal content.[189] At most, what can be said is that considerations of humanity are a tool for interpreting the exercise of States' competences in a human rights-friendly manner. In these cases, the law of the sea dispute settlement bodies have *de facto* merged the law of the sea with human rights law in order to produce common standards.[190] In this section, however, the focus is

[183] Papanicolopulu, 'Human Rights' (n 29) 518.

[184] *Arctic Sunrise Arbitration (The Netherlands v Russian Federation) (Merits)* [Award, 14 August 2015] PCA Case No. 2014-02, §§ 227–28.

[185] In the case law of the ICJ, see *Corfu Channel (United Kingdom v Albania) (Merits)* [Judgment, 9 April 1949] ICJ Rep 4, 22, where 'considerations of humanity' was the chapeau to foster the creation of a maritime environment safe for human beings: Irini Papanicolopulu, 'Considerations of Humanity in the *Enrica Lexie* Case' (2015) 22 *Questions of International Law – Zoom-In* 25, 27].

[186] *M/V 'Saiga' (No. 2) (Saint Vincent and the Grenadines v Guinea)* [Judgment, 1 July 1999] ITLOS Rep 10, §§ 155ff; *Idem*, 'Separate Opinion of Judge Mensah', § 20, referring to the human dignity and human rights of individuals.

[187] *'Juno Trader' (Saint Vincent and the Grenadines v Guinea-Bissau)* [Judgment, 18 December 2004] ITLOS Rep 17, § 77; *Idem*, 'Joint Separate Opinion of Judges Mensah and Wolfrum', § 3, referring to fair trial and due process guarantees; ibid, 'Separate Opinion of Judge Treves', § 5, referring to the disproportionate use of force and fair trial guarantees. See also *Enrica Lexie Incident (Italy v India)* [Order, 24 July 2015] ITLOS Rep 176, § 133.

[188] *'Tomimaru' (Japan v Russian Federation)* [Judgment, 6 August 2007] ITLOS Rep 74, § 76; *M/V 'Louisa' (Saint Vincent and the Grenadines v Kingdom of Spain)* [Judgment, 28 May 2013] ITLOS Rep 4, § 155.

[189] For a similar position, see Papanicolopulu, 'Considerations' (n 185) 28; Papanicolopulu, *International Law* (n 26) 166.

[190] Papanicolopulu, 'Human Rights' (n 29) 529; Papanicolopulu, 'Considerations' (n 185) 36.

not on these considerations of humanity, but rather on the two most prominent (human) rights assigned to individuals in the LOSC: the right not to be kept as a slave, serf, or forced labourer; and the right to life.

3.1. Repression of Slavery

3.1.1. What Amounts to Slavery?

Article 99 of the LOSC establishes that

> [e]very State shall take effective measures to prevent and punish the transport of slaves in ships authorized to fly its flag and to prevent the unlawful use of its flag for that purpose. Any slave taking refuge on board any ship, whatever its flag, shall *ipso facto* be free.

Although referring to the high seas, Article 99 of the LOSC is also applicable in the EEZ *ex vi* Article 58(2) of the LOSC. Moreover, Article 110(1)(b) of the LOSC empowers flag States with a right to intercept and visit a vessel on the high seas if there is 'reasonable ground for suspecting that: … (b) the ship is engaged in slave trade'.

In spite of being autonomous with regard to other treaties, these norms fit within a broader international policy of slavery and slave trade repression, which began with the 1890 General Act of the Brussels Conference,[191] and was resumed by the 1926 Slavery Convention, or the 1956 Supplementary Convention on the Abolition of Slavery, the Slave Trade and Institutions and Practices Similar to Slavery. Furthermore, the ICJ has already referred to repression of slavery as an *erga omnes* obligation binding upon all States in the international legal sphere.[192] Nonetheless, before the HSC and the LOSC were adopted, there was no international customary rule conferring on States a right of visit of vessels suspected of carrying slaves.[193]

Nonetheless, and taking into account the LOSC only, it is not entirely clear what the terms 'slavery' or 'slave' mean in this context. Although there is no *lex specialis* in the LOSC defining these terms, by taking systemic interpretation seriously, one must acknowledge that 'in many cases the verbal reconstruction

[191] Article XXII of this act conferred reciprocal rights of interception, visit and seizure of vessels in the Indian Ocean and the Red Sea whose tonnage is greater than 500 tons.

[192] *Barcelona Traction, Light and Power Company Limited (Belgium v Spain)* [Judgment, 5 February 1970] ICJ Rep 3, § 34.

[193] Douglas Guilfoyle, *Shipping Interdiction and the Law of the Sea* (CUP 2011) 75; Rosemary Rayfuse, *Non-Flag State Enforcement in the High Seas* (Brill 2004) 54; Robert Reuland, 'Interference with Non-National Ships on the High Seas: Peacetime Exceptions to the Exclusivity Rule of Flag-State Jurisdiction' (1989) 22 *Vanderbilt Journal of Transnational Law* 1161, 1190. Against, see Yoshifumi Tanaka, *The International Law of the Sea* (3rd edn, CUP 2019) 200.

of legal rules necessarily takes us outside of the immediate context of a single treaty'.[194] As such, the concepts of 'slavery' or 'slave' from other fields of international law can be operational in the law of the sea realm.[195] This is a good example of legislation or incorporation by reference, whereby an international treaty (*in casu*, the LOSC) refers to a concept set forth in different international instruments in order to avoid entropy and promote the integrity of the international legal order.[196] In fact, some treaties have adopted a definition of slavery, all of them having the core element of the existence of rights of ownership over individuals. According to the 1926 Slavery Convention, 'Slavery is the status or condition of a person over whom any or all of the powers attaching to the right of ownership are exercised'.[197] This is the classic meaning of slavery, as acknowledged for centuries, and which was received by human rights instruments as an authoritative definition within the international legal order. However, it does not reflect contemporary problems of repression of slavery, since no positive legal order accepts, at least *de iure*, the existence of ownership rights over individuals. Thus, an evolutionary definition of slavery is required, one that takes into account the new practices and necessities of the twenty-first century and considers practices akin to slavery.[198] In the *Rantsev* and the *Chowdury* cases, for instance, the ECtHR adopted this evolutionary approach and included in the *fattispecie* of Article 4 of the ECHR a case of human trafficking.[199]

Furthermore, slavery (together with servitude and forced labour) is also the object of several human rights and international criminal law instruments.[200] In the *Siliadin* case, the ECtHR stated that Article 4 of the ECHR encapsulates

[194] Ulf Linderfalk, 'State Responsibility and the Primary-Secondary Rules Terminology – The Role of Language for an Understanding of the International Legal System' (2009) 78 *Nordic Journal of International Law* 53, 58.

[195] Efthymios Papastavridis, *The Interception of Vessels on the High Seas – Contemporary Challenges to the Legal Order of the Oceans* (Hart Publishing 2014) 267.

[196] Alan Boyle and Christine Chinkin, *The Making of International Law* (OUP 2007) 247.

[197] Article 1(a). For its part, the concept of servitude, which is forbidden as a 'particularly serious form of denial of freedom', includes, 'in addition to the obligation to perform certain services for others, … the obligation for the "serf" to live on another person's property and the impossibility of altering his condition': *Siliadin v France* (App no. 73316/01) ECtHR 26 July 2005, § 124. On the other hand, according to § 1 of Article 2 of Convention No. 29 of the International Labour Organization (ILO), forced or compulsory work shall mean 'all work or service which is exacted from any person under the menace of any penalty and for which the said person has not offered himself voluntarily'. Unlike forced or compulsory work, slavery and servitude are a continuing personal *status*, although not necessarily permanent: Mark Janis, Richard Kay and Anthony Bradley, *European Human Rights Law – Texts and Materials* (3rd edn, OUP 2008) 231; Rainey, Wicks and Ovey, *European Convention* (n 104) 220–21.

[198] Efthymios Papastavridis, '"Fortress Europe" and Frontex: Within or Without International Law?' (2010) 79 *Nordic Journal of International Law* 75, 85; Papastavridis, *Interception* (n 195) 269–70.

[199] *Rantsev* [2010] §§ 281–82; *Chowdury and Others v Greece* (App no. 21884/15) ECtHR 30 March 2017, § 67.

[200] Article 4 of the ECHR; Article 4 of the Universal Declaration of Human Rights (UDHR); Article 6 of the ACHR; and Article of the African Charter on Human and Peoples' Rights (ACHPR).

the core of human dignity and 'enshrines one of the fundamental values of democratic societies', and as such deserves special international protection.[201] Therefore, the right not to be held in slavery is absolute and non-derogable,[202] and demands from States a *negative* obligation to refrain from maintaining a person under slavery, servitude or forced labour, but also a *positive* obligation to take all effective measures for the prevention, repression, prosecution and penalisation of any act aimed at maintaining a person in such a situation.[203]

In the *Rantsev* case, the ECtHR declared that, if appropriate and necessary, States might be required to take specific operational measures to protect (actual or potential) victims of slavery.[204] When wording this positive obligation of taking operational measures, what the ECtHR had in mind were the cases of human trafficking, some of them carried out through the sea. Despite its core importance, no human rights instrument defines slavery.[205] Yet, it is clear that a historical definition of slavery, embodying those cases where a claim to an ownership right over a person is made, is part of Articles 99 and 110(1)(b) of the LOSC. The vexed question is whether other cases, sufficiently similar, are to be incorporated in the notion of slavery as defined in those provisions. In this context, there is a trend in scholarship and case law to equate slavery to other contemporary manifestations, such as servitude, human trafficking and human smuggling. However, there is no State practice or an authoritative precedent in case law that per se can justify the match.[206] This incorporation would be useful to provide a meaningful content to Articles 99 and 110(1)(b) of the LOSC, but also to equip flag States with enhanced tools for fighting practices of human trafficking and smuggling. Moreover, this incorporation would be useful to give a human face to the flag States' policies of interception of ships.[207] Of course, this does not mean that all cases of human smuggling and trafficking equate

[201] *Siliadin* [2005] § 112; *C.N. v United Kingdom* (App no. 4239/08) ECtHR 13 November 2012, § 65.

[202] David Harris, Michael O'Boyle, Ed Bates and Carla Buckley, *Harris, O'Boyle, and Warbrick: Law of the European Convention on Human Rights* (4th edn, OUP 2018) 281; Janis et al, *Human Rights* (n 197) 230; Rainey et al, *European Convention* (n 104) 219.

[203] *Siliadin v France* [2005] § 112; *Rantsev* [2010] § 218; *C.N.* [2012] § 66. See also *Hadijatou Mani Koraou v The Republic of Niger* (ECW/CCJ/JUD/06/08) Economic Community of West African States Community Court of Justice, Judgment 27 October 2008, §§ 83–85.

[204] *Rantsev* [2010] § 218; *C.N.* [2012] § 67; *L.E. v Greece* (App no. 71545/12) ECtHR 21 January 2016, § 58; *Chowdury* [2017] § 88.

[205] *Prosecutor v Kunarac et al* [Judgment, 22 February 2001] ICTY Case No. IT-96-23-T, §§ 533–43. In contrast, Article 7(2)(c) of the International Criminal Court (ICC) Statute defines enslavement as 'the exercise of any or all of the powers attaching to the right of ownership over a person and includes the exercise of such power in the course of trafficking in persons, in particular women and children'. If the silence of human rights treaties is a tool for promoting its adaption to new necessities of society, the narrow definition of the ICC Statute aims at addressing the specific concerns with the principle of legality in the context of criminal law.

[206] Guilfoyle, *Shipping Interdiction* (n 193) 228; Papastavridis, *Interception* (n 195) 267.

[207] Papastavridis, *Interception* (n 195) 267.

to modern manifestations of slavery, but rather that sometimes these practices result in slavery if the elements overlap.[208] In fact, the difference between old and new forms of slavery is that nowadays people are enslaved by violence and kept captive for economic exploitation purposes against their will, even if they keep freedom *de iure*.[209] When practices (eg human trafficking and smuggling) also promote this kind of *de facto* enslavement, the concepts overlap and are relevant for the purpose of Articles 99 and 110(1)(b) of the LOSC.[210]

3.1.2. *The Obligational Scope of Articles 99 and 110(1)(b) of the LOSC*

From these norms one can derive some States' obligations, entailing State responsibility in case of non-compliance,[211] although their obligational scope is not entirely clear. In addition, at least a specific entitlement is enjoyed by individuals under Article 99 of the LOSC.

Article 99 of the LOSC, *in fine*, establishes that 'Any slave taking refuge on board any ship, whatever its flag, shall *ipso facto* be free'. This means, on the one hand, that if an individual, kept on board as slave, manages to flee and find refuge on board a different vessel, he must be recognised *ipso facto* as free.[212] However, this individual does not become free after taking refuge on board a different ship; finding refuge on board a different ship only grants him a right to demand protection in the ship where he took refuge. Hence, Article 99 of the LOSC, *in fine*, not only qualifies that individual as already free by his human nature, but also articulates the individual's *erga omnes* (and inter-individual) right to freedom from any manifestation of slavery and establishes a guarantee of that freedom. Compared with Article 110(1)(b) of the LOSC, Article 99 has at first sight a broader-scope *ratione personae* in terms of rights-holders: whereas Article 110(1)(b) only refers to persons transported for the purpose of slave trade, Article 99 includes any person kept as a slave (eg seafarers used as slaves on board).

Furthermore, Article 99 of the LOSC establishes a duty of repression of slavery at sea (to 'take effective measures to prevent and punish') but delegates its materialisation to domestic law.[213] At first sight, it seems that the duty imposed

[208] ibid 275; Tanaka, *Law of the Sea* (n 193) 200, considering that there is room for arguing that an evolutionary concept of slavery encompasses all forms of slavery, as mentioned in Article 4 of the UDHR, which seems to be the case for human trafficking and smuggling.

[209] Papastavridis, *Interception* (n 195) 274.

[210] ibid 275–78.

[211] John Norton Moore, Myron Nordquist, Satyam Nandan and Shabtai Rosenne (eds), *United Nations Convention on the Law of the Sea 1982 – A Commentary*, III (Martinus Nijhoff 1995) 179. The ILC affirmed that this duty of States is generally recognised in international law. See ILC, 'Report of the International Law Commission on the Work of its 8th Session' (23 April–4 April 1956) UN Doc. A/3159, 281–82. The wording of the ILC was generically transposed into the HSC and the LOSC.

[212] Churchill and Lowe, *Law of the Sea* (n 58) 212.

[213] Moore et al (eds), *UN Convention*, III (n 211) 180–81.

upon flag States is meagre, since under the LOSC only flag States have primary jurisdiction over ships flying their flag, and can seize the ship and arrest those on board.[214] At most, Article 110(1)(b) of the LOSC empowers non-flag States only with a right to intercept and visit a ship on the high seas when there is 'reasonable ground for suspecting that: … (b) the ship is engaged in slave trade', regardless of being directly affected by the suspicious ship's conduct. However, since slavery is not analogous to piracy, and since no right of interference apart from visit and inspection is conferred on non-flag States, where the ship is actually engaged in slave trade, the interfering State can solely report its findings to the flag State.[215] The only exception might derive from (multilateral or bilateral) treaties that confer reciprocal rights on flag States to seize the vessel and arrest those on board. This reading squares well with an orthodox view of international law, under which rights and competences are assigned to States to accomplish their goals in the international arena, whereas their obligations are crafted as *non facere*. A sound example of this traditional narrative could be found in Article 110(1)(b) of the LOSC: it equips States with a power to visit and inspect non-national ships and an obligation not to interfere with flag States' primary jurisdiction, but does not establish an obligation to exercise the power of interference with foreign navigation. Consequently, if a State has reasonable grounds to suspect that a foreign ship is engaged in slave trade, it has authority to intercept and visit the ship, but has no obligation to do so. The same seems to result from Article 8 of the 2000 Protocol against the Smuggling of Migrants by Land, Sea and Air, applicable to cases where a vessel is suspected of being engaged in migrant smuggling.

However, a different approach should be tested. The argument of protection of flag States' primary jurisdiction is on shaky ground. If it were absolute, no interference would be accepted, and specifically, repression of slavery would not be a legitimate ground to intercept a vessel at sea. Nevertheless, Article 110(1)(b) of the LOSC clearly empowers all States to visit and inspect vessels suspected of being engaged in slave trade. One narrow interpretation of this provision is that it only admits foreign States to visit, inspect and report the evidence collected, trusting that the flag State will then take the appropriate measures to free those individuals on board and punish those exploiting them. But a legal order committed to the value of human dignity cannot be comfortable with that solution. Can the legal system ask States' agents visiting and inspecting the ship

[214] Churchill and Lowe, *Law of the Sea* (n 58) 212; Malcolm Evans, 'The Law of the Sea', in Evans *International Law* (n 48) 635, 649, highly critical of this solution; Guilfoyle, *Shipping Interdiction* (n 193) 76.

[215] Article 99 of the LOSC. See also Article 13 of the HSC. Churchill and Lowe, *Law of the Sea* (n 58) 212; Guilfoyle, *Shipping Interdiction* (n 193) 76; Natalie Klein, *Maritime Security and the Law of the Sea* (OUP 2012) 122; Papastavridis, '"Fortress Europe"' (n 198) 93; Tullio Treves, 'High Seas', in *Max-Planck Encyclopaedia of Public International Law*, § 19; Tanaka, *Law of the Sea* (n 193) 200.

only to report their findings to the flag State (perhaps, a flag state of convenience) and proceed without freeing those kept captive?

A different interpretation could arise from the interaction between human rights treaties and the LOSC. In fact, Article 99 of the LOSC works as a hinge between the law of the sea and human rights law, namely concerning freedom from slavery.[216] As a gateway of human rights into the law of the sea, Article 99 of the LOSC encapsulates in the law of the sea those States' obligations concerning repression of slavery that have been unfolded by human rights treaties and bodies. And, in an Hohfeldian perspective, where there is an entitlement to freedom from slavery, there must be a corresponding duty.

With regard specifically to the ECHR, an individual might complain that his rights and freedoms under Article 4 of the ECHR were breached where the flag State – also a party to the ECHR – did not adopt the necessary measures to repress slavery, after receiving a report from the State that exerted the right of visit and inspection under Article 110(1)(b) of the LOSC. In this case, flag States hold an obligation (under the LOSC) with a corresponding right (under the ECHR and the LOSC, read together) allocated to individuals.

This reasoning is apparently straightforward with respect to the flag State of the ship engaged in slave trade, but not necessarily with regard to the interfering State. However, the case law of the ECtHR on the extraterritorial jurisdiction of States is helpful to establish a framework of positive obligations of the interfering State. In this light, when a State intercepts a foreign flagged ship and exerts its right of visit and inspection, the ship is (as are the persons on board it) *de facto* under its jurisdiction pursuant to Article 1 of the ECHR. As a result, positive obligations deriving from Article 4 of the ECHR emerge, including the duty to free those held captive on board. When exercising its right of interception, visit and inspection over a ship suspected of being engaged in slave trade, under Article 110(1)(b) of the LOSC, a State *de facto* controls those on board the ship, and thus individuals on board that ship fall *ipso facto* under the interfering State's jurisdiction pursuant to provisions such as Article 1 of the ECHR. Therefore, the interfering State is required to enforce the human rights of those individuals under its jurisdiction – which implies that if on board there are individuals kept captive as slaves, then the interfering State is obliged to free these individuals if there are (eg military, physical) conditions to do so. Moreover, this obligation arises even if interference is grounded on other provisions (eg the statelessness of a ship, to repress piracy).

This interpretation is possible under Articles 1 and 4 of the ECHR alone, which equip individuals with a specific entitlement deriving from the freedom from slavery when they are at sea – which could not be derived from Article 110(1)(b) of the LOSC. But appealing to both the ECHR and the LOSC

[216] Moore et al (eds), *UN Convention*, III (n 211) 180.

together has one merit that should not be downplayed: since Article 110(1)(b) of the LOSC cannot be read in a vacuum, but rather in consistency with other provisions of the same system of international law, States claiming to exercise the right enshrined in this provision ought to be aware that it automatically entails jurisdiction pursuant to Article 1 of the ECHR – and therefore the application of Article 4 of the ECHR and the ECtHR's case law on repression of slavery, servitude and forced labour. In this sense, not only hidden in Article 99 is a human right not to be kept slave – derived *ipso jure* from this provision but strengthened by reference to Article 4 of the ECHR whenever a foreign State exercises its competences under Article 110(1)(b) of the LOSC – but also States are aware that, when they exercise their powers under this latter provision, they are still bound by the ECHR.

At first sight, this conclusion is not particularly exciting in terms of regime interaction, since it ultimately states that provisions of (and obligations deriving from) the LOSC and the ECHR exist in parallel, but do not shape each other, for the structure and scope of the entitlements enshrined in Articles 99 of the LOSC and 4 of the ECHR are still determined autonomously. In fact, treaty interpretation needs to consider extrinsic provisions as a guiding tool to interpret a specific treaty provision: eg to resort to Article 4 of the ECHR as a tool for determining the meaning of Article 99 of the LOSC. This cross-regime interpretation is part of a systemic view of international law, openly (although restrictively) admitted by Article 31(3)(c) of the VCLT,[217] but it is only useful in individual cases of implementation of treaty provisions by a State party to both treaties: eg enlightening the interfering State of the obligations deriving from Article 4 of the ECHR whenever exercising its competence under Article 110(1)(b) of the LOSC. At most, cross-regime interpretation is helpful to set out common standards as a result of a cross-fertilisation process,[218] but even this process is of limited value since the parties to the LOSC and the ECHR (and other human rights treaties) do not match: applying human rights standards in the interpretation and/or implementation of Article 110(1)(b) of the LOSC would equate to applying the ECHR to non-parties.

Nonetheless, there is at least one particular aspect that should be considered. If the right of visit and inspection is not exerted – as it seems it falls within the State's discretion whether or not to exercise this power – it would seem that no right could be claimed by the individuals in question as a result of the non-exercise of the State's competence. This would mean that if States do not exercise their powers of interference with navigation, even if there is a suspicion that a vessel is engaged in slave trade, individuals would seem not to have any entitlement to be freed under current law of the sea and human rights law. But this is only partially correct. The keywords are characterised knowledge of the fact (something more than a mere suspicion) and real capacity of the State to interfere and

[217] Matz-Lück, 'Norm Interpretation' (n 34) 209–10.
[218] ibid 232.

free the persons kept as slaves on board. If no knowledge exists, or the State has no real capacity to free those kept as slaves on board, then there is no duty to intercept the vessel suspected of being engaged in slave trade. But if there is both knowledge and real capacity to free the individuals kept slave on board, then the State ought to exercise its power of interception under Article 110(1)(b) of the LOSC, or otherwise it will fail to comply with its obligations under Article 4 of the ECHR. In this sense, cross-regime interaction in this case implies the transmogrification of a right to exercise a competence into a duty to exercise the said competence:[219] this is the major impact of human rights law in the law of the sea: to transform its 'language and substance', and require new duties towards individuals, including the duty to exercise the competences assigned to States under law of the sea rules.[220]

3.2. The Protection of Life at Sea

A principle of protection of human life is articulated in two provisions of the LOSC.[221] Article 98 frames a duty to render assistance to individuals at sea, namely to assist vessels in distress or shipwrecked persons. This duty is also applicable to the EEZ,[222] and there is room to claim that the duty incorporated in this provision embodies a universal obligation pursuant to international customary law,[223] which prevails over any consideration of sovereignty, and therefore should also apply in the territorial sea.[224] Article 146 establishes in broad terms that, with regard to activities carried out in the Area, 'necessary measures shall be taken to ensure effective protection of human life': in particular, 'the Authority shall adopt the appropriate rules, regulations and procedures to supplement existing international law as embodied in relevant treaties'.

The core importance of the right to life is almost self-explanatory. In the case law of the ECtHR, it has been conceived as 'the supreme value in the international hierarchy of human rights',[225] 'an inalienable attribute of human beings';[226]

[219] On this 'slow' transformation process, see Papanicolopulu *International Law* (n 26) 201.
[220] ibid 204–05.
[221] Papanicolopulu, *International Law* (n 26) 187ff; Papanicolopulu, 'Human Rights' (n 29) 516; Vukas, 'Droit de la mer' (n 40) 73–74.
[222] *Ex vi* Article 58(2) of the LOSC. For some authors, it is valid in all maritime zones: Moore et al (eds), *UN Convention*, III (n 211) 170; Seline Trevisanut, 'The Principle of *Non-Refoulement* at Sea and the Effectiveness of Asylum Protection' (2008) 12 *Max-Planck Yearbook of United Nations Law* 205, 235.
[223] Oxman, 'Human Rights' (n 39) 415.
[224] Richard Barnes, 'Refugee Law at Sea' (2004) 53 *ICLQ* 47, 52; Sophie Cacciaguidi-Fahy, 'The Law of the Sea and Human Rights' (2007) 19 *Sri Lanka Journal of International Law* 85, 95; Oxman, 'Human Rights' (n 39) 414. Pursuant to Article 18(2) of the LOSC, ships on course of innocent passage on the territorial sea can stop 'for the purpose of rendering assistance to persons, ships, or aircraft in danger of distress'.
[225] *Streletz, Kessler and Krenz v Germany* (App nos. 34044/96, 35532/97 and 44801/98) ECtHR 22 March 2001, §§ 87 and 94.
[226] ibid § 94.

and the ECtHR has resorted to expressions such as the 'sanctity of life'[227] to qualify the right to life.[228] This human right has a negative and a positive dimension: *grosso modo*, the negative obligation, binding upon States, not to intentionally and unlawfully end an individual's life; and the positive obligation, also binding upon States, to take the appropriate measures in order to protect the human life of the individuals under their jurisdiction, and to adopt the appropriate investigations in some cases of deprivation of life.[229]

3.2.1. Protection of Life under Article 98 of the LOSC

Article 98 of the LOSC seeks to encapsulate an immemorial moral duty to render assistance to persons in distress at sea[230] – an obligation that had already been transposed into international customary and treaty law,[231] namely the HSC,[232] the SOLAS Convention,[233] the 1989 International Convention on Salvage,[234] and the SAR Convention.[235] Since they all pertain to the same legal order, Article 98 of the LOSC has to be systemically interpreted with exogenous provisions from these treaties. Although Article 98 of the LOSC is systematically incorporated in Part VII (High Seas), it is applicable in other maritime areas.[236]

[227] *Pretty v the United Kingdom* (App no. 2346/02) ECtHR 29 April 2002, § 65.

[228] For its part, the UN Human Rights Committee qualified the right to life as the 'supreme right of the human being': *Baboeram and others v Suriname* (Communications nos. 146/1983 and 148 to 154/1983) Human Rights Committee 4 April 1985, UN Doc. Supp. No. 40 (A/40/40), § 14.3.

[229] *L.C.B. v United Kingdom* (App no. 23413/94) ECtHR 9 June 1998, § 36; *Öneryildiz v Turkey* (App no. 48939/99) ECtHR [GC] 30 November 2004, § 72.

[230] See generally Tullio Scovazzi, 'Human Rights and Immigration at Sea', in Rubio-Marín (ed), *Human Rights and Immigration* (OUP 2014) 212, 225, who includes this obligation in the list of general principles of international law for the purposes of Article 38(c) of the ICJ Statute. The core relevance of this duty explains why 'No remuneration is due from persons whose life was saved' (Article 16(1) of the 1989 International Salvage Convention).

[231] Barnes, 'Refugee Law' (n 224) 49; Cacciaguidi-Fahy, 'Law of the Sea' (n 224) 90; Aldo Chircop, 'Assistance at Sea and Places of Refuge for Ships: Reconciling Competing Norms', in Henrik Ringbom (ed), *Jurisdiction* (n 67) 141, 141; Fischer-Lescano et al, 'Border Controls' (n 136) 289; Myron Nordquist, Satya Nandan, Shabtai Rosenne and Neal Grandy (eds), *United Nations Convention on the Law of the Sea 1982 – A Commentary*, II (Martinus Nijhoff 1993) 193; DP O'Connell, *The International Law of the Sea*, I (Clarendon 1982) 813–14; Oxman, 'Human Rights' (n 39) 414, Papastavridis, *Interception* (n 195) 294; Seline Trevisanut, 'Search and Rescue Operations in the Mediterranean: Factor of Cooperation or Conflict?' (2010) 25 *International Journal of Marine and Coastal Law* 523, 527.

[232] Article 12.

[233] Chapter V, Regulation 33.

[234] Articles 8 and 10.

[235] Annex, Chapter 2, 2.1.10.

[236] Richard Barnes, 'The International Law of the Sea and Migration Control', in Bernard Ryan and Valsamis Mitsilegas (eds), *Extraterritorial Immigration Control – Legal Challenges* (Martinus Nijhoff 2010) 103, 137; Papanicolopulu, *International Law* (n 26) 187–88; Papastavridis, *Interception* (n 195) 295; Scovazzi, 'Human Rights' (n 230) 226; Tullio Scovazzi, 'La tutela della vita umana in mare, con particolare riferimento agli immigrati clandestini diretti verso l'Italia' (2005) 88 *Rivista di diritto internazionale* 106, 107.

What is not entirely clear is who the recipient of the duty enshrined in this provision is. At first sight, it seems to be the State:[237] paragraph 2 of this provision is clearly addressed to coastal States; and paragraph 1 begins with the expression 'Every [flag] State shall …'. However, this crystal-clear reading is far from correct, for otherwise Article 98 of the LOSC would set out a mere reciprocal obligation of adopting domestic measures binding upon masters of vessels, or aimed at ensuring the search and rescue of persons in distress at sea. Nevertheless, such interpretation is not consistent with the detailed obligational scope set out in paragraph 1(a) to (c). Thus, my suggestion is to divide and tailor this provision in as many duties as it encompasses, and then assess what its exact content is and who the legal person responsible for its performance is.

A first set of duties enshrined in Article 98(1) of the LOSC is, 'in so far as [the master] can do so without danger to the ship, the crew or the passengers', '(a) to render assistance to any person at sea in danger of being lost', '(b) to proceed with all possible speed to the rescue of persons in distress, if informed of their need of assistance, in so far as such action may reasonably be expected from him', and '(c) after a collision, to render assistance to the other ship, crew and its passengers'. According to the SAR Convention, a rescue operation is 'An operation to retrieve persons in distress, provide for their initial medical or other needs, and deliver them to a place of safety'.[238] The first sentence of Article 98 of the LOSC refers to the flag State and to the master, but implies that the immediate recipient of the duty is the flag State, which would seem to have the duty not to rescue persons in distress, but rather to oblige masters of vessels flying its flag to do so under domestic law (obligation of due diligence).[239]

However, this provision cannot be read in a vacuum. In particular, the wording of Article 10(1) of the 1989 International Convention on Salvage is clear in setting out that 'Every master is bound, so far as he can do so without serious danger to his vessel and persons thereon, to render assistance to any person in danger of being lost at sea'; under paragraphs 2 and 3 of the said provision, 'The States Parties shall adopt the measures necessary to enforce the duty set out in paragraph 1', whilst 'The owner of the vessel shall incur no liability for a breach of the duty of the master under paragraph 1'. Even though this reference comes from a different treaty, the fact that it was adopted and ratified by a portion of the States parties to the LOSC makes it possible to resort to cross-regime interpretation and shed some light on the obligational scope of Article 98(1) of the LOSC. In this vein, it is curious to note that, under Article 10 of the 1989 International Convention on Salvage, a rational distribution of duties between the master and the flag State is outlined, whereby the immediate recipient of the duty to render assistance to persons in distress at sea is the master of a vessel

[237] By implication, see Barnes, 'Migration Control' (n 236) 137; Papanicolopulu, *International Law* (n 26) 85.
[238] Annex, Chapter III, 1.3.2.
[239] Papanicolopulu, 'Human Rights' (n 29) 510 and 516; Vukas, 'Droit de la mer' (n 40) 78.

(provided that it is realistically possible to perform it without undue danger for the vessel and persons thereon), whereas the flag State has an indirect obligation (under due diligence) for ensuring the performance of this duty through its domestic law. Pursuant to Chapter V, Regulation 33 of the SOLAS Convention, the same allocation to the master of a vessel of the duty to render assistance is articulated.[240] In both cases, the duty to render assistance is clearly assigned to the master of the vessel *only*. Under these provisions, however, the scope of the master's duty of assistance is left open to an operational judgement made by the master, whereby he might assess if his vessel can assist a person in distress with due regard for the safety of his own vessel and crew-members.[241] This is the only reading that provides meaningful content to the right of being rescued to persons in distress at sea, or otherwise these latter would have to communicate with the State agents, through appropriate (but not expeditious) channels, to ask for rescue.

In this vein, read in conjunction with Article 10 of the International Convention on Salvage and Chapter V, Regulation 33 of the SOLAS Convention, it is possible to ascertain that under Article 98 of the LOSC the same distribution of (non-overlapping) obligations between the master of the vessel and the flag State is implicit in the LOSC:[242] the master is the recipient of the duty of providing expeditious assistance to a person in distress at sea, provided that undue danger is not caused to his vessel or the persons thereon; the flag State is the bearer of an indirect obligation (of conduct) to ensure, through its domestic law, that dereliction of duty from the master in performing that obligation is punished, and an obligation of due diligence to monitor masters in the performance of this obligation. In any case, if the obligation of rendering assistance is not performed properly by the master, the assessment of this non-performance is made through domestic courts. Nonetheless, this ought not to be seen as evidence that Article 98(1) of the LOSC is addressed to the flag State and not to the master: it only means that the appropriate forum to seek compensation, or to punish dereliction of duty, is the domestic court, in order to protect freedom of navigation and the exclusive jurisdiction of the flag State.

On a different level, pursuant to Article 98(2) of the LOSC a positive obligation is assigned to coastal States, so that they 'promote the establishment, operation and maintenance of an adequate and effective search and

[240] See also Irene Khan, 'Trading in Human Misery: A Human Rights Perspective on the *Tampa* Incident' (2003) 12 *Pacific Rim Law & Policy Journal* 9, 14.

[241] Cacciaguidi-Fahy, 'Law of the Sea' (n 224) 94.

[242] See also ibid 93–94; Kirchner et al, 'Coastal State Obligations' (n 108) 63–65; Laurent Lucchini and Michel Vœlckel, *Droit de la mer*, I (Pedone 1990) 124; Patricia Mallia, *Migrant Smuggling by Sea – Combating a Current Threat to Maritime Security through the Creation of a Cooperative Network* (Martinus Nijhoff 2010) 99–101. Against, see Barnes, 'Refugee Law' (n 224) 50, who, however, acknowledges that this obligation will be performed by 'private mariners in practice'; Papanicolopulu, *International Law* (n 26) 85ff, for whom the LOSC only creates reciprocal obligations between States.

rescue service regarding safety on and over sea and, where circumstances so require, … cooperate with neighbouring States for this purpose'. The same positive obligation underlies Chapter V of the SOLAS Convention and the entire SAR Convention. These obligations are also of means and of due diligence, not of result.[243]

The rationale behind these provisions is self-explanatory: effective rescue of persons at sea might in practice be difficult since individuals might not have the chance to ask for help; irregular migrants and potential asylum-seekers are more concerned with fleeing from their State of origin by whatever means possible, including overcrowded and unseaworthy vessels; it might be the case that no vessel or aircraft is close to render assistance; and flag States of convenience are not even likely to be vigilant and comply with their due diligence obligation. As such, some individuals at sea 'die not because they are targeted by states of destination, but because they are ignored'.[244] This explains the importance of positive obligations, including the adoption of general measures aimed to protect an undetermined number of individuals (eg those set out in the SOLAS Convention or in the SAR Convention), such as the creation of shore-based search and rescue services, capable of being ready on-call to provide assistance: because the intention is to save human lives (not to govern inter-State relations), the establishment of search and rescue zones shall not prejudice the demarcation of States' maritime boundaries;[245] and they are not mutually exclusive, which entails that if a ship is in distress within the search and rescue zone of a State, other coastal States or masters of vessels in the same zone can also have the duty to intervene.[246] In this case, however, the right to life ensured through these positive obligations has no subject-holder, since these requirements are prior to the existence of an individual being actually affected by the lack of these measures.

Furthermore, the right to life might also require from coastal States the adoption of individual measures aimed at protecting the life of a specific person who, in a particular circumstance, is at risk, provided that 'the authorities knew or ought to know at the time of the existence of a real and immediate risk to the life of an identified individual or individuals': States' accountability will arise if 'they failed to take measures within the scope of their powers which, judged reasonably, might have been expected to avoid that risk',[247] eg if they fail to

[243] Efthymios Papastavridis, 'Is There a Right to Be Rescued at Sea? A Skeptical View' (2014) 4 *Questions of International Law – Zoom In* 17, 22.

[244] Thomas Spijkerboer, 'Wasted Lives. Borders and the Right to Life of People Crossing Them' (2017) 86 *Nordic Journal of International Law* 1, 27.

[245] Chapter 2, paragraph 2.1.7 of the Annex to the SAR Convention. This implies that search and rescue activities can be undertaken extraterritorially. However, when performed in the territorial waters of third States, these operations need the consent of the coastal State (Chapter 3, paragraph 3.1.2. of the Annex to the SAR Convention).

[246] Kees Wouters and Maarten den Heijer, 'The *Marine I* Case: A Comment' (2010) 22 *International Journal of Refugee Law* 1, 4–5.

[247] *Osman v United Kingdom* (App no. 23452/94) ECtHR 28 October 1998, §§ 115–16; *Kontrová v Slovakia* (App no. 7510/04) ECtHR 31 May 2007, §§ 49–50; *Branko Tomašić and Others v Croatia*

provide assistance to a specific person in distress at sea who has asked for rescue to coastal States' authorities. Moreover, Article 98 of the LOSC also being a hinge between the LOSC and human rights treaties, it embodies, by the technique of incorporation by reference, the positive obligation of States to protect human life defined in the ECHR and the case law of the ECtHR.

Pursuant to Article 98 of the LOSC (as with the other treaties referred to), the obligation of rescue is due to individuals at sea, and is to be observed without exception and without any discrimination regarding the status of the person to be rescued.[248] One may question if individuals are mere beneficiaries of this duty (as objects of protection), but not necessarily creditors (or subjects of law). If one adopts a reading of Article 98 of the LOSC as entailing reciprocal, inter-State obligations only, then individuals are conceived of as objects of protection solely. However, considering the wording of these provisions, referring to a duty to provide for assistance, 'An Hohfeldian might conclude that international law establishes a right to be rescued at sea'.[249]

My claim is that, under these provisions, individuals are the actual holders of a right to life, opposable to the master, the flag or the coastal State, in the terms outlined above. In scholarship, however, there are those who contend that no right to be rescued at sea is afforded to individuals by the LOSC and other treaties (which only convey inter-State obligations), since no remedy is conferred on individuals in these treaties;[250] at most, one could derive an apparent right to disembarkation in a place of safety.[251] A right to be rescued at sea could only be derived from human rights treaties.[252] Technically, this position rests upon the idea of rights without holders. But this is clearly not the view of this book. As said in Chapter 2, the absence of a remedy in the international legal order is not proof of the absence of an entitlement, for the existence of a right to be rescued is solely dependent upon defining who is the addressee of a legal norm. In this case, the obligation to render assistance to individuals in distress at sea logically implies a right to be rescued held by those individuals. The absence of a remedy in the international legal order is evidence only that the proper place to claim and enforce this right – in the view of the drafters of the LOSC – is the national court.

(App no. 46598/06) ECtHR 15 January 2009, §§ 50–51; *Opuz v Turkey* (App no. 33401/02) ECtHR 9 June 2009, §§ 128–29; *Mikayil Mammadov v Azerbaijan* (App no. 4762/05) ECtHR 17 December 2009, §§ 99–100.

[248] Barnes, 'Refugee Law' (n 224) 50; Scovazzi, 'Human Rights' (n 230) 225; Scovazzi, 'La tutela' (n 236) 107. See Article 11, paragraph 1 of the 1910 Brussels International Convention for the Unification of Certain Rules of Law relating to Assistance and Salvage at Sea, which refers to the duty of rendering assistance to 'an enemy'.

[249] Oxman, 'Human Rights' (n 39) 414. See also Papanicolopulu, 'Human Rights' (n 29) 517.

[250] Papastavridis, 'Is There a Right' (n 243) 21–24. See also Papanicolopulu, *International Law* (n 26) 43 and 49–50.

[251] Papastavridis, 'Is There a Right' (n 243) 22–23.

[252] ibid 24ff.

The obligation of rescue (as the right to be rescued) set out in these treaties is 'incomplete',[253] since several elements of the obligational scope are absent. For example, there is no reference to where persons rescued should be disembarked, and no coastal or flag State has the duty to accept the persons rescued at sea:[254] this issue tends to be solved on an ad hoc basis.[255] But this incompleteness of the rule does not preclude a minimum content to arise: the right to be rescued, and the corresponding duty to rescue.

One practice has been to disembark persons saved in the next port of call, notably due to commercial considerations, except if a medical urgency requires stopping at the nearest port[256] – a solution in line with the idea that the holder of the duty to render assistance is the master of the vessel, and not the flag State.[257] Despite the core importance of saving human life at sea, treaties do acknowledge the relevance of commercial concerns, as is implied in Article 8(1) of the 1989 International Convention on Salvage, according to which the master has a 'duty to the owner of the vessel or other property in danger: (a) to carry out the salvage operations with due care'.[258] Moreover, under Article 98 of the LOSC and the SAR Convention there is no obligation of the next port of call to accept rescued persons onto their territory.[259] At most, the State with jurisdiction for search and rescue is the most likely place of disembarkation, but no legal duty is established.[260] Nonetheless, the main question with the place of disembarkation refers not to regular seafarers, but rather to irregular migrants or potential asylum-seekers,[261] who may invoke the principle of *non-refoulement*: as established in the *Hirsi Jamaa* case, the objective test of *de facto* authority means that the rescuing State has jurisdiction under Article 1 of the ECHR, and therefore cannot disembark the individuals rescued in a place where they face a threat or risk of torture, or degrading or inhumane treatment. As such, the notion of place of safety has been interpreted as being more than just 'a place free from distress', but also 'free from *refoulement*'.[262]

This is a case where interaction between different international law fields is relevant: whereas under the law of the sea the only obligation binding upon the master and/or the State is to disembark the rescued persons in a place where they

[253] Barnes, 'Refugee Law' (n 224) 49.

[254] Papastavridis, 'Is There a Right' (n 243) 19; James Z Pugash, 'The Dilemma of the Sea Refugee: Rescue Without Refuge' (1977) 18 *Harvard Journal of International Law* 577, 578.

[255] Papastavridis, '"Fortress Europe"' (n 198) 87.

[256] Barnes, 'Refugee Law' (n 224) 51–52 and 63; Klein, 'Case' (n 171) 797; Wouters and den Heijer, '*Marine I* Case' (n 246) 5.

[257] Khan, 'Trading' (n 240) 14.

[258] Against, see Kirchner et al, 'Coastal State Obligations' (n 108) 75–76.

[259] Klein, 'Case' (n 171) 797.

[260] Kirchner et al, 'Coastal State Obligations' (n 108) 66. Highlighting that the notion of 'nearest port' needs to take into account several factors, such as weather conditions and the capacity and features of the port, see Klein, 'Case' (n 171) 797.

[261] Spijkerboer, 'Wasted Lives' (n 244) 16.

[262] Fischer-Lescano et al, 'Border Controls' (n 136) 290; Klein, 'Case' (n 171) 811.

can avail for themselves, under human rights and refugee law States have the obligation to disembark rescued persons only in a place of safety from several factors, including *refoulement*.[263] However, this second obligation is only binding upon States, not upon masters. This means that if rescued persons are on board a merchant vessel, only the first, rudimentary obligation of disembarkation is applicable, unless the flag State determines otherwise through domestic legislation; *non-refoulement* is only relevant if individuals are rescued at sea by warships or public-owned or public-operated vessels. This conclusion can only change if the master is considered, according to the appropriate domestic law, a State organ or a person exercising elements of governmental authority.[264]

Having said this, the right to life as protected under Article 98 cannot be reduced to a mere reciprocal obligation between States parties to render assistance to persons of their nationality, or on board a vessel flying their flag. More important is the State–individual dimension that derives from the fact that Article 98 of the LOSC embodies a human right to life. If the obligation is not performed by the master, the flag or the coastal State, then individuals might resort to the remedies available under domestic law. Furthermore, because the same right to life is afforded under Article 2 of the ECHR, if this provision is triggered also (ie if jurisdiction pursuant to Article 1 of the ECHR exists, and the failure to perform the obligation is attributable to States, and not to the master, since the ECHR has no horizontal effect) individuals are entitled to resort to the ECtHR and submit a complaint against that State.

3.2.2. Protection of Life under Article 146 of the LOSC

Article 146 of the LOSC refers to the adoption of 'necessary measures … to ensure effective protection of human life' with respect to deep seabed mining activities. 'To this end the Authority shall adopt the appropriate rules, regulations and procedures to supplement existing international law as embodied in relevant treaties'. From this, two ideas immediately come forward: this provision covers positive obligations (in a sense at least analogous to the one developed by the ECtHR in its case law) aimed at protecting human life; it makes clear that the recipient of this obligation is the Authority.

But 'what is the effective protection of human life?' It is curious that the drafters of the LOSC did not use a reference to the effective protection of the *right to life*, which at least would reproduce a well-known formula of international law. Instead, they preferred to use the wording 'protection of human life'. A possible explanation could be that the drafters were not comfortable with outlining a 'right' whose nature clearly points to being held by individuals. But a different reading is that 'human life' is more comprehensive than 'right to life',

[263] Wouters and Heijer, 'The *Marine I* Case' (n 246) 6.
[264] See Articles 4 and 5 of the ARSIWA.

and thus encompasses the right to life hand in hand with other human rights and freedoms necessary to the development of a human person and connected with his human dignity: eg right to privacy, physical integrity, labour conditions, or prohibition of slavery, servitude and forced labour. In scholarship, this second reading seems to be preferred,[265] and a policy argument favours this interpretation: whereas individuals under a (flag, coastal or port) State's jurisdiction are presumed to be armoured with the constitutional judiciary apparatus of human rights, and possibly with the chance of resorting to an international human rights body, individuals engaged in activities in the Area might, in fact, lack the armour of an effective human rights machinery, and therefore depend upon the Authority to ensure their human rights and freedoms. On dry land, within their enclosed territory, States' institutional machinery and legitimate violence is the ultimate guarantee of human rights protection. At sea, the effectiveness of being armoured by States' machinery is lower. But with respect to the activities in the Area, the fact that these activities take place outside States' territory and jurisdiction does not prevent the existence of human rights of the individuals engaged in those activities, but requires a different institutional apparatus to protect and ensure their human rights: that explains why the LOSC encumbers the Authority with the task of ensuring the protection of human life.

The first use of the wording 'protection of human life' seems to have been introduced by the United States delegation.[266] Right after that, the Tanzania delegation proposed that, under this chapeau, the Authority should adopt measures aimed at protecting 'human health' and minimising 'danger to life:'[267] this already suggests that, although the connection with the right to life is conspicuous, it encompasses broader interests. The wording of this provision was further discussed, but mostly with respect to the exact nature and extent of the Authority's powers – and not with respect to the meaning of 'protection of human life'. This suggests that implicit in the mind of the drafters of the LOSC was a vague notion that the formula 'protection of human life' should be broader than 'right to life', but no reference was explicitly made to this respect.

Under Article 146 of the LOSC, the minimum content of this right is composed of the 'existing international law as embodied in relevant treaties' – a formula that is a 'masterpiece of vagueness',[268] but ought to include provisions deriving from international labour conventions, the SOLAS Convention or the 1972 Convention on the International Regulations for Preventing Collisions at Sea.[269] Afterwards, when writing the draft regulations on prospection,

[265] ED Brown, *Sea-Bed Energy and Minerals: The International Legal Regime*, vol 2, *Sea-Bed Mining* (Martinus Nijhoff 2001) 86; Myron Nordquist, Satya Nandan, Shabtai Rosenne and Michael Lodge (eds), *United Nations Convention on the Law of the Sea 1982 – A Commentary*, VI (Martinus Nijhoff 2003) 201; Papanicolopulu, *International Law* (n 26) 191.

[266] Doc. A/AC.138/25.

[267] Doc. A/AC.138/33.

[268] Brown, *Sea-Bed Energy* (n 265) 86.

[269] ibid.

exploitation and exploration, the Special Commission 3 of the Preparatory Commission listed rules on health, labour and safety standards.[270] Furthermore, in the regulations adopted by the Authority, 'safety, labour, and health standards' is the formula used to convey the obligations deriving from Article 146 of the LOSC, and binding upon the contractor.[271] Although this wording suggests that human rights of individuals engaged in activities in the Area are meagre, the fact that these individuals do not establish their centre of life on the high seas (it is rather a transient labour status) implies that the level of human rights to be protected and ensured is comparatively minor, and might not include those meant to be applicable in the framework of a political community (eg the right to constitute or adhere to political parties).

Therefore, the absence of State machinery that might armour the legal status of individuals engaged in activities in the Area explains why the Authority (instead of the sponsoring State) is specifically encumbered with the task of ensuring human rights of these individuals, namely through the regulations applicable to the contractors involved in those activities. For that reason, its scope is broader than that of Article 98 of the LOSC, and includes not only the right to life, but also the right to physical integrity, prohibition of slavery, servitude and forced labour, the right to health, the right to privacy, and labour conditions and safety conditions. Other human rights might not be of immediate relevance – eg the right to education (except proper training for the exercise of one's job), freedom of elections, freedoms of expression and association, and to constitute trade unions – but cannot be discarded *tout court*.[272]

4. CONCLUSION

The goal of this chapter is to evidence that, if systemic interpretation is taken seriously, the legal status of private actors at sea can be fostered by the interaction between law of the sea rules and human rights law. The first exercise in this chapter was to assess the reading of Article 1 of the ECHR (an exercise that is replicable with regard to the twin clauses from human rights treaties), which establish that, once within the *de facto* jurisdiction of a State, individuals engaged in maritime activities are entitled to the human rights and freedoms listed in human rights treaties, although subject to a condition of severability. The second exercise was to assess how human rights law can impact the reading of the LOSC – not as a mere interpretative tool (as the ITLOS has done under

[270] Doc. LOS/PCN/SCN.3/WP.6/Add.8.

[271] See Sections 15 of Annexes 4 (Standard Clauses for Exploration Contracts) to the Nodules, the Sulphides, and the Cobalt Regulations, and Regulation 30 of the Draft Exploitation Regulations.

[272] eg if a citizen from State A is working on a platform engaged in deep seabed mining, and it is possible for him to vote by electronic means available to him, then his right to participate in elections must be respected.

the umbrella of 'considerations of humanity') but as a means to identify human rights directly in the wording of the LOSC (eg the rights not to be kept as slave and to the protection of human life).

What both exercises evidence is an alignment between human rights law and the law of the sea: sharing a common genetic code facilitates a systemic reading that includes human rights considerations in the interpretation of the LOSC, and resorts to the intricacies of law of the sea rules to determine States' human rights jurisdiction vis-à-vis individuals at sea. The fact that both exercises are autonomous suggests that fragmentation is still a methodological deadlock, but it does not preclude cross-regime interaction as required by Article 31(3)(c) of the VCLT with the resulting identification of new human rights by means of an extended *de facto* maritime jurisdiction of States, on the one hand, and of States' duties towards individuals at sea (with the corresponding individuals' rights), on the other. However, if fragmentation per se is not an obstacle to cross-regime interaction, something must explain the lack of a proper systemic interpretation, with the result of that interpretative process being to equip private actors with rights and duties. An implicit interpretative bias is one explanation, especially in light of the different matrix of legal regimes: ie a State-centred law of the sea vs an individual-centred human rights law.

6

Conclusion

THE TWENTY-FIRST CENTURY was announced as the time for private actors in international law.[1] However, fulfilling this prophecy was always going to be a difficult task in the context of a legal order characterised by the impregnable presence of States. True that private actors have some robust forms of participation under the traditional narratives of international law, but they are often seen with suspicion and conceived of as exo-subjects: ie they are not natural members of the international law environment and their participation is condoned only with particular restrictions; they cannot make the law; they have limited access to international dispute settlement institutions; and only in limited situations do they hold primary rights and duties under international law rules. As a result of this adamant narrative, private actors have been in the 'grey area'[2] of international law. However, the claim of this book is that private actors can be direct recipients of international law rules, since a State-centred narrative is only possible by means of an implicit interpretative bias against private actors. To that end, this book takes rules from the law of the sea – a domain that is traditionally considered to have been 'designed *by* States *for* States'[3] – to provide evidence that, if one follows a conception of international law neutral but open to private actors, one can unveil private actors' rights and duties under the already existing rules of international law.

Chapter 2 defines the method of observation for this book, by establishing the cases in which private actors are conceived of as subject of law under the rules of international law (ie when they are considered recipients of international law rules). After verifying that the concept of *international* legal personality is methodologically inaccurate, this book upholds the idea that private actors have a unique legal personality, prior to a given legal order, which implies that they are *ipso facto* legal persons under all legal orders, including therefore under the international legal system. Hence, the elasticity of a legal order to provide or decline relevance to a particular legal person is to be found not in its subjectivity, but rather in the legal capacities assigned to it. Accordingly, private actors are

[1] See generally Christoph Schreuer, 'The Waning of the Sovereign State: Towards a New Paradigm for International Law?' (1993) 4 *European Journal of International Law* 447.

[2] Anne Peters, *Beyond Human Rights – The Legal Status of the Individual in International Law* (CUP 2016) 37.

[3] Irini Papnicolopulu, *International Law and the Protection of People at Sea* (1st edn, OUP 2018) 84.

legal persons with international legal capacities whenever they are the recipients of an international norm, ie holders of rights and duties valid in the international legal order irrespective of being coupled with a remedy (rather in the domestic or in the international sphere). This should be a simple task of treaty interpretation based on the canons set out in Articles 31–33 of the VCLT, but implicit interpretative biases also play a role. As a result, this study is conducted having in mind the cases in which private actors hold entitlements under treaty-based law of the sea provisions (notably in the LOSC), regardless of having any remedy or procedural rights assigned for the protection of such entitlements. In order to avoid an interpretative bias against or in favour of private membership in international law, this study shares a conception of international law that is neutral but open to private actors.

Chapter 3 analyses the navigational rights and freedoms enshrined in the LOSC, with specific attention being paid to the detailed legal regimes of the right of innocent passage and the right to compensation. Surprising as it might be, in the legal regime set out in the LOSC, these entitlements are assigned to ships – not to flag States or the ship-owners. However, if one looks to the normative structure of these rights and to the *ex ante* and *ex post* responsibility for failure to comply with any rule or standard set out in the LOSC, one concludes that flag States and private actors hold concurrent, but still autonomous navigational entitlements – despite the ambiguous wording of the provisions of the LOSC. This conclusion is not in line with the practice and scholarship produced. However, assessing navigational entitlements and the right to compensation for interferences with navigation was key to pointing out one of the *modus operandi* of the implicit interpretative bias attached to orthodox, State-centred views of international law: the exclusion of private actors' entitlements, not because the provision cannot accommodate such interpretation under the canons established in Articles 31–33 of the VCLT, but rather as a result of the implicit bias that clouds the interpreter. In this context, the major finding of Chapter 2 is that if one is neutral but open to private actors (ie if one sets aside a Vattelian, State-to-State conception of international law), one can unveil new private actors' entitlements under the already *existing* rules of international law.

Chapter 4 deals with the rights emerging from the activities in the Area and the right to submit applications for the prompt release of vessels and crew members on behalf of the flag State. Whereas Chapter 3 is concerned with cases where the semantic element is unclear, the wording of the rights assessed in Chapter 4 is straightforward in assigning rights and duties to private miners and applicants. In fact, the legal regime of the Area is the best example of the participation of private actors in international law: contrary to other fields of international law that have created entitlements as a shield against States, Part XI of the LOSC (like its Annex III and the Implementation Agreement) adopted a new legal regime purposively subjected to the principle of the common heritage of mankind (ie entailing the binding nature of values transcendent and autonomous to States), created the Authority (an international organisation responsible for exercising the public function of governance of the Area, and thereby creating the ontological predicate for fostering the international status of private miners), admitted jural relations directly established between the Authority and private miners, assigned new entitlements to these latter, and therefore established that liability for damages caused by deep seabed mining rests primarily with private miners and the Authority. The ultimate evidence of such audacity is the drafting of the first regime of international property law in the absence of a sophisticated machinery to guarantee property. However, in its advisory opinion, the SDC expressed a view which is not consistent with the pivotal role of private miners in deep seabed mining, by adopting a State-centred perspective of how private mining shall be conducted. This is evidence of the second *modus operandi* of the interpretative bias against private participation in international law: the limitation or exclusion of private actors' entitlements in spite of the clear wording. The same can be said with respect to the institution of proceedings for the prompt release of vessels and crew members by private applicants: although the semantic element points to the possibility of submission of prompt release applications by private actors on behalf of the flag State, practice and scholarship produced do not support that reading of Article 292(2) of the LOSC.

Finally, Chapter 5 assesses the impact of cross-regime interaction following the canons of Article 31(3) of the VCLT, and particularly the interaction between the law of the sea and human rights law. The first conclusion of this chapter is that the emergence of self-contained regimes is a natural phenomenon in all legal orders (including domestic legal systems) but does not preclude that rules from one particular international legal regime may exercise a reciprocal gravitational force over rules from a different international legal regime. This can be illustrated with respect to human rights law and the law of the sea. This chapter assesses how human rights treaties (notably the ECHR) are shaped by rules of the law of the sea, on the one hand, and how the LOSC must also be interpreted in light of the relevant rules from human rights law, on the other. In the first case, this chapter demonstrates that the notion of jurisdiction under human rights treaties (ie the *de facto* authority of a State over an individual) implies assessing the *de iure* competences assigned to States under the law of the sea treaties. Only with a clear picture of the powers of States at sea and of their legal framework can one understand how a human rights treaty applies to a particular situation at sea (and in addition define what rights and freedoms are relevant in that particular situation). In the second case, this chapter notes that several provisions of the LOSC suggest that human rights are not foreign to the law of the sea, and afterwards assesses how the LOSC can be impacted by human rights law. For that purpose, this chapter analyses the entitlements under the aegis of repression of slavery and protection of human life at sea in order to conclude that, if rules from both domains are concurrently applicable, the obligations incumbent on States correspond to symmetrical, human rights-like entitlements of private actors. If humankind is the alpha and omega of international law, sovereign powers cannot be an empty shield: therefore, the conclusion of this chapter is that cross-regime interaction implies the transformation of States' powers into States' obligations towards individuals. This is the direct outcome of the fact that, under human rights law, the existence of *de iure* jurisdiction entails *ipso facto* State obligations towards individuals. However, practice and the scholarship produced do not always take systemic interpretation seriously, especially when the legal regimes at stake are State- and individual-centred (ie when there is an apparent mismatch between the matrix of both regimes). That, in the view of this book, is also the by-product of an interpretative bias.

These, in short, are the core conclusions of this book. This study is based on two bedrocks. First is the idea that the Vattelian society is obsolete and cannot work as a 'theory of everything' under international law, and, more importantly, is no longer responsive to the needs of an enlarged constituency of international law. Second is the idea that private actors have *de facto* conquered their own space in the realms of international law. If international law is a human creation, it is not a fossilized reality: it can comprise alternative conceptions that are neutral but open to private actors. The only limits to this task are human imagination and ingeniousness. If the State (which is a legal fiction with no natural or biological existence) can be a proper member of the international community, why cannot individuals (who at least have that very physical existence) be recognized as proper members also? The claim of this book is that an implicit interpretative bias against private actors has been a very efficient tool to provide a negative answer to that question. Therefore, an effort of openness is necessary to provide a full picture of private participation and membership in international law.

Nonetheless, this book does not aim to be a Panglossian exercise for endorsing the position of private actors as the sole or the major subjects of the law of the sea, or even as the substitutes of States in a brave new world. Dramatic changes are occurring in the international community, but the sovereign State will remain the central player of international law for a long time. And that should not be surprising, for the bureaucratic State is the most successful and efficient societal tool to cope with the ordeals of domestic and international life. In this vein, the only purpose of this book is another: just as '[t]he breaking of a wave cannot explain the whole sea',[4] an inter-State narrative is not a proper account of international law: it cannot provide a complete view of the entire building of international law, or depict accurately the very fabric of this legal order. A narrative neutral but open to private actors and entities other than States is an attempt to fill that gap.

[4] Vladimir Nabokov, *The Real Life of Sebastian Knight* [1941] (Penguin 1982) 87.

Bibliography

Abi-Saab, Georges, 'Cours général de droit international public', *Collected Courses of the Hague Academy of International Law* 207 (1987) 9–463

—— 'Fragmentation or Unification: Some Concluding Remarks', *New York University Journal of International Law and Politics* 31 (1999) 919–33

Accioly, Hildebrando, *Tratado de Direito Internacional Público*, vol I (Rio de Janeiro: Imprensa Nacional, 1933)

Akl, Joseph, 'Article 110', in Chandrasekhara Rao and Phillipe Gautier (eds), *The Rules of the International Tribunal for the Law of the Sea* (Leiden: Martinus Nijhoff, 2006) 305–10

—— 'Jurisprudence of the International Tribunal for the Law of the Sea in Prompt Release Proceedings', in Holger Hestermeyer, Doris König, Nele Matz-Lück, Volker Röben, Anja Seibert-Fohr, Peter-Tobias Stoll and Silja Vöneky (eds), *Coexistence, Cooperation and Solidarity – Liber Amicorum Rüdiger Wolfrum*, vol II (Leiden: Martinus Nijhoff, 2012) 1591–614

Althusius, Johannes, *Iuris romanis, libri duo. Ad leges Methodi Ramear conformati* (Basel: 1586) (available at Google Books)

—— *Politica – An Abridged Translation of Politics Methodically Set Forth and Illustrated with Sacred and Profane Examples* [1603] ed Frederick Carney ((Indianapolis, IN: Liberty Fund, 1995)

Amerasinghe, Chittharanjan, *Jurisdiction of International Tribunals* (The Hague: Kluwer Law, 2003)

Anderson, Andrew, 'Jurisdiction over Stateless Vessels on the High Seas: An Appraisal under Domestic and International Law', *Journal of Maritime Law and Commerce* 13 (1982) 323–42

Anderson, David, 'Investigation, Detention and Release of Foreign Vessels under the UN Convention on the Law of the Sea of 1982 and Other International Agreements', *International Journal of Marine and Coastal Law* 11 (1996) 165–77

—— 'Freedoms of the High Seas in the Modern Law of the Sea', in David Freestone, Richard Barnes and David Ong (eds), *The Law of the Sea – Progress and Prospects* (Oxford: Oxford University Press, 2006) 327–46

Anton, Donald, 'The Principle of Residual Liability in the Seabed Disputes Chamber of the International Tribunal for the Law of the Sea: The Advisory Opinion on Responsibility and Liability for International Seabed Mining (ITLOS Case No. 17)', *McGill International Journal of Sustainable Development Law and Policy* 7 (2012) 241–57

Anzilotti, Dionisio, *Corso de diritto internazionale*, vol I, *Introduzione – Teorie Generali* (Padua: Cedam, 1955)

Arangio-Ruiz, Gaetano, 'Stati e altri enti (Soggettività internazionale)', Antonio Azara and Ernesto Eula (eds), *Novissimo Digesto Italiano*, vol XVIII (Turin: Unione Tipográfico – Editrice Torinese, 1971) 132–213

Arendt, Hannah, '"The Rights of Man": What Are They?' (1949) 3 *Modern Review* 24–37

Attard, David and Mallia, Patricia, 'The High Seas', in David Joseph Attard (general ed), Malgosia Fitzmaurice and Norman A Martínez Gutiérrez (eds), *The IMLI Manual on International Maritime Law*, vol I, *The Law of the Sea* (Oxford: Oxford University Press, 2014) 239–75

Barberis, Julio, 'Nouvelles questions concernant la personnalité juridique international', *Collected Courses of the Hague Academy of International Law* 179 (1983) 145–285

Barnes, Richard, 'Refugee Law at Sea', *International and Comparative Law Quarterly* 53 (2004) 47–77

—— *Property Rights and Natural Resources* (Oxford and Portland, OR: Hart Publishing, 2009) Studies in International Law

—— 'Entitlement to Marine Living Resources in Areas beyond National Jurisdiction', in Erik Jaap Molenaar and Alex Oude Elferink (eds), *The International Legal Regime of Areas beyond National Jurisdiction: Current and Future Developments* (Leiden: Martinus Nijhoff Publishers, 2010) 83–141

—— 'The International Law of the Sea and Migration Control', in Bernard Ryan and Valsamis Mitsilegas (eds), *Extraterritorial Immigration Control – Legal Challenges* (Leiden: Martinus Nijhoff, 2010) 103

—— 'Flag States', in Donald Rothwell, Alex Oude Elferink, Karen Scott and Tim Stephens (eds), *The Oxford Handbook of the Law of the Sea* (Oxford: Oxford University Press, 2015) 304–24

—— 'Article 17', in Alexander Proelß (ed), *United Nations Convention on the Law of the Sea – A Commentary* (Munich: CH Beck, 2017) 176–81

—— 'Article 18', in Alexander Proelß (ed), *United Nations Convention on the Law of the Sea – A Commentary* (Munich: CH Beck, 2017) 181–86

—— 'Article 19', in Alexander Proelß (ed), *United Nations Convention on the Law of the Sea – A Commentary* (Munich: CH Beck, 2017) 186–96

—— 'Article 24', in Alexander Proelß (ed), *United Nations Convention on the Law of the Sea – A Commentary* (Munich: CH Beck, 2017) 217–22

—— 'Article 25', in Alexander Proelß (ed), *United Nations Convention on the Law of the Sea – A Commentary* (Munich: CH Beck, 2017) 222–26

—— 'Article 26', in Alexander Proelß (ed), *United Nations Convention on the Law of the Sea – A Commentary* (Munich: CH Beck, 2017) 226–29

Baslar, Kemal, *The Concept of the Common Heritage of Mankind in International Law* (The Hague: Martinus Nijhoff Publishers, 1998) Developments in International Law

Benvenisti, Eyal, 'The Interplay between Actors as a Determinant of the Evolution of Administrative Law in International Institutions', *Law and Contemporary Problems* 68 (2005) 319–40

Besson, Samantha, 'The Extraterritoriality of the European Convention on Human Rights: Why Human Rights Depend on Jurisdiction and What Jurisdiction Amounts To', *Leiden Journal of International Law* 25 (2012) 857–84

Bianchi, Andrea, 'The Fight for Inclusion: Non-State Actors and International Law', in Ulrich Fastenrath, Rudolf Geiger, Daniel-Erasmus Khan, Andreas Paulus, Sabine von Schorlemer and Christoph Vedder (eds), *From Bilateralism to Community Interest: Essays in Honour of Bruno Simma* (Oxford: Oxford University Press, 2011) 39–57

Birnie, Patricia, Boyle, Alan and Redgwell, Catherine, *International Law and the Environment*, 3rd edn (Cambridge: Cambridge University Press, 2009)

Blackstone, William, *The Commentaries on the Laws of England* [1753], ed George Sharswood (Indianapolis, IN: Liberty Fund, 2004)

Bogdandy, Armin von and Venzke, Ingo, 'Beyond Dispute: International Institutions as Lawmakers', *German Law Journal* 12 (2011) 979–1003

Boyle, Alan and Chinkin, Christine, *The Making of International Law* (Oxford: Oxford University Press, 2007) Foundations of Public International Law

Brabandere, Eric de, 'The Use of Precedent and External case Law by the International Court of Justice and the International Tribunal for the Law of the Sea', *The Law and Practice of International of International Courts and Tribunals* 15 (2016) 24–55

Brierly, James Leslie, 'Règles générales du droit de la paix', *Collected Courses of the Hague Academy of International Law* 58 (1936-IV) 5–237

—— *The Law of Nations – An Introduction to the International Law of Peace*, 6th edn (Oxford: Clarendon Press, 1963)

Brown, Edward D, *The International Law of the Sea*, vol I (Aldershot: Dartmouth, 1994)

—— 'The M/V 'Saiga' Case on Prompt Release of Detained Vessels – The First Judgment of the International Tribunal for the Law of the Sea', *Marine Policy* 22 (1998) 307–27

—— *Sea-Bed Energy and Minerals: The International Legal Regime*, vol 2, *Sea-Bed Mining* (The Hague: Martinus Nijhoff, 2001)

Brownlie, Ian and Crawford, James, *Brownlie's Principles of Public International Law*, 9th edn (Oxford: Oxford University Press, 2019)
Cacciaguidi-Fahy, Sophie, 'The Law of the Sea and Human Rights', *Sri Lanka Journal of International Law* 19 (2007) 85–107
Calvo, Carlos, *Derecho internacional teórico y práctico de Europa y América*, vol 1 (Paris: Amyot, 1868)
Cannone, Andrea, *Il Tribunale Internazionale del Diritto del Mare* (Bari: Cacucci Editore, 1991)
Carreau, Dominique and Marrella, Fabrizio, *Droit international*, 11th edn (Paris: Pedone, 2012)
Carty, Anthony, *Philosophy of International Law* (Edinburgh: Edinburgh University Press, 2007)
Cassese, Antonio, *International Law*, 2nd edn (Oxford: Oxford University Press, 2005)
—— 'States: Rise and Decline of the Primary Subjects of the International Community', in Bardo Fassbender and Anne Peters (eds), *The Oxford Handbook of the History of International Law* (Oxford: Oxford University Press, 2014) 49–70
Cassese, Sabino, 'Administrative Law without the State? The Challenge of Global Regulation', *International Law and Politics* 35 (2007) 663–94
Charney, Jonathan, 'Is International Law Threatened by Multiple International Tribunals?', *Collected Courses of the Hague Academy of International Law* 271 (1998) 101–382
Chazournes, Laurence Boisson de, 'Plurality in the Fabric of International Courts and Tribunals: The Threads for a Managerial Approach', *European Journal of International Law* 28 (2017) 13–72
Chen, Lung-chu, *An Introduction to Contemporary International Law – A Policy-Oriented Perspective*, 3rd edn (Oxford: Oxford University Press, 2015)
Cheng, Bin, 'Introduction to Subjects of International Law', in Mohammed Bedjaoui (ed), *International Law: Achievements and Prospects* (Leiden: Martinus Nijhoff, 1991) 23–40
Chetail, Vincent, 'The Legal Personality of Multinational Corporations, State Responsibility and Due Diligence: The Way Forward', in Denis Alland, Vincent Chetail, Olivier de Frouville and Jorge Viñuales (eds), *Unity and Diversity of International Law – Essays in Honour of Professor Pierre-Marie Dupuy* (Leiden: Martinus Nijhoff, 2014) 105–30
Chircop, Aldo, 'Assistance at Sea and Places of Refuge for Ships: Reconciling Competing Norms', in Henrik Ringbom (ed), *Jurisdiction over Ships – Post-UNCLOS Developments in the Law of the Sea* (Leiden: Brill Nijhoff, 2015) 141–53
Churchill, Robin, 'Some Reflections on the Operation of the Dispute Settlement System of the UN Convention on the Law of the Sea During Its First Decade', in David Freestone, Richard Barnes and David Ong (eds), *The Law of the Sea – Progress and Prospects* (Oxford: Oxford University Press, 2006) 388–416
—— 'Dispute Settlement under the UN Convention on the Law of the Sea: Survey for 2007', *International Journal of Marine and Coastal Law* 23 (2008) 601–42
—— 'Dispute Settlement in the Law of the Sea: Survey for 2011', *International Journal of Marine and Coastal Law* 27 (2012) 517–51
—— 'Dispute Settlement in the Law of the Sea: Survey for 2014', *International Journal of Marine and Coastal Law* 30 (2015) 585–653
Churchill, Robin and Hedley, Christopher, *The Meaning of the 'Genuine Link' Requirement in Relation to the Nationality of Ships: Project Report* (International Transport Workers Federation, 2000)
Churchill, Robin and Lowe, Vaughn, *The Law of the Sea*, 3rd edn (Manchester: Manchester University Press, 1999)
Clapham, Andrew, *Human Rights Obligations of Non-State Actors* (Oxford: Oxford University Press, 2006)
Gogliati-Bantz, Vincent, 'Disentangling the "Genuine Link": Enquiries in Sea, Air and Space Law', *Nordic Journal of International Law* 79 (2010) 383–432
Combacau, Jean, *Le droit international de la mer* (Paris: Presses Universitaires de France, 1985)
—— 'Pas une puissance, une liberté: La souveraineté internationale et l'État', *Pouvoirs* 67 (1993) 47–58

Combacau, Jean and Sur, Serge, *Droit international public*, 12th edn (Paris: LGDJ, 2016)
Conforti, Benedetto, *Il regime giuridico dei mari* (Naples: Casa Editrice Dott. Eugenio Jovene, 1957)
Cortês, António, *Jurisprudência dos Princípios – Estudo sobre os Fundamentos da Decisão Jurisdicional* (Lisbon: Universidade Católica Editora, 2010)
Cot, Jean-Pierre, 'Appearing "for" or "on behalf of" a State: The Role of Private Counsel before International Tribunals', in Nisuke Ando, Edward McWhinney and Rüdiger Wolfrum (eds), *Liber Amicorum Judge Shigeru Oda* (The Hague: Kluwer Law, 2002) 835–47
Crawford, James, *State Responsibility – The General Part* (Cambridge: Cambridge University Press, 2013) Cambridge Studies in International and Comparative Law
—— 'Chance, Order, Change: The Course of International Law – General Course on Public International Law', *Collected Courses of the Hague Academy of International Law* 365 (2013) 9–390
Daillier, Patrick, Forteau, Mathias, Pellet, Alain and Dinh, Ngyuen Quoc, *Droit international public*, 8th edn (Paris: LGDJ, 2009)
Dijk, Pieter van, Hoof, Fried van, Rijn, Arjen van and Zwaak, Leo (eds), *Theory and Practice of the European Convention on Human Rights*, 4th edn (Antwerp: Intersentia, 2006)
Djamchid, Momtaz, 'The High Seas', in René-Jean Dupuy and Daniel Vignes (eds), *A Handbook on the New Law of the Sea* (Dordrecht: Martinus Nijhoff Publishers, 1991) 383–423
Domingo, Rafael, *The New Global Law* (Cambridge: Cambridge University Press, 2010) ASIL Studies in International Legal Theory
Drenan, Matthew T, 'Gone Overboard: Why the Arctic Sunrise Case Signals an Over-Expansion of the Ship-as-a-Unit Concept in the Diplomatic Protection Context', *California Western International Law Journal* 45 (2014) 109–67
Dupuy, Pierre-Marie, 'The Danger of Fragmentation or Unification of the International Legal System and the International Court of Justice', *New York University Journal of International Law and Politics* 31 (1999) 791–807
—— 'L'unité de l'ordre juridique international', *Collected Courses of the Hague Academy of International Law* 297 (2002) 9–490
Dupuy, Pierre and Kerbrat, Yann, *Droit international public*, 13th edn (Paris: Dalloz, 2016)
Dupuy, René-Jean, 'The Sea Under National Competence', in René-Jean Dupuy and Daniel Vignes (eds), *A Handbook on the New Law of the Sea* (Dordrecht: Martinus Nijhoff Publishers, 1991) 247–313
—— *Le droit international* [1963], 12th edn (Paris: Presses Universitaires de France, 2001) Que sais-je?
Dworkin, Ronald, *Law's Empire* (Oxford and Portland, OR: Hart Publishing, 1998)
Eiriksson, Gudmundur, *The International Tribunal for the Law of the Sea* (The Hague: Martinus Nijhoff, 2000)
El-Baghdadi, Mahdi, 'The Binding Nature of the Disputes Settlement Procedure in the Third U.N. Convention on the Law of the Sea: The International Seabed Authority', *Journal of Mineral Law & Policy* 6 (1990–91) 173–83
Elferink, Alex Oude, 'The Genuine Link Concept: Time for a *Post Mortem*?', in Ige Dekker and Harry Post (eds), *On the Foundations and Sources of International Law* (The Hague: Asser Press, 2003) 41–63
Emmerich-Fritsche, Angelika, *Vom Völkerrecht zum Weltrecht* (Berlin: Duncker & Humblot, 2007) Rechtsfragen der Globalisierung
Endicott, Timothy, 'The Logic of Freedom and Power', in Samantha Besson and John Tasioulas (eds), *The Philosophy of International Law*, reprint (Oxford: Oxford University Press, 2013) 245–59
Evans, Malcolm (ed), *International Law*, 5th edn (Oxford: Oxford University Press, 2018)
—— 'The Law of the Sea', in Malcolm Evans (ed), *International Law*, 5th edn (Oxford: Oxford University Press, 2018)
Espaliú Berdud, Carlos, *Le passage inoffensive des navires de guerre étrangers dans la mer territoriale – Portée du régime contenu dans la Convention des Nations Unies sur le droit de la mer* (Brussels: Bruylant, 2006)

Fauchille, Paul, *Traité de Droit International Public*, vol I, 2nd part (Paris: Rousseau and Cie. Editeurs 1925)

Fischer-Lescano, Andreas, Löhr, Tillmann and Tohidipur, Timo, 'Border Controls at Sea – Requirements under International Human Rights Law and Refugee Law', *International Journal of Refugee Law* 21 (2009) 256–96

Fourlanos, Gerasimos, 'Subjectivity in International Law and the Position of the Individual', *Nordisk Tidsskrift for International Ret* 53 (1984) 9–25

Freestone, David, 'Responsibilities and Obligations of States Sponsoring Persons and Entities with Respect to activities in the Area', *American Journal of International Law* 105 (2011) 755–60

Gadamer, Hans-Georg, *Truth and Method*, 2nd edn (London: Bloomsbury, 1989)

Gardiner, Richard, *Treaty Interpretation*, 2nd edn (Oxford: Oxford University Press, 2017)

Gavouneli, Maria, *Functional Jurisdiction in the Law of the Sea* (Leiden: Martinus Nijhoff, 2007) Publications on Ocean Development

Geiß, Robin and Petrig, Anna, *Piracy and Armed Robbery at Sea – The Legal Framework for Counter-Piracy Operations in Somalia and the Gulf of Aden* (Oxford: Oxford University Press, 2011)

Geiss, Robin and Tams, Christian, 'Non-Flag States as Guardians of the Maritime Order: Creeping Jurisdiction of a Different Kind?, in Henrik Ringbom (ed), *Jurisdiction over Ships – Post-UNCLOS Developments in the Law of the Sea* (Leiden: Brill Nijhoff, 2015) 19–49

Gentili, Alberico, *De Iure Belli Libri Tres*, ed John C Rolfe (Oxford: Clarendon Press, 1933) Classics of International Law

Gidel, Gilbert, *Le droit international public de la mer – Les temps de paix*, vol I, *Introduction – La haute mer* [1932], reprint (Vaduz and Paris: Topos Verlag/Librairie Edouard Duchemim, 1981)

Gondek, Michał, *The Reach of Human Rights in a Globalising World: Extraterritorial Application of Human Rights Treaties* (Antwerp: Intersentia, 2009) School of Human Rights Research

Grotius, Hugo, *The Free Sea, or A Disputation Concerning the Right which the Hollanders Ought to Have to the Indian Merchandise for Trading* [*Mare liberum, sive de iure quod quod Baravis competit an Indicana commercial, Dissertatio*: 1609], ed David Armitage (Indianapolis, IN: Liberty Fund, 2004) Natural Law and Enlightenment Classics

—— *The Rights of War and Peace* [*De Jure Belli ac Pacis*: 1625], ed Richard Tuck (Indianapolis, IN: Liberty Fund, 2005) Natural Law and Enlightenment Classics

—— *Commentary on the Law of Prize and Booty* [*De Iure Praedae Commentarius*: 1604–05] (Oxford: Clarendon Press, 1950)

Guggenheim, Paul, *Traité de droit international public*, vol I (Geneva: Librairie de l'Université, 1953)

Guillaume, Gilbert, 'The Future of International Judicial Institutions', *International and Comparative Law Quarterly* 44 (1995) 848–62

Guilfoyle, Douglas, 'Counter-Piracy Law Enforcement and Human Rights', *International and Comparative Law Quarterly* 59 (2010) 141–69

—— *Shipping Interdiction and the Law of the Sea*, reprint (Cambridge: Cambridge University Press, 2011) Cambridge Studies in International and Comparative Law

—— 'Human Rights Issues and Non-Flag State Boarding of Suspect Ships in international Waters', in Clive R Symmons (ed), *Selected Contemporary Issues in the Law of the Sea* (Leiden: Martinus Nijhoff, 2011) 83–104

—— 'The High Seas', in Donald Rothwell, Alex Oude Elferink, Karen Scott and Tim Stephens (eds), *The Oxford Handbook on the Law of the Sea* (Oxford: Oxford University Press, 2015) 203–25

—— 'Article 106', in Alexander Proelß (ed), *United Nations Convention on the Law of the Sea – A Commentary* (Munich: CH Beck, 2017) 753–55

—— 'Article 110', in Alexander Proelß (ed), *United Nations Convention on the Law of the Sea – A Commentary* (Munich: CH Beck, 2017) 767–72

Hafner, Gerhard, 'Pros and Cons Ensuing from Fragmentation of International Law', *Michigan Journal of International Law* 25 (2004) 849–63

—— 'Some Thoughts on the State-Oriented and Individual-Oriented Approaches in International Law', *Austrian Review of International and European Law* 14 (2009) 27–39

—— 'The Emancipation of the Individual from the State under International Law', *Collected Courses of the Hague Academy of International Law* 358 (2011) 263–453

Hakapää, Kari, *Marine Pollution in International Law – Material Obligations and Jurisdiction* (Helsinki: Suomalainen Tiedeakatemia, 1981)

Hall, William, *A Treatise on International Law*, 8th edn (Oxford: Clarendon Press, 1924)

Harris, David, O'Boyle, Michael, Bates, Ed and Buckley, Carla, *Harris, O'Boyle, and Warbrick: Law of the European Convention on Human Rights*, 4th edn (Oxford: Oxford University Press, 2018)

Harrison, James, 'Judicial Law-Making and the Developing Order of the Oceans', *International Journal of Marine and Coastal Law* 22 (2007) 283–302

—— *Making the Law of the Sea – A Study in the Development of International Law* (Cambridge: Cambridge University Press, 2011) Cambridge Studies in International and Comparative Law

Higgins, Rosalyn, *Problems and Process – International Law and How We Use It* (Oxford: Clarendon Press, 1995)

—— 'A Babel of Judicial Voices? Ruminations from the Bench', *International and Comparative Law Quarterly* 55 (2006) 791–804

Hobbes, Thomas, *Leviathan* [1651], ed Richard Tuck (Cambridge: Cambridge University Press, 1996) Cambridge Texts in the History of Political Thought

—— *On the Citizen* [*De Cive*: 1642], ed Richard Tuck (Cambridge: Cambridge University Press, 2002) Cambridge Texts in the History of Political Thought

Ipsen, Knut, *Völkerrecht*, 6th edn (Munich: CH Beck, 2014)

Janis, Mark, Kay, Richard and Bradley, Anthony, *European Human Rights Law – Text and Materials* (Oxford: Oxford University Press, 2008)

Jennings, Robert, 'The Role of the International Court of Justice', *British Yearbook of International Law* 68 (1997) 1–63

Jenks, CW, 'Conflict of Law-Making Treaties', *British Yearbook of International Law* 30 (1953) 401–53

—— *The Common Law of Mankind* (London: Stevens & Sons, 1958)

Jessup, Philip, 'The Subjects of a Modern Law of Nations', *Michigan Law Review* 45 (1947) 383–408

—— *A Modern Law of Nations – An Introduction* (New York: The Macmillan Company, 1950)

Johnson, Lindy, *Coastal State Regulation of International Shipping* (Dobbs Ferry, NY: Oceana Publications, 2004)

Jouannet, Emmanuelle, *The Liberal-Welfarist Law of Nations – A History of International Law* (Cambridge: Cambridge University Press, 2012)

—— *A Short Introduction to International Law* [*Le droit international*: 2013] (Cambridge: Cambridge University Press, 2014)

Kamto, Maurice, 'La nationalité des navires en droit international', in Daniel-Heywood Anderson, Vincent Bantz, Geneviéve Bastid-Burdeau, Mohammed Bedjaoui and Josette Beer-Gabel (eds), *La mer et son droit – Mélanges offerts à Laurent Lucchini et Jean-Pierre Quéneudec* (Paris: Pedone, 2003) 343–73

Karaman, Igor, *Dispute Resolution in the Law of the Sea* (Leiden: Martinus Nijhoff, 2012) Publications on Ocean Development

Kaufmann, Wilhelm, *Die Rechtskraft des Internationales Rechtes und das Verhältnis der Staatsgesetzgebungen und der Staatsorgane zu demselben* (Stuttgart: F Enke, 1899)

Kelsen, Hans, *Das Problem der Souvenatität und die Theorie des Völkerrechts* (Tübingen: JCB Mohr/P Siebeck, 1920)

—— 'Les rapports de système entre le droit interne et le droit international public', *Collected Courses of the Hague Academy of International Law* 14 (1926-IV) 227–331

—— 'Théorie générale du droit international public – Problèmes choisis', *Collected Courses of the Hague Academy of International Law* 42 (1932-IV) 117–352

—— *Reine Rechtslehre* [1960], 2nd edn (Vienna: Verlag Österreich, 2000)

Khaliq, Urfan, 'Jurisdiction, Ships and Human Rights Treaties', in Henrik Ringbom (ed), *Jurisdiction over Ships – Post-UNCLOS Developments in the Law of the Sea* (Leiden: Brill Nijhoff, 2015) 324–60
Khan, Irene, 'Trading in Human Misery: A Human Rights Perspective on the *Tampa* Incident', *Pacific Rim Law and Policy Journal* 12 (2003) 9–22
King, Hugh, 'The Extraterritorial Human Rights Obligations of States', *Human Rights Law Review* 9 (2009) 521–56
Kingsbury, Benedict and Casini, Lorenzo, 'Global Administrative Law Dimensions of International Organizations Law', *International Organizations Law Review* 6 (2009) 319–58
Kingsbury, Benedict, Krisch, Nico and Stewart, Richard, 'The Emergence of Global Administrative Law' *Law & Contemporary Problems* 68 (2005) 15–61
Kirchner, Stefan, Geler-Noch, Katarzyna, Frese, Vanessa, 'Coastal State Obligations in the Context of Refugees at Sea under the European Convention on Human Rights', *Ocean and Coastal Law Journal* 20 (2015) 57–82
Kjeldgaard-Pedersen, Astrid, *The International Legal Personality of the Individual*, 1st edn (Oxford: Oxford University Press, 2018)
Klabbers, Jan, 'The Concept of Legal Personality', *Jus Gentium* 11 (2005) 35–66
—— 'Setting the Scene', in Jan Klabbers, Anne Peters and Geir Ulfstein (eds), *The Constitutionalization of International Law* (Oxford: Oxford University Press, 2009) 1–44
—— *International Law*, 3rd edn (Cambridge: Cambridge University Press, 2021)
Klabbers, Jan, Peters, Anne and Ulfstein, Geir (eds), *The Constitutionalization of International Law* (Oxford: Oxford University Press, 2009)
Klein, Natalie, *Dispute Settlement in the UN Convention on the Law of the Sea* (Cambridge: Cambridge University Press, 2005) Cambridge Studies in International and Comparative Law
—— *Maritime Security and the Law of the Sea* (Oxford: Oxford University Press, 2012) Oxford Monographs in International Law
—— 'A Case for Harmonizing Laws on Maritime Interceptions of Irregular Migrants', *International and Comparative Law Quarterly* 63 (2014) 787–814
Kolb, Robert, 'Une observation sur la détermination de la subjectivité international', *Zeitschrift für öffentliches Recht* 52 (1997) 115–25
—— 'Nouvelle observation sur la détermination de la personnalité juridique international', *Zeitschrift für öffentliches Recht* 57 (2002) 229–41
König, Doris, 'Flag of Ships', *Max Planck Encyclopedia of Public International Law*
Koskenniemi, Martti and Leino, Päivi, 'Fragmentation of International Law: Postmodern Anxieties', *Leiden Journal of International Law* 15 (2002) 553–79
Krabbe, Hugo, *Die moderne Staats-Idee* (The Hague: Martinus Nijhoff, 1919)
Kulesza, Joanna, *Due Diligence in International Law* (Leiden: Brill Nijhoff 2016) Queen Mary Studies in International Law
Lagoni, Rainer, 'The Prompt Release of Vessels and Crews before the International Tribunal for the Law of the Sea: A Preparatory Report', *International Journal of Marine and Coastal Law* 11 (1996) 147–64
Larsen, Kjetil, 'Territorial Non-Application of the European Convention on Human Rights', *Nordic Journal of International Law* 78 (2009) 73–93
Lauterpacht, Hersch, *Private Law Sources and Analogies of International Law* (London: Longmans, Green, & Co, 1927)
—— 'The Grotian Tradition in International Law', *British Yearbook of International Law* 23 (1946) 1–53
—— *International Law and Human Rights* (London: Stevens & Sons Ltd., 1950)
—— 'The Subjects of International Law', in Elihu Lauterpacht (ed), *International Law – Being the Collected Papers of Hersch Lauterpacht*, vol I (Cambridge: Cambridge University Press, 1970) 136–50 [Subjects I]
—— 'The Subjects of International Law', in Elihu Lauterpacht (ed), *International Law – Being the Collected Papers of Hersch Lauterpacht*, vol I (Cambridge: Cambridge University Press, 1970) 279–307 [Subjects II]

Le Gurun, Gwénaëlle, 'Annex III, Article 4', in Alexander Proelß (ed), *United Nations Convention on the Law of the Sea – A Commentary* (Munich: CH Beck, 2017) 2135–47

Linderfalk, Ulf, 'State Responsibility and the Primary-Secondary Rules Terminology – The Role of Language for an Understanding of the International Legal System', *Nordic Journal of International Law* 78 (2009) 53–72

Lindpere, Heiki, 'Prompt Release of Detained Foreign Vessels and Crews in Matters of Marine Environmental Protection', *International Journal of Legal Information* 33 (2005) 240–55

Lindroos, Anja, 'Addressing Norm Conflicts in a Fragmented Legal System: The Doctrine of *Lex Specialis*', *Nordic Journal of International Law* 74 (2005) 27–66

Lobel, Jules, 'Courts as Forums for Protest', *UCLA Law Review* 52 (2004) 477–561

Lodge, Michael, 'The Deep Seabed', in Donald Rothwell, Alex Oude Elferink, Karen Scott and Tim Stephens (eds), *The Oxford Handbook of the Law of the Sea* (Oxford: Oxford University Press, 2015) 226–53

Loucaides, Loukis, 'Determining the Extra-Territorial Effect of the European Convention: Facts, Jurisprudence and the *Banković* Case', *European Human Rights Law Review* 4 (2006) 391–407

Lowe, Vaughan, *International Law* (Oxford: Oxford University Press, 2007) Clarendon Law Series

—— 'The Function of Litigation in International Society', *International and Comparative Law Quarterly* 61 (2012) 209–22

—— 'Ships', in Nerina Boschiero, Tullio Scovazzi, Cesare Pitea and Chiara Ragni (eds), *International Courts and the Development of International Law – Essays in Honour of Tullio Treves* (Berlin: Springer, 2013) 291–98

Lowe, Vaughan and Staker, Christopher, 'Jurisdiction', in Malcolm Evans (ed), *International Law*, 5th edn (Oxford: Oxford University Press, 2018) 313–39

Lowe, Vaughan and Tzanakopoulos, Antonios, 'The Development of the Law of the Sea by the International Court of Justice', in Christian Tams and James Sloan (eds), *The Development of International Law by the International Court of Justice* (Oxford: Oxford University Press, 2013) 177–93

Lucchini, Laurent and Vœlckel, *Droit de la mer*, vol I, *La mer et son droit. Les espaces maritimes* (Paris: Pedone, 1990)

Mallia, Patricia, *Migrant Smuggling by Sea – Combating a Current Threat to Maritime Security through the Creation of a Cooperative Framework* (Leiden: Martinus Nijhoff Publishers, 2010) Publications on Ocean Development

Marten, Bevan, 'Port State Jurisdiction, International Conventions and Extraterritoriality: An Expansive Interpretation', in Henrik Ringbom (ed), *Jurisdiction over Ships – Post-UNCLOS Developments in the Law of the Sea* (Leiden: Brill Nijhoff, 2015) 105–39

Massé, Gabriel, *Le Droit commercial dans ses rapports avec le droits de la gens et le droit civil*, vol I (Paris: Guillaumin, 1844)

Matz-Lück, Nele, 'Norm Interpretation across International Regimes: Competences and Legitimacy', in Margaret Young (ed), *Regime Interaction in International Law – Facing Fragmentation* (Cambridge: Cambridge University Press, 2012) 201–34

McCorquodale, Robert, 'The Individual and the International Legal System', in Malcolm Evans (ed), *International Law*, 5th edn (Oxford: Oxford University Press, 2018) 284–310

McDougal, Myres, 'International Law, Power, and Policy: A Contemporary Conception', *Collected Courses of the Hague Academy of International Law* 82 (1953-I) 133–260

McDougal, Myres and Burke, William T, *The Public Order of the Oceans – A Contemporary International Law of the Sea*, reprint (New Haven, CT: New Haven Press, and Dordrecht: Martinus Nijhoff Publishers, 1987)

McDougal, Myres, Burke, William and Vlasic, Ivan, 'The Maintenance of Public Order at Sea and the Nationality of Ships', *American Journal of International Law* 54 (1960) 25–116

McDougal, Myres and Lasswell, Harold, 'The Identification and Appraisal of Diverse Systems of Public Order', *American Journal of International Law* 53 (1959) 1–29

McDougal, Myres, Lasswell, Harold and Chen, Lung-Chu, *Human Rights and World Public Order* (New Haven, CT: Yale University Press, 1980)

Mensah, Thomas, 'The Tribunal and the Prompt Release of Vessels', *International Journal of Marine and Coastal Law* 22 (2007) 425–49

Meron, Theodor, *The Humanization of International Law* (Leiden: Martinus Nijhoff, 2006) The Hague Academy of International Law Monographs

Merrills, JG, *International Dispute Settlement*, 5th edn (Cambridge: Cambridge University Press, 2011)

Milanović, Marko, 'From Compromise to Principle: Clarifying the Concept of State Jurisdiction in Human Rights Treaties', *Human Rights Law Review* 8 (2008) 411–48

—— *Extraterritorial Application of Human Rights Treaties – Law, Principles, and Policy* (Oxford: Oxford University Press, 2011) Oxford Monographs in International Law

—— '*Al-Skeini* and *Al-Jedda* in Strasbourg', *European Journal of International Law* 23 (2012) 121–39

Miller, Sarah, 'Revisiting Extraterritorial Jurisdiction: A Territorial Justification for Extraterritorial Jurisdiction under the European Convention', *European Journal of International Law* 20 (2009) 1223–46

Molenaar, Erik Jaap, *Coastal State Jurisdiction over Vessel-Source Pollution* (The Hague: Wolters Kluwer, 1998) International Environmental Law and Policy Series

—— 'Multilateral Hot Pursuit and Illegal Fishing in the Southern Ocean: The Pursuits of the *Viarsa 1* and the *South Tomi*', *International Journal of Marine and Coastal Law* 19 (2004) 19–42

—— 'Port State Jurisdiction: Towards Mandatory and Comprehensive Use', in David Freestone, Richard Barnes and David Ong (eds), *The Law of the Sea – Progress and Prospects* (Oxford: Oxford University Press, 2006) 192–209

Moore, John Norton, Nordquist, Myron, Nandan, Satya and Rosenne, Shabtai (eds), *United Nations Convention on the Law of the Sea 1982 – A Commentary*, vol III (The Hague: Martinus Nijhoff Publishers, 1995)

Mosler, Hermann, 'Réflexions sur la personnalité juridique en droit international public', in *Mélanges offerts a Henri Rolin – Problèmes de droit des gens* (Paris: A Pedone, 1964) 228–51

Nandan, Satya, 'Administering the Mineral Resources of the Deep Seabed', in David Freestone, Richard Barnes and David Ong (eds), *The Law of the Sea – Progress and Prospects* (Oxford: Oxford University Press, 2006) 75–92

Nelson, LDM, 'The New Deep Sea-Bed Mining Regime', *International Journal of Marine and Coastal Law* 10 (1995) 189–203

Nijman, Janne E, *The Concept of International Legal Personality* (The Hague: TMC Asser Press, 2004)

Nollkaemper, André, *National Courts and the International Rule of Law* (Oxford: Oxford University Press, 2012)

—— 'The Duality of Direct Effect of International Law', *European Journal of International Law* 25 (2014) 105–25

Nollkaemper, André and Jacobs, Dov, 'Shared Responsibility in International Law: A Conceptual Framework', *Michigan Journal of International Law* 34 (2013) 359–438

Nordquist, Myron H (editor-in-chief), Nandan, Satya N, Rosenne, Shabtai and Grandy, Neal R (volume editors), *United Nations Convention on the Law of the Sea 1982 – A Commentary*, vol II (Dordrecht: Martinus Nijhoff Publishers, 1993)

Nordquist, Myron H (editor-in-chief), Rosenne, Shabtai and Yankov, Alexander (volume editors), *United Nations Convention on the Law of the Sea 1982 – A Commentary*, vol IV (Dordrecht: Martinus Nijhoff Publishers, 1991)

Nordquist, Myron H (editor-in-chief), Rosenne, Shabtai and Sohn, Louis B (volume editors), *United Nations Convention on the Law of the Sea 1982 – A Commentary*, vol V (Dordrecht: Martinus Nijhoff Publishers, 1989)

Nordquist, Myron H (editor-in-chief), Nandan, Satya, Rosenne, Shabtai and Lodge, Michael (volume editors), *United Nations Convention on the Law of the Sea 1982 – A Commentary*, vol VI (Dordrecht: Martinus Nijhoff Publishers, 2003)

Noyes, John, 'The International Tribunal for the Law of the Sea', *Cornell International Law Journal* 32 (1998) 109–82

Nørgaard, Carl Aage, *The Position of the Individual in International Law* (Copenhagen: Munksgaard, 1962)

O'Connell, Daniel P, *International Law*, vol I (London: Stevens & Sons, 1965)

—— *International Law*, vol II, 2nd edn (London: Stevens & Sons, 1970)

—— *The International Law of the Sea*, vol I, ed Ivan A Shearer (Oxford: Clarendon Press, 1982)

—— *The International Law of the Sea*, vol II, reprint, ed Ivan A Shearer (Oxford: Clarendon Press, 1988)

Oda, Shigeru, 'Dispute Settlement Prospects on the Law of the Sea', *International and Comparative Law Quarterly* 44 (1995) 863–72

Oppenheim, Lassa, *International Law – A Treatise*, 2nd edn (London: Longmans, Green and Co., 1912)

Orakhelashvili, Alexander, 'The Position of the Individual in International Law', *California Western International Law Journal* 31 (2001) 241–76

—— 'Restrictive Interpretation of Human Rights Treaties in the Recent Jurisprudence of the European Court of Human Rights', *European Journal of International Law* 14 (2003) 529–68

Oxman, Bernard, 'Observations on Vessel Release under the United Nations Convention on the Law of the Sea', *International Journal of Marine and Coastal Law* 11 (1996) 201–15

—— 'Human Rights and the United Nations Convention on the Law of the Sea', *Columbia Journal of Transnational Law* 36 (1998) 399–432

Pagden, Anthony and Lawrance, Jeremy (eds), *Vitoria – Political Writings*, 12th printing (Cambridge: Cambridge University Press, 2010) Cambridge Texts in the History of Political Thought

Pancracio, Jean-Paul, *Droit de la mer*, 1st edn (Paris: Dalloz, 2010)

Papanicolopulu, Irini, 'La nozione di giurisdizione ai sensi dell'art. 1 della Convenzione Europea dei Diritti Umani nella recente giurisprudenza della Corte Europea dei Diritti Umani', in Tulio Scovazzi, Irini Papanicolopulu and Sabrina Urbinati (eds), *I diritti umani di fronte al giudice internazionale – Atti della giornata di studio in memoria di Carlo Russo* (Milan: Giuffrè Editore, 2009) 83–130

—— 'The Law of the Sea Convention: No Place for Persons?', *International Journal of Marine and Coastal Law* 27 (2012) 867–874

—— 'Hirsi Jamaa v. Italy', *American Journal of International Law* 107 (2013) 417–23

—— 'Human Rights and the Law of the Sea', in Nerina Boschiero, Tullio Scovazzi, Cesare Pitea and Chiara Ragni (eds), *International Courts and the Development of International Law – Essays in Honour of Tullio Treves* (Berlin: Springer, 2013) 535–44

—— 'A Missing Part of the Law of the Sea Convention: Addressing Issues of State Jurisdiction over Persons at Sea', in Clive Schofield, Seokwoo Lee and Moon-Sang Kwon (eds), *The Limits of Maritime Jurisdiction* (Leiden: Martinus Nijhoff Publishers, 2014) 387–404

—— 'Human Rights and the Law of the Sea', in David Joseph Attard (general ed), Malgosia Fitzmaurice and Norman A Martínez Gutiérrez (eds), *The IMLI Manual of International Maritime Law*, vol I, *The Law of the Sea* (Oxford: Oxford University Press, 2014) 509–32

—— 'Considerations of Humanity in the *Enrica Lexie* Case', *Questions of International Law – Zoom-In* 22 (2015) 25–37

—— *International Law and the Protection of People at Sea* (Oxford: Oxford University Press, 2018)

Papastavridis, Efthymios, '"Fortress Europe" and Frontex: Within or Without International Law?', *Nordic Journal of International Law* 79 (2010) 75–111

—— 'European Convention on Human Rights and the Law of the Sea: The Strasbourg Court in Unchartered Waters?', in Malgosia Fitzmaurice and Panos Merkouris (eds), *The Interpretation and Application of the European Convention o Human Rights – Legal and Practical Implications* (Leiden: Martinus Nijhoff, 2012) 115–46

—— *The Interception of Vessels on the High Seas – Contemporary Challenges to the Legal Order of the Oceans* (Oxford and Portland, OR: Hart Publishing, 2014)

—— 'Is There a Right to Be Rescued at Sea? A Skeptical View', *Questions of International Law – Zoom-In* 4 (2014) 17–32

Parlett, Kate, *The Individual in the International Legal System – Continuity and Change in International Law* (Cambridge: Cambridge University Press, 2011) Cambridge Studies in International and Comparative Law

Pauwelyn, Joost, 'Bridging Fragmentation and Unity: International Law as a Universe of Inter-Connected Islands', *Michigan Journal of International Law* 25 (2004) 903–16

—— 'Fragmentation of International Law', *Max Planck Encyclopaedia of Public International Law*

Pellet, Alain, 'The Definition of Responsibility in International Law', in James Crawford, Alain Pellet and Simon Olleson (eds), *The Law of International Responsibility* (Oxford: Oxford University Press, 2010) 3–16

Peters, Anne, 'International Dispute Settlement: A Network of Cooperational Duties', *European Journal of International Law* 14 (2003) 1–34

—— 'Membership in the Global Constitutional Community', in Jan Klabbers, Anne Peters and Geir Ulfstein (eds), *The Constitutionalization of International Law* (Oxford: Oxford University Press, 2009) 153–262

—— *Völkerrecht*, 3rd edn (Zurich, Basel and Geneva: Schulthess, 2012)

—— *Beyond Human Rights – The Legal Status of the Individual in International Law* (Cambridge: Cambridge University Press, 2016) Cambridge Studies in International and Comparative Law

Petrig, Anna, 'Piracy', in Donald Rothwell, Alex Oude Elferink, Karen Scott and Tim Stephens (eds), *The Oxford Handbook of the Law of the Sea* (Oxford: Oxford University Press, 2015) 843–65

Plakokefalos, Ilias, 'Seabed Disputes Chamber of the International Tribunal for the Law of the Sea: Responsibilities and Obligations of States Sponsoring Persons and Entities with respect to Activities in the Area', *Journal of Environmental Law* 24 (2012) 133–43

—— 'Environmental Protection of the Deep Seabed', in André Nollkaemper, Ilias Plakokefalos, Jessica Schechinger (eds), *The Practice of Shared Responsibility in International Law* (Cambridge: Cambridge University Press, 2017) 380–98

Politis, Nicolas, *Les nouvelles tendances du droit international* (Paris: Hachette, 1927)

Portmann, Roland, *Legal Personality in International Law* (Cambridge: Cambridge University Press, 2010) Cambridge Studies in International and Comparative Law

Pufendorf, Samuel von, *De Jure Naturae et Gentium*, ed CH Oldfather and WA Oldfather (Oxford: Clarendon Press, 1934) Classics of International Law

Pugash, James Z, 'The Dilemma of the Sea Refugee: Rescue Without Refuge', *Harvard Journal of International Law* 18 (1977) 577–604

Quadri, Rolando, 'Cours général de droit international public', *Collected Courses of the Hague Academy of International Law* 113 (1964-III) 237–483

—— *Corso di diritto internazionale pubblico* (Naples: Libreria Scientifica Editrice, 1966)

Rachel, Samuel, *De Jure Naturae et Gentium Dissertationes*, ed Ludwig von Bar (Washington D C: Carnegie Institute of Washington, 1916) Classics of International Law

Rainey, Bernardette, Wicks, Elizabeth and Ovey, Clare, *Jacobs, White, and Ovey: The European Convention on Human Rights*, 7th edn (Oxford: Oxford University Press, 2017)

Rao, Chandrasekhara, 'The International Tribunal for the Law of the Sea: An Evaluation', in Nisuke Ando, Edward McWhinney and Rüdiger Wolfrum (eds), *Liber Amicorum Judge Shigeru Oda* (The Hague: Kluwer Law, 2002) 667–81

Rao, Pemmaraju Sreenivasa, 'Multiple International Judicial Forums: A Reflection of the Growing Strength of International Law or Its Fragmentation?', *Michigan Journal of International Law* 25 (2004) 929–61

Rawls, John, *The Law of Peoples* (Cambridge, MA: Harvard University Press, 1999)

Rayfuse, Rosemary, *Non-Flag State Enforcement in the High Seas* (Leiden: Brill, 2004) Publications on Ocean Development

—— 'The Anthropocene, Autopoiesis and the Disingenuousness of the Genuine Link: Addressing Enforcement Gaps in the Legal Regime for Areas beyond National Jurisdiction', in Erik Jaap

Molenaar and Alex Oude Elferink (eds), *The International Legal Regime of Areas beyond National Jurisdiction: Current and Future Developments* (Leiden: Martinus Nijhoff Publishers, 2010) 165–90

—— 'Differentiating the Commons? The Responsibilities and Obligations of States Sponsoring Deep Seabed Mining Activities in the Area', *German Yearbook of International Law* 54 (2011) 459–88

Reuland, Robert, 'Interference with Non-National Ships on the High Seas: Peacetime Exceptions to the Exclusivity Rule of Flag-State Jurisdiction', *Vanderbilt Journal of Transnational Law* 22 (1989) 1161–229

—— 'The Customary Right of Hot Pursuit onto the High Seas. Annotation to Article 111 of the Law of the Sea Convention', *Virginia Journal of International Law* 33 (1993) 557–89

Riley, Patrick, *Leibniz – Political Writings*, 2nd edn, reprint (Cambridge: Cambridge University Press, 2006) Cambridge Texts in the History of Political Thought

Ringbom, Henrik, 'Ship-Source Marine Pollution', in André Nollkaemper, Ilias Plakokefalos, Jessica Schechinger (eds), *The Practice of Shared Responsibility in International Law* (Cambridge: Cambridge University Press, 2017) 265–93

Rocha, Armando, *O Contencioso dos Direitos do Homem no Espaço Europeu – O Modelo da Convenção Europeia dos Direitos do Homem* (Lisbon: Universidade Católica Editora, 2010)

—— 'They Have Rights, Don't They? – As Fronteiras (da CEDH) Também Se Abatem', *O Direito* 144 (2012) 449–85

Ross, Alf, *A Textbook of International Law* (London: Longmans, 1947)

—— *On Law and Justice* (Clark, NJ: The Lawbook Exchange, 2012)

Rothwell, Donald and Stephens, Tim, 'Illegal Southern Ocean Fishing and Prompt Release', *International and Comparative Law Quarterly* 53 (2004) 171–87

—— *The International Law of the Sea*, 2nd edn (Oxford and Portland, OR: Hart Publishing, 2016)

Roucounas, Emmanuel, 'Facteurs privés et droit international public', *Collected Courses of the Hague Academy of International Law* 299 (2002) 9–420

Roxstrom, Erik, Gibney, Mark and Einarsen, Terje, 'The NATO Bombing Case (Banković et al. v. Belgium et al.) and the Limits of Western Human Rights Protection', *Boston University International Law Review* 23 (2005) 55–136

Rüth, Alexandra and Trilsch, Mirja, 'Banković v. Belgium (Admissibility)', *American Journal of International Law* 97 (2003) 168–72

Ryngaert, Cedric, *Jurisdiction in International Law*, reprint (Oxford: Oxford University Press, 2012) Oxford Monographs in International Law

—— 'Clarifying the Extraterritorial Application of the European Convention on Human Rights', *Merkourios – Utrecht Journal of International and European Law* 28 (2012) 57–60

Scelle, Georges, 'Règles générales du droit de la paix', *Collected Courses of the Hague Academy of International Law* 46 (1933-IV) 331–697

—— *Précis de droit des gens – Principes et systématique* (Paris: Sirey, 1932)

Schaefer, Max, '*Al-Skeini* and the Elusive Parameters of Extraterritorial Jurisdiction', *European Human Rights Law Review* 16 (2011) 566–81

Shaw, Malcolm N, *International Law*, 8th edn (Cambridge: Cambridge University Press, 2017)

Schmitt, Carl, *Der Nomos der Erde im Völkerrecht des Jus Publicum Europaeum*, 5th edn (Berlin: Duncker and Humblot, 2011)

Scovazzi, Tullio, 'The Evolution of International Law of the Sea: New Issues, New Challenges', *Collected Courses of the Hague Academy of International Law* 286 (2000) 39–243

—— 'La tutela della vita umana in mare, con particolare riferimento agli immigrati clandestini diretti verso l'Italia', *Rivista di diritto internazionale* 88 (2005) 106–20

—— 'Human Rights and Immigration at Sea', in Ruth Rubio-Marín (ed), *Human Rights and Immigration* (Oxford: Oxford University Press, 2014) 212–60

Schreuer, Christoph, 'The Waning of the Sovereign State: Towards a New Paradigm for International Law?', *European Journal of International Law* 4 (1993) 447–71

Seeberg-Elverfeldt, Niels-J, *The Settlement of Disputes in Deep Seabed Mining* (Baden-Baden: Nomos, 1998)

Sellers, Mortimer, 'International Legal Personality', *Ius Gentium* 11 (2005) 67–78

Sequeira, Elsa Vaz de, *Da Contitularidade de Direitos no Direito Civil – Contributo para a sua Análise Morfológica* (Lisbon: Universidade Católica Editora, 2015)

Shany, Yuval, *The Competing Jurisdiction of International Courts and Tribunals* (Oxford: Oxford University Press, 2003) International Courts and Tribunals Series

Shearer, Ivan, 'Problems of Jurisdiction and Law Enforcement against Delinquent Vessels', *International and Comparative Law Quarterly* 35 (1986) 320–43

Simma, Bruno and Pulkowski, Dirk, 'Of Planets and the Universe: Self-Contained Regimes in International Law', *European Journal of International Law* 17 (2006) 483–529

Singh, Nagendra, 'Maritime Flag and State Responsibility', in Jerzy Makarczyk (ed), *Essays in Honour of Judge Manfred Lachs* (The Hague: Martinus Nijhoff, 1984) 657–69

Sohn, Louis B, 'Settlement of Law of the Sea Disputes', *International Journal of Marine and Coastal Law* 10 (1995) 205–17

Spijkerboer, Thomas, 'Wasted Lives. Borders and the Right to Life of People Crossing Them', *Nordic Journal of International Law* 86 (2017) 1–29

Steinberg, Philip E, *The Social Construction of the Ocean* (Cambridge: Cambridge University Press, 2001) Cambridge Studies in International Relations

Stephan, Paul B, 'Privatizing International Law', *Virginia Law Review* 97 (2011) 1573–664

Sudre, Frédéric, 'Les obligations "positives" dans la jurisprudence européenne des droits de l'homme', in Paul Mahoney (ed), *Protection des droits de l'homme: La perspective européenne – Mélanges à la memoire de Rolv Ryssdal* (Cologne: Carl Heymanns, 2000) 1359–76

—— *Droit européen et international des droits de l'homme*, 14th edn (Paris: Presses Universitaires de France, 2019)

Takei, Yoshinobu, 'Assessing Flag State Performance in Legal Terms: Clarifications of the Margin of Discretion', *International Journal of Marine and Coastal Law* 28 (2013) 97–133

Tanaka, Yoshifumi, 'Prompt Release in the United Nations Convention on the Law of the Sea: Some Reflections on the ITLOS Jurisprudence', *Netherlands International Law Review* 51 (2004) 237–71

—— 'Obligations and Liability of Sponsoring States concerning Activities in the Area: Reflections on the ITLOS Advisory Opinion of 1 February 2011', *Netherlands International Law Review* 60 (2013) 205–30

—— 'Navigational Rights and Freedoms', in Donald Rothwell, Alex Oude Elferink, Karen Scott and Tim Stephens (ed), *The Oxford Handbook of the Law of the Sea* (Oxford: Oxford University Press, 2015) 536–58

—— *The International Law of the Sea*, 3rd edn (Cambridge: Cambridge University Press, 2019)

Tavernier, Paul, 'La Cour européenne des droits de l'homme et la mer', in Daniel-Heywood Anderson, Vincent Bantz, Geneviéve Bastid-Burdeau, Mohammed Bedjaoui and Josette Beer-Gabel (eds), *Le mer et son droit – Mélanges offerts à Laurent Lucchini et Jean-Pierre Quéneudec* (Paris: Pedone, 2003) 575–89

Teitel, Ruti, *Humanity's Law* (Oxford: Oxford University Press, 2011)

Thurman, Aleksandra Elizabeth, *The Justification of the Law of the Sea in Early Modern Europe*, PhD dissertation (Ann Arbor, MI: The University of Michigan, 2010)

Tomuschat, Christian, 'International Law: Ensuring the Survival of Mankind on the Eve of a New Century – General Course on Public International Law', *Collected Courses of the Hague Academy of International Law* 281 (1999) 9–438

—— 'International Law as a Coherent System: Unity or Fragmentation?', in Mahnoush Arsanjani, Jacob Katz Cogan, Robert Sloane and Siegfried Wiessner (eds), *Looking to the Future – Essays on International Law in Honor of W. Michael Reisman* (Leiden: Martinus Nijhoff, 2011) 323–54

Tourme-Jouannet, Emmanuelle, 'Des origines du droit international: à propos du droit des gens modern au 18ème siècle', in Pierre-Marie Dupuy and Vincent Chetail (eds), *The Roots of International Law / Les fondements du droit international – Liber Amicorum Peter Haggenmacher* (Leiden: Martinus Nijhoff, 2014) 649–71Treves, Tullio, 'High Seas', in *Max-Planck Encyclopaedia of Public International Law*

—— 'Navigation', in René-Jean Dupuy and Daniel Vignes (eds), *A Handbook on the New Law of the Sea*, vol II (Dordrecht: Martinus Nijhoff Publishers, 1991) 835–988
—— 'The Proceedings Concerning Prompt Release of Vessels and Crews before the International Tribunal for the Law of the Sea', *International Journal of Marine and Coastal Law* 11 (1996) 179–200
—— 'Flags of Convenience before the Law of the Sea Tribunal', *San Diego International Law Journal* 6 (2004–5) 179–89
—— *Diritto internazionale – Problemi fondamentali* (Milan: Giuffrè Editore, 2005)
—— 'Fragmentation of International Law: The Judicial Perspective', *Agenda Internacional* 27 (2009) 213–53
—— 'Human Rights and the Law of the Sea', *Berkeley Journal of International Law* 28 (2010) 1–14
—— 'Article 292', in Alexander Proelß (ed), *United Nations Convention on the Law of the Sea – A Commentary* (Munich: CH Beck, 2017) 1881–92
Trevisanut, Seline, 'The Principle of *Non-Refoulement* at Sea and the Effectiveness of Asylum Protection', *Max Planck Yearbook of United Nations Law* 12 (2008) 205–46
—— 'Search and Rescue Operations in the Mediterranean: Factor of Cooperation or Conflict?', *International Journal of Marine and Coastal Law* 25 (2010) 523–42
—— 'The Exercise of Administrative Functions by ITLOS: A Comment on Prompt Release Cases', in Nerina Boschiero, Tullio Scovazzi, Cesare Pitea and Chiara Ragni (eds), *International Courts and the Development of International Law – Essays in Honour of Tullio Treves* (Berlin: Springer, 2013) 311–23
Trindade, Antônio Cançado, 'A consolidação da personalidade e da capacidade jurídicas do indivíduo como sujeito do direito internacional', in *Anuario Hispano-Luso-Americano de Derecho Internacional* 16 (2003) 237–88
—— *International Law for Humankind: Towards a New Jus Gentium* (Leiden: Martinus Nijhoff, 2010) The Hague Academy of International Law Monographs
—— *The Access of Individuals to International Justice* (Oxford: Oxford University Press, 2011)
Tuerk, Helmut, *Reflections on the Contemporary Law of the Sea* (Leiden: Martinus Nijhoff, 2012) Publications on Ocean Development
—— 'The International Seabed Area', in David Joseph Attard (general ed), Malgosia Fitzmaurice and Norman A Martínez Gutiérrez (eds), *The IMLI Manual of International Maritime Law*, vol I, *The Law of the Sea* (Oxford: Oxford University Press, 2014) 276–303
Tully, Stephen, *Corporations and International Lawmaking* (Leiden: Martinus Nijhoff, 2007)
Ulfstein, Geir, 'The International Judiciary', in Jan Klabbers, Anne Peters and Geir Ulfstein (eds), *The Constitutionalization of International Law* (Oxford: Oxford University Press, 2009) 126–52
Vattel, Emer de, *The Law of Nations* [*Le droit des gens, Ou principes de la loi naturelle, appliqués à la conduit et aux affaires des nations et des souverains*: 1758], ed Béla Kapossy and Richard Whatmore (Indianapolis, IN: Liberty Fund, 2008) Natural Law and Enlightenment Classics
Verdross, Alfred, *Die Verfassung der Völkerrechtsgemeinschaft* (Vienna: Springer, 1926)
—— 'Règles générales du droit international de la paix', *Collected Courses of the Hague Academy of International Law* 30 (1929-V) 275–507
—— *Völkerrecht*, 5th edn (Vienna: Springer Verlag, 1964)
Verzijl, JHW, *International Law in Historical Perspective*, Part II, *International Persons* (Leiden: AW Sijthoff, 1969)
Vicuña, Francisco Orrego, 'The Régime for the Exploration and Exploitation of Sea-Bed Mineral Resources', in René-Jean Dupuy and Daniel Vignes (eds), *A Handbook on the New Law of the Sea* (Dordrecht: Martinus Nijhoff Publishers, 1991) 635–687
—— 'Individuals and Non-State Entities before International Courts and Tribunals', *Max Planck Yearbook of United Nations Law* 5 (2001) 53–66
—— *International Dispute Settlement in an Evolving Global Society – Constitutionalization, Accessibility, Privatization*, reprint (Cambridge: Cambridge University Press, 2006) Hersch Lauterpacht Memorial Lectures

Visscher, Charles de, *Théories et réalités en droit international public*, 4th edn (Paris: Éditions A Pedone, 1970)
—— 'Cours général de droit international public', *Collected Courses of the Hague Academy of International Law* 136 (1972-II) 1–202
Vöneky, Silja and Höfelmeier, Anja, 'Article 136', in Alexander Proelß (ed), *United Nations Convention on the Law of the Sea – A Commentary* (Munich: CH Beck, 2017) 949–57
—— 'Article 137', in Alexander Proelß (ed), *United Nations Convention on the Law of the Sea – A Commentary* (Munich: CH Beck, 2017) 957–64
—— 'Article 139', in Alexander Proelß (ed), *United Nations Convention on the Law of the Sea – A Commentary* (Munich: CH Beck, 2017) 968–76
Vukas, Budislav, 'Droit de la mer et droits de l'homme', in *The Law of the Sea – Selected Writings* (Leiden: Martinus Nijhoff Publishers, 2004) 71–9
Waldron, Jeremy, *The Right to Private Property* (Oxford: Clarendon Press, 1990)
Walter, Christian, 'Subjects of International Law', *Max Planck Encyclopedia of Public International Law*
Wegelein, Florian, 'The Rules of the Tribunal in the Light of Prompt Release of Vessels', *Ocean Development & International Law* 30 (1999) 255–96
Weil, Prosper, 'Le droit international en quête de son identité – Cours générale de droit international public', *Collected Courses of the Hague Academy of International Law* 237 (1992-VI) 9–370
Wendel, Philipp, *State Responsibility for Interferences with the Freedom of Navigation in Public International Law* (Berlin: Springer, 2007) Hamburg Studies on Maritime Affairs
Westlake, John, *Chapters on the Principles of International Law* (Cambridge: Cambridge University Press, 1894)
Wilde, Ralph, 'Legal "Black Hole"? Extraterritorial State Action and International Treaty Law on Civil and Political Rights', *Michigan Journal of International Law* 26 (2005) 739–806
—— 'The "Legal Space" or "Espace Juridique" of the European Convention on Human Rights: Is It Relevant to Extraterritorial State Action?', *European Human Rights Law Review* 2 (2005) 115–24
—— 'Triggering State Obligations Extraterritorially: The Spatial Test in Certain Human Rights Treaties', *Israel Law Review* 40 (2007) 503–26
Wolff, Christian, *Jus Gentium Methodo Scientifica Pertractatum*, ed Joseph H Drake (Oxford: Clarendon Press, 1934) The Classics of International Law
Wolfrum, Rüdiger, 'Reflagging and Escort Operations in the Persian Gulf: An International Law Perspective', *Virginia Journal of International Law* 29 (1989) 387–99
—— 'The Settlement of Disputes before the International Tribunal for the Law of the Sea – A Progressive Development of International Law or Relying on Traditional Mechanisms?', *Japanese Yearbook of International Law* 51 (2008) 140–63
—— 'Obligation of Result Versus Obligation of Conduct: Some Thoughts About the Implementation of International Obligations', in Mahnoush Arsanjani, Jacob Katz Cogan, Robert Sloane and Siegfried Wiessner (eds), *Looking to the Future – Essays on International Law in Honor of W. Michael Reisman* (Leiden: Martinus Nijhoff, 2011) 363–83
Wouters, Kees and Heijer, Maarten den, 'The *Marine I* Case: A Comment', *International Journal of Refugee Law* 22 (2010) 1–19
Yang, Haijiang, *Jurisdiction of the Coastal State over Foreign Merchant Ships in Internal Waters and the Territorial Sea* (Dordrecht: Springer, 2006) Hamburg Studies on Maritime Affairs
Zemanek, Karl, 'The Legal Foundations of the International System – General Course on Public International Law', *Collected Courses of the Hague Academy of International Law* 266 (1997) 21–335
—— 'Does the Prospect of Incurring Responsibility Improve the Observance of International Law?', in Maurizio Ragazzi (ed), *International Responsibility Today – Essays in Memory of Oscar Schachter* (Leiden: Martinus Nijhoff, 2005) 125–34
Zhang, Hui, 'The Sponsoring State's "Obligation to Ensure" in the Development of the International Seabed Area', *International Journal of Marine and Coastal Law* 28 (2013) 681–99

Index

Note: Alphabetical arrangement is word-by-word, where a group of letters followed by a space is filed before the same group of letters followed by a letter, eg '*ex post* will appear before 'exclusion. In determining alphabetical arrangement, initial articles and prepositions are ignored.

absolute concept:
legal personality, 41
abstract aptitude of entities:
holding rights or duties, legal personality, 41
abstraction, States as, 30
access:
democracy of, 20
information, to, 104
Accioly, Hildebrando, 66
accountability:
autonomous, ship-owners, 84
deep seabed mining, LOSC, 111
ex post facto, 67–71
flag States, *see* flag States
non-compliance, 70
private actors:
Liability for Oil Pollution Convention, 70
private miners, 111, 112–13
shared, *see* shared accountability
ship-owners, flag States, 76
sponsoring States, 111, 113–18
States, 180–81
ACtHR, *see* **African Court of Human Rights**
active nationality, 147
activities in the Area, 99
activity limitations:
freedom of the seas, 52
addressees:
rules of international law, States, 26
international norms, 38
adjudication:
judicial law-making natural effect of, 133
administration, international, 104
administrative law, global, 103–104
administrative measures, 115
adversarial notion of international legal personality, 37
African Court of Human Rights (ACtHR):
consular and diplomatic communication as human right, 166–67
Agreement on Illicit Traffic by Sea, 90, 91
***Al-Saadoon* case, ECtHR,** 152
***Ali Samatar* case, ECtHR,** 162
Althusius, Johannes, 26
ambiguous wording:
exclusion of private actors for international law, 2
American Convention on Human Rights (ACHR), 43
anomalies, historical, 25
Anzilotti, Dionisio, 28
apartheid of private actors, 7–13
applicants' proposals:
Authority, the, examining, 102
arbitral tribunals, commercial, 109–10
arbitration:
deep seabed mining, 106, 109
archipelagic waters, 53, 72, 147
architecture of legal systems, 133
***Arctic Sunrise* arbitration case, LOSC,** 168
Area, the:
activities carried out in, 99, 176, 184, 185, 188–89
Authority, *see* Authority, the
common heritage of mankind principle governing activities in, 96–97
equitable sharing of benefits for exploitation of resources, 96
exploitation of, 95
exploration for, 95
freedom of navigation in superjacent waters, 53
human life protection, 176
international management of resources rule, 96
legal regime, 101–102
maritime zones beyond national jurisdiction, 53
mining activities in, 103
non-appropriation rules, 96
peaceful use rule, 96

private miners' participation in activities in, 98–101
resource management in, 104
resources, 96, 134
rule of law in, 114
sponsoring States compliance with legal regime of, 116
sponsoring States' responsibilities for ensuring activities in, 113
wrongful acts in, liability for, 112

Arendt, Hannah, 49
ARSIWA, *see* **Articles on Responsibility of States for Internationally Wrongful Acts**
artefacts, social, 11
Articles on Responsibility of States for Internationally Wrongful Acts (ARSIWA):
attribution of conduct to States, 69, 84, 129, 130

artificial islands, EEZ, 158
artificial legal persons, 9, 26
assessment:
criteria for private actors, 32–41
tests, objective, ECtHR, 165

association, freedom of, 166, 185
associations:
'private actors' term, inclusion in, 2

attribution, 69–151
Austin, John, 34
***aut dedere aut judicare* principle,** 148
authority:
constitutional, 39
prevention of exercising, States, 154
ships, over, 83

Authority, the:
accountability of private miners and, 112–13
applicants' proposals, examining, 102
arbitration rules, 106
authorisation for deep seabed mining operations, 105
competence over other States and private actors, 98
contractors, 105–106, 113–14, 185
decisions, 98
discrimination avoidance, 102
enforcement tools, 97
Enterprise, 99–100
forced labour prohibition, 185
freedom of association, 185
freedom of elections, 185
freedom of expression, 185
freedom to constitute trade unions, 185
functions, discrimination avoidance, 102
health standards, 185
human life protection, 176, 183, 184
human rights and freedoms, dependency on, 184, 185
incidental powers, 97
inspecting powers limits, 115
internal management of the Area's resources, 97
labour conditions, 185
legal regime of exploration for and exploitation of resources, 97
non-discriminatory procedure before contracts award, 102
objective procedure before contracts award, 102
positive obligations, 183
powers, discrimination avoidance, 102
prescriptive tools, 97
primary liability for wrongful and harmful acts in the Area, 112
private miners, 103–104, 112
prospective contractors and, SDC jurisdiction, 109
Regulations adopted by, 101, 104
resource management, 104
responsibility, 111
right to education, 185
right to health, 185
right to life, 185
right to physical integrity, 185
right to privacy, 185
safety conditions, 185
servitude prohibition, 185
slavery prohibition, 185
State-like entity, as, 98

authority of international law, 73
autonomous accountability:
ship-owners, 84

autonomous interests:
flag States, 83
private actors, 11

autonomous liability:
damage arising from mining activities, for, 113

autonomy of international legal system, 47, 48
***Avena* case, ICJ,** 38

***Banković* case, ECtHR,** 155, 156, 157
***Barcelona Traction* case, *dictum*, ICJ,** 46

barriers to cross-regime interaction, 140
bearers:
navigational entitlements, private actors, LOSC implicit recognition, 71
beneficial owners:
ship-owners, 67
beneficiaries of international law:
private actors as, 11, 23
benefits, *see* **equitable sharing of benefits**
biases:
assigning rights and duties to entities other than States, against, 13
different conclusions, leading to, 14–15
exclusion of private actors from international law, 143
international legal personality, impacting, 15
interpretive, *see* interpretive bias
intrinsic to every human being, 14
private actors, against, 2
private membership in international law, against, 13, 15, 31
private participation in international law, against, 96, 131
treaty interpretation interference, 93–94
bilateral procedure relations, LOSC, 131
binding norms, 104
Blackstone, William, 10
bonds, *see* **prompt release applications**
Bonello, Judge, 151–52
boosting private actors, 24
breach of due diligence, 86
breach of international legal rules, 76
Brierly, James Leslie, 30
broadcasting, illegal, 89
burdens, flag States bearing, 83

capacité juridique, *see* **legal capacity**
capacity:
different, conferred on same subjects, international legal system, 48
international legal subjectivity and, 42
legal, *see* legal capacity
case law:
convergent and consistent, 138
ECtHR, *see* European Court of Human Rights
impact, subjects of law influencing downstream production of law through, 132
Cavaglieri, Arrigo, 28
centre of rights and duties:
legal persons as, 47
centrepiece of international law:
States as, 24–27
Chamber of Summary Procedure, ITLOS, 122
Charney, Jonathan I, 141
charterers, *see* **ships**
choice of law, 105
***Chowdury* case, ECtHR,** 170
civilisation:
high seas as place outside, 10
coastal States:
activities prejudicial to, LOSC, 56
authorisation, 73
customs laws, infringement prevention, 55
EEZs, *see* Exclusive Economic Zones
enforcement, 118, 148, 158
facts prejudicial to, preventative measures, 56–57
fiscal laws, infringement prevention, 55
flag State vessels arrested by, 167
flag States' interests and, 65
human rights, 153, 158
immigration laws, infringement prevention, 55
innocent passage, 53–54, 57–58, 61
interception of vessels on high seas, 153
international fair trial standards, 167
jurisdiction:
de facto, 143, 158
de iure, 143, 161
extraterritorial, 147
functional, 147
law of the sea, 157
non-discrimination, 167
sea, at, 144, 146
spatial, 147, 157
laws and regulations, 55, 57–58
LOSC provisions, structure and obligational scope, ship-owners' compliance, 67–71
marine resources conservation, 55
maritime spaces under territorial sovereignty of, 53
maritime zones, 53, 158–59
moral duty to render assistance to persons in distress at sea, 177
positive obligations:
search and rescue, 179–80
prescriptive jurisdiction over ships exercising innocent passage as right, 57
prescriptive measures, 158
prompt release applications, LOSC, 120
regulations, *see* laws and regulations *above*

right to life, 180
safety of navigation, 55
sanitary laws, infringement prevention, 55
sea lanes, 55
sovereignty, 54
spatial enforcement jurisdiction, 119
territorial sea sovereignty, 54
see also Exclusive Economic Zones
collected resources, Area, the, 134
collisions, 178
command as law, 34
commercial arbitral tribunals, 109–10
commercial concerns:
International Convention on Salvage, 182
common genetic code:
human rights, law of the sea, 137–43
common heritage of mankind:
deep seabed mining, LOSC, 96
principle, 5, 96–97
community acceptance, 21
comparative law methodology, 22
compensation:
creditors for rights to, 92
damage covered by right to, 90
discouraging interferences with navigation, 92
dispute settlement system, 92
Fish Stocks Agreement, 91
flag States, to, 92
holders of rights to, 90–93
illegal hot pursuit, for, LOSC, 90
interfering States' accountability, 91
Intervention Convention, 91–92
lawful but unfounded interference with navigation, 90
navigational entitlements and, 92
private actors as creditors, 93
remedies delegated to domestic level, 92
shared responsibilities, 90
ship-owners creditors for, 92
ships entitled to, law of the sea treaties, 62
SUA Convention, 91
unlawful interference with navigation, for, LOSC, 65
competence:
assumption, sponsoring States, 115
conferred, responsibility *ex ante facto*, LOSC, 82
due diligence, international law equipping States with, 85
duty to exercise, 176
jurisdiction, flag States, 83
right to exercise, 176
compliance:
human rights, port States, 158
mechanisms, international law, in, 44
composite concept, 33–36
composite nature of innocent passage as right, 55
compulsory and exclusive jurisdiction, SDC, 108–11
concepts of international legal personality, 27, 33–41
conclusions:
different, biases leading to, 14–15
conduct of operations:
private miners' liability for wrongful acts in, 112
conflicting norms, legal systems, 39
consistency, legal systems, 133
constitutional authority, 39
constraints, innocent passage, 68
consular communication as human right, 166–67
contiguous zone, 147
continental shelf, 53, 147
contractors:
deep seabed mining, *see* deep seabed mining
private miners' selection, plan of work approval, 102
sponsoring States, 117–18
contracts:
deep seabed mining areas subject to, 99
entitlements, private miners, 104–108
governed by ICJ laws chosen by parties, 106
private miners, *see* private miners
contradictions between legal systems, 139
control:
deep seabed mining, 100
flag States over ships, 80
performance, *see* performance control
Convention on the International Regulations for Preventing Collisions at Sea, 184
core importance, right to life, 176–77
***Corfu Channel* case, ICJ,** 55
corporations:
'private actors' term, inclusion in, 2
cosmopolitan view of international law, 31
courts:
competence, general international law jurisdiction, 145
international rules, illuminating contests of, 133
jurisdiction of, human rights treaties, 146
national, 181

proliferation dangers, 140
protest forum, as, 37
role in making international law, 133
creditors:
compensation, for, 92, 93
crews:
detention, 118–23
prompt release applications, *see* prompt release applications
criminal guarantees:
human rights, ECHR, 166
criminal law:
private actors' rights or duties at, 12
cross-fertilisation, 175
cross-regime:
interaction, 2, 140, 176, 186, 189–90
interpretation, 175–76, 178, 186
customary international law:
VCLT legal regime reflecting, 14
customary law:
source of law, as, 133
customs laws:
infringement prevention, coastal States, 55

damage:
caused to by interference, 91
covered by right to compensation, 90
liability cases where secondary obligations refer to, 77
sustained, LOSC, 90–91
***Danzig* case, PCIJ,** 28
***de facto* authority, objective test of,** 182
***de facto* enslavement,** 172
***de facto* jurisdiction,** 150, 159
coastal States, 143, 158
ECHR, 149
flag States, 143, 154, 160, 165
human rights treaties, 149, 152
port States, 143
States, 157, 186
***de facto* maritime jurisdiction of States,** 186
***de iure* jurisdiction,** 149, 150
coastal States, 143, 161
ECHR, 153–54
EEZ, 158
flag States,143, 159–60, 161, 165
general international law, 149
human rights treaties, 152
port States, 143
States, 148, 150, 153–54, 157
de-Vattellisation of international law, 11
decisions:
the Authority, 98
judges, of add to tradition, 133
reasoned, rights to, 104
review of, rights to, 104
decommissioning justice to private actors, 129
deep seabed:
freedom of access rule, 96
governance, 98
mining, *see* deep seabed mining
quasi-Stateless relations of international law with private miners, 98
vertical integration, 98
see also Area, the
deep seabed mining:
accountability regime, LOSC, 111
activities in the Area, LOSC, 99
arbitration, 106, 109
areas subject to contract, 99
Authority, the, authorisation for operations, 105
choice of law, LOSC, 105
commercial arbitral tribunals, 109–10
common heritage of mankind, LOSC, 96
contract for security of tenure, LOSC, 105
contractors, 99–100, 106, 112, 185
control, 100
disputes arising out of, 95, 108–11
Enterprise, 99–100
extracted minerals object of property rights, LOSC, 106–107
human life, protection of, 183–85
Implementation Agreements, 100, 101, 102, 104, 107, 111
joint ventures, 100
Legal and Technical Commission recommendation, 101
legal regime, 99
mandatory referral, 110
minerals:
extracted, object of property rights, 106–107
resources, 98
multiple nationalities, 101
nationality, 100–101
pivotal role given to sponsoring States, 117
plans of work, 101
precautionary approach, LOSC, 114
private actors on behalf of flag States, LOSC, 127–28, 129
private miners, *see* private miners

procedures before approval, LOSC, 101
property rights, LOSC, 106–107
reserved areas, 99
resources referred to as minerals, 99
SDC jurisdiction, 109
sea-bed and ocean floor and subsoil thereof, LOSC, 96, 97
sponsoring States, 95
sponsorship, 100–101
State parties of nationality or control, 100
technology transfer, 100
default judges of international law, 38
democracy of access, 20
detaining States:
interests for penalty or compensation, prompt release applications, LOSC, 119
international judiciary interference limitations, 123
not requested for prompt release applications bonds, 121, 122–23
detention of vessels and crews, *see* **prompt release applications**
different conclusions:
biases leading to, 14–15
differentiated international capacity, 48
dignity, human, 171
diligence:
flag States, 69
see also due diligence
diplomatic communication as human right, 166–67
diplomatic protection rules, 44
diplomatic States:
protection, 11, 35, 44
direct effect, 73
treaties, 12
direct obligations:
flag States, 81
sponsoring States, 114
discrimination avoidance:
Authority, the, functions, 102
disembarkation of rescued persons, 182
disenfranchisement of private actors:
international legal system, 45, 134
dispute settlement:
bodies, 138–39, 141
compensation system, 92
inter-State system, LOSC, 70
international, *see* international dispute settlement
ITLOS pivotal role, 134
system, LOSC, 137–38
disputes:
deep seabed mining, arising out of, 95, 108–11
navigational entitlements, private actors, 72
settlement, *see* dispute settlement
domestic authorities, 71–72
domestic courts, 38, 40, 75
domestic institutions, 39
domestic law:
duties existing under, 28
enforcement remedies under, ship-owners, 71
international law and, 30, 45, 74
jural relations, 39, 65
juristic persons as full persons with limited capacities, 45
private actors within, international rules favouring, 12
rights existing under, 28
rules:
international law rules and, 12, 39
domestic legal contexts, 23
domestic legal orders:
international legal orders and, 22, 80
legal personality granted or recognised, 24
private actors invoking, applying and enforcing rights and duties in, 36
subjects of law, 22
domestic legal persons, 26, 47
domestic legal spheres:
individuals, 42, 43
juristic persons, 42, 43
domestic legal systems:
institutional protection to property rights, 107
international rules invoked as part of, 39
legal personality concept common to, 22
domestic level:
compensation remedies delegated to, 92
enforcement, ICJ, 38
domestic model:
genuine link requirement, 79–80
domestic procedures guarantees:
prompt release applications, 121
domestic secondary norms:
primary international norms coupled with, 40
domestic societies:
international societies not separate from, 45
domestic statutes:
rights adopted by, enjoyment after, 28

domestic statutory law:
incorporating LOSC provisions, dualism, 73
downstream mechanisms of production of law, 23
downstream production, 6, 132, 133
Draft Articles on Responsibility of States for Internationally Wrongful Acts, 139
***Drieman* case, ECtHR,** 161–62
drugs trafficking, 89
dualism, 73
due diligence:
breach of, 86
duties of, 84
ex ante responsibilities, sponsoring States, 116
flag States, 69–70, 86, 179
flexible notion, 85
international law equipping States with competence, 85
lack of, from flag States, 86
non-performance of obligations, sponsoring States, 116
obligation of, 84–87
sponsoring States, 114, 117
standards, flag States' failure to comply, 87
ultimate purpose, 85
Dupuy, René-Jean, 8
duties:
aptitude of entities to be recipient of, 42
assigning to entities other than States, biases against, 13
centre of, *see* centre of rights and duties
criminal law, private actors, 12
distribution between masters and flag States, 178–79
domestic law, existing under, 28
due diligence, of, 84
enforcement in international legal order, 36
exercise competence, 176
human rights law, private actors, 12
international, 34, 39
international law, under, 19–20
investment law, private actors, 12
juristic persons, 42
legal norms, conferring, 47
legal orders allocation to, 41
legal personality aptitude to hold under legal system, 38
primary:
secondary claims entailed, 40
private actors, 187
held under *ius gentium*, 4
international level, at, 12
invoking, applying and enforcing in domestic legal orders, 36
private miners' complex web of, 107
rescue, 182
rules equipping private actors with, 28
sovereign States, LOSC, 3
that entities can hold, legal capacity measure of, 42
treaty provisions conferred on private actors, 28
validity, 36
see also rights
duty-bearers:
private miners as, under law of the sea, 98

ECHR, *see* **European Convention on Human Rights**
ECJ, *see* **European Court of Justice**
economic interests, LOSC, 118–19
ECtHR, *see* **European Court of Human Rights**
education:
human rights to, ECHR, 166
EEZ, *see* **Exclusive Economic Zones**
elections:
free, human rights to, ECHR, 166
elements exogenous to international legal order, 47
enforceability:
rights, 35, 36
enforcement:
authority:
difficulties, flag States, 148
bodies:
human rights treaties, 146
coastal States, 118, 148, 158
domestic level, ICJ, 38
international law by domestic courts, 40
international legal system, secondary norms devolving to domestic courts, 40
international level, ICJ, 38
jurisdiction, 147
limited, jurisdiction, 147
mechanisms, 37, 44, 83
navigational entitlements:
national authorities, by, 71
port States, *see* port States
primary jurisdiction, flag States, 52
damage caused to, 91
remedies under domestic law:
ship-owners, 71

rights, LOSC, 33
third-party, 37
tools:
Authority, the, 97
enhancing instruments of governance, 103
enslavement, *see* **slavery**
Enterprise:
Authority, the, 99–100
deep seabed mining, 99–100
entitlements:
conferred on private actors, HSC, 66
private miners, 101–11
epistemological status, 23
equitable sharing of benefits:
for exploitation of resources, Area, the, 96
European Convention on Human Rights (ECHR), 43, 130–31
human dignity, 171
human rights:
criminal and fair trial guarantees, 166
to education, 166
equality between spouses, 166
to free elections, 166
freedom from slavery when at sea, 174–75
freedom of association, 166
freedom of expression, 166
freedom of religion, 166
to human freedom, 166
to life, 166, 183
to marry, 166
non-refoulement principle, 166, 182
to physical integrity, 166
human trafficking, 170
jurisdiction:
de facto, 149
de iure, 153–54
personal terms, 150
spatial terms, 150
standard of, 166
territorial, 153–54
LOSC interaction, 142
norms:
interaction with norms of LOSC, 142
rescuing States' jurisdiction under, 182
European Court of Human Rights (ECtHR), 43, 130–31
Al-Saadoon case, 152
Ali Samatar case, 162
Banković case, 155, 156, 157
case law, 153, 155–66, 174–77
Chowdury case, 170
Drieman case, 161–62
effective overall control, 155
general international law, falling back on, 142
Hassan cases, 162
Hirsi Jamaa case, 161, 164–65, 182
human dignity, 171
human rights:
criminal and fair trial guarantees, 166
to education, 166
equality between spouses, 166
to free elections, 166
freedom from slavery when at sea, 174–75
freedom of association, 166
freedom of expression, 166
freedom of religion, 166
to human freedom, 166
to life, 166, 183
to marry, 166
non-refoulement principle, 166, 182
to physical integrity, 166
human trafficking, 170
Ilaşcu case, 153–54, 160–61
Issa case, 157
jurisdiction:
de facto, 149
de iure, 153–54
personal terms, 150
spatial terms, 150
standard of, 166
territorial, 153–54
LOSC interaction, 142
marine environment special features, 163
Medvedyev case, 163–64
norms:
interaction with norms of LOSC, 142
objective assessment tests, 165
positive obligations, 160–61
Rantsev case, 170, 171
rescuing States' jurisdiction under, 182
Rigopoulos case, 163–64
Siliadin case, 170–71
territoriality, meaning, 155
vacuum in system, 156
Vassis, case, 164
Women of Waves case, 162, 164
Xhavara decision, 166
European Court of Justice (ECJ):
ships not attached to States, no freedom of navigation, 66–67
evidence rules:
diplomatic States protection, 44
flag States protection, 35

ex ante responsibilities, 115
due diligence obligation, sponsoring States, 116
***ex post facto* breach of international law rules,** 76–77
***ex post facto* accountability:**
non-compliance with provisions, LOSC, 67–71
***ex post* responsibilities,** 115
non-performance of due diligence obligations, sponsoring States, 116
exclusion of private actors for international law, 2
exclusive and compulsory jurisdiction, SDC, 108–11
Exclusive Economic Zones (EEZs):
artificial islands, structures and platforms, 158
fishing activities, 158, 167
freedom of navigation, 53
individuals at sea, duty to render assistance, 176
jurisdiction, *de iure*, 158
limited prescriptive and enforcement jurisdiction, 147
maritime zones under jurisdiction of coastal States, 53
spatial-functional jurisdiction, 147
exclusive exploitation rights, 134
exo-subjects, 187
expectations:
protection of, 104
exploitation:
Area, the, of, 95
contracts, private miners, 105
resources, 5, 97
rights, exclusive, 134
exploration:
the Area, for, 95
contracts, private miners, 105
resources, for, 97
rights, 5, 106, 134
expression:
freedom of, *see* freedom of expression
extracted minerals:
deep seabed mining, object of property rights, LOSC, 106–107
extraterritorial action, States, 156
extraterritorial jurisdiction:
coastal States, 147
human rights treaties, 152, 156
States, 74, 146, 154, 156, 157
facts:
prejudicial to coastal States, 56–57
succinct statements of, *see* succinct statements of facts
fair trial guarantees:
human rights, ECHR, 166
fall-back mechanisms, LOSC, 142
feasibility:
jurisdiction and, 151
tests, flag States, 160
feudal relations:
patrimonial States and, international society of, 9
fictional legal persons:
States as, 9
financial security:
posting, prompt release applications, 118
fiscal laws:
coastal States, infringement prevention, 55
Fish Stocks Agreement, 62, 82, 91, 167
fisheries laws, 167
fishing activities, 158, 167
flag States:
accountability, 84
active nationality, 147
burdens, bearing, 83
communication rights, LOSC, coastal States' EEZs, 167
compensation to, 92
control over ships, 80, 159
diligence, 69
direct obligations, 81
due diligence, 69–70, 86, 179
enforcement, 83, 148
failure to comply, due diligence, 87
feasibility tests, 160
foreign flags of convenience, 79
genuine link requirement, 80–81, 83
high seas:
governance and jurisdiction on, enforcement, 52
human smuggling:
enhanced tools for fighting, 171
human trafficking:
enhanced tools for fighting, 171
indirect obligation, 179
indirect responsibilities, 81–84
interception of ships, 169, 171
interests:
autonomous, 83
coastal States and, 65

international community and, 65
transcendent, 83
interference with navigation of private miners, 115
international responsibilities, 87
jurisdiction, 54
competence to exercise, 83
de facto, 143, 154, 160, 165
de iure, 143, 159–60, 161, 165
difficulties in exercising, 154
effective exercise, 82–83
exclusive on high seas, ships subject to, 81
Fish Stocks Agreement, 82
high seas, on, 5
international law, under, 82
law of the sea, 155
LOSC, 80, 81–82, 87–88, 161
not exclusive, 87
obligation to exercise, 83
primary, 81–82, 173
sea, at, 144, 146
search and rescue operations, 165
ships, over, 59, 78, 80, 161
law of the sea responsibilities, 86
LOSC provisions, structure and obligational scope, nationals compliance, 67–71
merchant vessels and, 65
nationality, 76
nationality of ships, 60, 76, 79, 160
navigational entitlements rights and freedoms held by, 93
navigational rights-holders, as, 64–65
non-compliance with international law, 87
primary enforcement jurisdiction, 52, 91
private actors:
authorised by, 125
on behalf of, deep seabed mining, LOSC, 127–28, 129
prompt release applications, 70, 118–19, 122, 123–31, 134
protection, 11, 35, 44
rendering assistance to persons in distress at sea, LOSC, 179
responsibility deriving from jurisdiction over flagged ships, 115
rights held by ships flying their flags, protection of, 76
seaworthiness conditions, 58–59
ship-owners:
conduct not directly attributable to, 69
foreigners, 79
genuine link requirement, *see* genuine link requirement
and, intertwining positions, 75–87
shared accountability, 76
ships and, relationships between, 80
slavery, 6, 169, 172–73
submitting, prompt release applications, ITLOS, 124–25, 135
ubi commoda ibi incommoda principle, 83
UN Consultative Group on Flag State Implementation, *ante facto* obligations, 69
vessels arrested by coastal States, 167
flagged ships, ***see*** **ships**
flexible notion of due diligence, 85
forced labour, 158, 170, 185
foreign flags of convenience, 79
foreign merchant vessels, 65
foreign ships, 54, 88
foreign vessels, 64, 162
foreigners:
ship-owners, flag States, 79
foreseeability:
legal systems, courts responsibility for providing, 133
formal notion of legal personality, 23
former subjects of law
transforming into objects of protection, 11
foundations:
'private actors' term, inclusion in, 2
fragmentation:
international law atomisation into autonomous fields, 138–42
international legal orders, 137
international legal personality, 137
legal capacity, private actors, 43
legal orders, international law as, 139
legal personality, 43
freedom:
conferred on private actors, 40
freedom from slavery, 174
freedom of access rule:
deep seabed, 96
freedom of association, 166, 185
freedom of elections:
Authority, the, 185
freedom of expression:
Authority, the, 185
human rights, ECHR, 166
freedom of high seas, 66
freedom of navigation, 51–53, 66
freedom of religion, 166

freedom of slaves:
taking refuge on ships, LOSC
freedom of the seas, 52
freedom to constitute trade unions, 185
freedoms
navigational, *see* navigational rights and freedoms
full international legal personality, 42
full international legal subjectivity, *see* **international legal subjectivity**
functional jurisdiction:
coastal States, 147
functionally defined issue-areas of international law, 140

gateway into human rights:
law of the sea, 174
general international law:
falling back on, ITLOS, 142
jurisdiction, *see* jurisdiction
norms of, fall-back on, 141
general theory of law, 22
genetic code, common, *see* **common genetic code**
genetic legacy of positivism, 34
***Genocide* case, ICJ,** 86
Gentili, Alberico, 53, 93
genuine link requirement:
absence:
denial of nationality of ships on, 80
case law, ITLOS, 79
domestic model, 79–80
effective jurisdiction rules and, 80
flag States, 80–81, 83
guideline rather than hard rule, 80
HSC, 77–78
international model, 79–80
ITLOS, 79
LOSC, 77–80
minimum national element requirement, 78
purpose:
flag State jurisdiction effectiveness, 77
undetermined notion of, 80
vagueness, 80
geographical limitations:
freedom of the seas, 52
geometrically rigid legal personality, 41
global administrative law, 103–104
good faith:
VCLT treaty interpretation rules, 14
governance:
deep seabed, 98
enhancing instruments of, 103
high seas, on, flag States enforcement, 52
government ships:
assigned to States, 65
immunities, LOSC, 61
Grotius, Hugo, 53, 93
guarantees:
domestic procedures, 121
human rights treaties, 167

***Handlungs-*, *see* legal capacity**
hard dualists, 73
harmful acts in the Area:
Authority, the, primary liability for, 112
***Hassan* cases, ECtHR,** 162
health standards:
Authority, the, 185
Heilborn, P, 28
high seas:
active nationality – flag state jurisdiction, 147
enforcement jurisdiction, 147
freedom of, 66
freedom of navigation, 52
governance on:
flag States enforcement, 52
interception of ships on, 163–64
jurisdiction on, 5, 52
limited prescriptive and enforcement jurisdiction, 147
maritime zones beyond national jurisdiction, 53
navigational entitlements held by private actors, LOSC, 68
non-flag States, 88, 89
place outside society and civilisation, as, 10
rights of passage, 66
ships on:
no navigational rights and freedoms, 63
ships subject to flag States' exclusive jurisdiction, 81
universal jurisdiction, 147
vessels interception on, coastal States, 153
warships' interception of vessels on, 149
see also oceans; sea; seas
***Hirsi Jamaa* case, ECtHR,** 161, 164–65, 182
historical anomalies, 25
historical evolution of international legal system, 22
historical misconception in international law, 23

historical redundancy, 24–32
Hobbes, Thomas, 25, 26
Hohfeld, Wesley Newcomb, 174, 181
holders:
navigational entitlements, *see* navigational entitlements
rights, *see* rights
HSC:
entitlements conferred on private actors, 66
genuine link, 77–78
moral duty to render assistance to persons in distress at sea, 177
slavery, 169
human beings:
biases intrinsic to, 14
'private actors' term, inclusion in, 2
human dignity, ECHR, 171
human freedom:
human rights to, ECHR, 166
interests, prompt release applications, LOSC, 118
human life protection:
Area, the, 176
Authority, the, 176, 183
LOSC, 184
deep seabed mining, 183–85
LOSC, 5, 176
human rights:
bound by:
coastal States and port States, 158
common genetic code of, law of the sea, 137–43
compliance, port States, 158
consideration in interpretation of, LOSC, 186
consular and diplomatic communication as, ActHR, 166–67
covered by ECHR, coastal States, 153
criminal and fair trial guarantees, ECHR, 166
to education, ECHR, 166
enjoyment of, 145
equality between spouses, ECHR, 166
to free elections, ECHR, 166
freedom from slavery when at sea, ECHR, 174–75
freedom of association, ECHR, 166
freedom of expression, ECHR, 166
freedom of religion, ECHR, 166
gateway into, law of the sea, 174
to human freedom, ECHR, 166
to life, 166, 183
jurisdiction at sea, 145–66
law, *see* human rights law
law of the sea and, 186
LOSC, in, 166–69, 172–85
maritime activities, 143, 145
to marry, ECHR, 166
nationality of ships, obligations, flag States, 160
negative obligations, 153, 177
non-refoulement principle, 166, 182
to physical integrity, ECHR, 166
positive obligations, 153, 177
precondition of human rights application, as, 143–45
private actors, of, Fish Stocks Agreement, 167
prohibition of torture, States, 162
protection:
life at sea, 176–85
vacuum in system, 156
rescue:
disembarkment obligations, 183
rights to liberty, States, 162
rights to life, States, 162
slavery repression, 169–76
SUA Convention, 167
treaties and, LOSC, 181
human rights and freedoms:
dependency on, The Authority, 184, 185
human rights law:
common genetic code of law of the sea, 137–43
cross-fertilisation process, 175
cross-regime interaction, 176, 186
cross-regime interpretation, 175–76, 186
individual-centred vs State-centred law of the sea, 142, 186
jurisdiction:
established at sea, 136–37
individual protection means, 148–49
law of the sea and:
alignment between, 186
common genetic code of, 137–43
LOSC reading impact, 185
overall control test, 86
primary rights assigned to private actors, 143
private actors:
fragmented legal personality, 43
rights or duties at, 12
subjects of, 43

State-centred vs individual-centred law of the sea, 142, 186
treaties, 136
human rights treaties:
enforcement bodies, 146
guarantees, 167
jurisdiction:
de facto, 149, 152
de iure, 152
extraterritorial, 152, 156
courts, of, 146
personal relations between and States, 150
States, 146, 150
territoriality, 152
regional scope, 156
sea, at, 143–66
universal scope, 156
universality, 156
see also European Convention on Human Rights
human smuggling, 171–72
human trafficking, 89, 170, 171–72
humanisation of international law, 12
humanitarian interests:
flag States, prompt release applications, LOSC, 118–19
humanity:
considerations of, ITLOS, 168, 185–86

ICCPR (International Covenant on Civil and Political Rights), 155
ICJ, *see* **International Court of Justice**
ICTY, *see* **International Criminal Tribunal for the former Yugoslavia**
***Ilaşcu* case, ECtHR,** 153–54, 160–61
ILC, *see* **International Law Commission**
illegal broadcasting, 89
illegal hot pursuit, 90
immigration laws:
coastal States, infringement prevention, 55
IMO, *see* **International Maritime Organization**
Implementation Agreements, *see* **deep seabed mining**
incidental powers, Authority, the, 97
inclusive concept(ion):
legal capacity and legal personality, 48–49
individual-centred human rights law vs State-centred law of the sea, 186
individual legal subjectivity, 15
individual protection means, 148–49
individualisation of international norms, 34
individualist theories of international law, 28
individuals:
domestic legal spheres:
pursuit of any lawful end, 43
holders of right to life, as, 181
membership in political communities, 78
sea, at:
duty to render assistance, EEZ, 176
duty to render assistance, LOSC, 176, 181
States' duties to, 186
States and:
analogy between in international law, 24–25
creation by as domestic legal persons, 47
similarities between, 25
States compared to, international legal scholarship, 25
States' jurisdiction over based on nationality principle, 59–60
subjection to jurisdiction, States, 149
subjects of international law, 30–31
individuals-only conception of international legal personality:
private actors' advent, 30–32
information:
access to, 104
rights to, LOSC, 54
innocent passage, 54
archipelagic waters, 53
assurance by ship-owners, 68
coastal States, 53–54, 57–58, 61
concept unclear, 55
constraints, addressed to ship-owners, 68
continuous and expeditious, 55
definition amended in UNCLOS III, 56
facts depriving passage of innocence, 56
foreign ships through territorial sea, 54
non-suspendable rights, international straits, 53
permitted by coastal States, 53–54
right, as, 54–55, 57–58, 70, 72
rights of:
archipelagic waters, 53
LOSC, 29
invoking against other State parties, 72
territorial sea, through, 61
territorial sea, 53, 54

sea lanes, 55
ship-owners:
constraints, addressed to ship-owners, 68
non-compliance accountability, 70
submarines, 55
territorial sea, 53
under-water vehicles, 55
inspecting powers limits:
Authority, the, 115
inspection of facilities:
contractors and the Authority, 113–14
integrity, physical, 166
inter-State law, 3
intercepting States:
jurisdiction, 162, 163–64
slavery, 174
interdiction operations, 162
interests:
economic, LOSC, 118–19
flag States, *see* flag States
human freedom, *see* human freedom
humanitarian, *see* humanitarian interests
ships, represented in, *see* ships
States, 5, 25
interfering States:
accountability, compensation, 91
capacity, 175–76
ships engaged in slave trade, 174
internal management:
the Area's resources, 97
internal waters, 53, 54, 147
international adjudicating bodies, 138
international administration activity, 104
international bodies, 137
international capacity, differentiated, 48
international community:
flag States' interests and, 65
private membership in, 46
International Convention for the Prevention of Pollution from Ships (MARPOL)
port State jurisdiction, 148
ports, admission conditions, 68
ships entitled to compensation, 62
International Convention for the Safety of Life at Sea (SOLAS):
duty to render assistance to persons in distress at sea, 177, 179
navigational rights and freedoms assigned to ships, 61
positive obligations, 161, 180
rescue, 11, 182
ships entitled to compensation, 62
International Convention on Civil Liability for Oil Pollution Damage, 67
International Convention on Liability and Compensation for Damage in Connection with the Carriage of Hazardous and Noxious Substances by Sea, 67
International Convention on Maritime Search and Rescue (SAR Convention):
moral duty to render assistance to persons in distress at sea, 177
positive obligations, 161, 180
rescue:
disembarkation of rescued persons, 182
duty to, 178, 182
International Convention on Salvage:
commercial concerns, 182
distribution of duties between masters and flag States, 178–79
rendering assistance, 177, 178
International Court of Justice (ICJ), 6
assessment criteria for private actors, 32–33
Avena case, 38
Barcelona Traction case, *dictum*, 46
contracts governed by laws chosen by parties, 106
Corfu Channel case, 55
domestic level enforcement, 38
Genocide case, 86
international legal persons, composite criteria to qualify, 32–33
international level enforcement, 38
international rights recognition, 38
LaGrand case, 38
Reparation for injuries case advisory opinion, 18, 19, 42
slavery, repression, 169
treaty interpretation, 14
International Covenant on Civil and Political Rights (ICCPR), 155
international criminal law:
overall control test, 86
International Criminal Tribunal for the former Yugoslavia (ICTY), 11, 140
international customary law:
international law interpretation, strict canons of, 28
moral duty to render assistance to persons in distress at sea, 177
universal obligation pursuant to, 176
international decision-making, 20

international dispute settlement:
bodies, 138–39
limited access to, 131
private miners access to, 95
State-to-State matrix of, 6
international duties, 34, 39
international fair trial standards:
coastal States, 167
international judicial proceeding:
private access to, interpretive bias, 131
international judiciary:
interference limitations, detaining States, 123
international labour conventions, 184
International Law Commission (ILC)
lex specialis in international law as self-contained regime, 139
international legal capacity:
measure of relevance, 47
private actors having, 49
remedies evidence of, 132
international legal orders:
domestic legal orders and, 22, 80
duties enforcement in, 36
elements exogenous to, 47
fragmented, 137
private actors exclusion from, 13
private memberships in, interpretive bias, 108
remedies absence, 181
international legal personality, 4, 187
adversarial notion of, 37
assessment criteria for private actors, 32–41
biases impacting, 15
composite concept, 33–36
concepts and conceptions of, 27, 33–41
epistemological status, 23
formal concept, 38–41
fragmented, 137
full, 42
individuals-only conception of, private actors' advent, 30–32
international law misconceptions, 42
limited, 42, 45
low-density, 42
partial, 42
private actors:
boosting, 24
ordeals of, 42–45
procedural concept, 36–38
ships deprived of, 62
States, *see* States
international legal persons, 1
composite criteria to qualify, ICJ, 32–33
'international legal subjects' used interchangeably, 2
'subjects of international law' used interchangeably, 2
international legal relationships, 21
international legal rules:
breach, 76
private actors beneficiaries of, 74
private actors recipients of, 49
international legal scholarship, 25
international legal sphere:
States creators and dominant players of, 10
States' natural access to, 27
international legal status:
private miners, 101
international legal subjectivity, 36, 38
aptitude of entities to be recipient of rights and duties, 42
capacity and, 42
criteria inferring, 22
disregarded by New Haven School, 20
existence, 19
full, States as template of, 18
parasitic notion of legal personality, 22
private actors, 23
usefulness of concept, 19
international legal subjects:
domestic legal persons, entities different from, 26
'international legal persons' used interchangeably, 2
ordinary, 25
private actors as, 19, 32, 43
'subjects of international law' used interchangeably, 2
typical, States, 25
international legal system:
autonomy of, 47, 48
customary law as source of law, 133
different capacities conferred on same subjects, 48
historical evolution, 22
law, between juristic persons, as, 22
legal personality notion prior to, 48
new tectonic movements in future, 49
openness, 47
private actors:
disenfranchisement, 134
legal subjects, as, 39

private participation in:
interpretation as tool for, 134
procedural substitution, 40
remedies function in, 131
secondary norms:
enforcement devolving to domestic courts, 40
social entities and, 19
States dominant players, 13
tectonic subjective transformation of, 49
international legal theory:
New Haven School challenges, 20
international level:
enforcement, ICJ, 38
private actors' rights or duties at, 12
international litigation:
Lowe's binary function of, 132
international management of resources rule:
the Area, 96
international management rule:
the Area resources, 96
International Maritime Organization (IMO):
freedom of navigation impacts on, 52
international model:
genuine link requirement, 79–80
international norms:
addressees of, 38
individualisation of, 34
primary coupled with domestic secondary norms, 40
State rights conferred by, not possessed, 43
international persons, normal, 27
international processes:
private actors' rights of participation in, 23
international realm:
individual legal subjectivity translation into, 15
International Regulations for Preventing Collisions at Sea, Convention on, 184
international remedies:
absence, LOSC, 39
available to private actors, 131
conferred on private actors, 35
international rights and duties coupling with, 34
international responsibilities:
ex post facto breach of international law rules, 76–77
flag States, 87
international rights:
recognition, ICJ, 38
international rights-holders:
States, 4
international rules:
courts' illuminating contests of, 133
invoked as part of domestic legal systems, 39
private actors within domestic law, favouring, 12
International Seabed Authority (ISA), 6
international societies:
domestic societies not separate from, 45
international society of patrimonial States and feudal relations, 9
international society of territorial and sovereign States, 9
international status:
private actors, interpretive bias against, 4
international straits, 53, 72
international subjectivity, 23, 25
International Tribunal for the Law of the Sea (ITLOS):
Chamber of Summary Procedure, 122
considerations of humanity, 168, 185–86
dispute settlement pivotal role, 134
general international law, falling back on, 142
genuine link requirement, 79
legal disputes settlement, 132
Louisa case, 168
open to entities other than States, 6, 127
private actors, 70–71
prompt release applications, 118, 120
amounts disputed, 122
bonds not posted, 130
bonds posted but vessels and crews not released, 122
Chamber of Summary Procedure dealing with, 122
detaining States not requested, 122–23
flag States submitting, 124–25, 135
jurisdiction compulsory, 122
priority, 122
private actors authorised by flag States submitting, 125, 128
private attorneys submitting on behalf of flag States, 124–25, 126, 135
State agents submitting on behalf of flag States, 124–25
succinct statements of facts submission, 122
variable powers, 123

prompt release procedures, 70, 140
Saiga (2) case, 79
Seabed Disputes Chamber (SDC), *see* Seabed Disputes Chamber
ship-as-a-unit concept, 3
States as parties before, 124
States' enforcement mechanisms, 83
Tomimaru case, 168
Virginia G case, 79
interpretation:
fall-back processes, LOSC: 141
question, 29
systemic, *see* systemic interpretation
tool for private participation, as, 134
treaties, *see* treaties
interpretive bias, 15, 93
freedom of navigation, 51
implicit, 50, 134, 186–88
law of the sea, 2
navigational entitlements, 135
not excluding private miners from being recipients of rights and duties under international law, 117–18
private access to international judicial proceeding, 131
private actors:
authorised by flag States submitting prompt release applications, 125
international status, against, 4
rights and freedoms recognition under international law, against, 71
private memberships in international legal order, 108
private miners' minor role, 111
private participation, against, 2, 134–35
process, in, 14
prompt release applications, 135
rule, 4
SDC, 111
Intervention Convention:
compensation, 91–92
interventions:
flag States, prompt release applications, LOSC, 131
sponsoring States, 111
investment law:
private actors, 12, 43
ISA (International Seabed Authority), 6
***Issa* case, ECtHR,** 157
ITLOS, *see* **International Tribunal for the Law of the Sea**
***ius cogens*,** 158
***ius gentium*:**
duties of private actors held under, 4
early international legal scholars, 8
law of nations to *ius inter gentes* from, 9
private actors subjects of, 8
rights of private actors held under, 4
sovereign ruler's person as subject of, 25
States as legal persons within realm of, 26
***ius inter gentes*:**
law of nations from *ius gentium* to, 9

Jessup, Philip, 31
***J.H.A. v Spain case*,** 164
joint and several liability:
Authority, the, and private miners, between, 112
joint ventures:
deep seabed mining, 100
judges:
decisions add to tradition, 133
judicial bodies:
case law, convergent and consistent, 138
common methodology, 138
judicial decisions:
no binding effect except between parties, LOSC, 132
judicial law-making:
natural effect of adjudication, 133
jural relations:
among nations, 9
contractors and the Authority, between, 106
domestic law, subject to, 39
governed by domestic law, 65
imbalance between States and private actors, 44
international law governing, 39
municipal law, subject to, 39
quasi-Stateless, 98
treaties, 87
jurisdiction:
active nationality, law of the sea, 147
attribution and, 151
'authority over' meaning, 151
coastal States, law of the sea, 157
compulsory:
prompt release applications, ITLOS, 122
conflicting meanings, 145
'control of' meaning, 151
de facto, 150, 159
coastal States, 143, 158
ECHR, 149
flag States,143, 154, 160, 165

port States, 143
States, 157, 186
de iure, 149, 150
coastal States, 143, 161
ECHR, 153–54
EEZ, 158
flag States, 143, 159–60, 161, 165
port States, 143
States, 148, 150, 153–54, 157
defined with respect to territories, PCIJ, 146
difficulties in exercising, flag States, 154
enforcement:
internal waters, 147
extraterritorial, *see* extraterritorial jurisdiction
feasibility and, 151
flag States, *see* flag States
functional, coastal States, 147
general international law, 145, 148–49
high seas, on, 5, 52
human rights at sea, 145–66
human rights law, *see* human rights law
human rights purposes, meaning, 159
human rights treaties, *see* human rights treaties
individuals' subjection to, States, 149
intercepting States, 162, 163–64
internal waters, 147
limited enforcement, 147
limited prescriptive, 147
maritime, of States, *de facto*, 186
maritime, *see* maritime jurisdiction
meaning, 157
non-discrimination, coastal States, 167
personal elements, model based on, 152
personal terms, ECHR, 150
persons at sea, over, States, 146
port States, *see* port States
precondition of human rights application, as, 143–45
prescriptive, 147
primary, flag States,173
private actors' claims, over, SDC, 6
protective, 147
rescuing States under ECHR, 182
responsibility and, 151
rules:
effective, genuine link requirement and, 80
sea, at, 144, 146
search and rescue operations, 165
ships:
flying flags, over, flag States, 161
over determined in spatial terms, 60
sovereign power, exercise of, 145–46
spatial, *see* spatial jurisdiction
spatial-functional, 147
sponsoring States, 115
standard of, ECHR, 166
States, law of the sea, 155
territorial, 147, 153–54
territories, States, 146
universal, law of the sea, 147
juristic persons:
domestic legal spheres, 42, 43
duties, 42
full persons with limited capacities, as, domestic law, 45
law between, international legal system, 22
'private actors' term, inclusion in, 2
rights, 42
States as, 9, 26
States' jurisdiction over based on nationality principle, 60
subjects of law, as, 22
jurists:
domestic legal contexts, trained in, 23
justice:
decommissioning to private actors, 129

kaleidoscopic reality, 138
Kantian view of international law, 31
Kaufman, Wilhelm, 30
Kelsen, Hans, 30
Krabbe, Hugo, 30

labour:
conditions, The Authority, 185
forced, 158, 170, 185
standards, The Authority, 185
***LaGrand* case, ICJ,** 38
land-locked States:
access to seas, LOSC, 65
Lapradelle, Albert Geouffre de, 30
Lauterpacht, Hersch, 31
law:
choice of, 105
command, as, 34
commandment adopted by sovereign States, as, 74
comparative, 22
domestic, *see* domestic law

downstream mechanisms of production of, 23
former subjects, transforming into objects of protection, 11
general theory of, 22
governing mankind:
human rights, *see* human rights law
international law as, 31
monist system of, 22
nations, of, *see* law of nations
private actors as proper subjects of, 5
sea, of, *see* law of the sea
States, 3
subjects of, *see* subjects of law
theory of, 21–24
upstream production, 6

law-making, 23, 24

law of nations:
concept confined to relations among States, 7
from *ius gentium* to *ius inter gentes*, 9
jural relations among nations, 9
private actors excluded, 7
States creator and sole subject of, 9

law of the sea:
common genetic code, human rights law, 137–43
cross-fertilisation process, 175
cross-regime interaction, 176, 186
cross-regime interpretation, 175–76
current law:
private actors' entitlements held under, 2
downstream production, 6
flag States' responsibilities, 86
history, 8
human rights, 137–43, 174, 186
human rights law and, 186
interpretative bias, 2
issues, experience accumulated of, LOSC, 134
jurisdiction and:
active nationality, 147
coastal States, 157
flag States, 155
port States, 147
protective, 147
spacial-functional, 147
States, 155
territorial, 147
universal, 147
nationality of ships pivotal in, 60
private actors:
entitlements held under current law, 2
exclusion as subjects of, 2, 8
limitation of status as subjects of, 2
meagre procedural relevance, 6
not subjects of, 43
participation, 3, 6–7
segregation from, 6
private miners as rights-holders and duty-bearers, 98
rescue:
disembarkment obligations, 182–83
rules, 186
servitude, Roman property law of, transposed into, 54
slavery, 170, 174
State-centred conception of international law, 2
State-centred vs individual-centred human rights law, 142, 186
State-to-State perspective, 97
tale between States or State-like communities, 8
treaties:
ships entitled to compensation, 62
upstream production, 6

Law of the Sea Convention (LOSC)**:**
addressees of provisions, 69
Arctic Sunrise arbitration case, 168
coastal States:
activities prejudicial to, 56
EEZs, 167
sovereignty, 54
collisions, after, rendering assistance, 178
common heritage of mankind principle, 5
compensation:
illegal hot pursuit, for, 90
unlawful interference with navigation, for, 65
competencies conferred:
responsibility *ex ante facto*, 82
consular and diplomatic communication as human right, 166–67
cross-regime interpretation, 178
damage sustained, 90–91
deep seabed mining, 95
accountability regime, 111
activities in the Area, 99
arbitration, 106
choice of law, 105
common heritage of mankind, 96
contract for security of tenure, 105

extracted minerals object of property rights, 106–107
precautionary approach, 114
private actors on behalf of flag States, 127–28, 129
private miners' liability caused by their conduct, 116
procedures before approval, 101
property rights, 106–107
sea-bed and ocean floor and subsoil thereof, 96
Authority, the, 97
dispute settlement system, 70, 137–38
ECHR interaction, 142
enforcement rights, 33
entitlements conferred on private actors, 66
ex post facto accountability for non-compliance with provisions, 67–71
experience accumulated of law of the sea issues, 134
fall-back mechanisms, 142
flag States:
interception of ships believed to be engaged in slave trade, 169
jurisdiction, 161
jurisdiction and control, 80, 81–82, 87–88
rendering assistance to persons in distress at sea, 179
genuine link requirement, 77–80
government ships, immunities, 61
guarantees, 167
high seas navigational entitlements held by private actors, 68
human life protection, 5, 176
human rights, 166–69
consideration in interpretation of, 186
law impact reading of, 185
protection of life at sea, 176–85
repression of slavery, 169–76
to life, 183
treaties and, 181
individuals at sea, duty to render assistance, 176, 181
innocent passage, 54
continuous and expeditious, 55
rights of, 29
invoking against other State parties, 72
territorial sea, through, 61
interference with navigation, toleration, 34
international remedies, absence, 39
interpretation fall-back processes, 141
judicial decisions:
no binding effect except between parties, 132
land-locked States:
access to seas, 65
local remedies, exhaustion of, 71–72
loss sustained, 90–91
maritime activities regulated, 12
maritime jurisdiction, 146
minerals recovered, property rights over, 40–41
moral duty to render assistance to persons in distress at sea, 177
municipal remedies, 39
nationality:
conferral on ships, 160
navigational entitlements, 58
allocation to ships, 61
areas under spatial jurisdiction, in, 63
rights held by ships, in negative wording, 6
navigational rights and freedoms, 39, 53, 63, 188
non-flag States, 34
norms:
interaction with norms of ECHR, 142
Nottebohm judgment, 78
obligational scope of provisions, 67–71
persons at sea in danger of being lost, rendering assistance to, 178
persons in distress, rendering assistance to, 178
pollution:
monetary penalties, 167
port State jurisdiction, 148
ports, admission conditions, 68
positive obligations, 161
private actors:
engaged in maritime activities, rights of, 167
exploitation of resources, 5
exploration rights, 5
maritime activities beneficiaries, 5
navigational entitlements, 5
as objects of protection, 5
participation in prompt release proceedings, 71
position in, 5–7
as proper subjects of law, 5
property rights over resources, 5
as rights holders, 5

private applicants' primary rights under, 132
prompt release applications:
bilateral procedure relations, 131
coastal States, 120
conditions, 120
detaining States' interests for penalty or compensation, 119
flag States:
economic and humanitarian interests, 118–19
interventions, 131
function in framework of, 118–23
human freedom interests, 118
private actors, by, 95, 127, 128–29
provisions identification, 120
release of vessels and crews, 118
rights for release on posting bonds, 120
ship-owners' or operators' financial interests, 118
prompt release proceedings, 70
property rights, 33, 40–41
protection of life, 177–85
provisions:
reading, helping, 134
systemic interpretation of, 141
remedies, 70
rescue:
disembarkation of rescued persons, 182
duty to, 182
obligation, 182
persons in distress at sea, 11
right to be rescued, 182
rights to information, 54
saving lives at sea, 161
search and rescue facilities, 161
ships:
assigning rights to, 64
entitled to compensation, 62
States' rights to sail, 65
slavery, 169–72
prohibition, 5, 6
repression at sea, 172–76
sovereign States' rights and duties, 3
structure of provisions, 67–71
visit, rights of, 162
warships, immunities, 61
lawful interference:
navigation, grounds for, 88–89
laws:
adoption, 115
laws and regulations:
coastal States, 55, 57–58
Le Fur, Louis, 30
Legal and Technical Commission:
deep seabed mining recommendation, 101
legal capacity:
elasticity to legal subjectivity, 41
fragmented, private actors, 43
inclusive concept(ion), 48–49
legal personality:
and legal subjectivity and, defined interchangeably, 42
status prior to given legal order, as, 46–48
legal persons:
differences between, shaping, 41
measure of rights and duties that entities can hold, 42
misconception source, 41–49
open and empty concept(ion), 48
quantitative feature of legal personality, 41
private actors' international legal personality, ordeals of, 42–45
relative feature of legal personality, 41
single (not multiple) legal personality, 45–46
legal disputes settlement:
ITLOS, 132
legal fiction:
States as, 30
legal norms, 47, 133
legal orders:
being legal persons, connection with, 47
characterised by impregnable presence of States, 187
different, single social orders regulation from, 46
domestic, *see* domestic legal orders
fragmented, 139
given, status as legal personality prior to, 46–48
legal persons:
derivation from norms of, 22
rights and duties, allocation to, 41
new, 9
private actors *ipso facto* legal persons under all, 187
remedies engagement in, 132
single, governing relations from separate social orders, 46
legal personality:
absolute concept, 41
abstract aptitude of entities to hold rights or duties, 41

aptitude to hold rights or duties under legal system, 38
concept common to domestic legal systems, 22
concept empty of meaningful content, 48
concept in theory of law, 21–24
participation of private actors as subjects of law, 18–19
different degrees of, 2
dimension of:
procedural capacities of private actors, 36
epistemological function of:
participation of private actors as subjects of law, 19–21
estates, conferred on, 62
fragmented, 43
full, domestic legal spheres, 42
geometrically rigid, 41
granted or recognised in domestic legal orders, 24
inclusive concept(ion), 48–49
individuals as model of, 42
international law, under, 18
international, *see* international legal personality
law-making capacities, 23
legal capacity, 41
legal subjectivity and legal capacity and, defined interchangeably, 42
misconception source, 41–49
notion of, formal, 23
notion prior to international legal system, 48
open and empty concept(ion), 48
parasitic notion of, international legal subjectivity, 22
private:
private membership implicit in, 46
private actors, of, 47, 49, 131
problem, international law pragmatic answer to, 26
qualitative concept, 41
right to have rights to be integrated into political communities, 49
ships, 62–63, 91
single (not multiple), 45–46, 49
sole requirement of, 38
status as, prior to given legal order, 46–48
study of, absence in international law, 23
theory of law, in, 21–24
things, conferred on, 62

legal persons:
artificial, 9, 26
being, 21, 47
centre of rights and duties, as, 47
differences between, legal capacity shaping, 41
domestic, 26, 47
legal capacity, 41
legal orders derivation from norms of, 22
list of, unitary, 47
notion of, unitary, 47
private actors, 49, 187
ships not, 64
ships, *see* ships
States as, 26, 32
theory of law, 22
legal regimes:
Area, the, 101–102
deep seabed mining, 99
VCLT, reflecting customary international law, 14
legal representatives:
private actors, of, States acting solely as, 44
legal scholars, 9
legal scholarship, international, 25
legal status of private actors in international law, 38
legal subjectivity, 18
legal capacity elasticity to, 41
legal personality and legal capacity and, defined interchangeably, 42
participation plus some form of community acceptance, 21
rights indicator of, 132
status of entities bestowed by legal system, 46
see also international legal subjectivity
legal subjects, 22
international, *see* international legal subjects
private actors as, international legal system, 39
legal systems:
conflicting norms, 39
consistency, courts responsibility for providing, 133
contradictions between, 139
foreseeability, courts responsibility for providing, 133
international, *see* international legal system
legal personality aptitude to hold rights or duties under, 38

legal subjectivity status of entities bestowed by, 46
new information attached to rule and architecture of, 133
normative elements, VCLT, 14
porosity, 46
stability, courts responsibility for providing, 133
systemic interpretation intrinsic feature of, 137
uniformity, courts responsibility for providing, 133
legitimacy of comparative law methodology, 22
Leibniz, Gottfried Wilhelm, 9, 26
***lex generalis* and *lex specialis*, relations between,** 142
***lex specialis*:**
different, relations among, 142
strong and weak cases of, 139
***lex specialis* and *lex generalis*, relations between,** 142
liability:
autonomous, 113
cases where secondary obligations refer to damage, 77
ex post facto breach of international law rules, 76–77
primary, 112
Liability for Oil Pollution Convention, 70
liberal access of private actors:
prompt release applications, in, 127
liberal system, international law as, 49
life:
human rights to, ECHR, 166, 183
protection of, 176–85
life at sea:
human rights protection, 176–85
limited access to international dispute settlement, 131
limited enforcement jurisdiction, 147
limited international legal personality, 42, 45
limited prescriptive jurisdiction, 147
limitedness of procedural capacity of private actors, 38
local remedies:
exhaustion of, LOSC, 71–72
***locus standi* of private actors:**
prompt release applications, in, 118–30
lords of international law:
States as, 26
LOSC, *see* **Law of the Sea Convention**
loss sustained, LOSC, 90–91
***Louisa* case, ITLOS,** 168
low-density international legal personality, 42
Lowe's binary function of international litigation, 132
Lucchini, Laurent, 55

magnetic force of States, 9
major international law-makers, 32
making international law, 27, 43
management, internal, 97
management rule:
international, 96
mandatory referral:
deep seabed mining, 110
mankind:
common heritage, *see* common heritage of mankind
international law as law governing, 31
marine environment:
protection, 89
special features, ECtHR, 163
marine resources:
conservation, coastal States, 55
maritime activities:
beneficiaries, private actors, LOSC, 5
human rights, 145
LOSC regulated, 12
private actors engaged in, 142–43
maritime jurisdiction:
LOSC, 146
States, 72, 73, 186
maritime law:
flagged ships compliance with, 83
maritime *lex mercatoria*, 4
maritime spaces:
territorial sovereignty of coastal States, under, 53
maritime zones, 53, 158–59
MARPOL, *see* **International Convention for the Prevention of Pollution from Ships**
marry:
human rights to, ECHR, 166
masters, ships, 66
meaningful content:
concept(ion) empty of, legal personality, 48
***Medvedyev* case, ECtHR,** 163–64
membership of international law, 4
merchant vessels, 65
Meron, Theodor, 12
meta-legal concepts, 22

Migrant Smuggling Protocol, 91
Milanović, Marko, 148
minerals:
collected, property rights over, 95
deep seabed mining, *see* deep seabed mining
extracted, 106–107
recovered, property rights over, LOSC, 40–41
resources referred to as, deep seabed mining, 99
miners, private, *see* **private miners**
mining:
activities in the Area, 103
deep seabed, *see* deep seabed mining
rights objects, private miners, 98
misconception:
historical, in international law, 23
international law, international legal personality, 42
legal personality source, 41–49
source, legal capacity, 41–49
monetary penalties:
pollution, LOSC, 167
monism:
international law and domestic laws, relations between, 73
LOSC applied as treaty, 73
new, legal effects within domestic legal orders, 73
true, 73
monist system of law, 22
moral duties:
rendering assistance to persons in distress at sea, LOSC, 177
moral persons:
States as, 26
multiple nationalities:
deep seabed mining, 101
municipal law:
jural relations subject to, 39
municipal remedies, LOSC, 39
myopia, self-protecting, of international law, 27–28

narrow reading of explicit private actors' entitlements, 95–96
locus standi of private actors in prompt release applications:
applications, submission on behalf of the flag State, 123–31
prompt release proceedings in LOSC framework, 118–23
remedies, importance of having, 131–34
rights emerging from activities in the Area, 96–97
ontological function of (state-like) authority, 97–98
private miners, *see* private miners
conclusion, 134–35
national courts:
right to life enforcement, 181
national law:
States enforcement jurisdiction immunity under, 71
national legal orders:
liberal and comfortable with third States' authority, 74
nationality:
active, 147
conferral on ships, LOSC, 160
core function, 59
deep seabed mining, 100–101
individuals' membership in political communities, 78
possession:
navigational entitlements conditions for enjoyment, 59
principle, 59–60
private miners, 100–101
ship-owners, 80
conferred, lawfulness of, 81
ships, *see* ships
nationals:
States, 30
nations:
jural relations among, 9
law of, *see* law of nations
natural persons:
conduct being considered as act of state, 69
navigation:
compensation discouraging interferences with, 92
freedom of, *see* freedom of navigation
interference with, toleration, LOSC, 34
lawful but unfounded interference with, compensation,90
lawful interference, grounds for, 88–89
safety of, coastal States navigation, 55
navigational entitlements, 58
allocation to ships, LOSC, 61
archipelagic waters, on, 72
areas under spatial jurisdiction, in, LOSC, 63
compensation and, 92
conditions for enjoyment of, 58–60
enforcement by national authorities, 71

existence regardless of coastal States' authorisation, 73
high seas, held by private actors, 68
holders, 59, 64, 92
hypothetical, held by private actors, 71
imposition among States, 73
international straits, 72
interpretive bias, 135
obligations assigned to ship-owners, 70
private actors:
bearers, LOSC implicit recognition, 71
disputes, 72
full enjoyment derived from flag State nationality, 76
LOSC, 5
protecting, 71
rights held by, 93
rights and freedoms held by flag States, 93
rights held by ships, in negative wording, LOSC, 6
ship-owners, 75, 76
ships, *see* ships
territorial sea, on, 72

navigational rights and freedoms:
contextual reading of provisions, LOSC, 63
exceptional, internal waters, 53
foreign vessels under, LOSC, 53
LOSC, 39, 188
ships, *see* ships
variable geometry, 52

navigational rights-holders:
flag States as, 64–65

negative obligations:
human rights, 177
nationality of ships, flag States, 160
refrain from maintaining persons from slavery, to, 171
States, 153

new forms of slavery, 172

New Haven School, 10, 20

new international legal system tectonic movements in future, 49

new legal order, 9

new monism:
legal effects within domestic legal orders, 73

NGO, *see* **non-governmental organisations**

non-appropriation rules:
the Area, 96

non-compliance:
accountability, innocent passage, ship-owners, 70
international law, with, 87

non-discrimination:
contracts award, 102
jurisdiction, coastal States, 167
LOSC, coastal States' EEZs, 167
private miners, 102

non-flag States:
competence to interfere with navigation of foreign ships, 88
interference on high seas, 89
jurisdiction on high seas, 88
LOSC, 34
public order reasons for interference with navigation, 88

non-governmental organisations (NGO):
'private actors' term, inclusion in, 2

non-innocent passage, TSC, 55–56

non-interference principles:
general international law jurisdiction, 148–49

non-national ships:
States visiting and inspecting, 173–74

***non-refoulement* principle,** 162, 166, 182

normal international persons, 27

normative instrument:
private miners' contracts as, 104–105

normative jungles, 138

norms:
binding, 104
conflicting, 39
ECHR, interaction with norms of LOSC, 142
general international law, of, fall-back on, 141
international:
primary coupled with domestic secondary norms, 40
legal, 47, 133
LOSC, interaction with norms of ECHR, 142
primary, 11, 39–40, 75
secondary, 11, 39–40, 70, 75

notice-and-comment, rights to, 104

***numerus clausus* not in international law,** 49

O'Connell, Daniel P, 31

objective assessment tests, ECtHR, 165

objective procedure:
contracts award, before, 102

objective test of *de facto* authority, 182

objects of international law:
private actors as, 23

obligations:
direct, *see* direct obligations
rescue, 182
sufficiently characterised, 41
observer effect, 27
ocean floor and sea-bed and subsoil thereof:
beyond limits of national jurisdiction, deep seabed mining, LOSC, 96
oceans:
governance, 8
transport surface, conception as, 64
see also high seas; seq; seas
old forms of slavery, 172
ontologically reduced reading of international law, 28
open and empty concept(ion), 48
operations:
rescue, SAR Convention, 178
operators:
financial interests, 118
ships, *see* ships
ordeals of private actors:
international legal personality, 42–45
ordinary international legal subjects, 25
overall control test, 86
owners, ships, *see* **ship-owners**
Oxman, Bernard, 126

parasitic notion of legal personality, 22
partial international legal personality, 42
participants:
international decision-making, 20
limitations, freedom of the seas, 52
see also relevant participants
participation of private actors as subjects of law, 18–19
epistemological function of legal personality, 19–21
legal personality concept in theory of law, 21–24
passage:
innocent, *see* innocent passage
rights of, 66
patriarchal system:
international law followed matrix of, 10
patrimonial States:
feudal relations and, international society of, 9
payments:
prompt release applications bonds, 131
PCIJ, *see* **Permanent Court of International Justice**
peaceful use rule:
Area, the, 96
penalisation of acts maintaining slavery, 171
penalty payments:
ship-owners, 83
performance control:
obligational scope, ship-owners, LOSC, 67–68
Permanent Court of International Justice (PCIJ):
Danzig case, 28
jurisdiction defined with respect to territories, 146
ships' nationality, 60
persistent non-compliance with international law, 87
***personae iure gentium*, States as,** 26
personal elements:
jurisdiction model based on, 152
personal terms:
jurisdiction, ECHR, 150
personality:
legal, *see* legal personality
States, 42
***Persönlichkeit*,** *see* **legal personality**
***personnalité juridique*,** *see* **legal personality**
persons:
legal, *see* legal persons
subjects and, difference between, 2
persons at sea:
danger of being lost, in:
rendering assistance to, 178
jurisdiction over, States, 146
persons in distress:
rendering assistance to, LOSC, 178
sea, at:
rendering assistance to, 177, 179
philosophers:
States creation of, 9
physical integrity:
human rights to, ECHR, 166
piracy, 10–11, 59, 66, 89, 91, 158
plans of work:
deep seabed mining, 101
form as contracts, in, private miners' contracts, 104
private miners, *see* private miners
platforms, EEZ:
persons subject to *de iure* of coastal States, 158

political communities:
right to have rights to be integrated into, 49
political convenience:
result of, international remedies conferred on private actors, 35
Politis, Nicolas, 30
pollution:
control, 162
monetary penalties, LOSC, 167
polymetallic nodules, 96, 98
porosity, legal systems, 46
port States:
enforcement:
authority, 148
measures, 158
human rights:
bound by, 158
compliance, 158
jurisdiction:
de facto, 143
de iure, 143
law of the sea, 147
limited enforcement, 147
LOSC, 148
MARPOL Convention, 148
sea, at, 144, 146
prescriptive measures, 158
ports:
admission conditions, 68
ships unable to leave, 68
positive obligations:
The Authority, 183
ECtHR, 160–61
human rights, 177
LOSC, 161
nationality of ships, flag States, 160
SAR Convention, 161, 180
SOLAS, 161, 180
States, 153
positivism:
genetic legacy of, 34
posting:
prompt release applications bonds, 118
***pouvoir constituants* of international law:**
States, 30
***pouvoir continués*:**
States as, 30
powers:
discrimination avoidance:
Authority, the, 102
incidental, Authority, the, 97
jurisdiction describing, States, 145
pragmatic reason:
assigning ships' rights, for, 64
pre-contractual rights:
applicant private miners, of, 101–104
precautionary approach:
deep seabed mining, LOSC, 114
sponsoring States, 117–18
prescriptive jurisdiction, 147
prescriptive measures, 158
prescriptive tools:
Authority, the, 97
preservation for future generations:
Area, the, resources, 96
prevention of acts maintaining slavery, 171
primary duties:
secondary claims entailed, 40
primary jurisdiction:
flag States, 173
persons and events on board their ships, over, 81–82
primary liability:
wrongful and harmful acts in the Area, for:
Authority, the, 112
primary norms, 11, 75
primary rights:
human rights law assigned to private actors, 143
secondary claims entailed, 40
primary State rights:
fictitious separation, 44
primary subject of international law:
States as, 26, 27
prior hearings, rights to, 104
private access to international judicial proceeding:
interpretive bias, 131
private applicants:
primary rights under LOSC, 132
procedural rights compensating private actors for law-making capacities lack, 134
private attorneys:
prompt release applications on behalf of flag States, ITLOS, 124–25, 126, 135
private international law, 3
private legal personality:
private membership implicit in, 46
private membership:
international community, in, 46
international law, in, biases against, 13, 15, 31

private miners:
accountability, 111, 112–13
activities performed by, 99
Authority, the, and, 103–104, 112–13
autonomous liability for damage arising from mining activities, 113
complex web of rights and duties, 107
conduct of operations, liability for wrongful acts in, 112
contractors' selection, plan of work approval, 102
contracts, 104–108
deep seabed mining, 95
direct relations with the Authority, 103–104
duties deriving from international law compliance, sponsorship ensuring, 114
duty-bearers, as, under law of the sea, 98
entitlements, 101–11
flag States interference with navigation of, 115
international dispute settlement, access to, 95
international legal status, 101
law of the sea rights-holders and duty-bearers, as, 98
liability caused by their conduct, LOSC, 116
locus standi in disputes arising out of deep seabed mining, 95, 108–11
mining rights objects, 98
minor role, interpretive bias, 111
nationality, 100–101
non-discrimination, 102
participation in activities in the Area, 98–101
plans of work, 102, 104, 105
pre-contractual rights of applicants, 101–104
procedural entitlements of applicants, 102–104
property rights, 107
responsibility, the Authority and sponsoring States, 111
accountability of private miners and the Authority, 112–13
accountability of sponsoring States, 113–18
rights-holders, as, under law of the sea, 98
SDC jurisdiction, 109
ships of its nationality, use of, 115
sponsorship, 100–101
subjection to sponsoring States, 117
transportation, 99
wrongful acts in conduct of operations, liability for, 112
private mining, 135
private participation:
international law, in:
biases against, 2, 96, 131
international legal system, in:
interpretation as tool for, 134
interpretive bias against, 134–35
private violence:
high seas as place of, 10
procedural capacity of private actors:
dimension of legal personality, 36
limitedness of, 38
procedural concept:
assessment criteria for private actors, 36–38
international legal personality, 36–38
procedural entitlements:
applicant private miners, of, 102–104
procedural rights, 36
helping changing reading of international law, 134
private actors:
before, ITLOS, 70–71
prompt release applications, 129–30, 132, 134
private applicants compensating private actors for law-making capacities lack, 134
SDC, before, 134
procedural substitution:
international legal system, 40
procedural transparency, rights to, 104
prohibition of piracy, 10–11
prohibition of torture, 162
prompt release applications, 118, 120, 167
amounts disputed, ITLOS, 122
bilateral procedure relations, LOSC, 131
bonds:
amounts disputed, 121, 122
detaining States not requested, 121, 122–23
not posted, ITLOS, 130
paid but vessels and crew not released, 121, 122
payment, 131
posted but vessels and crews not released, ITLOS, 122
posting, 118
Chamber of Summary Procedure dealing with, ITLOS, 122

coastal States:
detention powers, 120
failure to release, 120
spatial enforcement jurisdiction, 119
conditions, LOSC, 120
crews, detention, 118–23
detaining States:
not requested, ITLOS, 122–23
interests for penalty or compensation, LOSC, 119
detention of vessels and crews, 118–23
domestic procedures guarantees, 121
financial security, posting, 118
flag States, 122, 129–30, 134
economic and humanitarian interests, LOSC, 118–19
interventions, LOSC, 131
submitting, ITLOS, 124–25, 135
force used in detention, 121
function in framework of, LOSC, 118–23
human freedom interests, LOSC, 118
interpretive bias, 135
ITLOS, *see* International Tribunal for the Law of the Sea
jurisdiction compulsory, ITLOS, 122
liberal access of private actors in, 127
locus standi of private actors in, 118–30
LOSC, *see* Law of the Sea Convention
priority, ITLOS, 122
private actors:
authorised by flag States submitting, ITLOS, 125, 128
LOSC, 95, 127, 128–29
procedural rights, 129–30, 132, 134
private attorneys submitting on behalf of flag States, ITLOS, 124–25, 126, 135
provisions identification, LOSC, 120
release of vessels and crews, LOSC, 118
remedies, importance of having, 131–34
rights for release on posting bonds, LOSC, 120
ship-owners' or operators' financial interests, LOSC, 118
State agents submitting on behalf of flag States, ITLOS, 124–25
submission of applications on behalf of flag States, 123–31
succinct statements of facts submission, ITLOS, 122
urgency of proceedings, 126–27
variable powers, ITLOS, 123
vessels, detention, 118–23

prompt release proceedings:
crew members, LOSC and ITLOS, 70
ITLOS, 70, 140
LOSC, 70
private actors' participation in, LOSC, 71
ships, LOSC and ITLOS, 70
submitted on behalf of flag States, 70
proper legal persons, 4
property rights:
collected minerals, over, 95
deep seabed mining minerals extracted, object of, 106–107
domestic legal systems' institutional protection to, 107
international law no institutional protection to, 107
LOSC, 33, 40–41
minerals recovered, over, LOSC, 40–41
private miners, 107
resources, over, private actors, LOSC, 5
proportionality standards:
compliance with, rights to, 104
prosecution of acts maintaining slavery, 171
prospective contractors:
Authority, the, and, SDC jurisdiction, 109
protection:
diplomatic States, 11
expectations, of, 104
flag States, 11
former subjects of law transforming into objects of, 11
life, of, 176–85
private actors:
beneficiaries of, 3
objects of, 3, 5, 11
primary norms level, 11
special, 11
protective jurisdiction:
law of the sea, 147
protest:
courts as forum for, 37
third-party enforcement with autonomous function of, 37
Protocol against the Smuggling of Migrants by Land, Sea and Air, 167, 173
public order at sea, 88
public-owned vessels:
foreign vessels, limited but effective control over, 162
Pufendorf, Samuel von, 9, 26

qualitative concept:
legal personality, 41
***quasi*-Stateless jural relations of international law,** 98

Rachel, Samuel, 25
***Rantsev* case, ECtHR,** 170, 171
reality, kaleidoscopic, 138
reasoned decisions, rights to, 104
***Rechtsfähigkeit*, *see* legal capacity**
redundancy, historical, 24–32
referral, mandatory, 110
refugee law:
rescue, disembarkment obligations, 183
regional scope:
human rights treaties, 156
regionalisation of international law, 139
regulations:
adoption, 101, 104, 115
Rehm, Hermann, 30
relevance:
measure of, international legal capacities, 47
relevant participants:
international decision-making, 20
religion, freedom of, 166
remedies:
engagement in legal order, 132
function in international legal system, 131
importance of having, 131–34
international, *see* international remedies
LOSC, 70
rights, affording protection to, 132
subjects of law influencing downstream production of law through case law impact, 132
***Reparation for injuries* case advisory opinion, ICJ,** 18, 19, 42
representatives, legal, 44
repression of acts maintaining slavery, 171
repression of slavery, *see* slavery
***res communis gentium*:**
seas as, 96
rescue:
disembarkation, 182–83
duties, 182
obligation, 182
operations:
SAR Convention, 178
see also search and rescue
persons in distress at sea, 11
refugee law:
disembarkment obligations, 183
right to be rescued, 182
search and, *see* search and rescue
States, jurisdiction under ECHR, 182
reserved areas:
deep seabed mining, 99
residence, ship-owners, 80
resources:
Area, the, *see* Area, the
collected, 134
deep seabed mining minerals, 98
exploitation, 5, 97
management:
Area, the, in, 104
Authority, the, 104
referred to as minerals, deep seabed mining, 99
responsibility:
Authority, the, 111
jurisdiction and, 151
rules, States, 69
Responsibility of States for Internationally Wrongful Acts, Draft Articles on, 139
review of decisions, rights to, 104
revisionist theories of international law, 28
right:
innocent passage as, *see* innocent passage
right to be rescued:
SAR Convention, 182
right to education:
Authority, the, 185
right to health:
Authority, the, 185
right to life:
The Authority, 185
coastal States, 180
core importance, 176–77
enforcement, national courts, 181
individuals as holders of, 181
right to physical integrity:
Authority, the, 185
right to privacy:
Authority, the, 185
right-holders:
States as, 1–2
rights:
access to information, to, 104
adopted by domestic statutes, enjoyment after, 28

aptitude of entities to be recipient of international legal subjectivity, 42
assigning to entities other than States, biases against, 13
binding norms compliance, to, 104
centre of, *see* centre of rights and duties
conferral irrespective of direct effects, 71–75
conferred on private actors
rules. international law, 40
criminal law, private actors, 12
domestic law, existing under, 28
enforceability, 35
enforcement in international legal order, 36
exercise competence, 176
exploration, 5, 106, 134
held by private actors, 131
holders:
navigational, flag States, 64–65
private actors as, 5
private actors in special domains of international law, 11
private actors under international law, 48
private miners as, under law of the sea, 98
ships, apparent, 61–64
use of specific goods, 40
human rights law, private actors, 12
in personam, 40
in rem, 40
international, 38
international law, under, 19–20
investment law, private actors, 12
juristic persons, 42
legal norms, conferring, 47
legal orders allocation to, 41
legal personality aptitude to hold under legal system, 38
legal subjectivity, indicator of, 132
navigational, *see* navigational rights and freedoms
notice-and-comment, to, 104
primary:
secondary claims entailed, 40
prior hearings, to, 104
private actors, 187
engaged in maritime activities, LOSC 167
held under *ius gentium*, 4
international level, at, 12
invoking, applying and enforcing in domestic legal orders, 36
private miners' complex web of, 107
procedural, *see* procedural rights
procedural transparency, to, 104
property, *see* property rights
proportionality standards, compliance with, 104
protection of expectations to, 104
reasoned decisions, 104
remedies affording protection to, 132
review of decisions, 104
right to have, to be integrated into political communities, 49
rules equipping private actors with, 28
seafarers, *see* seafarers' rights
ships, *see* ships
sovereign States, LOSC, 3
States, *see* States
that entities can hold, legal capacity measure of, 42
treaty provisions conferred on private actors, 28
validity, 36
see also duties
rights of passage, 66
rights of transit, 53
rights to liberty, human rights, States, 162
rights to life, human rights, States, 162
***Rigopoulos* case, ECtHR,** 163–64
rule of law:
Area, the, in, 114
rule of legal systems:
new information attached to, 133
rule-makers:
private actors, 23
rule-takers:
private actors, 23
rules:
domestic law:
scope of application, international law rules overlapping, 39
equipping private actors with duties, 28
evidence, *see* evidence rules
guiding law enforcers' choice, 39
international law:
freedom conferred on private actors, 40
rights conferred on private actors, 40
responsibility, 69
shipping, *see* shipping rules
specialised, 139
treaty-based, *see* treaty-based rules

safety conditions:
Authority, the, 185
Safety of Life at Sea, International Convention for, *see* **International Convention for the Safety of Life at Sea**
safety standards:
Authority, the, 185
***Saiga (2)* case, ITLOS,** 79
sanctity of life, 177
sanitary laws:
coastal States infringement prevention, 55
SAR Convention, *see* **International Convention on Maritime Search and Rescue**
saving lives at sea, LOSC, 161
Scelle, Georges, 30
scholarship, legalz5
Schrödinger's cat paradox, 43
Scott, Walter, 11
SDC, *see* **Seabed Disputes Chamber**
sea:
human rights, 136–37, 143–66
individuals at, *see* individuals
jurisdiction at, 144, 146
law of, *see* law of the sea
life at, *see* life at sea
persons at, *see* persons at sea
persons in distress at, *see* persons in distress
public order at, 88
rescues of persons in distress at, 11
saving lives at, LOSC, 161
slavery repression at, flag States, 172–73
territorial, *see* territorial sea
treaties criminalising certain acts committed by private actors at, 66
sea lanes:
coastal States, 55
innocent passage, 55
ship-owners respecting, 68
seabed:
deep, *see* deep seabed
seabed and ocean floor and subsoil thereof:
beyond limits of national jurisdiction, deep seabed mining, LOSC, 96
Seabed Disputes Chamber (SDC):
deep seabed mining jurisdiction, 109
exclusive and compulsory jurisdiction, 108–11
interpretive bias, 111
jurisdiction, 6, 109
private actors' *locus standi* before, 110
procedural rights before, 134
sponsoring States, 114, 117, 135
State-centric view, 117
seafarers' rights:
flagged ships compliance with, 83
search and rescue:
facilities, LOSC, 161
operations, 162, 165
positive obligations, coastal States, 179–80
seas:
res communis gentium, as, 96
States' appropriation of, 8
see also high seas; oceans; sea
seaworthiness:
conditions, flag States, 58–59
flagged ships compliance with, 83
navigational entitlements conditions for enjoyment, 58
secondary norms, 11, 70, 75
secondary State rights:
fictitious separation, 44
security:
financial, 118
security of tenure, 105
seized ships:
owners' rights under international law, 66
self-contained regimes, 141
self-protecting myopia of international law, 27–28
servitude, 170, 171
prohibition, The Authority, 185
Roman property law of:
transposed into law of the sea, 54
setting the scene, 3–4, 15–17
private actors:
apartheid from international law and law of the sea, 7
gradual building of Vattelian Premise, 7–11
ongoing erosion of Vattelian Premise, 11–13
LOSC, in, 5–7
participation through interpretation, 13–15
scheme of the book, 15–17
shared accountability:
ship-owners, flag States, 76
shared responsibilities:
compensation, 90
shield effect, 75
ship-as-a-unit concept, ITLOS, 3
ship-owners:
accountability, 84

beneficial owners, 67
compensation, creditors for, 92
compliance:
coastal States LOSC provisions, structure and obligational scope, 67–71
conduct not directly attributable to, 69
enforcement remedies under domestic law, 71
entitlements deriving from freedom of navigation, 66
ex ante facto responsibility for performance of LOSC's obligational scope, 68
financial interests:
prompt release applications, LOSC, 118
flag States and:
genuine link requirement, *see* genuine link requirement
intertwining positions, 75–87
shared accountability, 76
freedom of high seas assigned to, 66
genuine link requirement, 80–81, 83
innocent passage:
constraints, addressed to ship-owners, 68
non-compliance accountability, 70
LOSC:
obligational scope performance control, 67–68
nationality, 80
conferred, lawfulness of, 81
navigational entitlements, 75
coastal States, against, 76
obligations assigned to, 70
penalty payments, 83
port admission conditions, 68
private actors, as, 67
residence, 80
right exercise as innocent passage, obligations addressed to, 70
rights of passage assigned to, 66
sea lanes, respecting, 68
seized ships, rights under international law, 66
substantive rights held by, 75
traffic separation schemes, respecting, 68
shipping rules:
flagged ships compliance with, 83
ships:
assigning rights to, LOSC, 64
authority over, 83
believed to be engaged in slave trade
flag States' interception of, LOSC, 169
charterers:
creditors for compensation, 92
private actors, as, 67
compensation:
entitled to, 62
conduct:
not directly attributable to States under State responsibility, 69
exercising innocent passage as right, 57
flag States:
relationships between, 80
interception of, 171
control over, 80, 159
jurisdiction over, 59, 78, 80
rights held by flying their flags, protection of, 76
flagged:
flag States' responsibility deriving from jurisdiction over, 115
maritime law, compliance with, 83
seafarers' rights, compliance with, 83
seaworthiness, compliance with, 83
shipping rules, compliance with, 83
flying flags, jurisdiction over, flag States, 161
foreign merchant vessels, 65
high seas, on:
no navigational rights and freedoms, 63
interception on high seas, 163–64
interests represented in:
damages caused to by interference, 91
State links with, 78
international law, States responsible for, 83
international legal personality, deprived of, 62
jurisdiction over determined in spatial terms, 60
legal personality, 91
recognising, 62–63
legal persons:
holding specific international legal rights and duties, as, 62
not seen as, 63
masters:
freedom of high seas assigned to, 66
rights of passage assigned to, 66
nationality, 59, 60
conferring, 80, 81
denial by States, 80
denial on genuine link requirement absence, 80
flag States, 60
granting, 79
human rights obligations, flag States, 160

PCIJ, 60
pivotal in law of the sea, 60
positive and negative obligations, flag States, 160
role of:
navigational entitlements conditions for enjoyment, 58–60
State jurisdiction identification, 83, 84
withdrawing, 79
navigational entitlements:
allocation to, 61
areas under spatial jurisdiction, in, 63
exercise of, 64
navigational rights and freedoms:
assigned to, SOLAS Convention, 61
not held, 63
non-national, 173–74
not attached to States, no freedom of navigation, ECJ, 66–67
not legal persons, 64
operators:
freedom of high seas assigned to, 66
private actors, as, 67
rights of passage assigned to, 66
owners, *see* ship-owners
ports:
admission conditions, 68
unable to leave, 68
private miners' nationality, of, use of, 115
prompt release applications, *see* prompt release applications
prompt release proceedings, LOSC and ITLOS, 70
puzzling reference to, 61–64
rights:
holders, apparent, 61–64
pragmatic reason for assigning, 64
seized:
owners' rights under international law, 66
slave trade, engaged in:
human rights enforcement, interfering States, 174
individuals on board under jurisdiction of interfering States, interfering States, 174
Stateless, 60
statelessness, 89
States' rights to sail, LOSC, 65
subject to flag States' exclusive jurisdiction on high seas, 81
subjects of law, as, 61
see also foreign vessels; vessels

***Siliadin* case, ECtHR,** 170–71
single (not multiple) legal personality:
legal capacity, 45–46
single legal orders:
governing relations from separate social orders, 46
single legal personality (not multiple), 45–46, 49
slavery, 158, 169–72
de facto enslavement, 172
freedom from, 174–75
freedom of slaves taking refuge on ships, LOSC
HSC, 169
intercepting States, 174
interception of ships believed to be engaged in slave trade, flag States, 169
law of the sea, 170, 174
meaning, 169–70
negative obligations to refrain from maintaining persons from, 171
new forms, 172
non-national ships:
States visiting and inspecting, 173–74
old forms, 172
positive obligations to take all effective measures for prevention, repression, prosecution and penalisation of acts maintaining, 171
prohibition:
LOSC, 5, 6
Authority, the, 185
repression, 89
human rights in LOSC, 172–76
ICJ, 169
ships engaged in slave trade, *see* ships
victims of, 171
Slavery Convention, 169, 170
smuggling, 158
human, 171–72
migrants, of, 167
Smuggling of Migrants by Land, Sea and Air, Protocol against, 167, 173
social artefacts, 11
social entities, 19
social orders:
single, regulation from different legal orders, 46
society:
high seas as place outside, 10
sociological importance:
international law, 4

SOLAS, *see* **International Convention for the Safety of Life at Sea**
sole requirement of legal personality, 38
sovereign membership of international law:
territorial entities, 26
sovereign power:
jurisdiction as exercise of, 145–46
sovereign ruler's person as subject of ***ius gentium*****,** 25
sovereign States, 8
conceived, 25
international law:
applicable within domestic legal order, 75
interpretation, application and enforcement by domestic courts, 75
law as commandment adopted by, 74
rights and duties, 9
LOSC, 3
solely and exclusively subjects of international law, 4
territorial States and, international society of, 9
treaties as part of law of the land, 75
sovereigns:
international law created for, 4
sovereignty, 74
by-product:
general international law jurisdiction, 148–49
coastal States, 54
States, 5, 9, 25, 26
sovereignty-freedom, 74
spacial-functional jurisdiction:
law of the sea, 147
spatial authority:
allocation to States, 8
spatial-functional jurisdiction, EEZ and continental shelf, 147
spatial jurisdiction:
areas under, navigational entitlements, ships, in, 63
coastal States, 147, 157
model, States, 152
spatial States:
jurisdiction:
search and rescue operations, 165
spatial terms:
jurisdiction, ECHR, 150
special protection:
private actors as objects of, 11
specialised rules and rule systems, 139
specific goods:
right holders' use of, 40
Spiropoulos, Jean, 30
sponsoring States:
accountability, 111, 113–18
competence assumption, 115
compliance with legal regime of the Area, 116
contractors:
damage from activities, appropriate measures to prevent, 117–18
deep seabed mining, 95
pivotal role given to, 117
direct obligations, 114
due diligence, 114, 117
ex ante responsibilities, 115
due diligence obligation, 116
ex post responsibilities, 115
non-performance of due diligence obligations, 116
intervention, 111
jurisdiction, 115
precautionary approach, 117–18
private miners' subjection to, 117
private mining, SDC, 135
purpose of sponsorship, 114
reasonably appropriate measures establishing, 115
responsibility for ensuring activities in the Area, 113
roles, SDC, 135
sponsorship:
deep seabed mining, 100–101
private miners, 100–101
duties deriving from international law compliance, ensuring, 114
purpose of, 114
spouses:
human rights equality between, ECHR, 166
stability:
legal systems, courts responsibility for providing, 133
standard-setting processes:
private actors taking part in, 23
State agents:
submitting prompt release applications on behalf of flag States, ITLOS, 124–25
State-centred conception of international law, 2, 93
State-centred law of the sea vs individual-centred human rights law, 186
State-centred narrative, 187

State-centric view, SDC, 117
State-like communities:
law of the sea history, tale between, 8
State-like entity:
Authority, the, as, 98
State parties of control:
deep seabed mining, 100
State parties of nationality:
deep seabed mining, 100
State-to-State conception of international law, 1
State-to-State perspective:
law of the sea, 97
Stateless ships, 60, 89
statements of facts:
succinct, *see* succinct statements of facts
States:
abstraction, as, 30
accountability, 180–81
acts infringing other States and its citizens, 43–44
addressees of rules of international law, 26
artificial legal person, as, 9
artificial persons, as, 26
attribution of conduct to, ARSIWA, 69, 84
authority, prevention of exercising, 154
coastal, *see* coastal States
centrepiece of international law, as, 24–27
competence conferred by international law, 72
creation by individuals as domestic legal persons, as, 47
creation of philosophers, statesmen and legal scholars, 9
creator and sole subject of law of nations, 9
de facto maritime jurisdiction of, 186
detaining, *see* detaining States
diplomatic, *see* diplomatic States
duties, assigning to entities other than, biases against, 13
enforcement:
jurisdiction immunity under national law, 71
mechanisms, ITLOS, 83
extraterritorial action, 156
extraterritorial jurisdiction, 74
fictional legal person, as, 9
flag, *see* flag States
freedom of navigation:
entitlements deriving from, 66
full international legal subjectivity, as template of, 18
governmental ships assigned to, 65
human rights:
non-refoulement principle, 162, 182
prohibition of torture, 162
rights to liberty, 162
rights to life, 162
treaties jurisdiction and, personal relations between, 150
individuals:
analogy between in international law, 24–25
at sea, duties to, 186
compared, international legal scholarship, 25
jurisdiction over based on nationality principle, 59–60
similarities between, 25
intercepting, *see* intercepting States
interests, 25
reconciling, 5
interfering, *see* interfering States
international law making, 43
control, 27
enforcement, 27
international law subjects, as, 22
international legal personality:
historical redundancy, 24–32
states-only conception of international legal personality, 27–30
template, 42–43
international legal sphere:
natural access to, 27
creators and dominant players of, 10
international legal system dominant players, 13
international rights-holders, 4
ITLOS open to entities other than, 6
jurisdiction:
de facto, 157, 186
de iure, 148, 150, 153–54, 157
extraterritorial, 146, 154, 156, 157
human rights treaties, 146, 150
identification, ships' nationality, 83, 84
individuals' subjection to, 149
law of the sea, 155
persons at sea, over, 146
sea, at, 144
spatial model, 152
territories, 146
juristic persons, as, 9, 26
jurisdiction over based on nationality principle, 60

land-locked, *see* land-locked States
law, 3
law-making competence, 24
law of the sea history, tale between, 8
legal fiction, as, 30
legal orders characterised by impregnable presence of, 187
legal person, as, 32
  within realm of *ius gentium*, 26
legal personality of private actors, exclusion, 47
legal representatives of private actors, acting solely as, 44
links with interests represented in ships, 78
lords of international law, as, 26
magnetic force of, 9
major international law-makers, as, 32
maritime jurisdiction:
  conveyed by international law instruments, 73
  over portions of sea conferred and demarcated by LOSC, 72
moral persons, as, 26
nationals, 30
navigational entitlements imposition among, 73
non-flag, *see* non-flag States
normal international persons, as, 27
obligations:
  negative, 153
  positive, 153
  realistic compliance, dependent on, 152
ocean governance, cooperation in, 8
only entities as subjects of international law, as, 27, 28
only subjects of international law, 9
ordinary international legal subjects, 25
parties before ITLOS, as, 124
personae iure gentium, as, 26
personality, 42
port, *see* port States
pouvoir constituants of international law, 30
pouvoir continués, as, 30
power:
  jurisdiction describing, 145
primary subject of international law, as, 26, 27
private actors:
  exclusive control of, under, 7
  jural relations, imbalance, 44
  legal personality exclusion, 47
  legal representatives of, acting solely as, 44
  subjectivity not dependent on States' benediction, 47
  subjects of, as, 7
relations among:
  law of nations concept confined to, 7
responsibility rules, 69
responsible for ships under international law, 83
right-holders, as, 1–2
rights:
  assigning to entities other than, biases against, 13
  conferred by international norms, not possessed, 43
  primary and secondary, fictitious separation, 44
seas, appropriation of, 8
ships:
  jurisdiction over determined in spatial terms, 60
  nationality denial by, 80
slavery:
  visiting and inspecting non-national ships, 173–74
sole subject of international law, as, 27
sovereign, *see* sovereign States
sovereignty, 5, 9, 25, 26
spatial authority allocation to, 8
sponsoring, *see* sponsoring States
State-to-State matrix of international dispute settlement, 6
territorial, 8
treaties, internationally bound by, 74
typical international legal subjects, 25
warships assigned to, 65
statesmen:
  States creation of, 9
straits, international, 53, 72
strict canons of international law interpretation:
  international customary law, 28
  VCLT, 28
structure of provisions, LOSC, 67–71
structures, EEZ:
  persons subject to *de iure* of coastal States, 158
study of legal personality
  absence in international law, 23
SUA Convention, *see* **Suppression of Unlawful Acts against the Safety of Maritime Navigation Convention**

subjectivity:
international, 23
international legal, 36
legal, *see* legal subjectivity
private actors, of:
not dependent on States' benediction, 47
subjects:
persons and, difference between, 2
subjects of international law, 24
difference from subjects of domestic law, private actors not included, 73–74
individuals, 30–31
'international legal persons' used interchangeably, 2
'international legal subjects' used interchangeably, 2
sovereign states solely and exclusively, 4
States only entities as, 27, 28
territorial entities only, 26
subjects of law:
domestic legal orders, 22
participation of private actors as, 18–19
epistemological function of legal personality, 19–21
influencing downstream production of law through case law impact, 132
juristic persons as, 22
legal personality concept in theory of law, 21–24
submarines:
innocent passage, 55
substantive entitlement:
private actors, ITLOS, 71
substantive rights:
ship-owners, held by, 75
substitution, procedural, 40
succinct statements of facts:
submission, prompt release applications, ITLOS, 122
superjacent waters:
continental shelf freedom of navigation in (not part of the continental shelf), 53
Supplementary Convention on the Abolition of Slavery, the Slave Trade and Institutions and Practices Similar to Slavery, 169
Suppression of Unlawful Acts against the Safety of Maritime Navigation (SUA) Convention
compensation, 62, 91
human rights, 167
supreme sovereignty, States, 26
systemic interpretation, 185–86
different *lex specialis*, relations among, 142
failure to take seriously, 143
human rights treaties at sea, application, 143
human rights jurisdiction at sea, 145–66
jurisdiction as precondition of human rights application, 143–45
common genetic code of law of the sea and human rights law, 137–43
human rights in the LOSC, 166–69
protection of life at sea, 176–85
repression of slavery, 169–76
international law, systemic view of, 175
intrinsic feature of legal systems, 137
lex generalis and *lex specialis*, relations between, 142
LOSC provisions, 141
private actors' standpoint, 136
taking seriously, 136–37
systemic view of international law, 175

Tanaka, Yoshifumi, 52
technology transfer:
deep seabed mining, 100
tectonic subjective transformation of international legal system, 49
territorial entities:
international law only subjects, 26
sovereign membership of international law, 26
territorial jurisdiction:
ECHR, 153–54
law of the sea, 147
territorial sea:
coastal States' sovereignty, 54
foreign ships' innocent passage through, 54
innocent passage, 53
foreign ships through, 54, 61
maritime spaces under territorial sovereignty of coastal States, 53
navigational entitlements on, 72
prescriptive and enforcement jurisdiction, 147
right of innocent passage, 53, 54
territorial jurisdiction, 147
Territorial Sea Convention (TSC):
coastal States' sovereignty, 54
non-innocent passage, 55–56

territorial States, 8
sovereign States and, international society of, 9
territorial jurisdiction, exclusive, 74
territoriality:
jurisdiction, human rights treaties, 152
meaning, ECtHR, 155
territories:
jurisdiction, States, 146
tests:
assessment, objective, ECtHR, 165
feasibility, flag States, 160
theory of law, 21–24
third-party enforcement, 37
tokenism, 23
Tolstoy, Leo, 3
***Tomimaru* case, ITLOS,** 168
torture, prohibition, 162
traffic separation schemes:
ship-owners respecting, 68
transit rights, 53
transnational governance:
private actors' rights of participation in, 23
transport surface:
oceans conception as, 64
transportation:
private miners, 99
treaties:
compliance with law, 87
criminalising certain acts committed by private actors at sea, 66
cross-fertilisation process, 175
cross-regime interaction, 176
cross-regime interpretation, 175–76
direct effect, 12
expression of will of sovereign States, 75
human rights law, 136
interpretation, 1, 188
extrinsic provisions, considering, 175
ICJ, 14
implicit interpretive bias, 188
interference biases, 93–94
objectivity and scientific character, VCLT, 29
private actors' participation obtained by means of, 13
rules, VCLT, biases interfering, 94
jural relations, 87
law of the sea:
ships entitled to compensation, 62
part of law of the land of sovereign States, as, 75
private actors' rights and duties under, 13
direct source, 12
private actors' rights under, 131
provisions:
rights and duties conferred on private actors, 28
States internationally bound by, 74
treaty-based rules:
application, domestic courts, 75
relevant rules of international law, VCLT, 137
treaty-derived entitlements:
domestic courts, private actors invoking, 75
tribunals:
arbitral, 109–10
competence:
general international law jurisdiction, 145
Triepel, Heinrich, 28
true monism, 73
TSC, *see* **Territorial Sea Convention**

***ubi commoda ibi incommoda*,** 55, 83
***ubi jus, ibi remedium*,** 132
UN Committee Against Torture:
J.H.A. v Spain case, 164
UN Consultative Group on Flag State Implementation, 69
UN Convention against the Illicit Traffic in Narcotic Drugs, 167
UN Security Council:
freedom of navigation impacts on, 52
UNCITRAL:
deep seabed mining arbitration in accordance with rules of, 106, 109
UNCLOS III:
innocent passage definition amended in, 56
under-water vehicles:
innocent passage, 55
unified legal orders:
common background transforming international law in, 141
uniformity:
legal systems, courts responsibility for providing, 133
unitary list of legal persons, 47
unitary notion of legal persons, 47
United Nations Convention against Illicit Traffic in Narcotic Drugs and Psychotropic Substances, 61, 163

universal jurisdiction:
high seas, limited enforcement jurisdiction, 147
universal obligation:
pursuant to international customary law, 176
universal scope:
human rights treaties, 156
universality:
human rights treaties, 156
unlawful outcomes, 77
unveiling private actors' entitlements, 51
compensation rights, 87–88
grounds for lawful interference with navigation, 88–89
holders of rights to compensation, 90–93
intertwining position of ship-owners and flag states, 75–77
due diligence obligation, 84–87
genuine link requirement, 77–81
indirect responsibilities of flag states, 81–84
navigation, freedom of, entitlements deriving from, 51–53
innocent passage, rights of, 53–58
role of nationality of vessels as condition for enjoyment of navigational entitlements, 58–60
puzzling reference to ships, 61
ships as apparent rights-holders, 61–64
pragmatic reason for assigning rights to ships, 64
States as navigational rights-holders, 64–65
private actors as navigational rights-holders, 66–67
conferral of rights irrespective of direct effect, 71–75
LOSC's provisions structure and obligational scope, 67–71
upstream production:
international law, 133
law of the sea, 6

vacuum in system, ECtHR, 156
validity:
duties, 36
private miners' plans of work, 105
rights, 36
variable powers:
prompt release applications, ITLOS, 123
***Vassis*, case, ECtHR,** 164
Vattel, Emer de, 7, 9, 26, 53
Vattelian conception of international law, 111, 129
Vattelian fiction, 43
Vattelian narrative of international law, 85, 128
Vattelian Premise, 7–13, 73
VCLT, *see* **Vienna Convention on the Law of Treaties**
vertical integration:
deep seabed, 98
vessels:
flag States, arrested by coastal States, 167
foreign, *see* foreign vessels
interception on high seas, coastal States, 153
nationality, *see* ships: nationality
prompt release applications, LOSC, 118
warships' interception on high seas, 149
see also ships
victims of slavery, 171
Vienna Convention on Consular Relations, 166
Vienna Convention on the Law of Treaties (VCLT), 1
context, 14
cross-regime interaction, 186
dispute settlement bodies, 141
intention of parties, 14
international law interpretation, strict canons of, 28
legal regime:
reflecting customary international law, 14
legal system normative elements, 14
object, 14
purpose, 14
spirit of treaty, 14
treaty-based rules:
relevant rules of international law, 137
treaty interpretation rules, 13–14, 135
biases interfering, 94
canons, 14, 134
good faith, 14
objectivity and scientific character, 29
ordinary meaning of terms used, 14
systemic interpretation, 14
two or more languages, authenticated in, 14
violence, private, 10
***Virginia G* case, ITLOS,** 79
Vœlckel, Michel, 66

warships:
assigned to States, 65
foreign vessels, limited but effective control over, 162
immunities, LOSC, 61
interception of vessels on high seas, 149

Wendel, Philipp, 66
Wolff, Christian, 9, 25, 26
***Women of Waves* case, ECtHR,** 162, 164
wrongful acts, 112

***Xhavara* decision, ECtHR,** 166

www.ingramcontent.com/pod-product-compliance
Lightning Source LLC
Chambersburg PA
CBHW071300180926
51613CB00001B/81